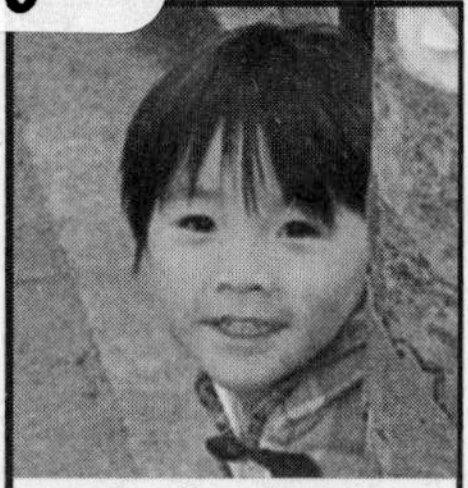

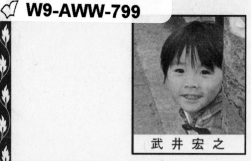

武井宏之

My son. This picture was taken about two years ago (which is why I figured it would be okay to show). He is entering the first grade this year, and recently he's started reading Weekly Shonen Jump too. Dad's going to draw a good manga so no one at school will make fun of you! But on the other hand, dad loves to draw embarrassing manga. What a conundrum. Well, just make sure your friends don't find out who your dad is.

—Hiroyuki Takei, 1999

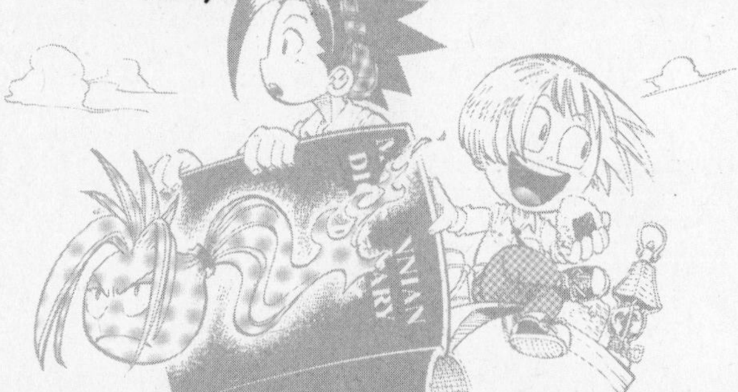

Unconventional author/artist Hiroyuki Takei began his career by winning the coveted Hop Step Award (for new manga artists) and the Osamu Tezuka Award (named after the famous artist of the same name). After working as an assistant to famed artist Nobuhiro Watsuki, Takei debuted in **Weekly Shonen Jump** in 1997 with **Butsu Zone**, an action series based on Buddhist mythology. His multicultural adventure manga **Shaman King**, which debuted in 1998, became a hit and was adapted into an anime TV series. Takei lists Osamu Tezuka, American comics and robot anime among his many influences.

SHAMAN KING VOL. 2
The SHONEN JUMP Graphic Novel Edition

This graphic novel contains material that was originally published in English in **SHONEN JUMP** #7-11.

STORY AND ART BY
HIROYUKI TAKEI

English Adaptation/Lance Caselman
Translation/Lillian Olsen
Touch-Up Art & Lettering/Dan Nakrosis
Cover & Graphics Design/Sean Lee
Editor/Jason Thompson

Managing Editor/Frances E. Wall
Editorial Director/Elizabeth Kawasaki
VP & Editor in Chief/Yumi Hoashi
Sr. Director of Acquisitions/Rika Inouye
Sr. VP of Marketing/Liza Coppola
Exec. VP of Sales & Marketing/John Easum
Publisher/Hyoe Narita

Printed in the U.S.A.

Published by VIZ Media, LLC
P.O. Box 77010 • San Francisco, CA 94107

SHONEN JUMP Graphic Novel Edition
10 9 8 7 6 5 4
First printing, December 2003
Second printing, September 2004
Third printing, May 2005
Fourth printing, July 2006

PARENTAL ADVISORY
SHAMAN KING is rated T for Teen.
It contains violence and tobacco usage.
It is recommended for ages 13 and up.

THE WORLD'S
MOST POPULAR MANGA

www.viz.com

www.shonenjump.com

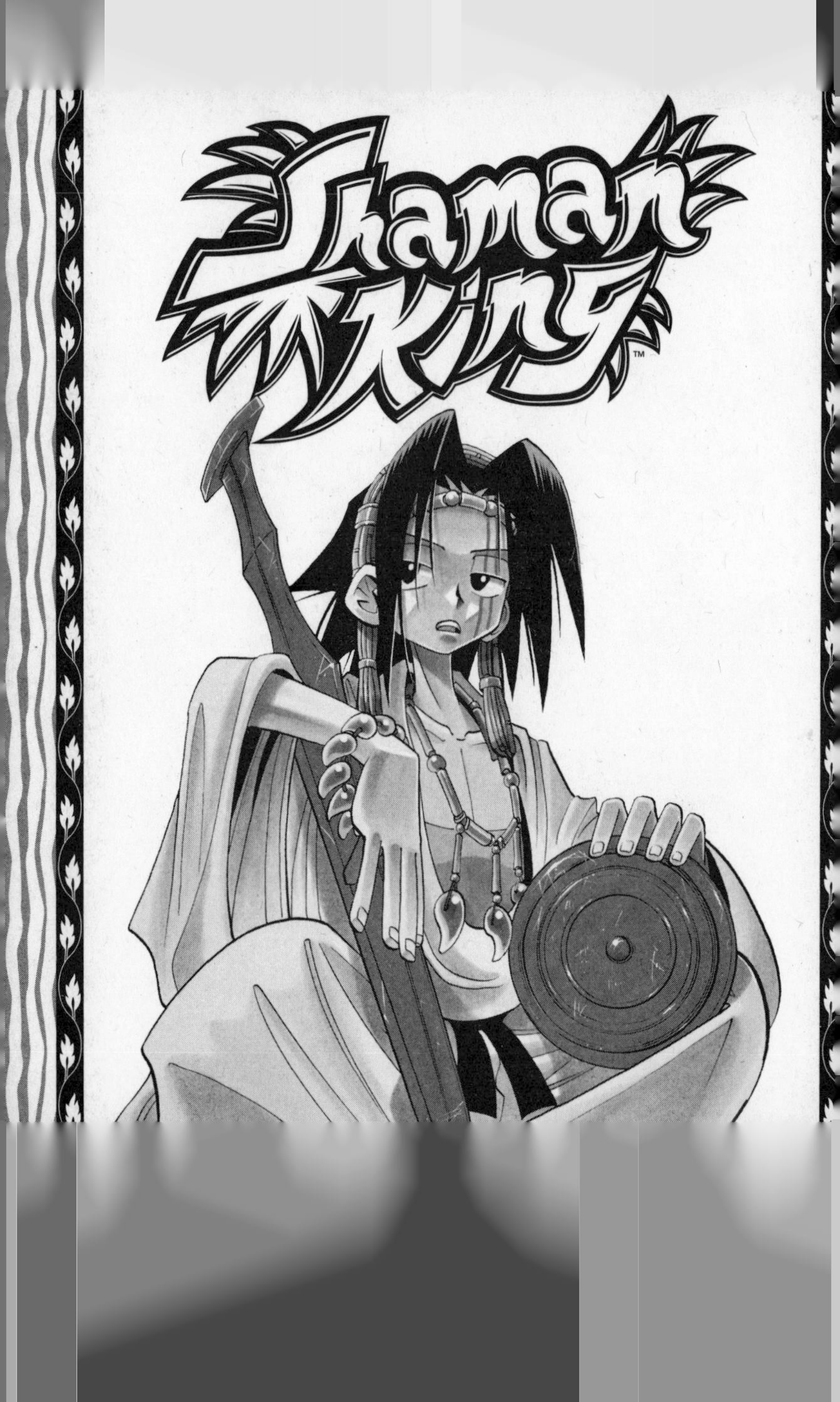
Shaman King™

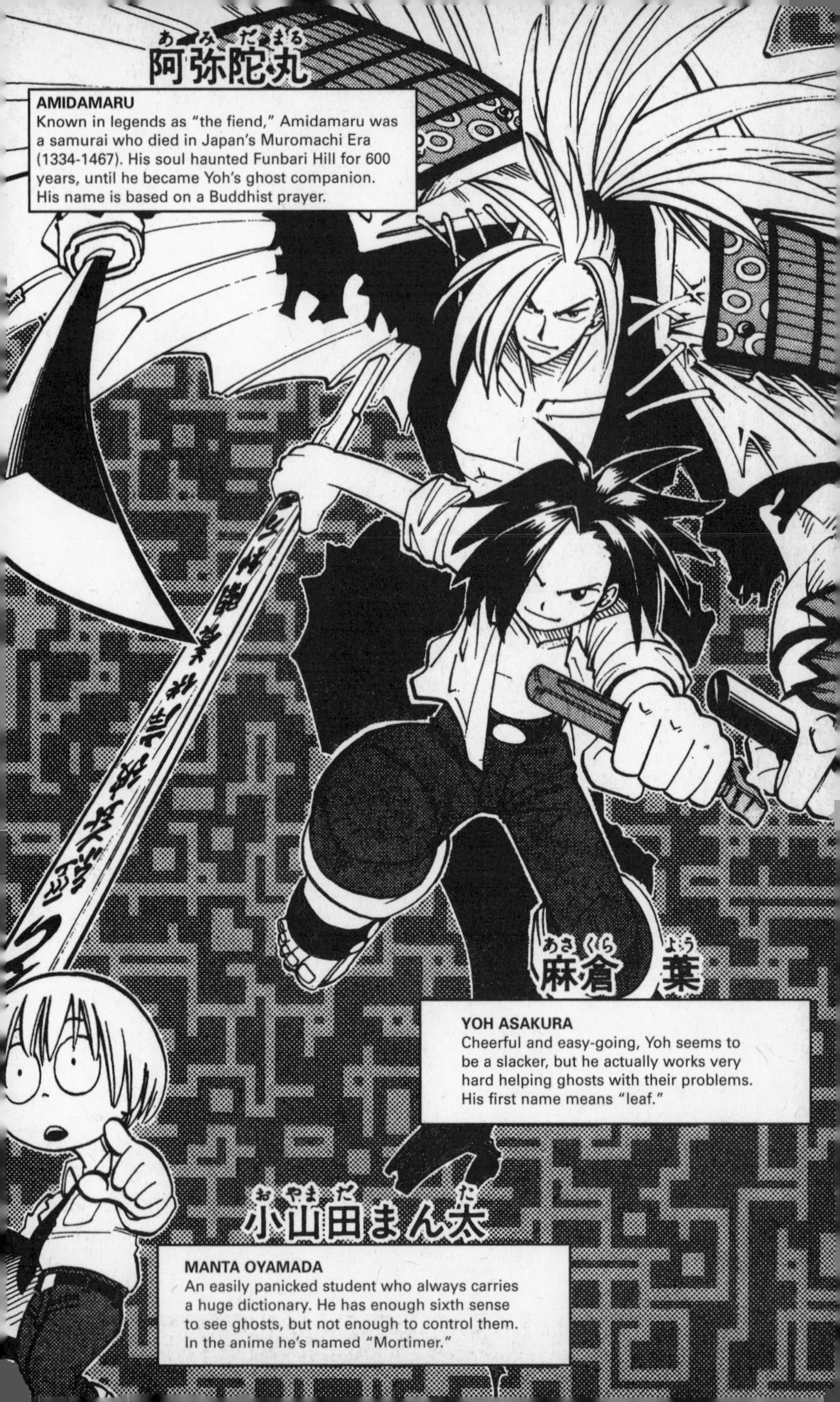

阿弥陀丸
AMIDAMARU
Known in legends as "the fiend," Amidamaru was a samurai who died in Japan's Muromachi Era (1334-1467). His soul haunted Funbari Hill for 600 years, until he became Yoh's ghost companion. His name is based on a Buddhist prayer.
麻倉 葉
YOH ASAKURA
Cheerful and easy-going, Yoh seems to be a slacker, but he actually works very hard helping ghosts with their problems. His first name means "leaf."
小山田まん太
MANTA OYAMADA
An easily panicked student who always carries a huge dictionary. He has enough sixth sense to see ghosts, but not enough to control them. In the anime he's named "Mortimer."

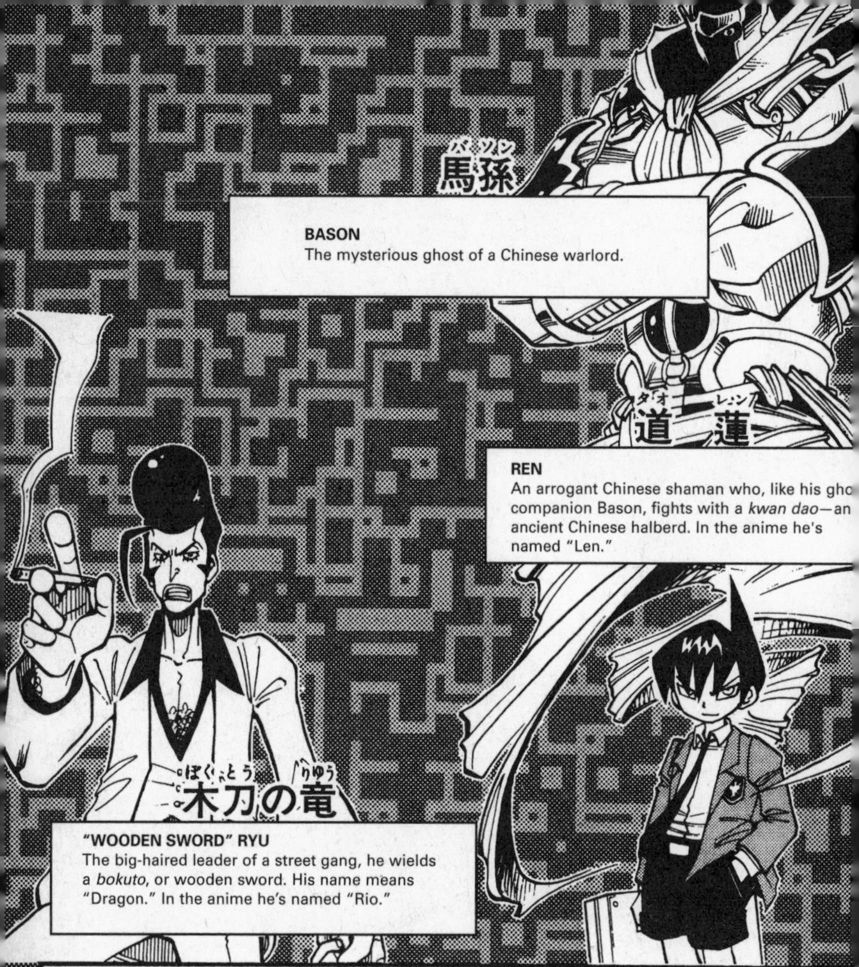
馬孫
道蓮
木刀の竜

BASON
The mysterious ghost of a Chinese warlord.

REN
An arrogant Chinese shaman who, like his gho companion Bason, fights with a *kwan dao*—an ancient Chinese halberd. In the anime he's named "Len."

"WOODEN SWORD" RYU
The big-haired leader of a street gang, he wields a *bokuto*, or wooden sword. His name means "Dragon." In the anime he's named "Rio."

THE STORY SO FAR...

Yoh Asakura is a *shaman*—one of the gifted few who, thanks to training or natural talent, can speak to spirits that most people can't even see. He can even channel them and use their powers! When Ren, a power-hungry Chinese shaman, attacked Yoh to take control of his ghost friend Amidamaru, Yoh used Amidamaru's samurai fighting techniques to defeat Ren...but was badly injured in the process. But why did Ren attack him in the first place? And who is the "ruler of all shamans"?

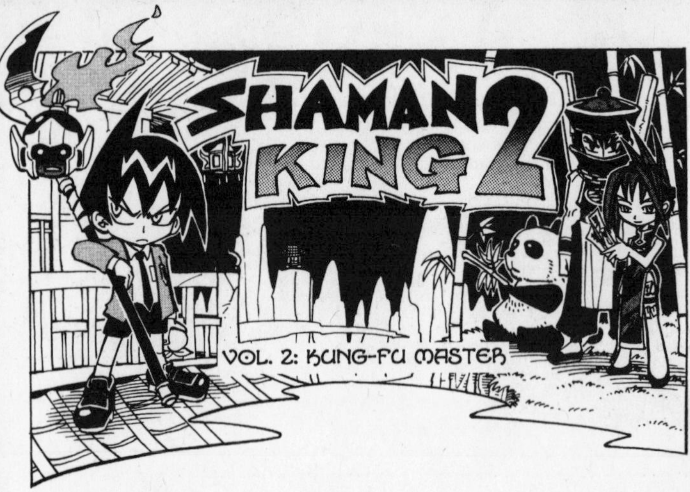
SHAMAN KING 2
VOL. 2: KUNG-FU MASTER

CONTENTS

REINCARNATION 9: THE SHAMAN KING

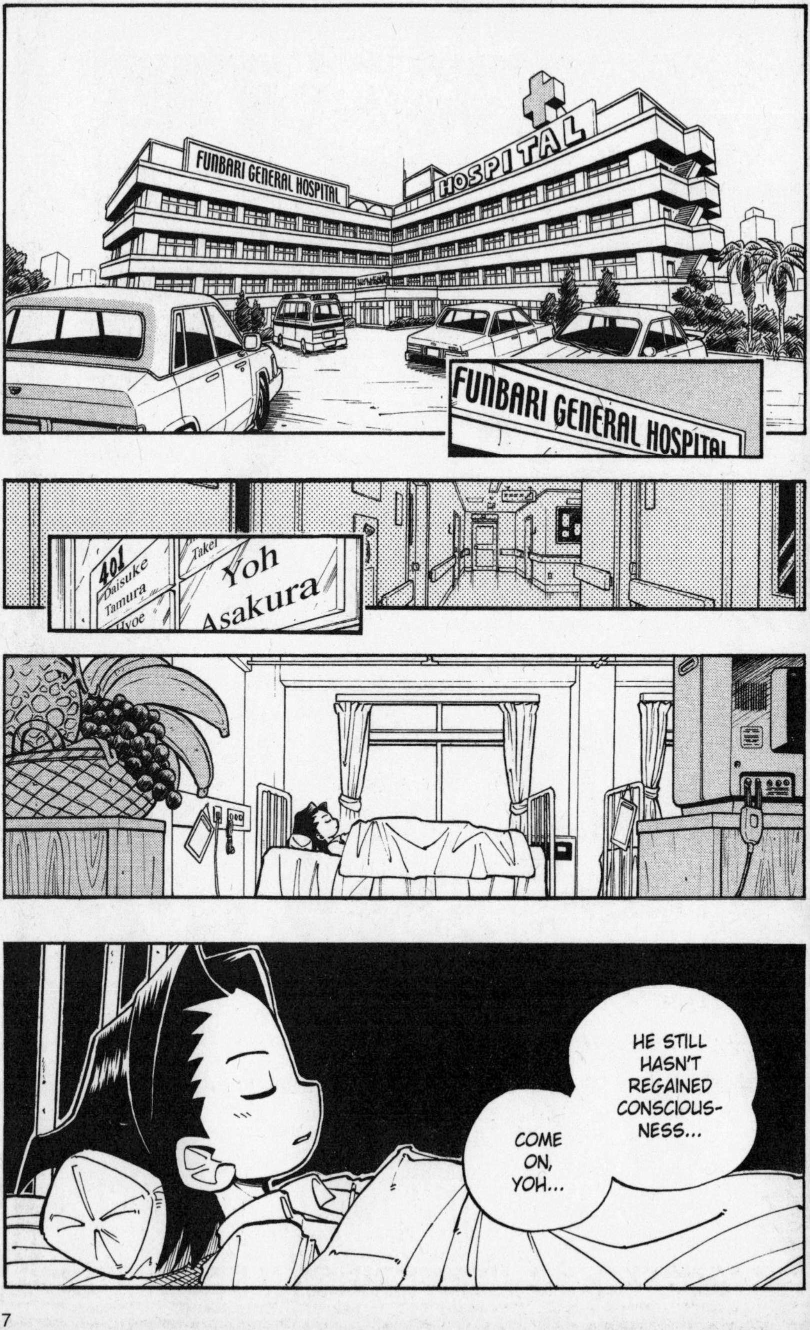
HOSPITAL
FUNBARI GENERAL HOSPITAL
FUNBARI GENERAL HOSPITAL
401
Daisuke Tamura
Takei
Yoh Asakura
HE STILL HASN'T REGAINED CONSCIOUS-NESS...
COME ON, YOH...

READ THIS WAY

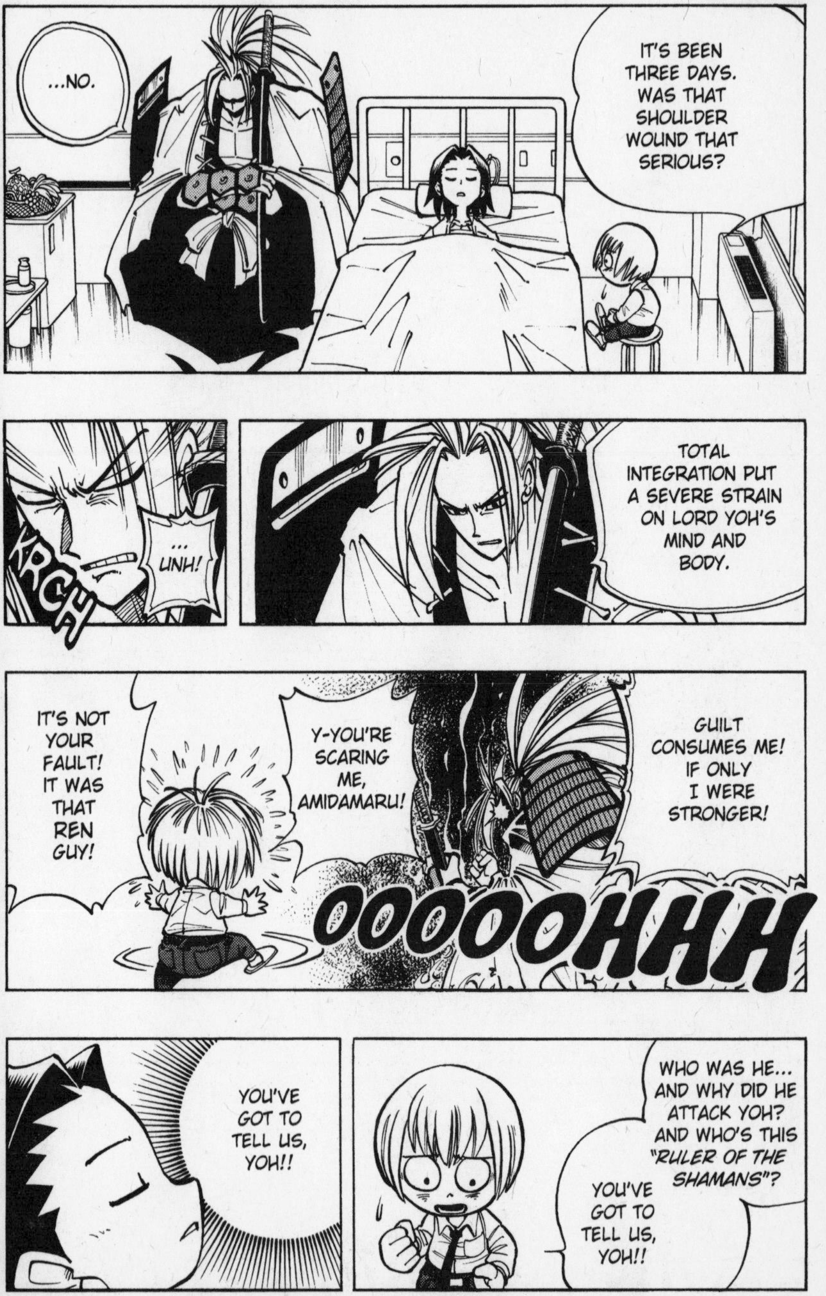

IT'S BEEN THREE DAYS. WAS THAT SHOULDER WOUND THAT SERIOUS?
...NO.
TOTAL INTEGRATION PUT A SEVERE STRAIN ON LORD YOH'S MIND AND BODY.
... UNH!
KRCH
GUILT CONSUMES ME! IF ONLY I WERE STRONGER!
OOOOOHHH
Y-YOU'RE SCARING ME, AMIDAMARU!
IT'S NOT YOUR FAULT! IT WAS THAT REN GUY!
WHO WAS HE... AND WHY DID HE ATTACK YOH? AND WHO'S THIS "RULER OF THE SHAMANS"?
YOU'VE GOT TO TELL US, YOH!!
YOU'VE GOT TO TELL US, YOH!!

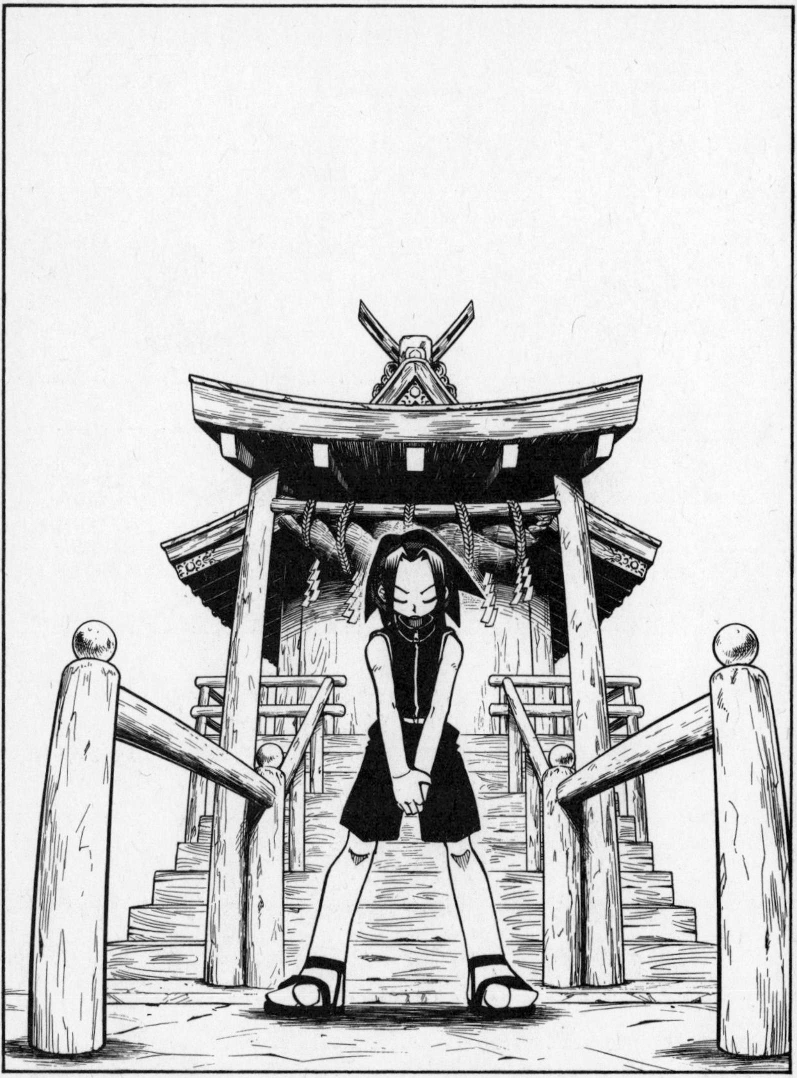

Reincarnation 9:
The Shaman King

READ THIS WAY

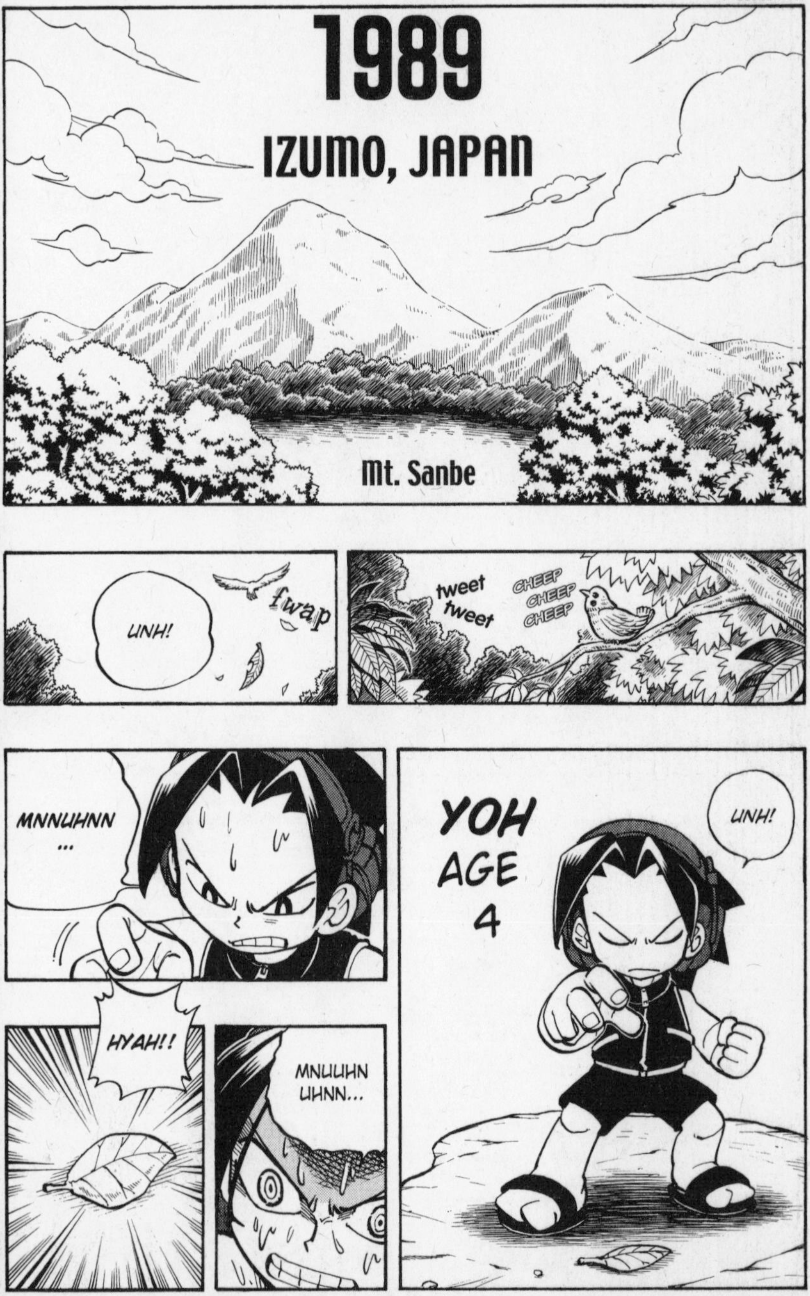
1989
IZUMO, JAPAN
Mt. Sanbe
tweet tweet
CHEEP CHEEP CHEEP
fwap
UNH!
YOH AGE 4
UNH!
MNNUHNN ...
MNUUHN UHNN...
HYAH!!

READ THIS WAY

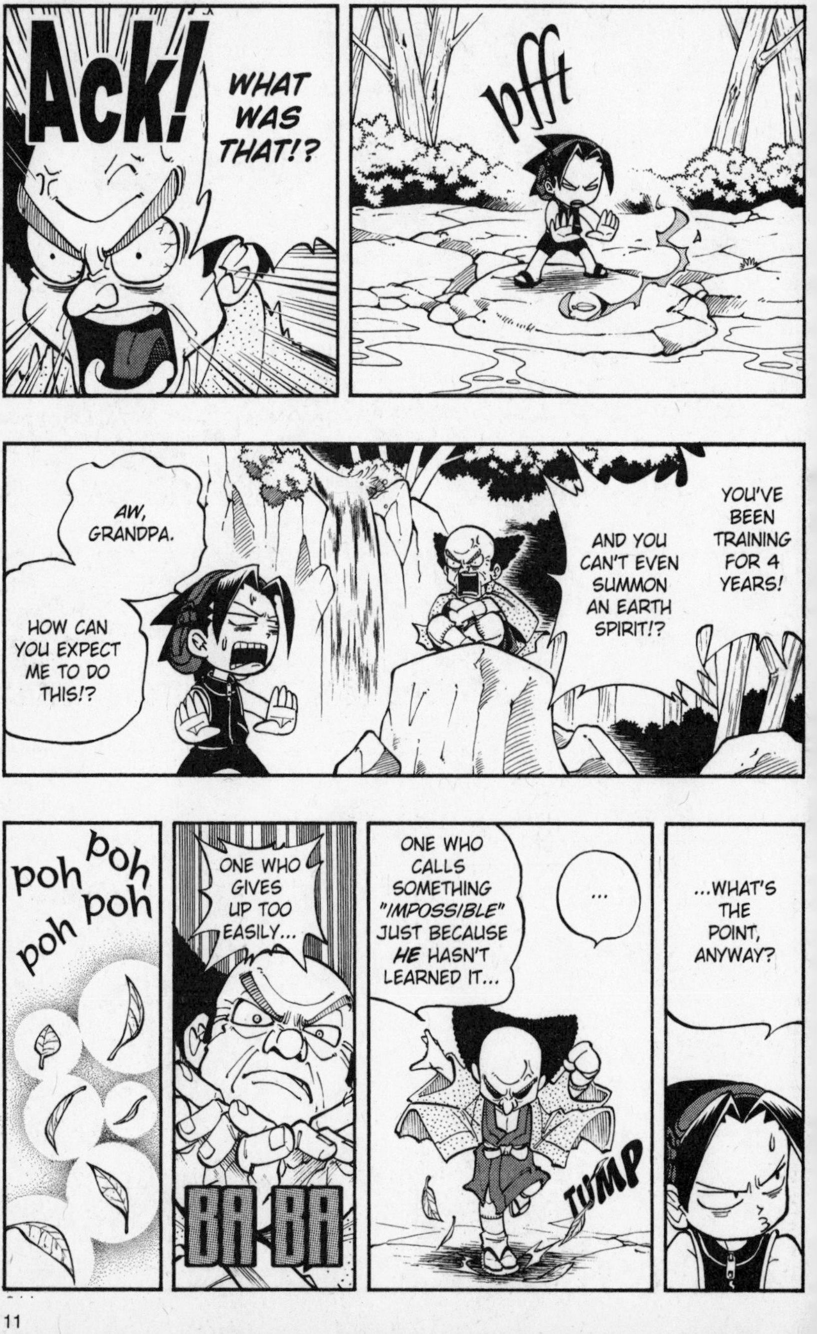

pfft
Ack!
WHAT WAS THAT!?
YOU'VE BEEN TRAINING FOR 4 YEARS!
AND YOU CAN'T EVEN SUMMON AN EARTH SPIRIT!?
AW, GRANDPA.
HOW CAN YOU EXPECT ME TO DO THIS!?
...WHAT'S THE POINT, ANYWAY?
...
ONE WHO CALLS SOMETHING "IMPOSSIBLE" JUST BECAUSE HE HASN'T LEARNED IT...
TUMP
ONE WHO GIVES UP TOO EASILY...
BA BA
poh poh poh poh

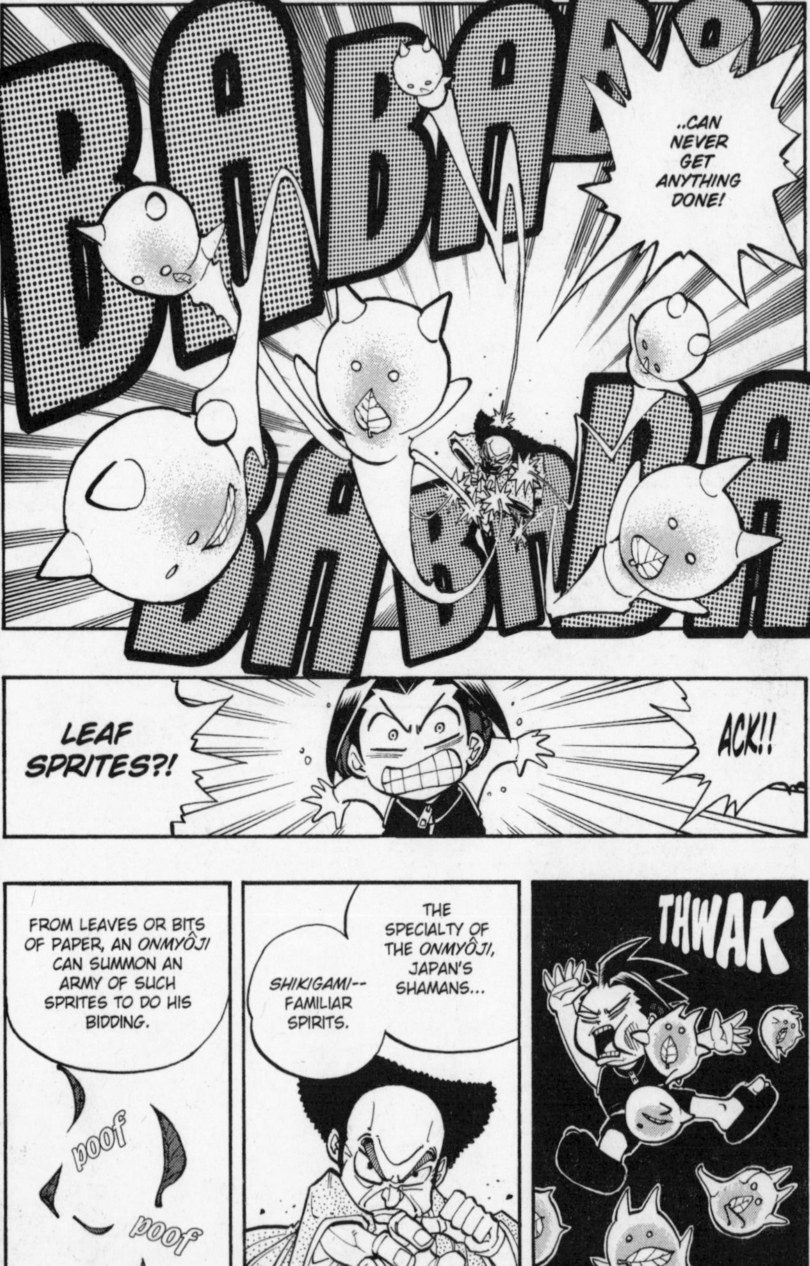
..CAN NEVER GET ANYTHING DONE!
ACK!!
LEAF SPRITES?!
THWAK
THE SPECIALTY OF THE *ONMYÔJI*, JAPAN'S SHAMANS...
SHIKIGAMI-- FAMILIAR SPIRITS.
FROM LEAVES OR BITS OF PAPER, AN *ONMYÔJI* CAN SUMMON AN ARMY OF SUCH SPRITES TO DO HIS BIDDING.
poof
poof

READ THIS WAY

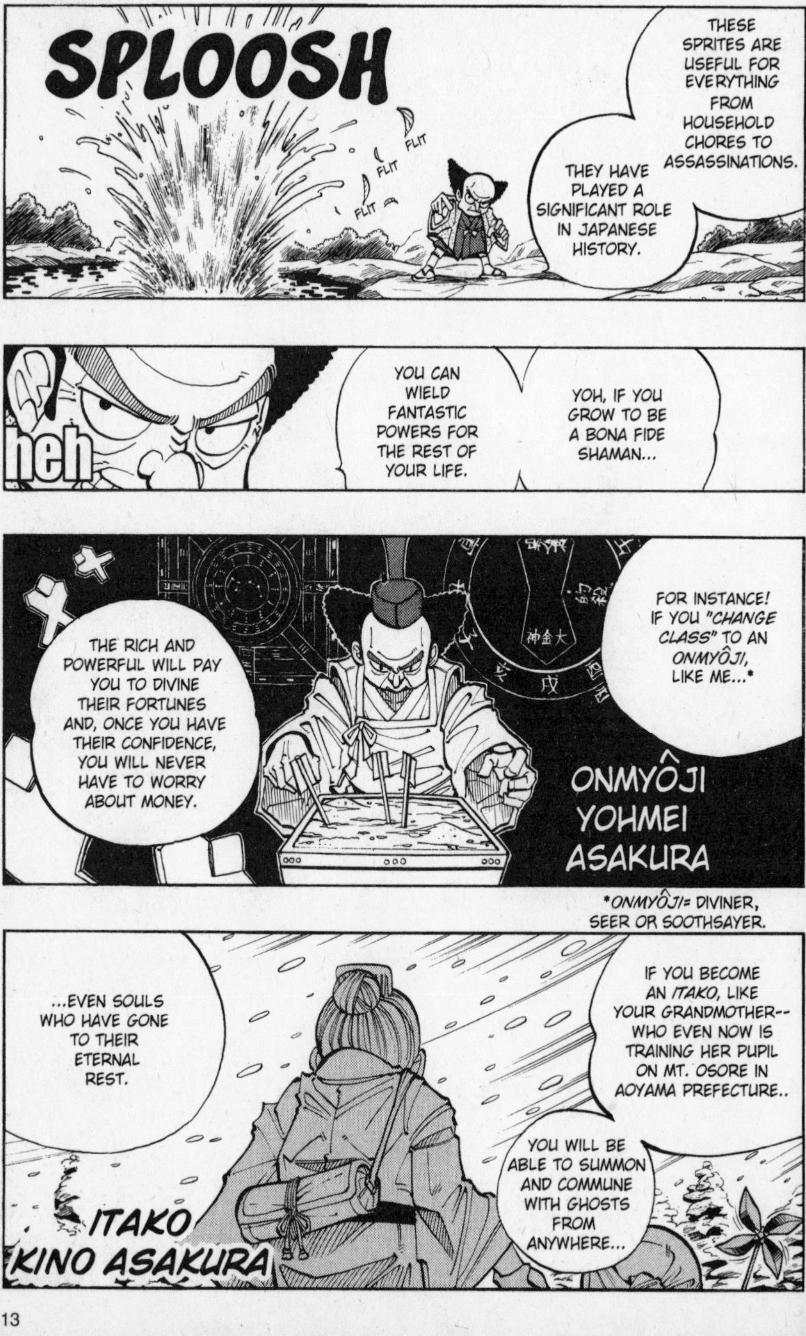
THESE SPRITES ARE USEFUL FOR EVERYTHING FROM HOUSEHOLD CHORES TO ASSASSINATIONS.
THEY HAVE PLAYED A SIGNIFICANT ROLE IN JAPANESE HISTORY.
FLIT FLIT FLIT
SPLOOSH
YOH, IF YOU GROW TO BE A BONA FIDE SHAMAN...
YOU CAN WIELD FANTASTIC POWERS FOR THE REST OF YOUR LIFE.
heh
FOR INSTANCE! IF YOU "CHANGE CLASS" TO AN ONMYÔJI, LIKE ME...*
ONMYÔJI YOHMEI ASAKURA
THE RICH AND POWERFUL WILL PAY YOU TO DIVINE THEIR FORTUNES AND, ONCE YOU HAVE THEIR CONFIDENCE, YOU WILL NEVER HAVE TO WORRY ABOUT MONEY.
IF YOU BECOME AN ITAKO, LIKE YOUR GRANDMOTHER-- WHO EVEN NOW IS TRAINING HER PUPIL ON MT. OSORE IN AOYAMA PREFECTURE..
YOU WILL BE ABLE TO SUMMON AND COMMUNE WITH GHOSTS FROM ANYWHERE...
...EVEN SOULS WHO HAVE GONE TO THEIR ETERNAL REST.
ITAKO KINO ASAKURA

*ONMYÔJI= DIVINER, SEER OR SOOTHSAYER.

READ THIS WAY

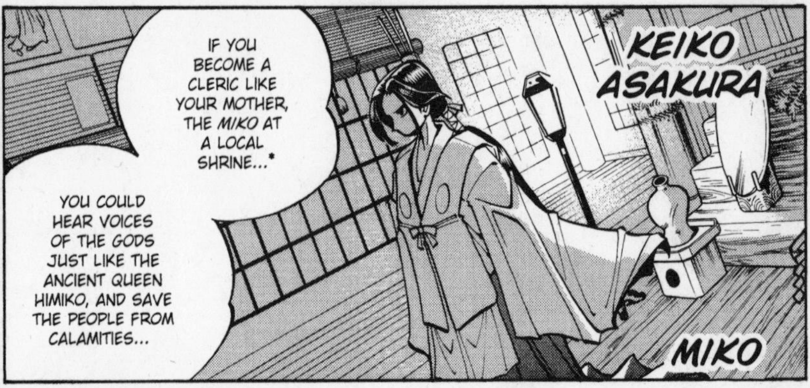

KEIKO ASAKURA
IF YOU BECOME A CLERIC LIKE YOUR MOTHER, THE *MIKO* AT A LOCAL SHRINE...*
YOU COULD HEAR VOICES OF THE GODS JUST LIKE THE ANCIENT QUEEN HIMIKO, AND SAVE THE PEOPLE FROM CALAMITIES...
MIKO

**MIKO* = SHRINE PRIESTESS

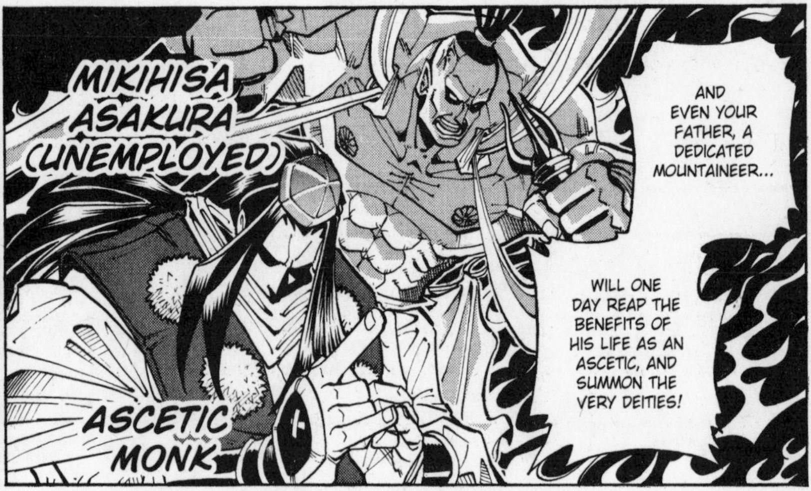

AND EVEN YOUR FATHER, A DEDICATED MOUNTAINEER...
MIKIHISA ASAKURA (UNEMPLOYED)
WILL ONE DAY REAP THE BENEFITS OF HIS LIFE AS AN ASCETIC, AND SUMMON THE VERY DEITIES!
ASCETIC MONK

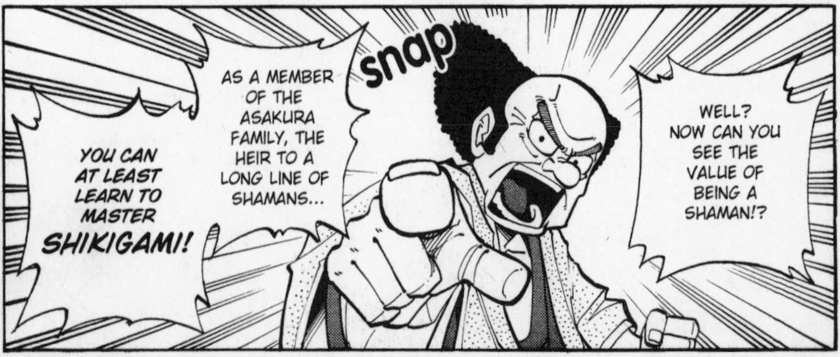

snap
WELL? NOW CAN YOU SEE THE VALUE OF BEING A SHAMAN!?
AS A MEMBER OF THE ASAKURA FAMILY, THE HEIR TO A LONG LINE OF SHAMANS...
YOU CAN AT LEAST LEARN TO MASTER SHIKIGAMI!

READ THIS WAY

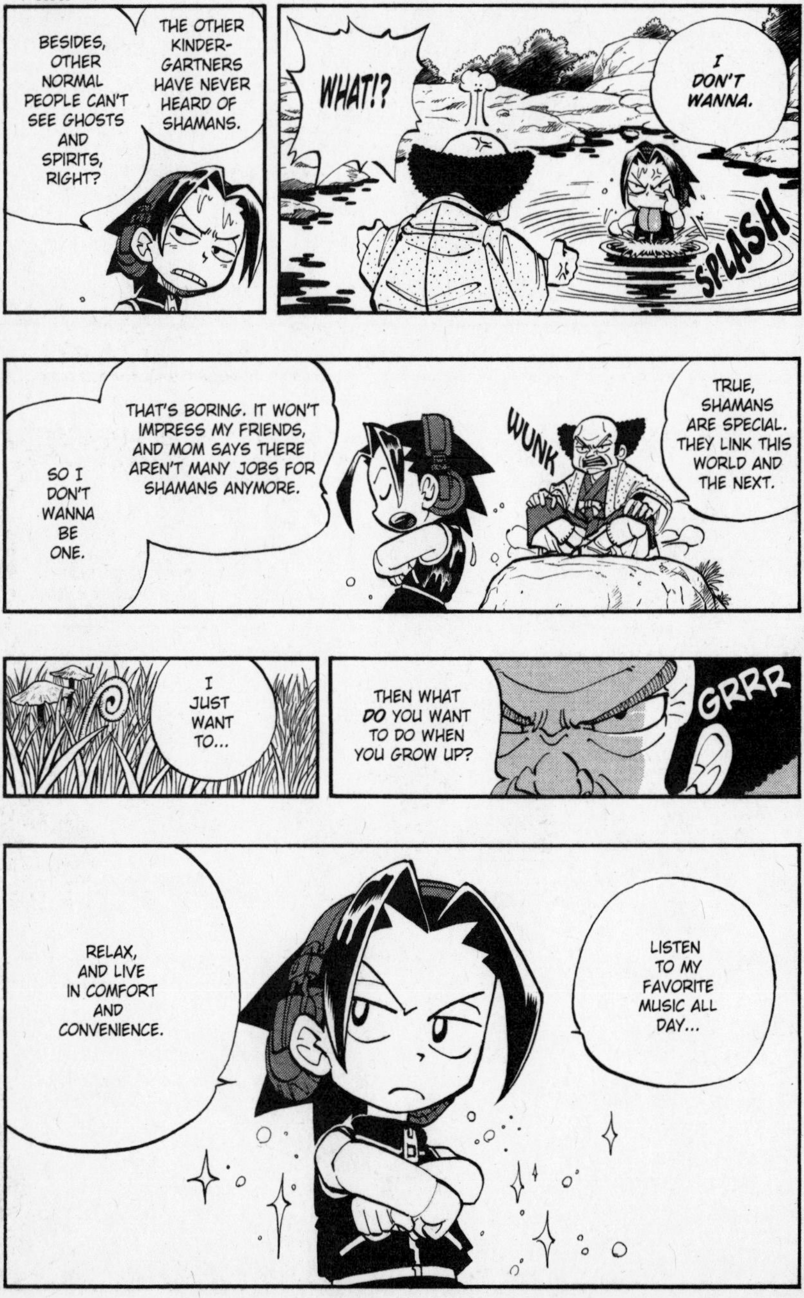
I DON'T WANNA.
WHAT!?
SPLASH
THE OTHER KINDER-GARTNERS HAVE NEVER HEARD OF SHAMANS.
BESIDES, OTHER NORMAL PEOPLE CAN'T SEE GHOSTS AND SPIRITS, RIGHT?
TRUE, SHAMANS ARE SPECIAL. THEY LINK THIS WORLD AND THE NEXT.
WUNK
THAT'S BORING. IT WON'T IMPRESS MY FRIENDS, AND MOM SAYS THERE AREN'T MANY JOBS FOR SHAMANS ANYMORE.
SO I DON'T WANNA BE ONE.
GRRR
THEN WHAT *DO* YOU WANT TO DO WHEN YOU GROW UP?
I JUST WANT TO...
LISTEN TO MY FAVORITE MUSIC ALL DAY...
RELAX, AND LIVE IN COMFORT AND CONVENIENCE.

READ THIS WAY

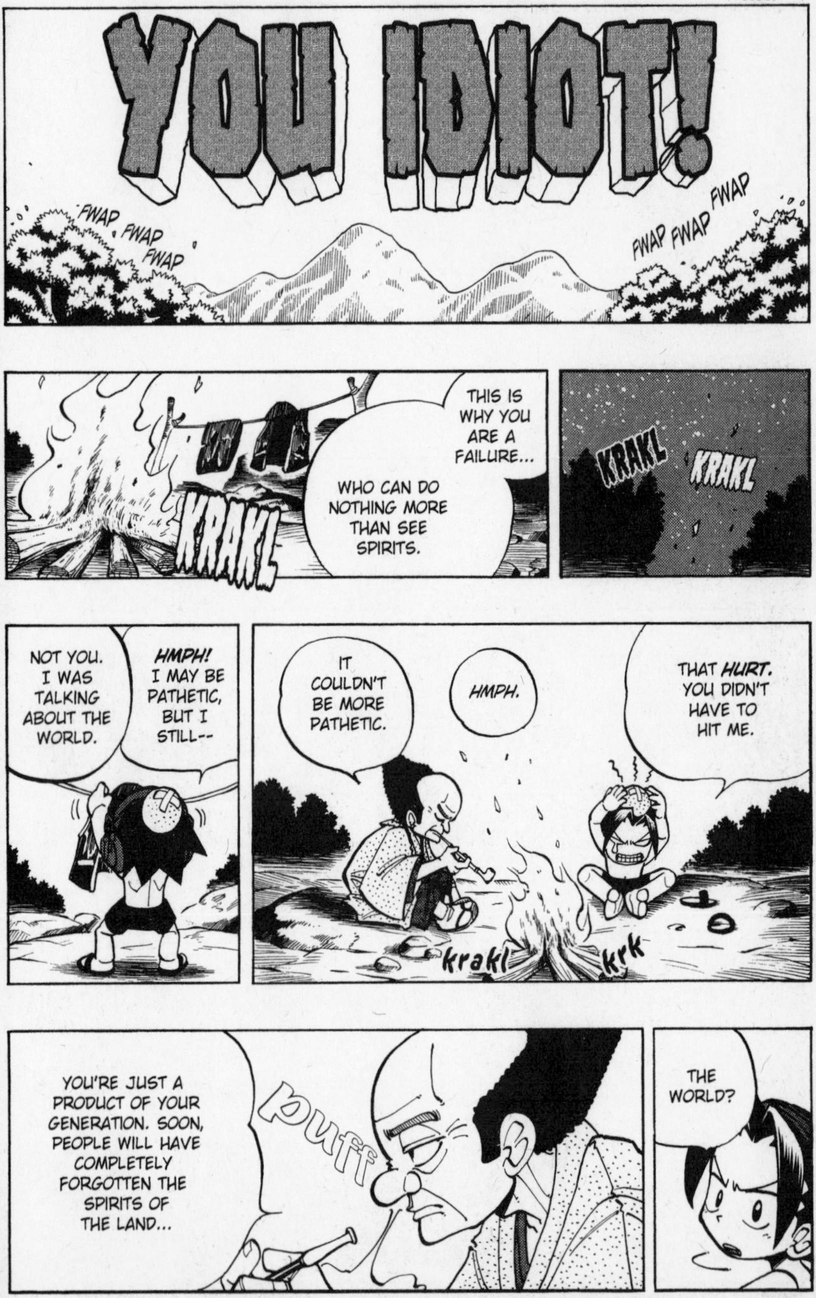
YOU IDIOT!
FWAP FWAP FWAP
FWAP FWAP FWAP
KRAKL
KRAKL
THIS IS WHY YOU ARE A FAILURE...
WHO CAN DO NOTHING MORE THAN SEE SPIRITS.
KRAKL
THAT ***HURT.*** YOU DIDN'T HAVE TO HIT ME.
HMPH.
IT COULDN'T BE MORE PATHETIC.
krakl
krk
HMPH! I MAY BE PATHETIC, BUT I STILL--
NOT YOU. I WAS TALKING ABOUT THE WORLD.
THE WORLD?
puff
YOU'RE JUST A PRODUCT OF YOUR GENERATION. SOON, PEOPLE WILL HAVE COMPLETELY FORGOTTEN THE SPIRITS OF THE LAND...

READ THIS WAY

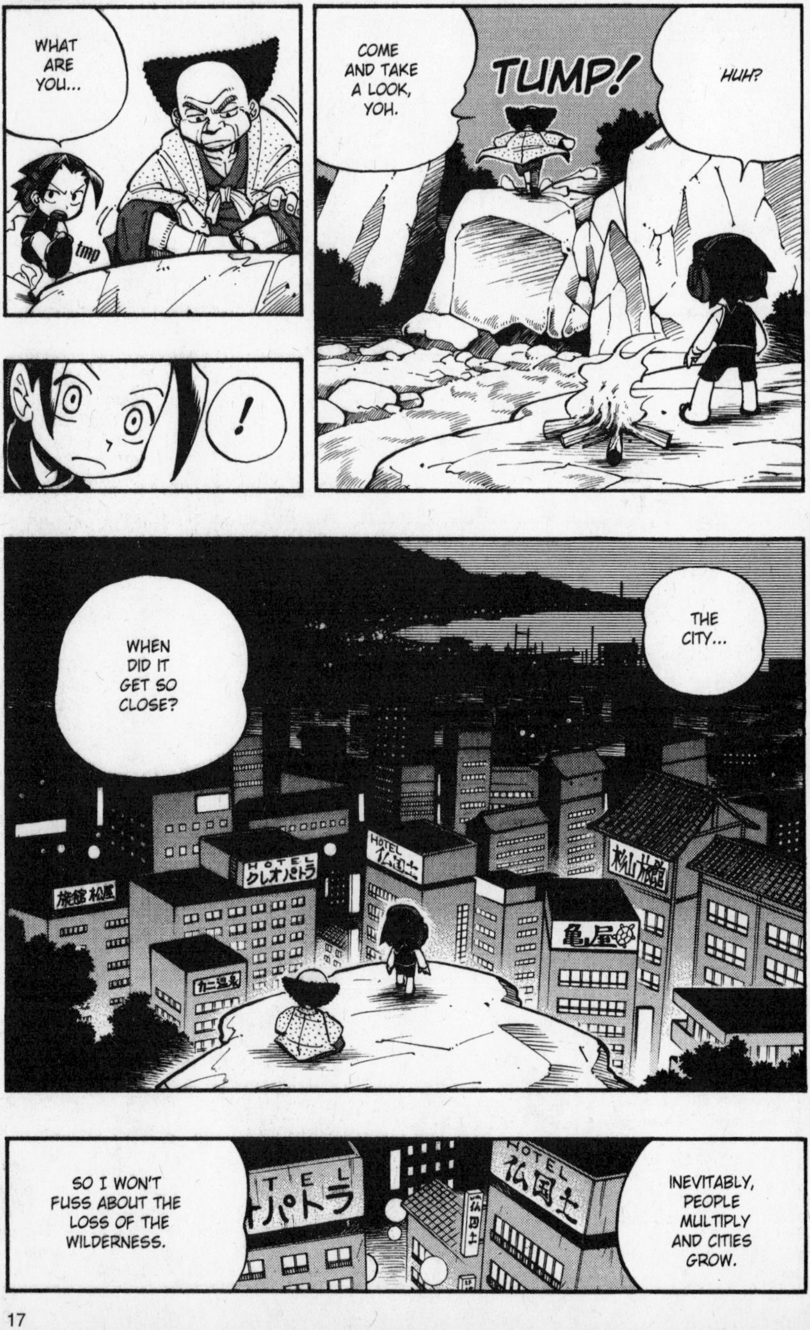

HUH?
TUMP!
COME AND TAKE A LOOK, YOH.
WHAT ARE YOU...
tmp
!
THE CITY...
WHEN DID IT GET SO CLOSE?
HOTEL クレオパトラ
旅館 松屋
亀屋
INEVITABLY, PEOPLE MULTIPLY AND CITIES GROW.
SO I WON'T FUSS ABOUT THE LOSS OF THE WILDERNESS.

READ THIS WAY

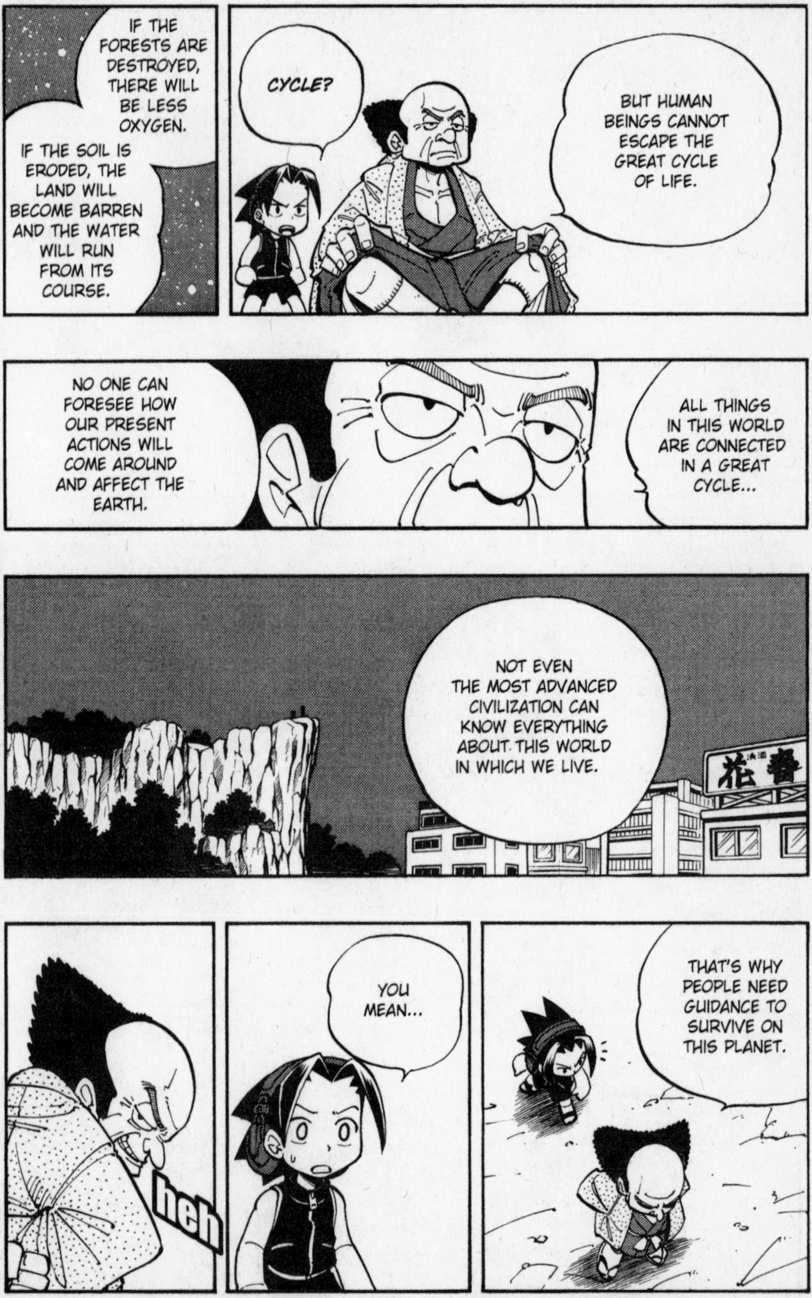
BUT HUMAN BEINGS CANNOT ESCAPE THE GREAT CYCLE OF LIFE.
CYCLE?
IF THE FORESTS ARE DESTROYED, THERE WILL BE LESS OXYGEN.
IF THE SOIL IS ERODED, THE LAND WILL BECOME BARREN AND THE WATER WILL RUN FROM ITS COURSE.
ALL THINGS IN THIS WORLD ARE CONNECTED IN A GREAT CYCLE...
NO ONE CAN FORESEE HOW OUR PRESENT ACTIONS WILL COME AROUND AND AFFECT THE EARTH.
NOT EVEN THE MOST ADVANCED CIVILIZATION CAN KNOW EVERYTHING ABOUT THIS WORLD IN WHICH WE LIVE.
THAT'S WHY PEOPLE NEED GUIDANCE TO SURVIVE ON THIS PLANET.
YOU MEAN...
heh

READ THIS WAY

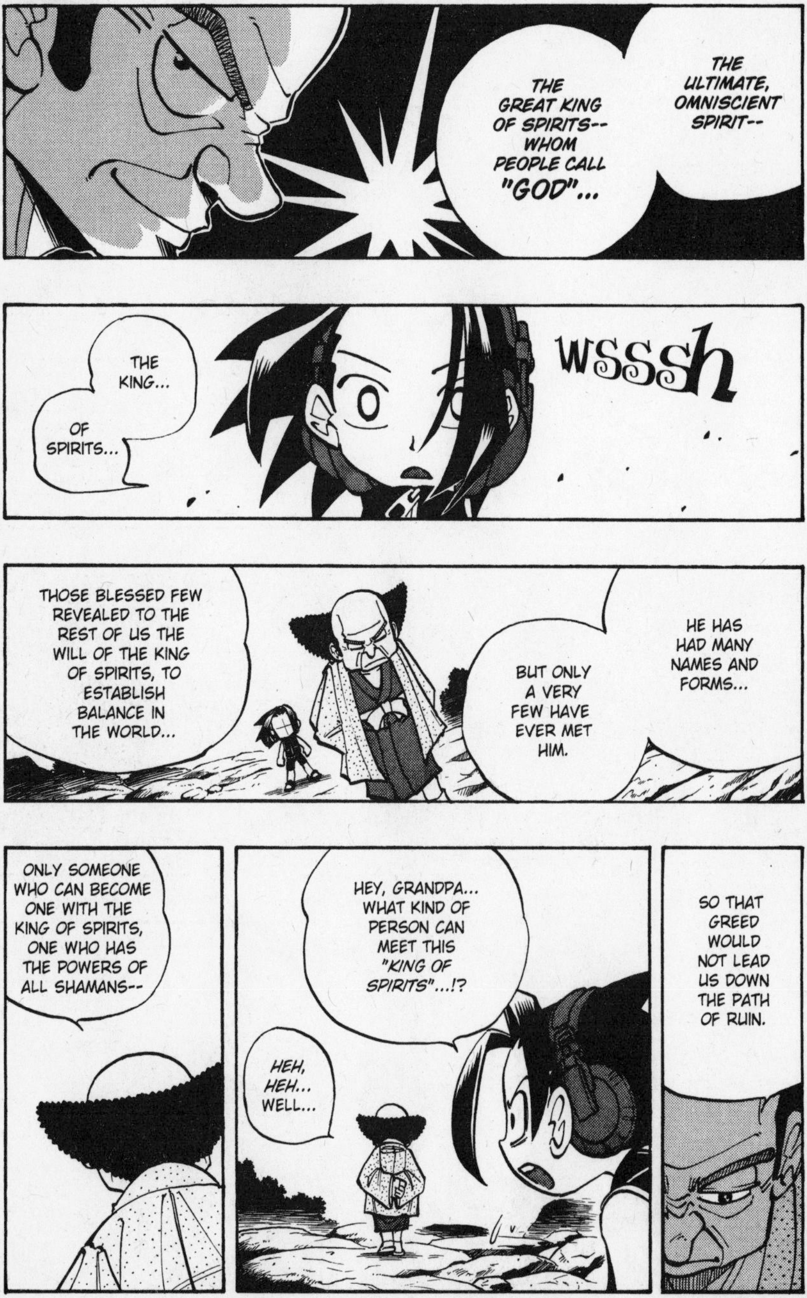

THE ULTIMATE, OMNISCIENT SPIRIT--
THE GREAT KING OF SPIRITS-- WHOM PEOPLE CALL "GOD"...
WSSSH
THE KING...
OF SPIRITS...
HE HAS HAD MANY NAMES AND FORMS...
BUT ONLY A VERY FEW HAVE EVER MET HIM.
THOSE BLESSED FEW REVEALED TO THE REST OF US THE WILL OF THE KING OF SPIRITS, TO ESTABLISH BALANCE IN THE WORLD...
SO THAT GREED WOULD NOT LEAD US DOWN THE PATH OF RUIN.
HEY, GRANDPA... WHAT KIND OF PERSON CAN MEET THIS "KING OF SPIRITS"...!?
HEH, HEH... WELL...
ONLY SOMEONE WHO CAN BECOME ONE WITH THE KING OF SPIRITS, ONE WHO HAS THE POWERS OF ALL SHAMANS--

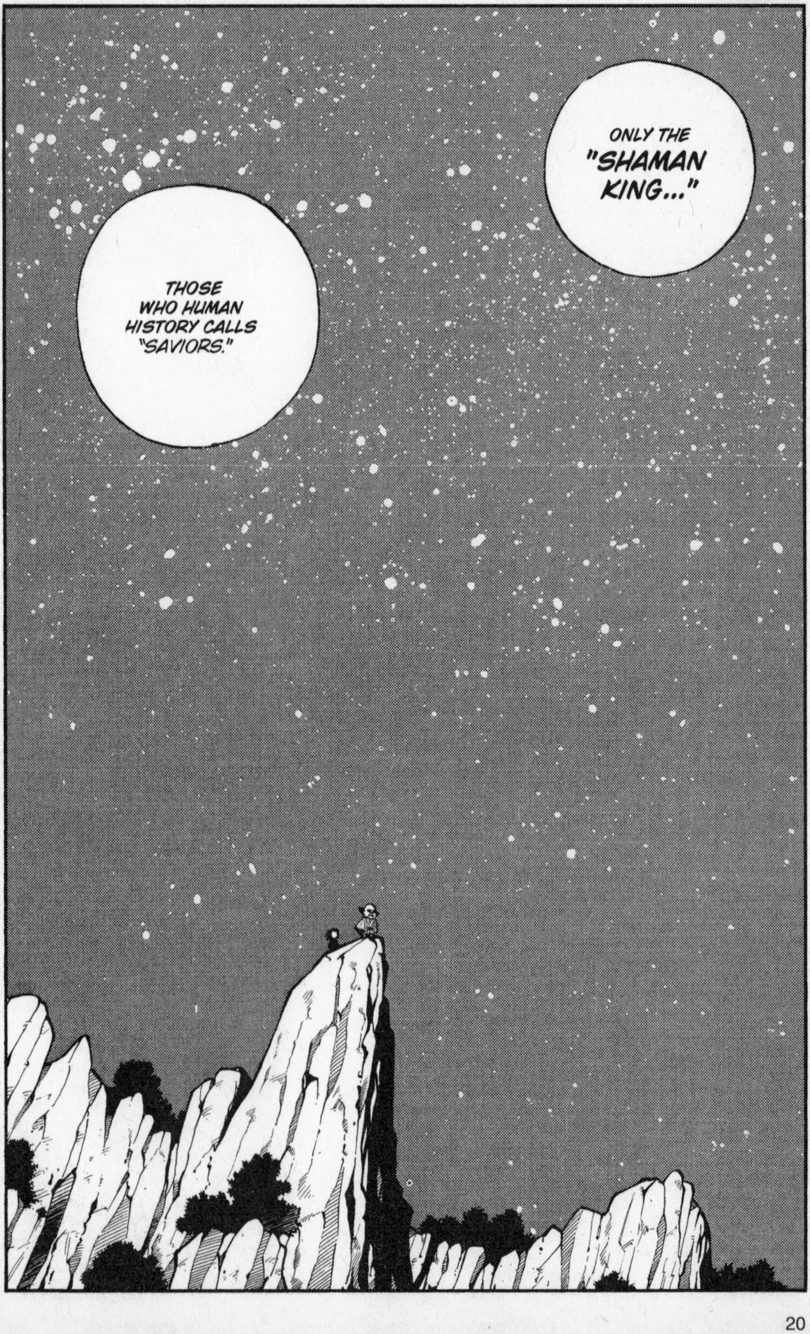

READ THIS WAY
ONLY THE "SHAMAN KING..."
THOSE WHO HUMAN HISTORY CALLS "SAVIORS."

READ THIS WAY

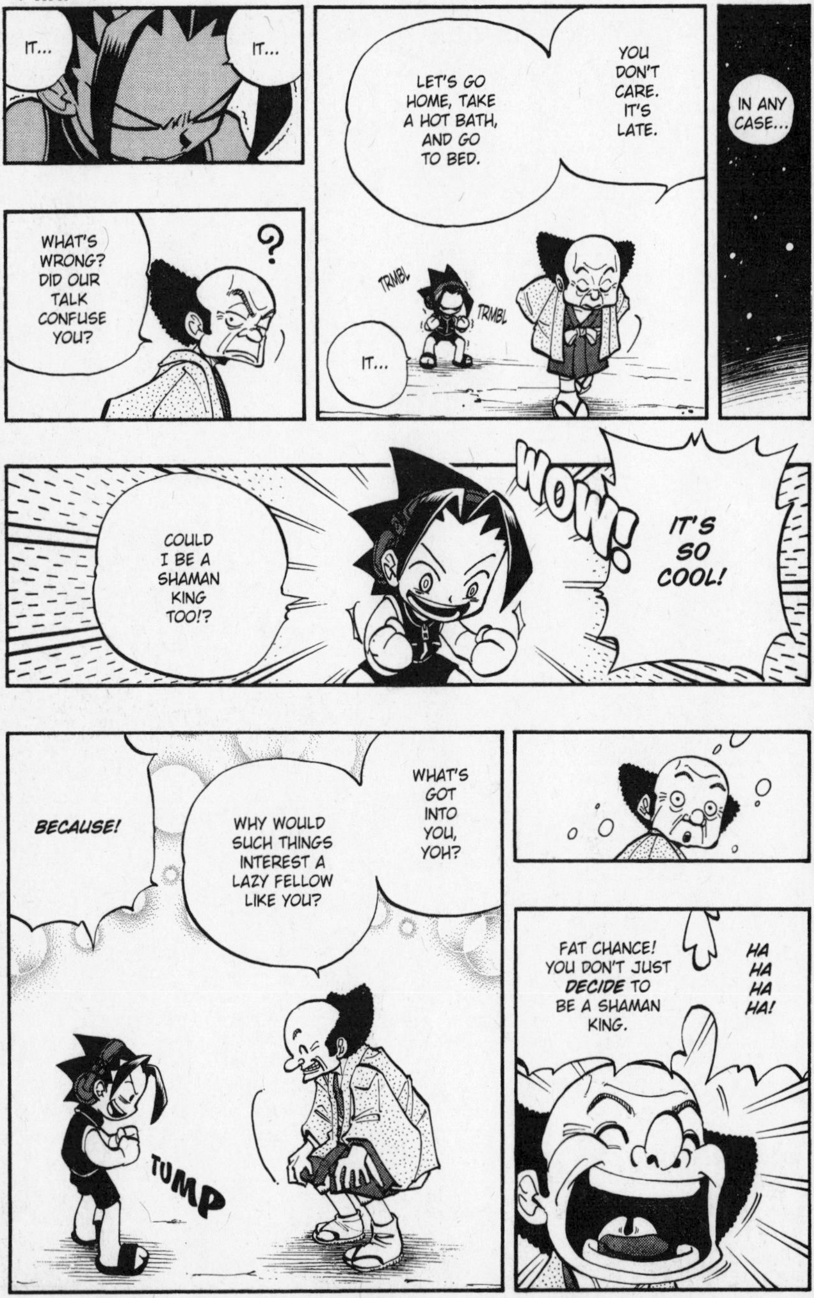
IN ANY CASE...
YOU DON'T CARE. IT'S LATE.
LET'S GO HOME, TAKE A HOT BATH, AND GO TO BED.
TRMBL
TRMBL
IT...
IT...
IT...
?
WHAT'S WRONG? DID OUR TALK CONFUSE YOU?
WOW!
IT'S SO COOL!
COULD I BE A SHAMAN KING TOO!?
HA HA HA HA!
FAT CHANCE! YOU DON'T JUST *DECIDE* TO BE A SHAMAN KING.
WHAT'S GOT INTO YOU, YOH?
WHY WOULD SUCH THINGS INTEREST A LAZY FELLOW LIKE YOU?
BECAUSE!
TUMP

READ THIS WAY

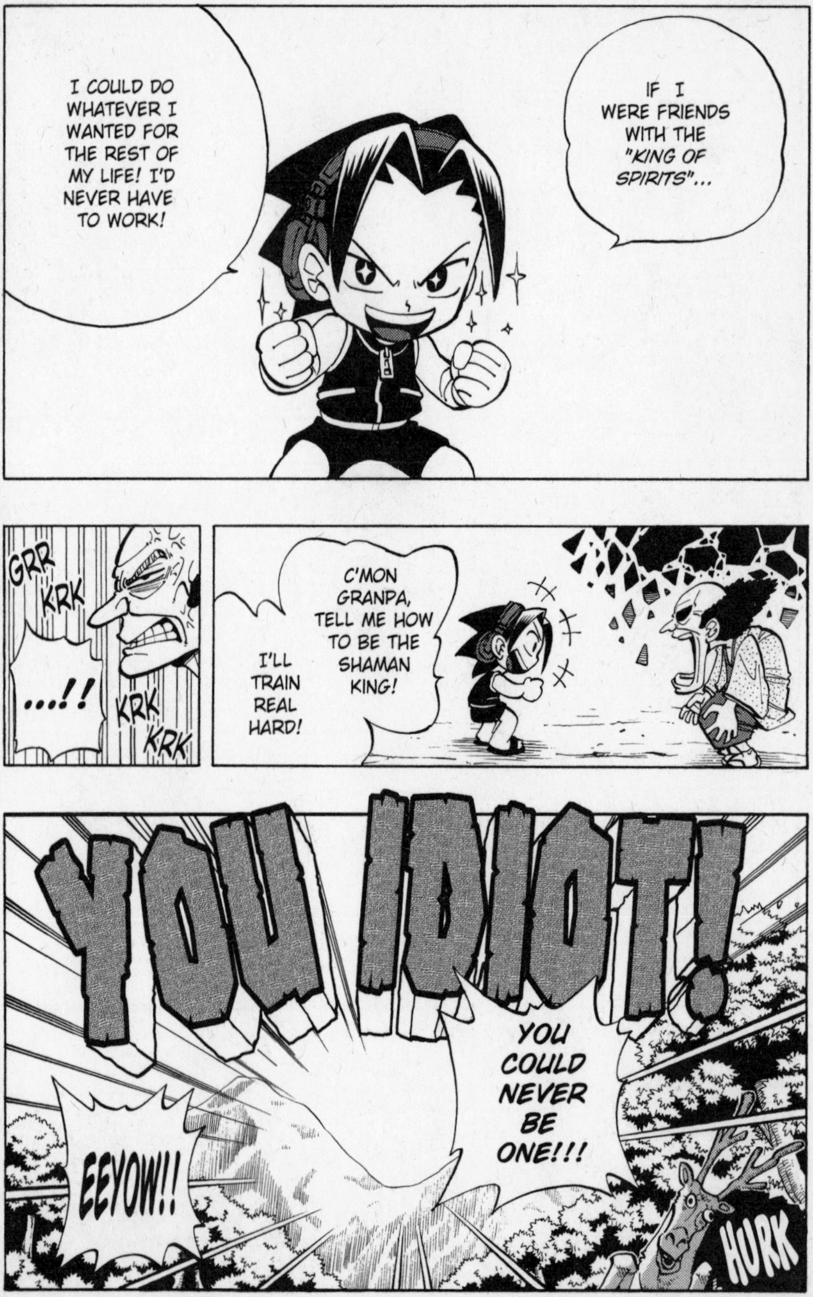
IF I WERE FRIENDS WITH THE "KING OF SPIRITS"...
I COULD DO WHATEVER I WANTED FOR THE REST OF MY LIFE! I'D NEVER HAVE TO WORK!
C'MON GRANPA, TELL ME HOW TO BE THE SHAMAN KING!
I'LL TRAIN REAL HARD!
GRR KRK
...!!
KRK KRK
YOU IDIOT!
YOU COULD NEVER BE ONE!!!
HURK
EEYOW!!

READ THIS WAY

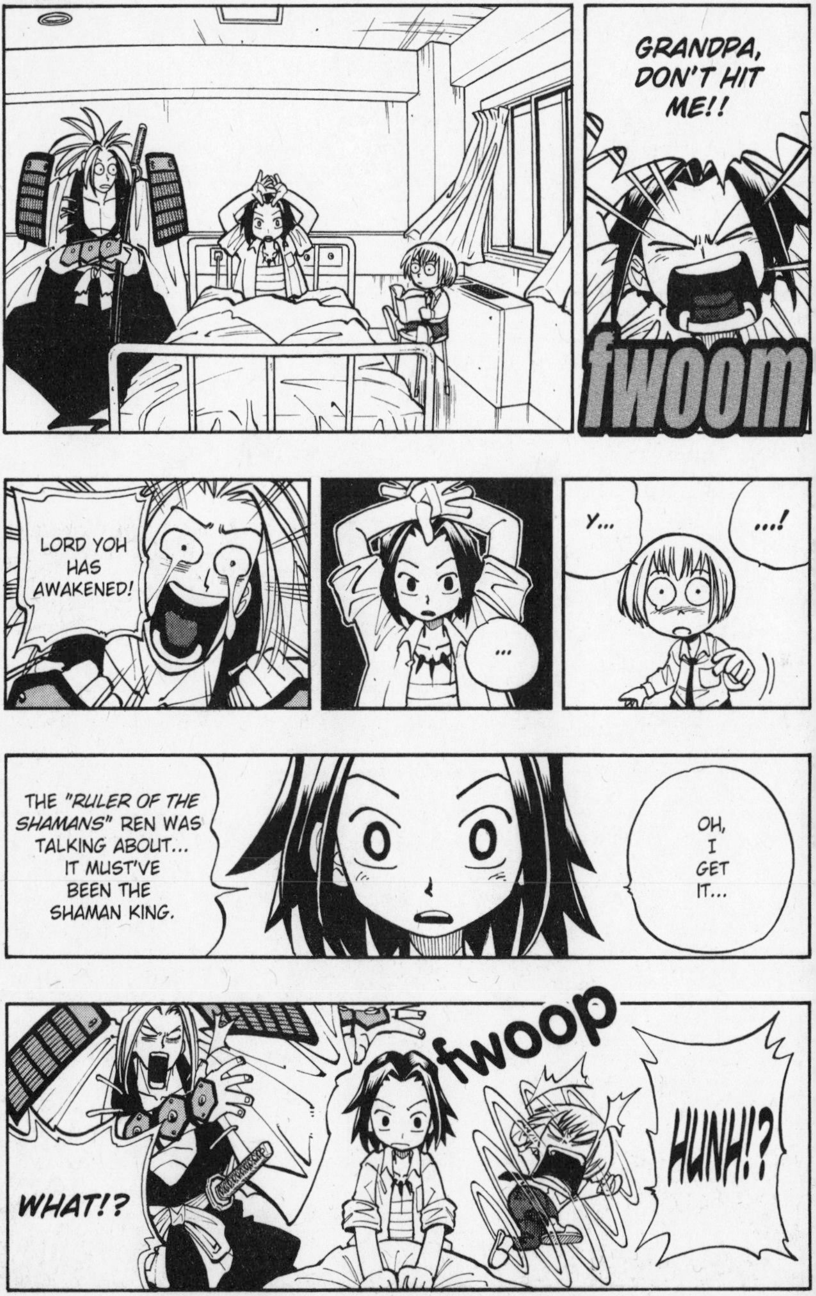
GRANDPA, DON'T HIT ME!!
fwoom
...!
Y...
...
LORD YOH HAS AWAKENED!
OH, I GET IT...
THE "RULER OF THE SHAMANS" REN WAS TALKING ABOUT... IT MUST'VE BEEN THE SHAMAN KING.
fwoop
HUNH!?
WHAT!?

READ THIS WAY

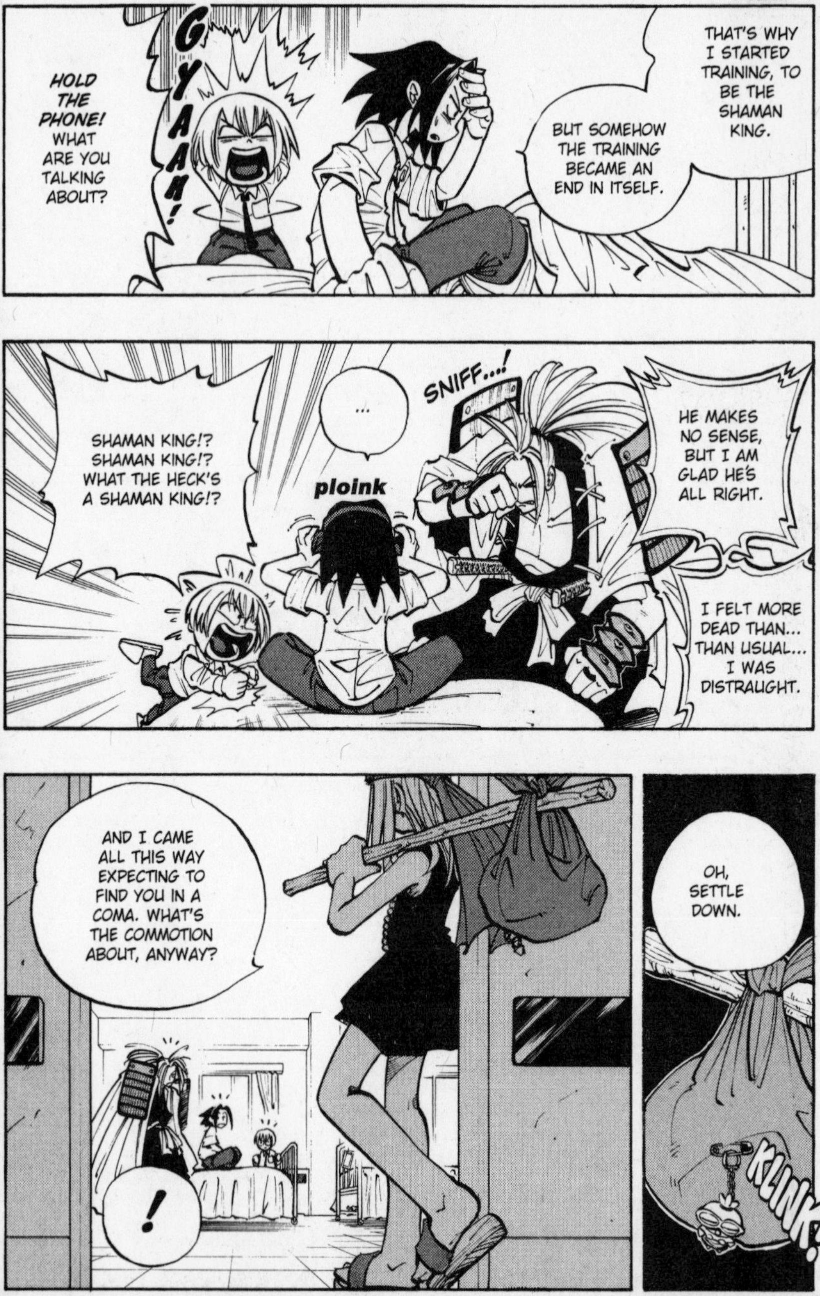
THAT'S WHY I STARTED TRAINING, TO BE THE SHAMAN KING.
BUT SOMEHOW THE TRAINING BECAME AN END IN ITSELF.
GYAAAH!
HOLD THE PHONE! WHAT ARE YOU TALKING ABOUT?
HE MAKES NO SENSE, BUT I AM GLAD HE'S ALL RIGHT.
I FELT MORE DEAD THAN... THAN USUAL... I WAS DISTRAUGHT.
SNIFF...!
...
ploink
SHAMAN KING!? SHAMAN KING!? WHAT THE HECK'S A SHAMAN KING!?
OH, SETTLE DOWN.
KLINK!
AND I CAME ALL THIS WAY EXPECTING TO FIND YOU IN A COMA. WHAT'S THE COMMOTION ABOUT, ANYWAY?
!

READ THIS WAY

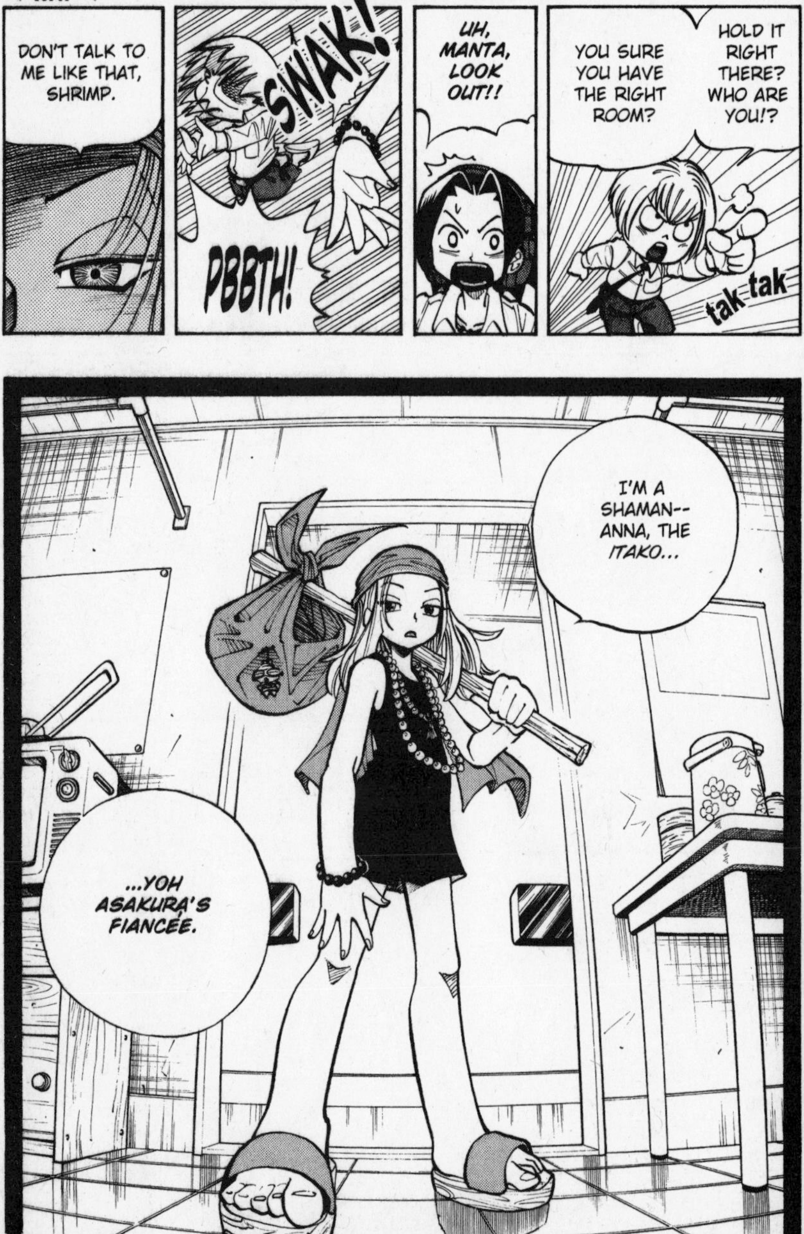
HOLD IT RIGHT THERE? WHO ARE YOU!?
YOU SURE YOU HAVE THE RIGHT ROOM?
tak tak
UH, MANTA, LOOK OUT!!
SWAK!
PBBTH!
DON'T TALK TO ME LIKE THAT, SHRIMP.
I'M A SHAMAN-- ANNA, THE *ITAKO*...
...YOH ASAKURA'S FIANCÉE.

SHAMAN KING CHARACTER FILE No.5

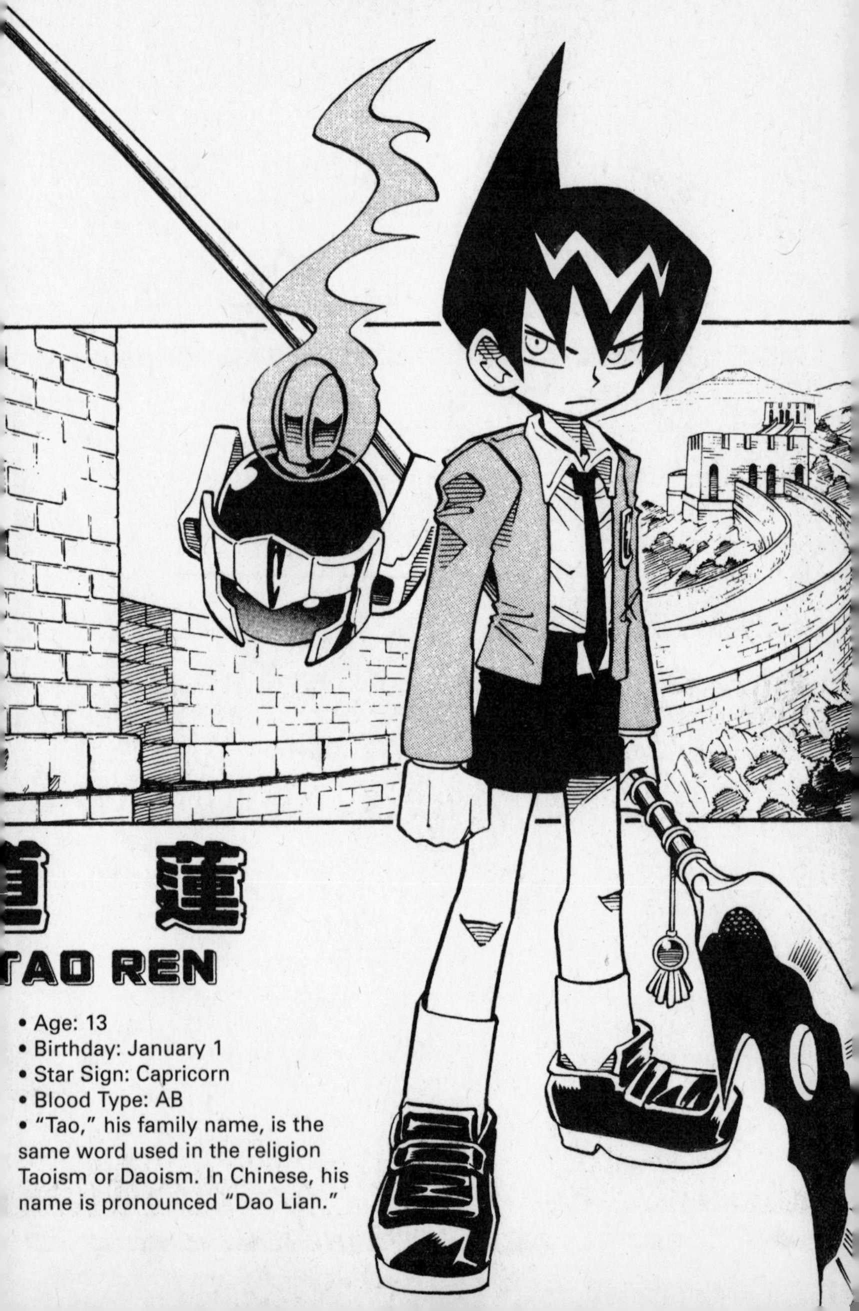

蓮

TAO REN

- Age: 13
- Birthday: January 1
- Star Sign: Capricorn
- Blood Type: AB
- "Tao," his family name, is the same word used in the religion Taoism or Daoism. In Chinese, his name is pronounced "Dao Lian."

REINCARNATION 10: SHAMAN'S AMBITION

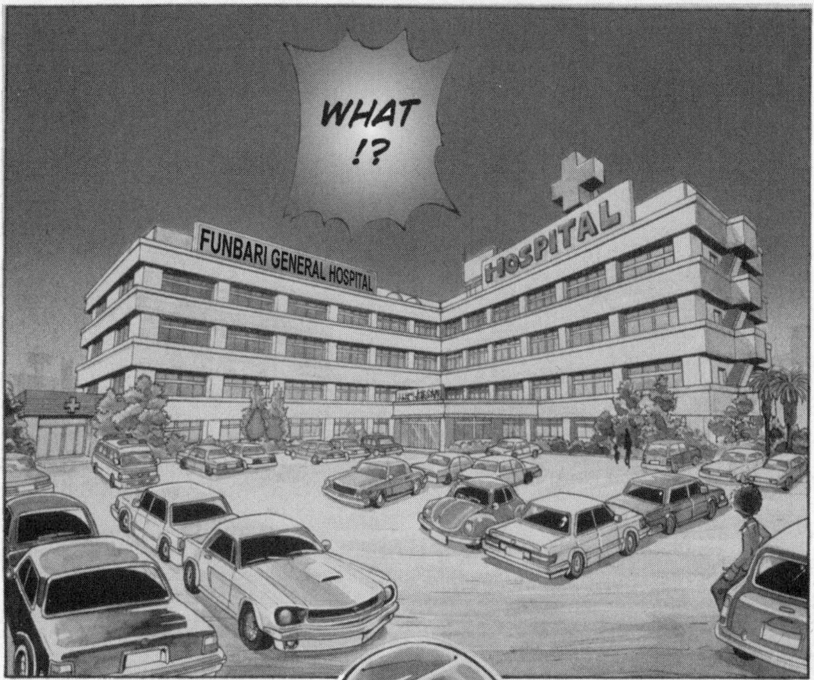
WHAT !?
HOSPITAL
FUNBARI GENERAL HOSPITAL

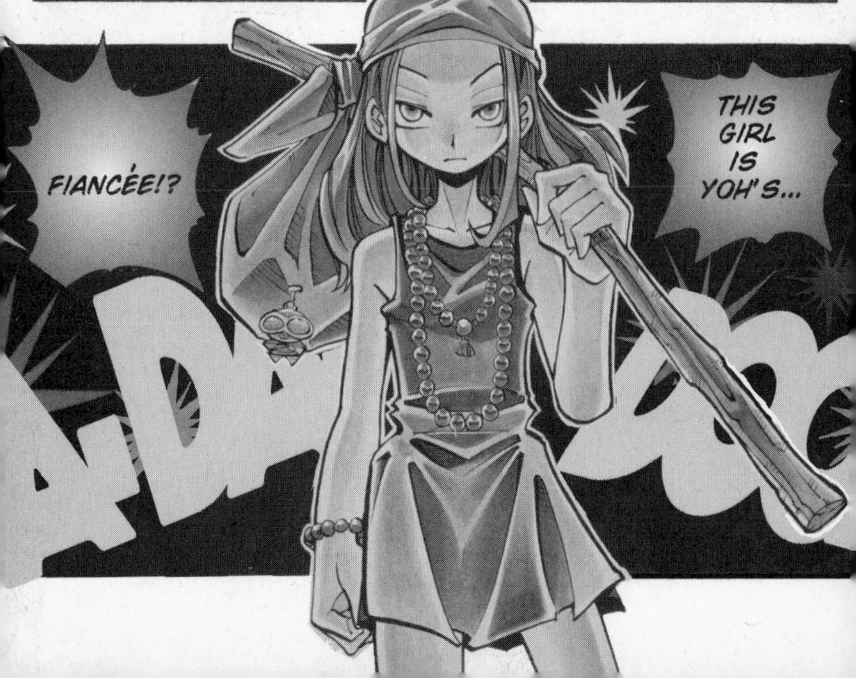
THIS GIRL IS YOH'S...
FIANCÉE!?

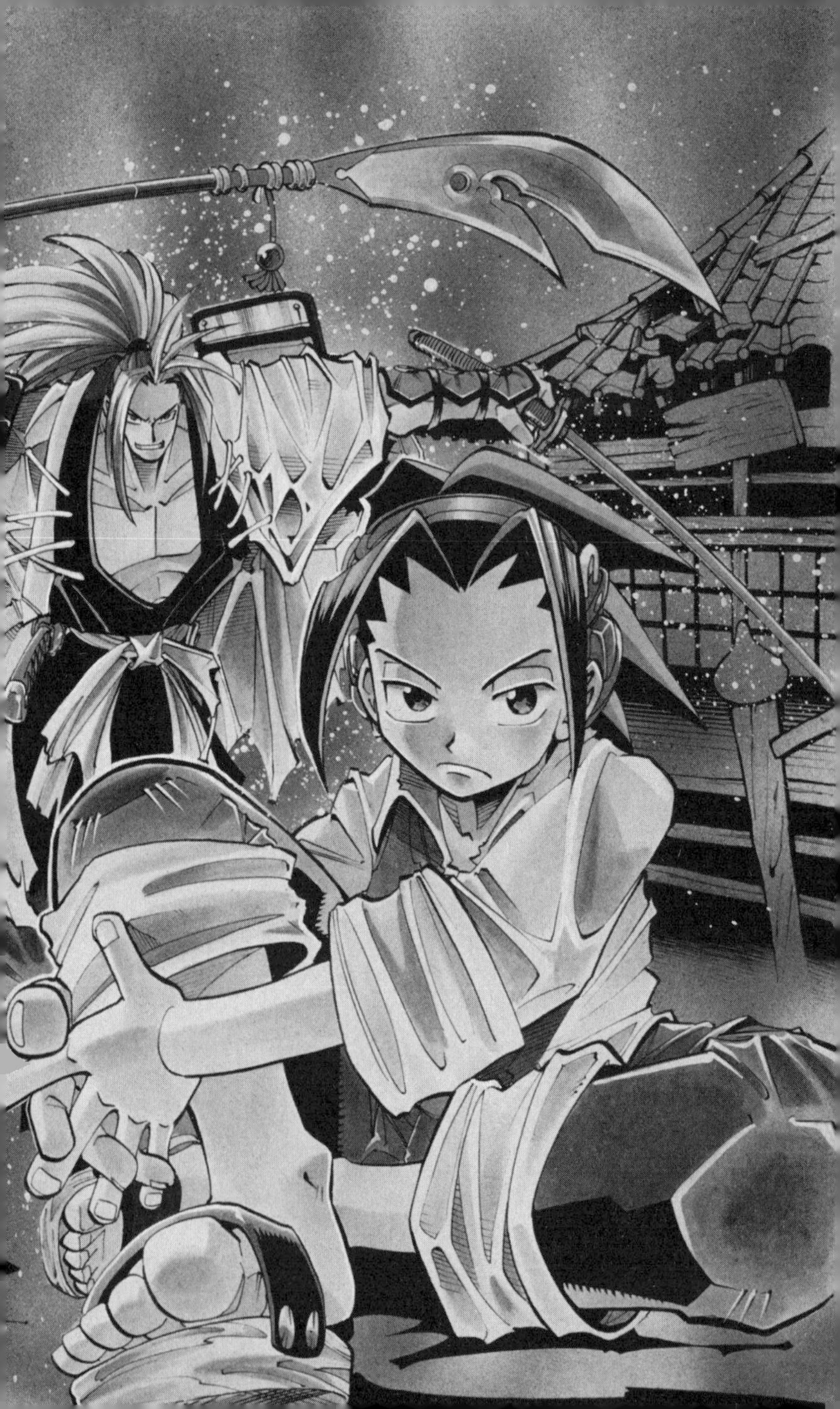

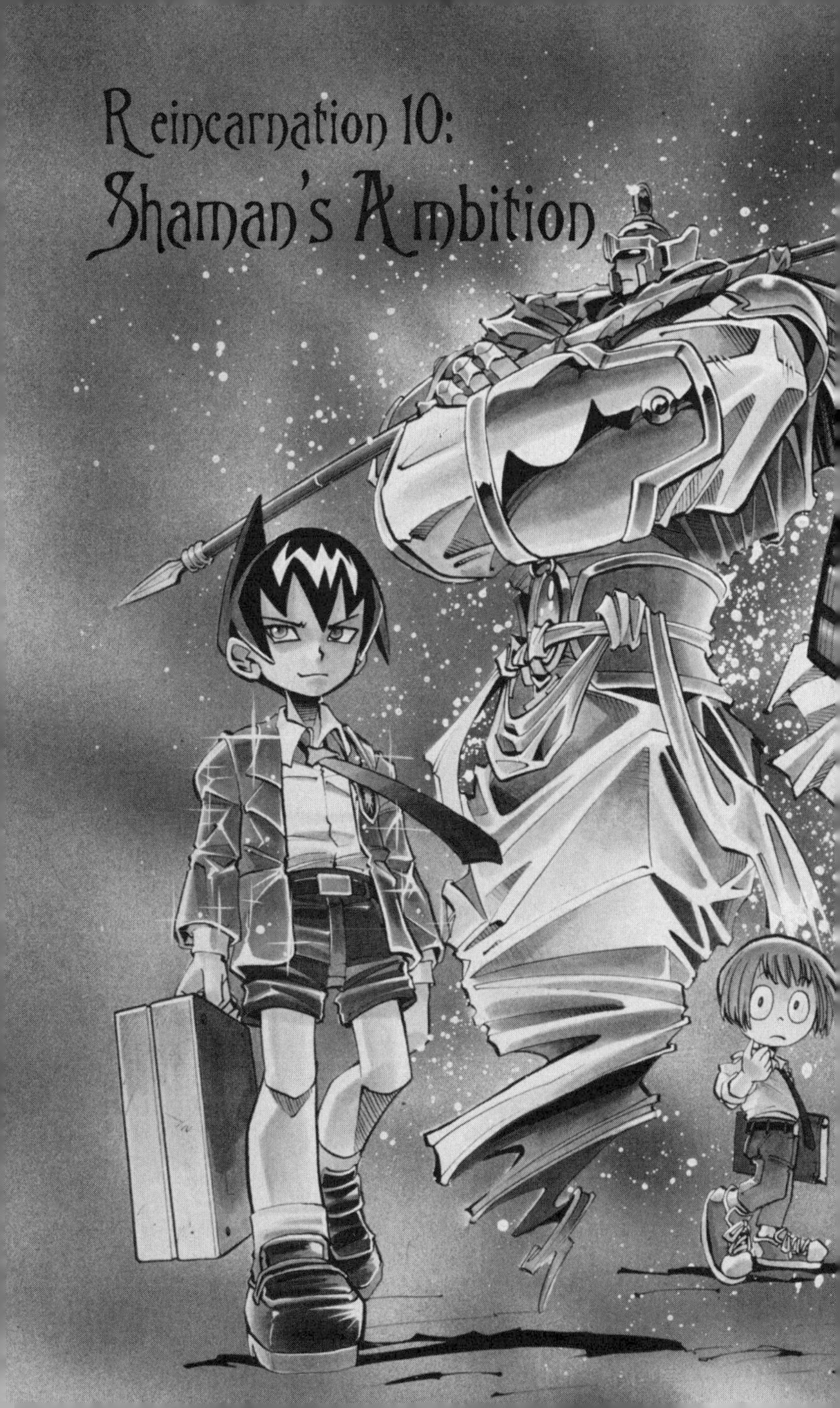
Reincarnation 10:
Shaman's Ambition

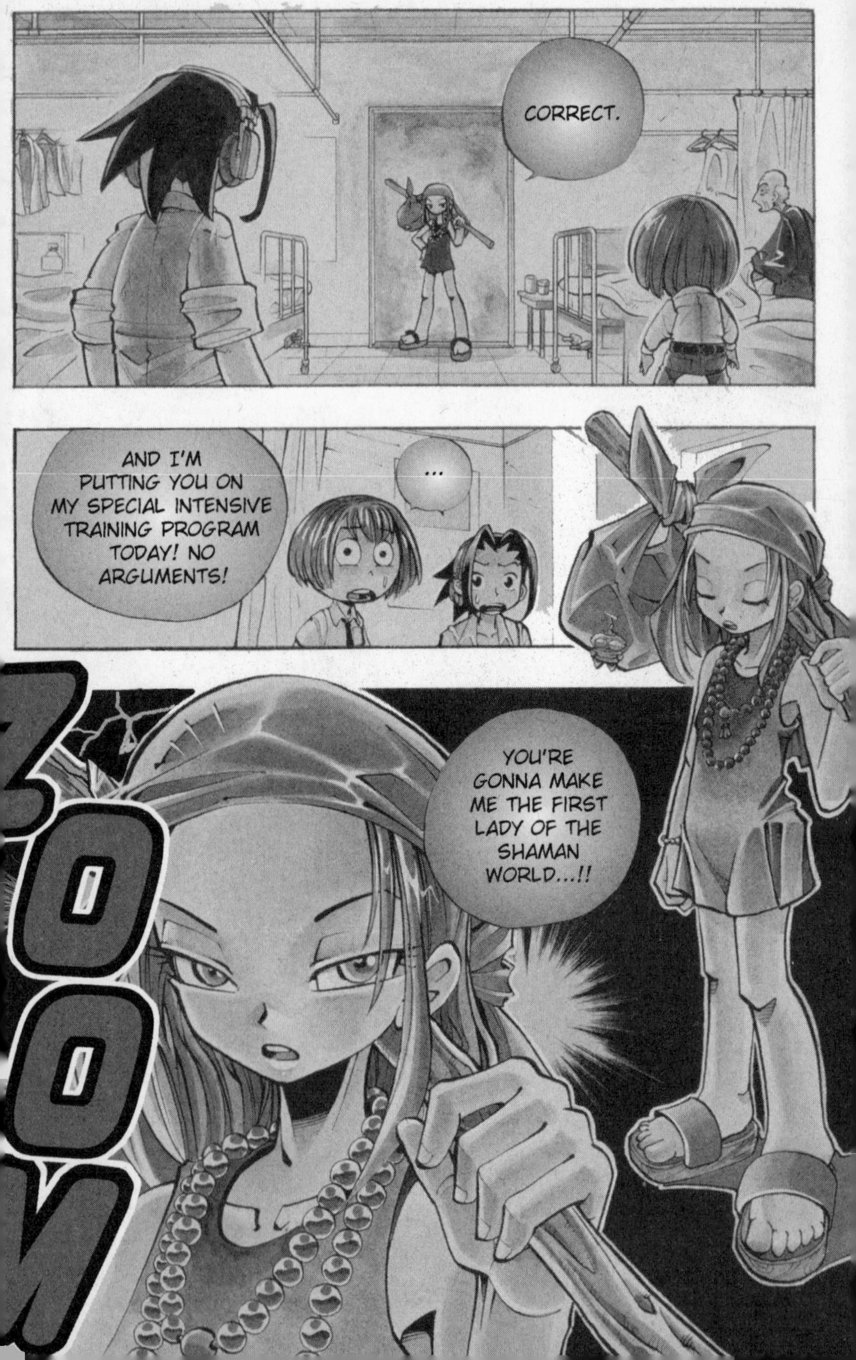
CORRECT.
...
AND I'M PUTTING YOU ON MY SPECIAL INTENSIVE TRAINING PROGRAM TODAY! NO ARGUMENTS!
YOU'RE GONNA MAKE ME THE FIRST LADY OF THE SHAMAN WORLD...!!

READ THIS WAY

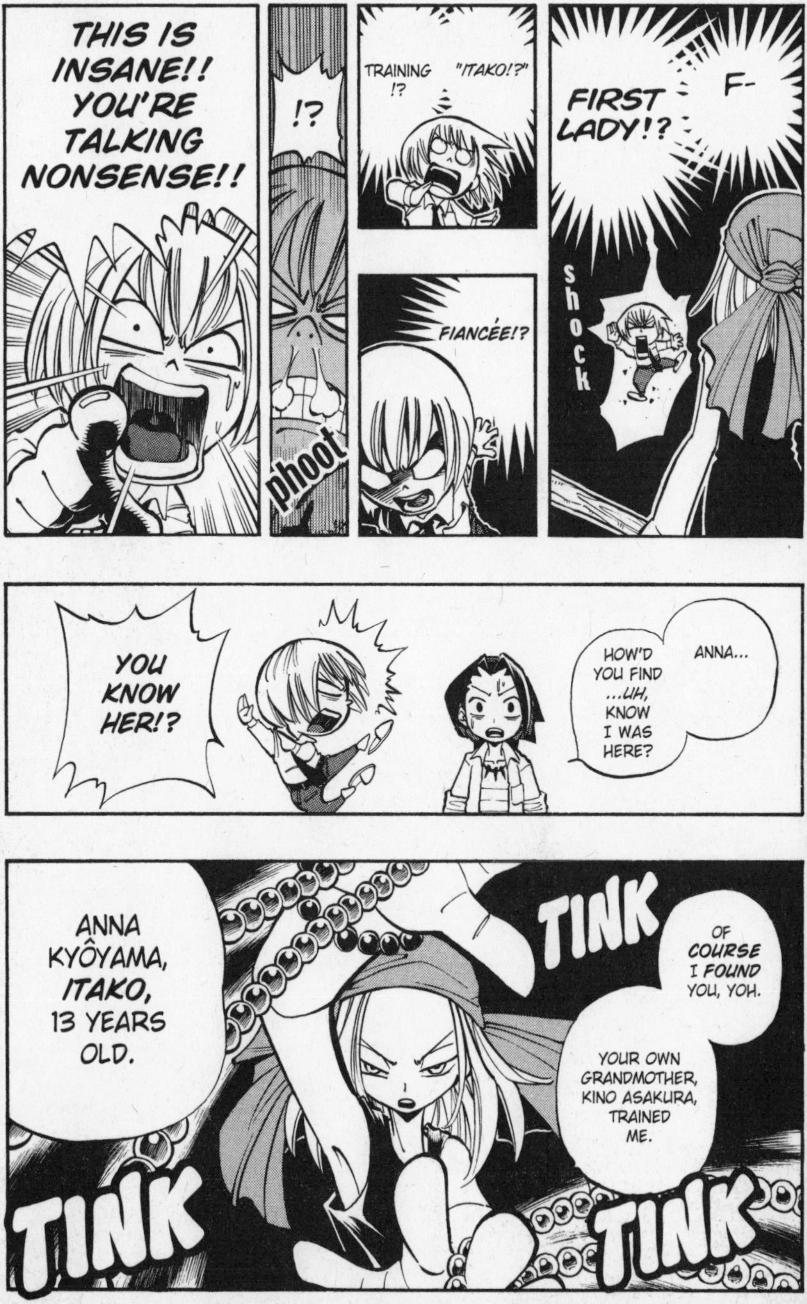

F-
FIRST LADY!?
shock
"ITAKO!?"
TRAINING !?
FIANCÉE!?
!?
phoot
THIS IS INSANE!! YOU'RE TALKING NONSENSE!!
ANNA...
HOW'D YOU FIND ...UH, KNOW I WAS HERE?
YOU KNOW HER!?
OF COURSE I FOUND YOU, YOH.
TINK
YOUR OWN GRANDMOTHER, KINO ASAKURA, TRAINED ME.
ANNA KYÔYAMA, ITAKO, 13 YEARS OLD.
TINK
TINK

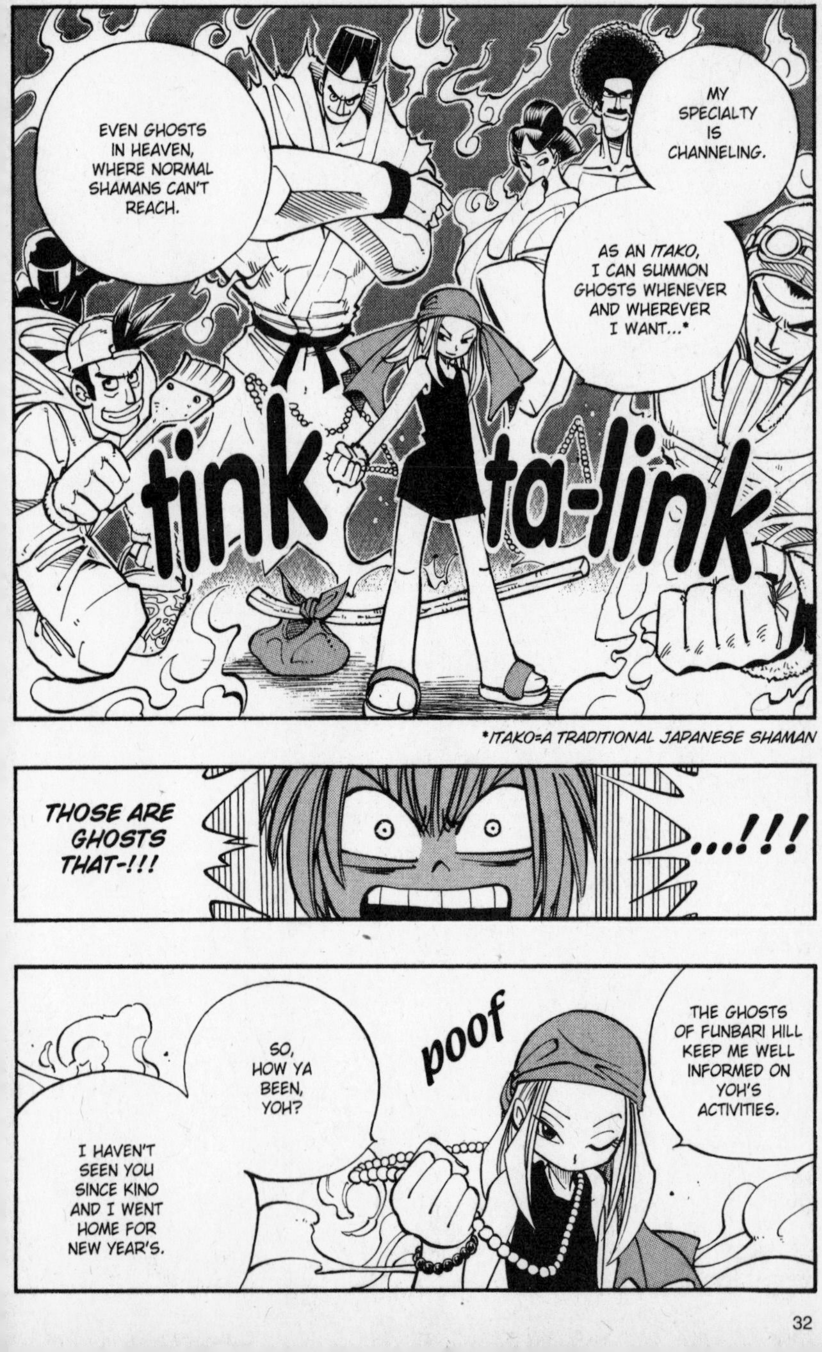
MY SPECIALTY IS CHANNELING.
AS AN *ITAKO*, I CAN SUMMON GHOSTS WHENEVER AND WHEREVER I WANT...*
EVEN GHOSTS IN HEAVEN, WHERE NORMAL SHAMANS CAN'T REACH.
tink ta-link
...!!!
THOSE ARE GHOSTS THAT-!!!
THE GHOSTS OF FUNBARI HILL KEEP ME WELL INFORMED ON YOH'S ACTIVITIES.
poof
SO, HOW YA BEEN, YOH?
I HAVEN'T SEEN YOU SINCE KINO AND I WENT HOME FOR NEW YEAR'S.

*ITAKO=A TRADITIONAL JAPANESE SHAMAN

READ THIS WAY

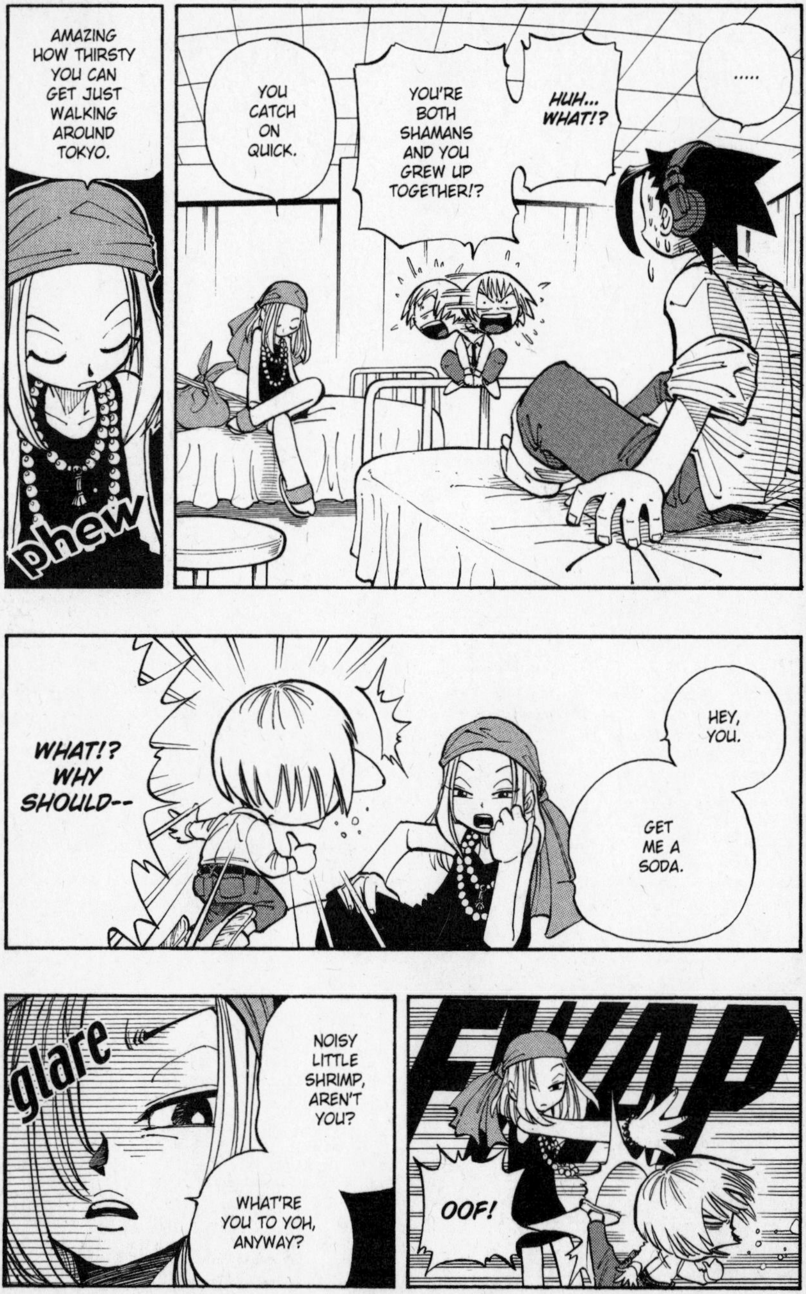
.....
HUH... WHAT!?
YOU'RE BOTH SHAMANS AND YOU GREW UP TOGETHER!?
YOU CATCH ON QUICK.
AMAZING HOW THIRSTY YOU CAN GET JUST WALKING AROUND TOKYO.
phew
HEY, YOU.
GET ME A SODA.
WHAT!? WHY SHOULD--
FWAP
OOF!
NOISY LITTLE SHRIMP, AREN'T YOU?
glare
WHAT'RE YOU TO YOH, ANYWAY?

READ THIS WAY

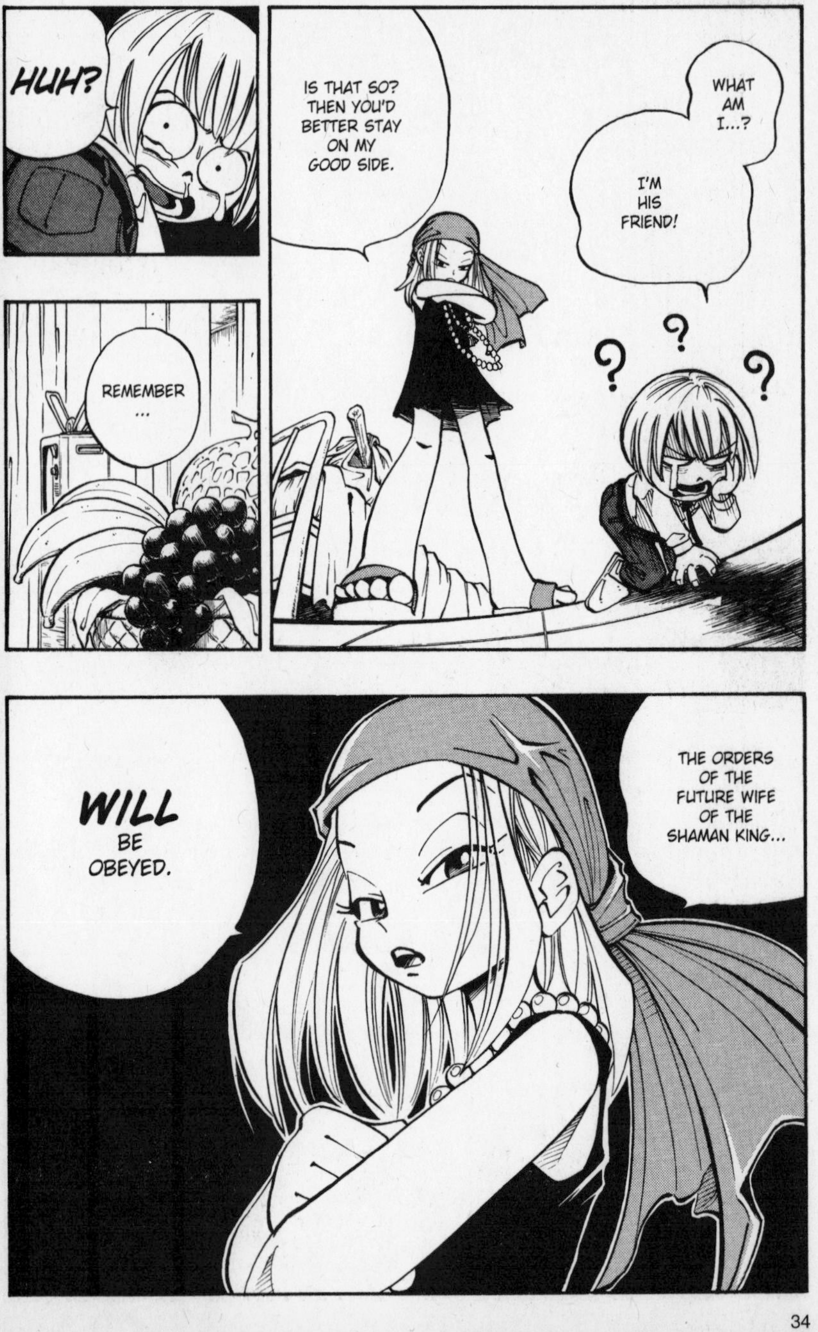

WHAT AM I...?
I'M HIS FRIEND!
IS THAT SO? THEN YOU'D BETTER STAY ON MY GOOD SIDE.
HUH?
REMEMBER ...
THE ORDERS OF THE FUTURE WIFE OF THE SHAMAN KING...
WILL BE OBEYED.

READ THIS WAY

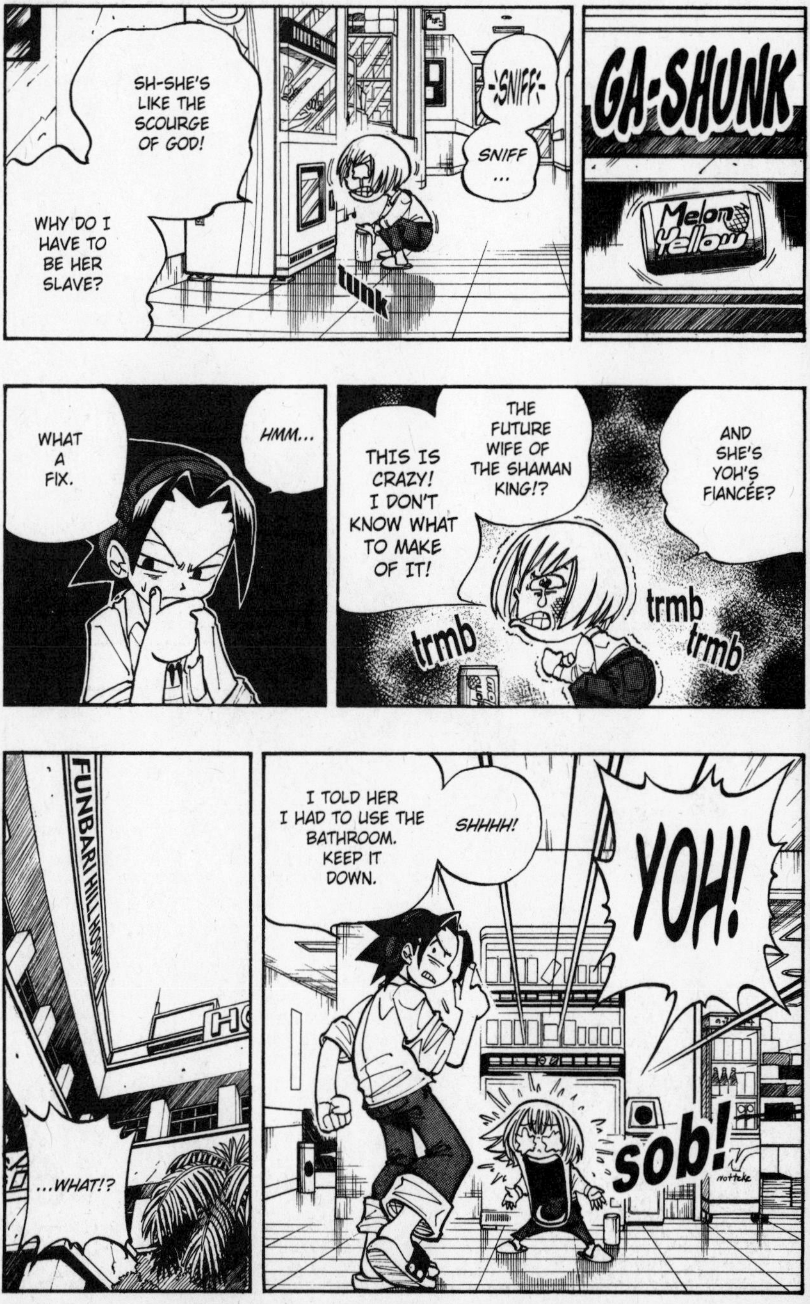

GA-SHUNK
Melon Yellow
-SNIFF-
SNIFF ...
SH-SHE'S LIKE THE SCOURGE OF GOD!
tunk
WHY DO I HAVE TO BE HER SLAVE?
AND SHE'S YOH'S FIANCÉE?
THE FUTURE WIFE OF THE SHAMAN KING!?
THIS IS CRAZY! I DON'T KNOW WHAT TO MAKE OF IT!
trmb
trmb
trmb
HMM...
WHAT A FIX.
YOH!
SHHHH!
I TOLD HER I HAD TO USE THE BATHROOM. KEEP IT DOWN.
sob!
FUNBARI HILL
...WHAT!?

READ THIS WAY

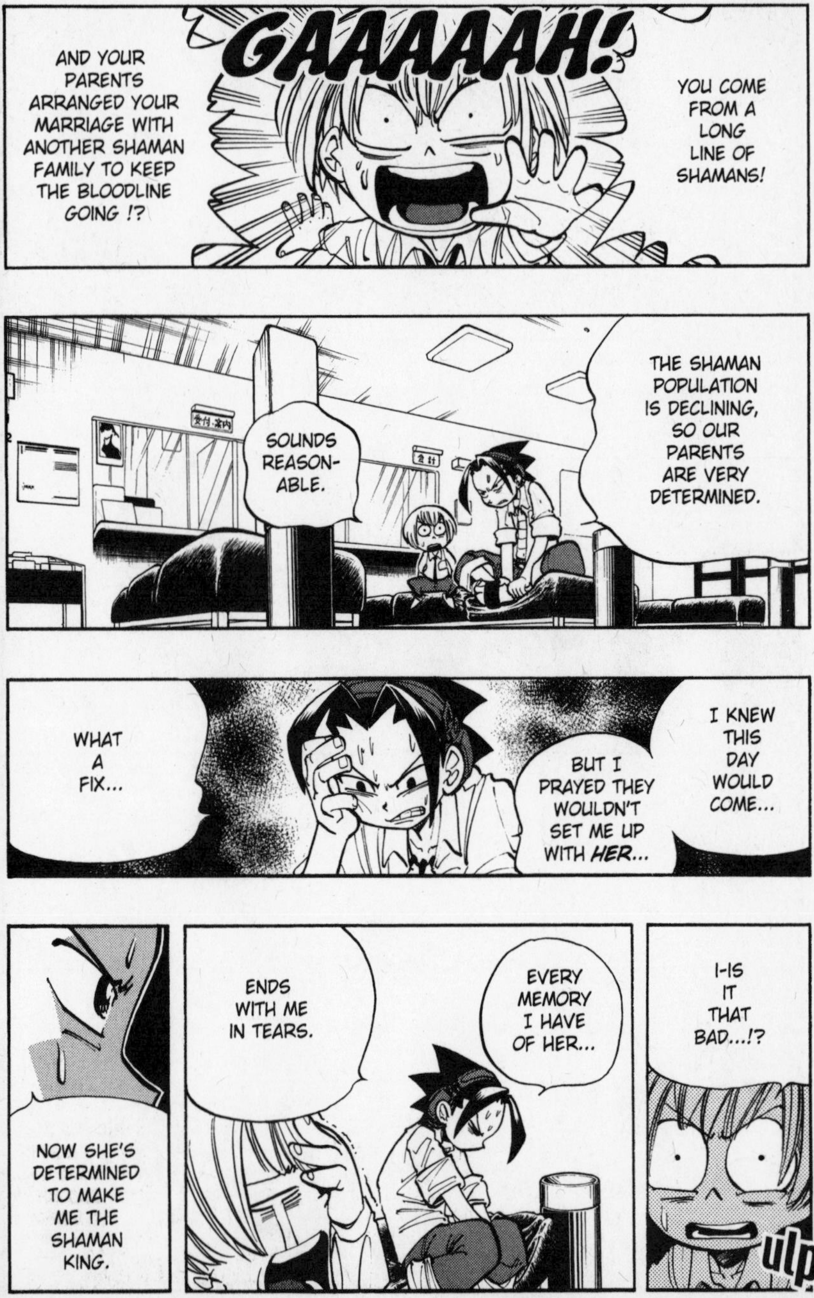

YOU COME FROM A LONG LINE OF SHAMANS!
AND YOUR PARENTS ARRANGED YOUR MARRIAGE WITH ANOTHER SHAMAN FAMILY TO KEEP THE BLOODLINE GOING !?
GAAAAAH!
THE SHAMAN POPULATION IS DECLINING, SO OUR PARENTS ARE VERY DETERMINED.
SOUNDS REASON-ABLE.
I KNEW THIS DAY WOULD COME...
BUT I PRAYED THEY WOULDN'T SET ME UP WITH *HER*...
WHAT A FIX...
I-IS IT THAT BAD...!?
ulp
EVERY MEMORY I HAVE OF HER...
ENDS WITH ME IN TEARS.
NOW SHE'S DETERMINED TO MAKE ME THE SHAMAN KING.

READ THIS WAY

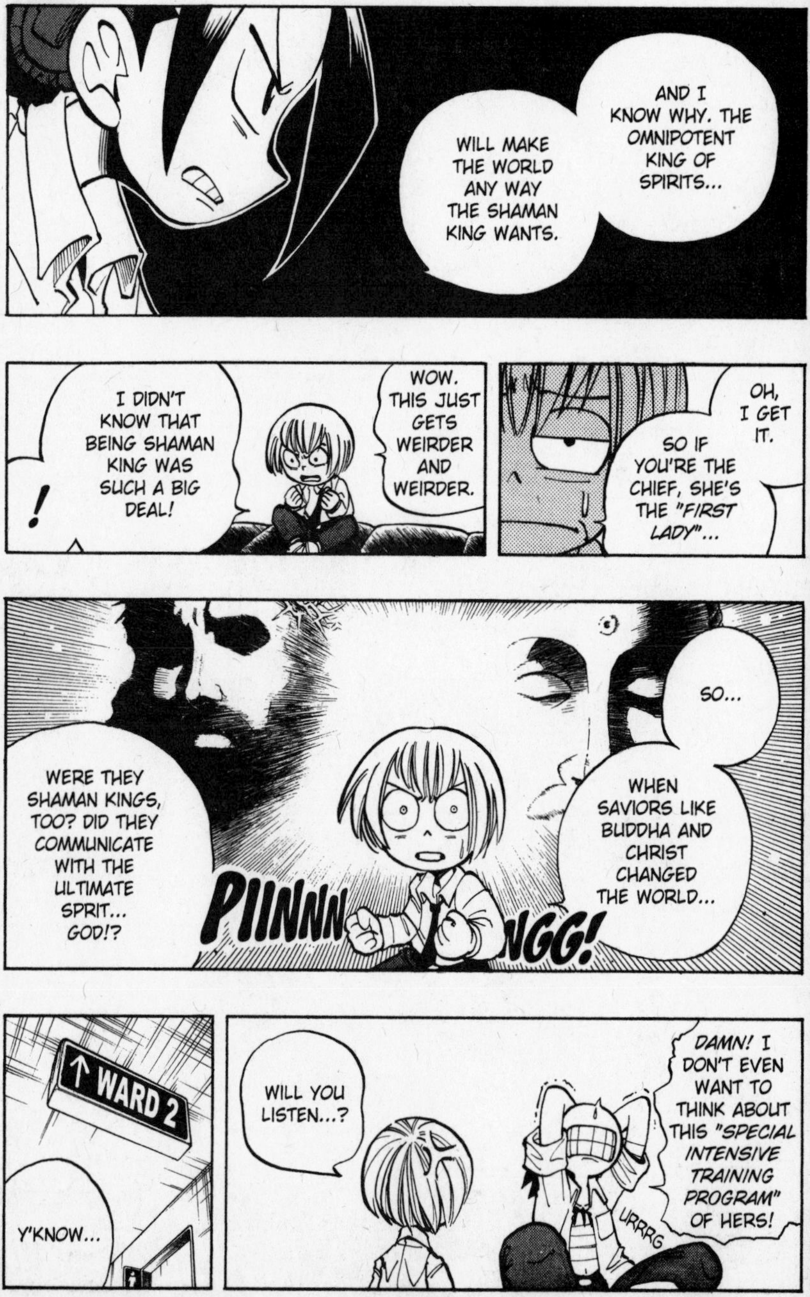
AND I KNOW WHY. THE OMNIPOTENT KING OF SPIRITS...
WILL MAKE THE WORLD ANY WAY THE SHAMAN KING WANTS.
OH, I GET IT.
SO IF YOU'RE THE CHIEF, SHE'S THE "FIRST LADY"...
WOW. THIS JUST GETS WEIRDER AND WEIRDER.
I DIDN'T KNOW THAT BEING SHAMAN KING WAS SUCH A BIG DEAL!
!
SO...
WHEN SAVIORS LIKE BUDDHA AND CHRIST CHANGED THE WORLD...
PIINNN
NGG!
WERE THEY SHAMAN KINGS, TOO? DID THEY COMMUNICATE WITH THE ULTIMATE SPRIT... GOD!?
DAMN! I DON'T EVEN WANT TO THINK ABOUT THIS "SPECIAL INTENSIVE TRAINING PROGRAM" OF HERS!
URRRG
WILL YOU LISTEN...?
↑ WARD 2
Y'KNOW...

READ THIS WAY

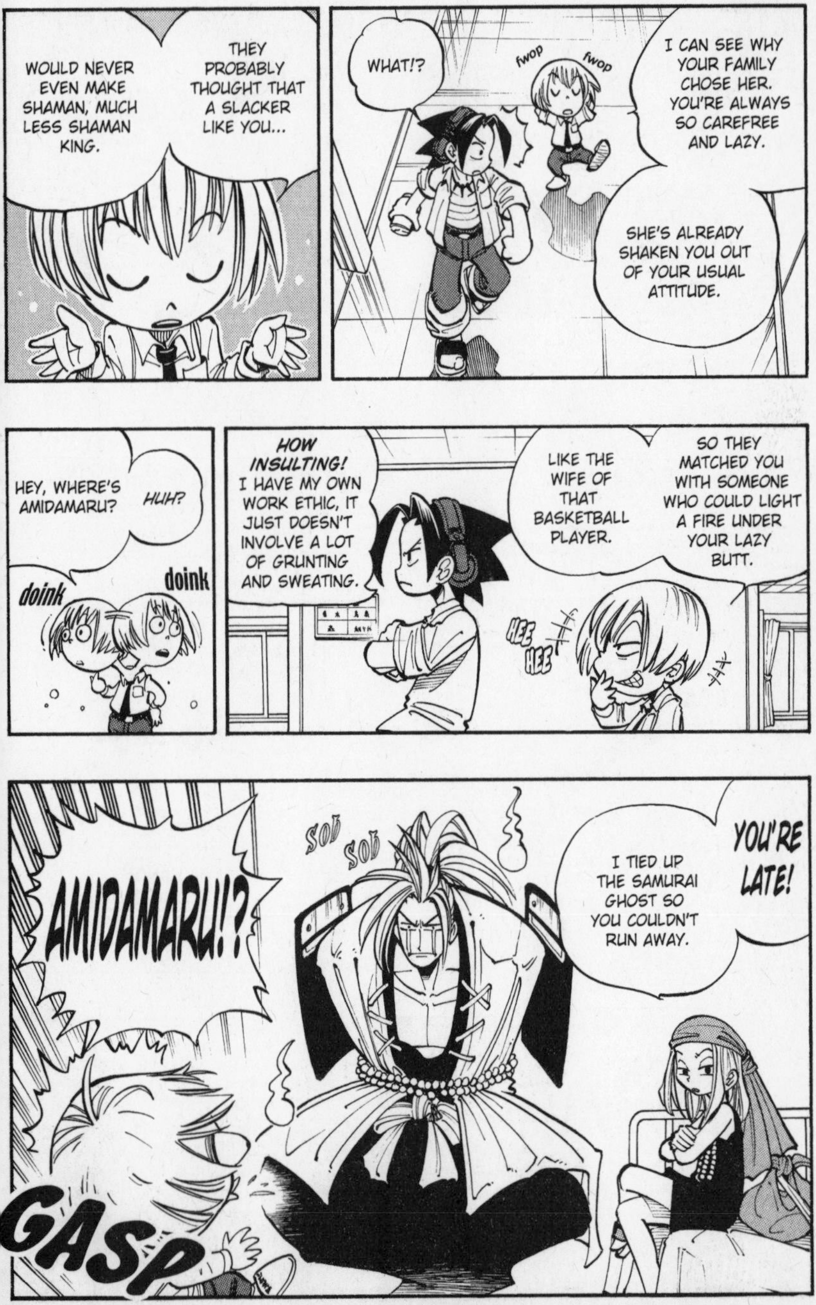
I CAN SEE WHY YOUR FAMILY CHOSE HER. YOU'RE ALWAYS SO CAREFREE AND LAZY.
SHE'S ALREADY SHAKEN YOU OUT OF YOUR USUAL ATTITUDE.
fwop fwop
WHAT!?
THEY PROBABLY THOUGHT THAT A SLACKER LIKE YOU...
WOULD NEVER EVEN MAKE SHAMAN, MUCH LESS SHAMAN KING.
SO THEY MATCHED YOU WITH SOMEONE WHO COULD LIGHT A FIRE UNDER YOUR LAZY BUTT.
LIKE THE WIFE OF THAT BASKETBALL PLAYER.
HEE HEE
HOW INSULTING! I HAVE MY OWN WORK ETHIC, IT JUST DOESN'T INVOLVE A LOT OF GRUNTING AND SWEATING.
HUH?
HEY, WHERE'S AMIDAMARU?
doink doink
YOU'RE LATE!
I TIED UP THE SAMURAI GHOST SO YOU COULDN'T RUN AWAY.
sob sob
AMIDAMARU!?
GASP

READ THIS WAY

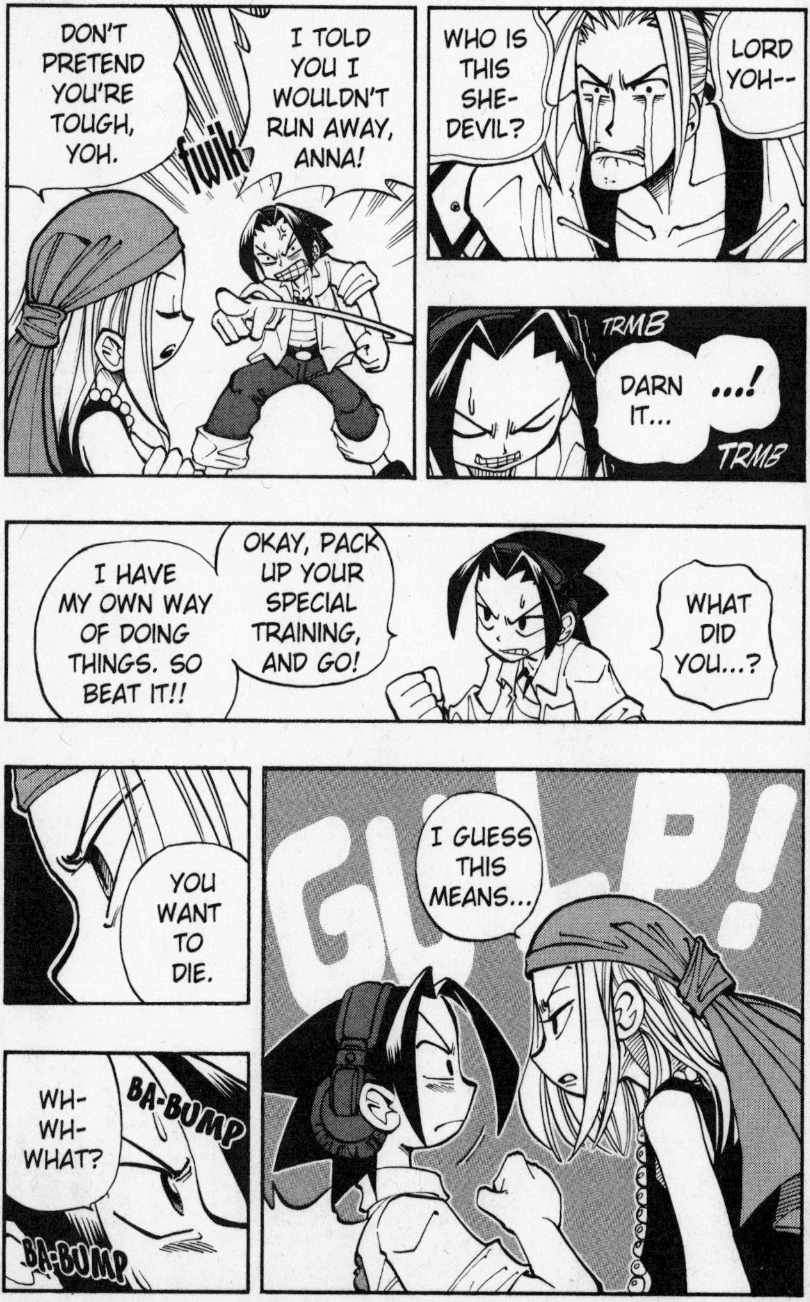

LORD YOH--
WHO IS THIS SHE-DEVIL?
TRMB
...!
DARN IT...
TRMB
I TOLD YOU I WOULDN'T RUN AWAY, ANNA!
fwik
DON'T PRETEND YOU'RE TOUGH, YOH.
WHAT DID YOU...?
OKAY, PACK UP YOUR SPECIAL TRAINING, AND GO!
I HAVE MY OWN WAY OF DOING THINGS. SO BEAT IT!!
GULP!
I GUESS THIS MEANS...
YOU WANT TO DIE.
BA-BUMP
WH-WH-WHAT?
BA-BUMP

READ THIS WAY

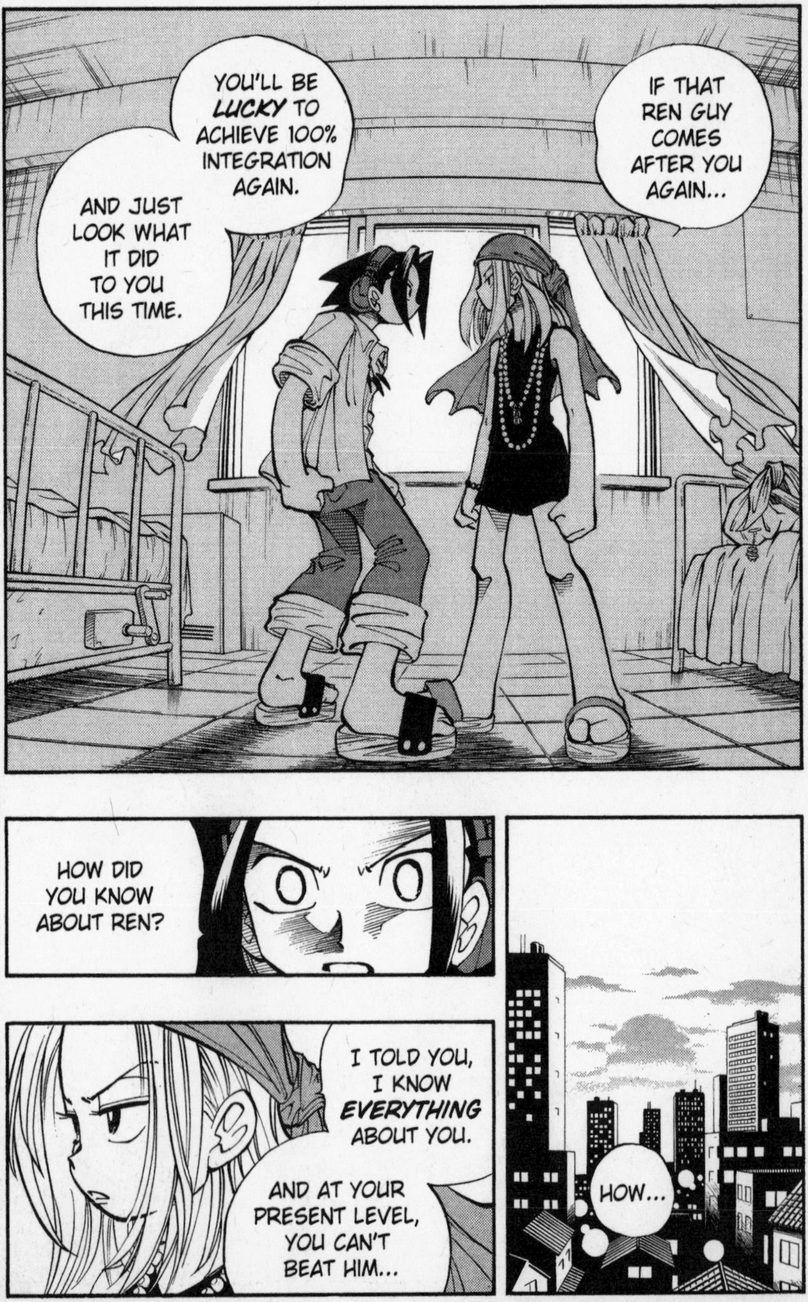

IF THAT REN GUY COMES AFTER YOU AGAIN...
YOU'LL BE LUCKY TO ACHIEVE 100% INTEGRATION AGAIN.
AND JUST LOOK WHAT IT DID TO YOU THIS TIME.
HOW...
HOW DID YOU KNOW ABOUT REN?
I TOLD YOU, I KNOW EVERYTHING ABOUT YOU.
AND AT YOUR PRESENT LEVEL, YOU CAN'T BEAT HIM...

READ THIS WAY

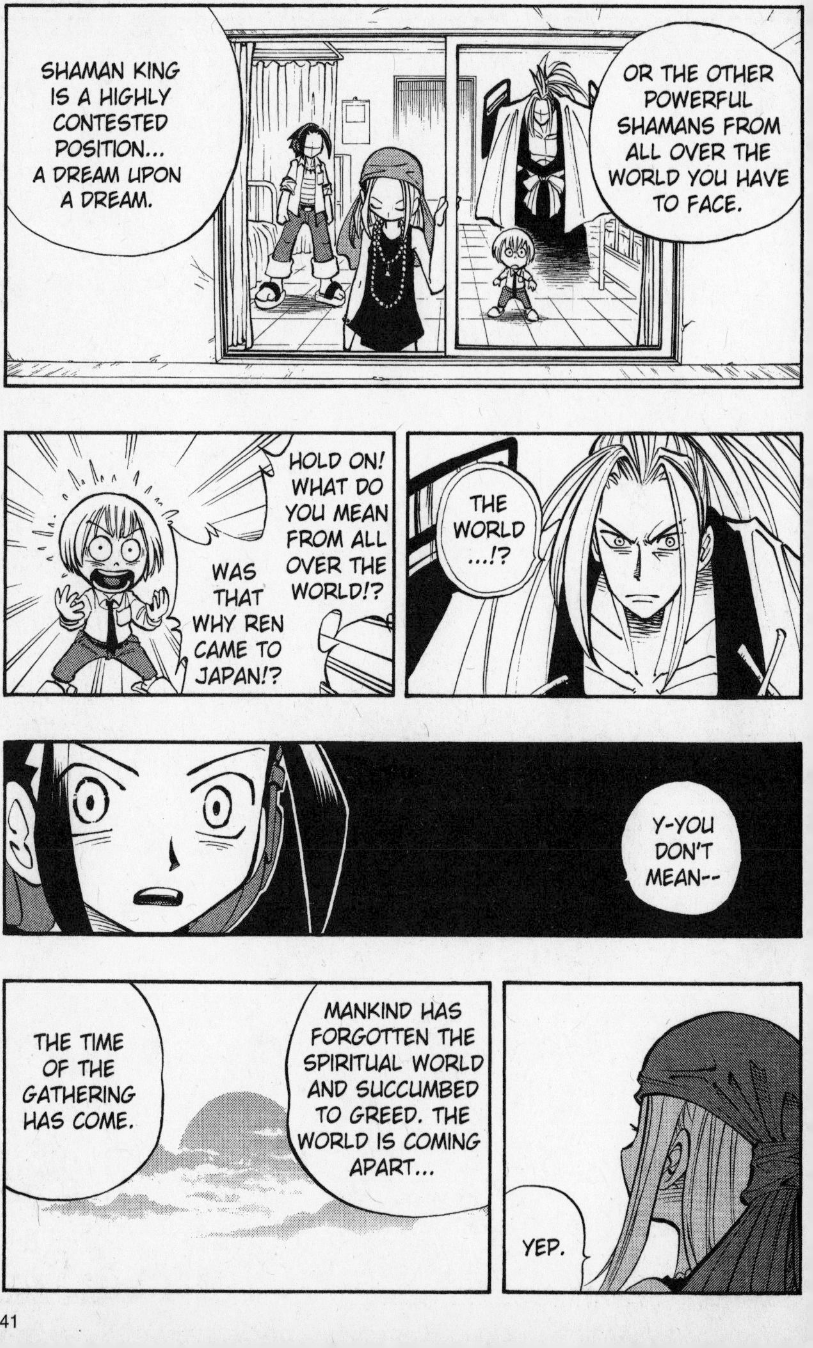

OR THE OTHER POWERFUL SHAMANS FROM ALL OVER THE WORLD YOU HAVE TO FACE.
SHAMAN KING IS A HIGHLY CONTESTED POSITION... A DREAM UPON A DREAM.
THE WORLD ...!?
HOLD ON! WHAT DO YOU MEAN FROM ALL OVER THE WORLD!?
WAS THAT WHY REN CAME TO JAPAN!?
Y-YOU DON'T MEAN--
YEP.
MANKIND HAS FORGOTTEN THE SPIRITUAL WORLD AND SUCCUMBED TO GREED. THE WORLD IS COMING APART...
THE TIME OF THE GATHERING HAS COME.

READ THIS WAY

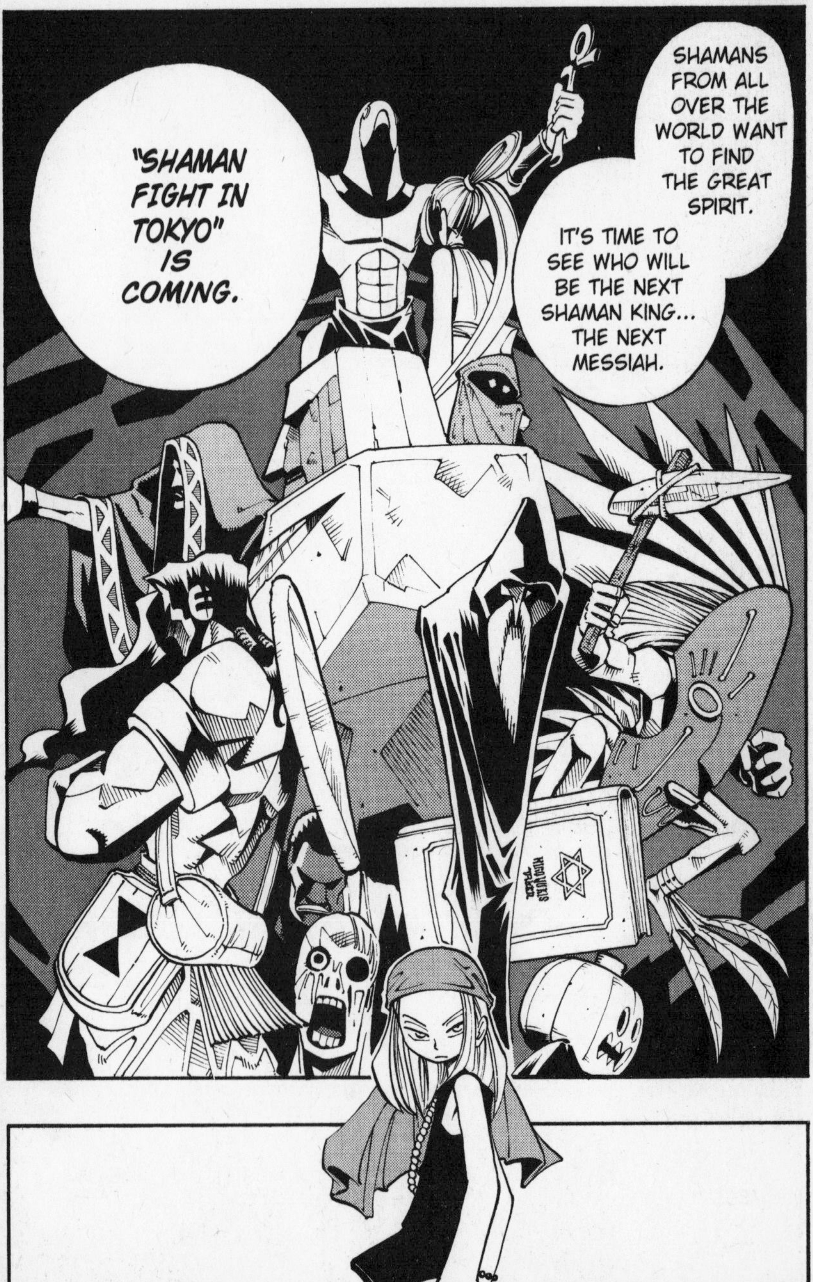
SHAMANS FROM ALL OVER THE WORLD WANT TO FIND THE GREAT SPIRIT.
IT'S TIME TO SEE WHO WILL BE THE NEXT SHAMAN KING... THE NEXT MESSIAH.
"SHAMAN FIGHT IN TOKYO" IS COMING.

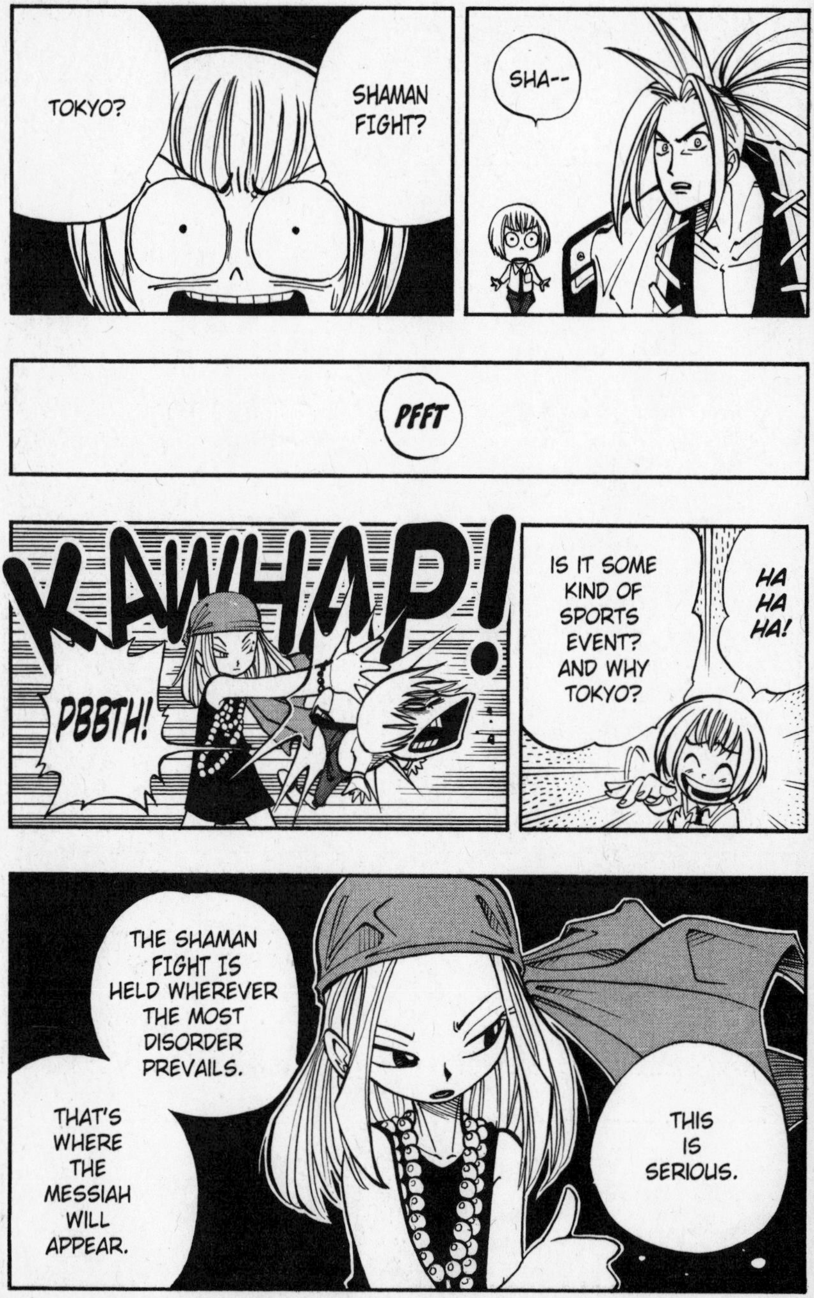
SHA--
SHAMAN FIGHT?
TOKYO?
PFFT
HA HA HA!
IS IT SOME KIND OF SPORTS EVENT? AND WHY TOKYO?
KAWHAP!
PBBTH!
THIS IS SERIOUS.
THE SHAMAN FIGHT IS HELD WHEREVER THE MOST DISORDER PREVAILS.
THAT'S WHERE THE MESSIAH WILL APPEAR.

READ THIS WAY

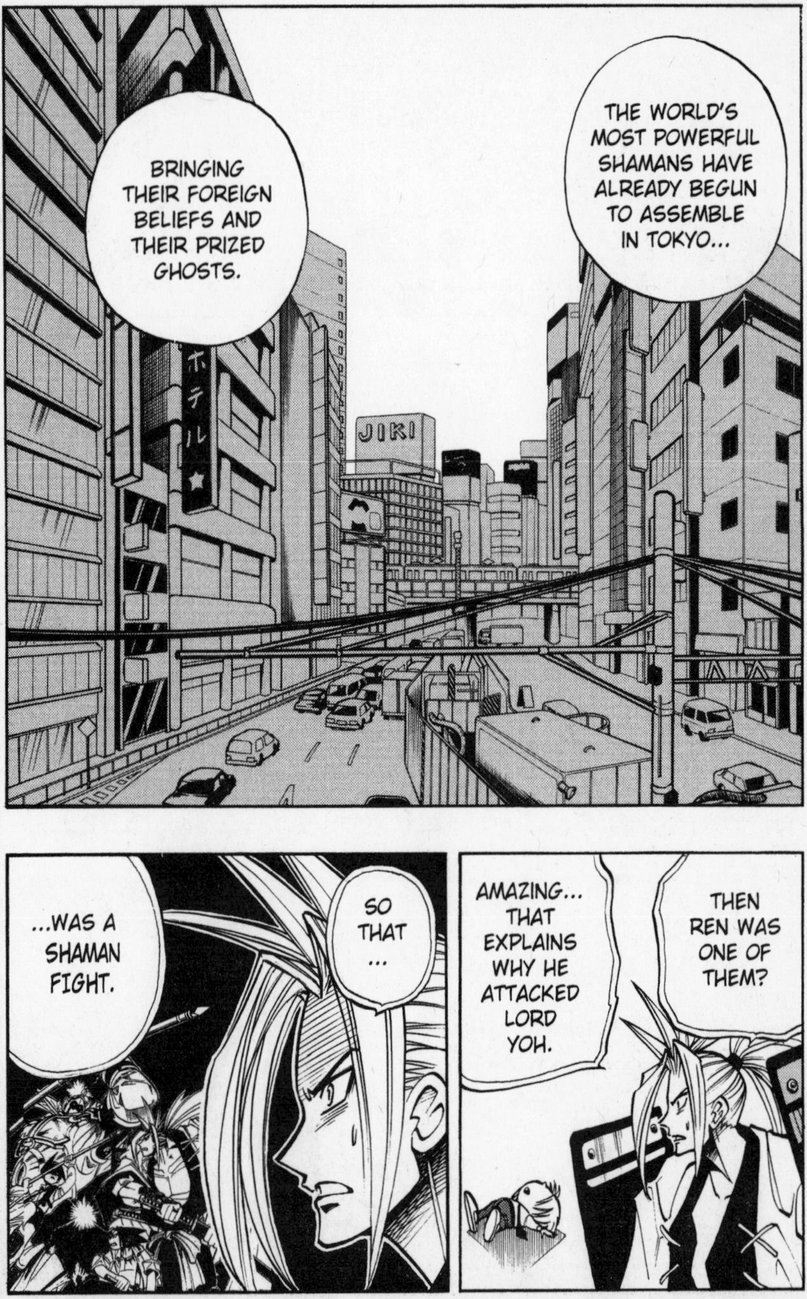

THE WORLD'S MOST POWERFUL SHAMANS HAVE ALREADY BEGUN TO ASSEMBLE IN TOKYO...
BRINGING THEIR FOREIGN BELIEFS AND THEIR PRIZED GHOSTS.
ホテル
JIKI
THEN REN WAS ONE OF THEM?
AMAZING... THAT EXPLAINS WHY HE ATTACKED LORD YOH.
SO THAT ...
...WAS A SHAMAN FIGHT.

READ THIS WAY

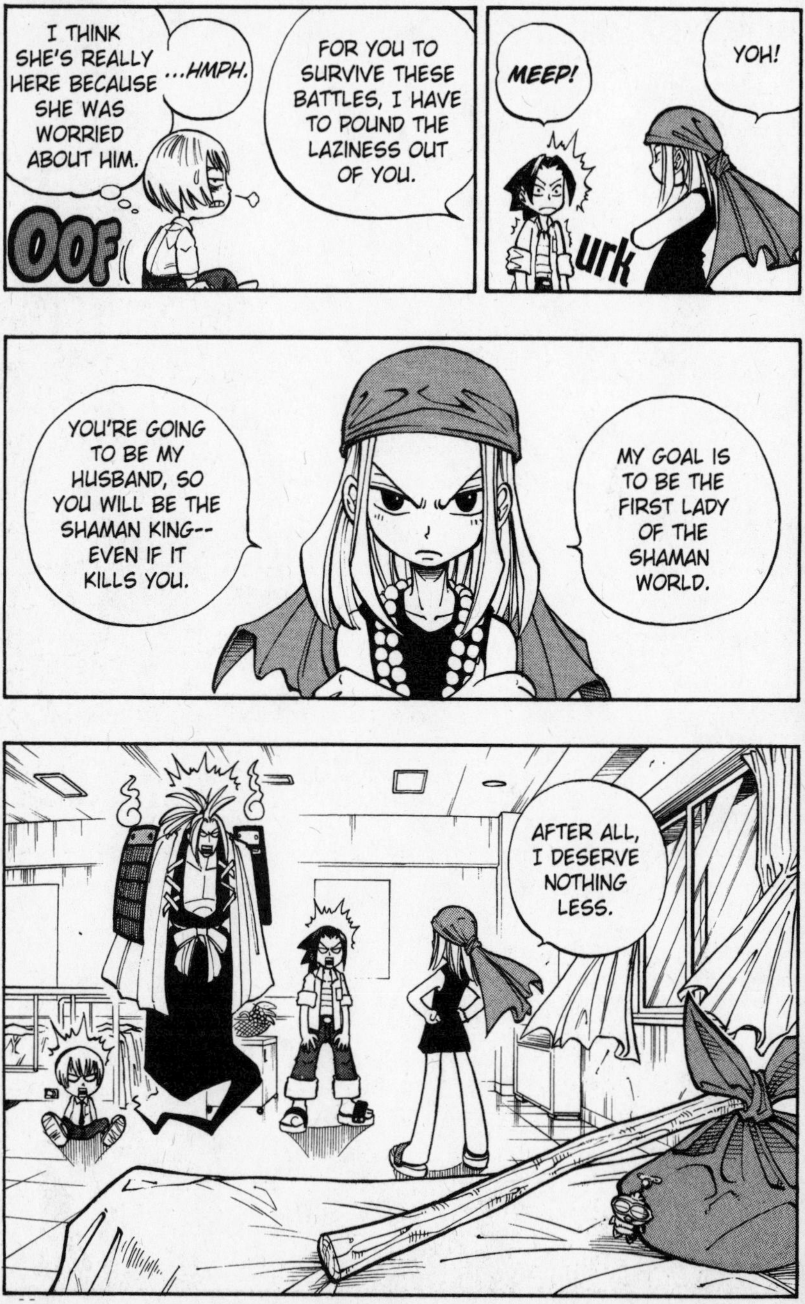
YOH!
MEEP!
urk
FOR YOU TO SURVIVE THESE BATTLES, I HAVE TO POUND THE LAZINESS OUT OF YOU.
...HMPH.
I THINK SHE'S REALLY HERE BECAUSE SHE WAS WORRIED ABOUT HIM.
OOF
MY GOAL IS TO BE THE FIRST LADY OF THE SHAMAN WORLD.
YOU'RE GOING TO BE MY HUSBAND, SO YOU WILL BE THE SHAMAN KING-- EVEN IF IT KILLS YOU.
AFTER ALL, I DESERVE NOTHING LESS.

SHAMAN KING
2

SHAKO-CHAN MASCOT
(A reproduction of a famous
Jomon-era (prehistoric)
Japanese figurine, sometimes
sold at tourist shops in Japan.)

REINCARNATION 11: THE SHAMAN LIFE

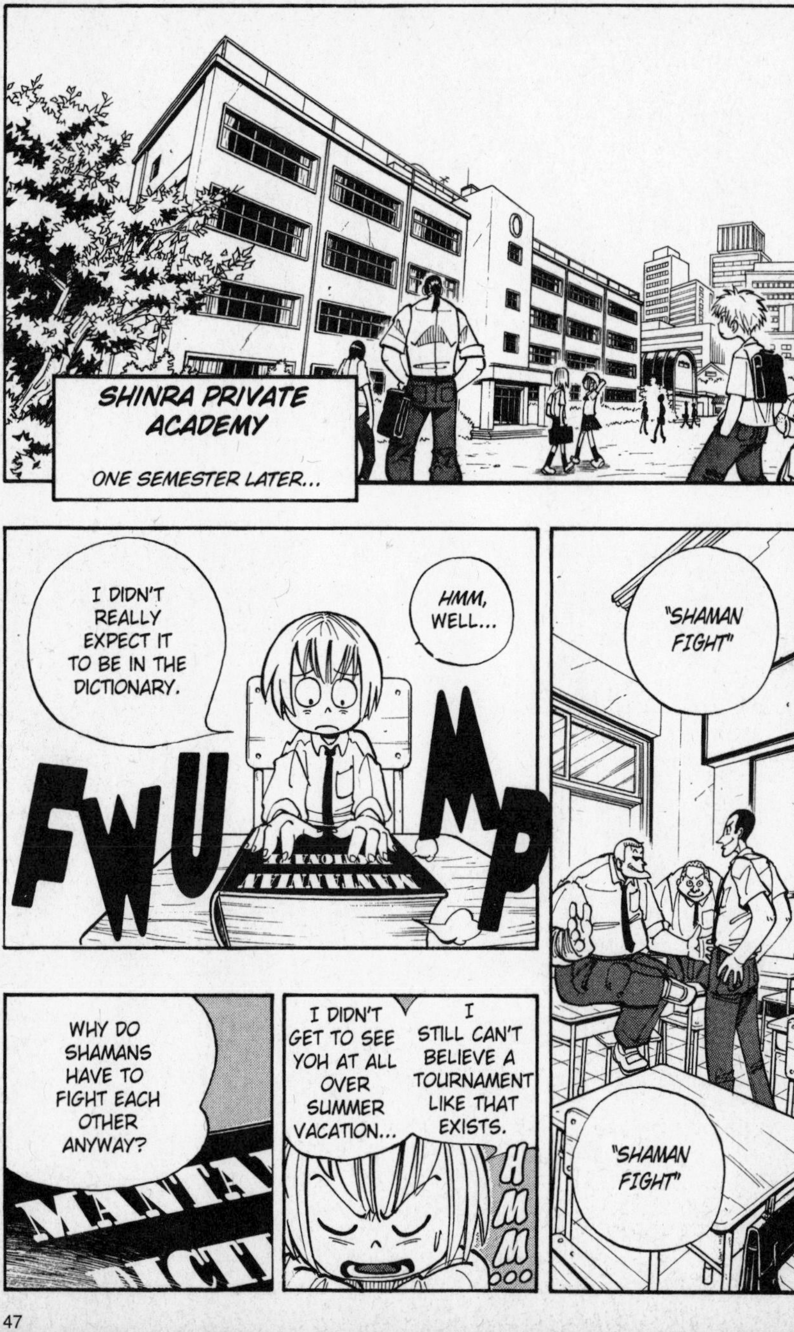

SHINRA PRIVATE ACADEMY
ONE SEMESTER LATER...
"SHAMAN FIGHT"
"SHAMAN FIGHT"
HMM, WELL...
I DIDN'T REALLY EXPECT IT TO BE IN THE DICTIONARY.
FWUMP
I STILL CAN'T BELIEVE A TOURNAMENT LIKE THAT EXISTS.
I DIDN'T GET TO SEE YOH AT ALL OVER SUMMER VACATION...
HMMM...
WHY DO SHAMANS HAVE TO FIGHT EACH OTHER ANYWAY?

READ THIS WAY

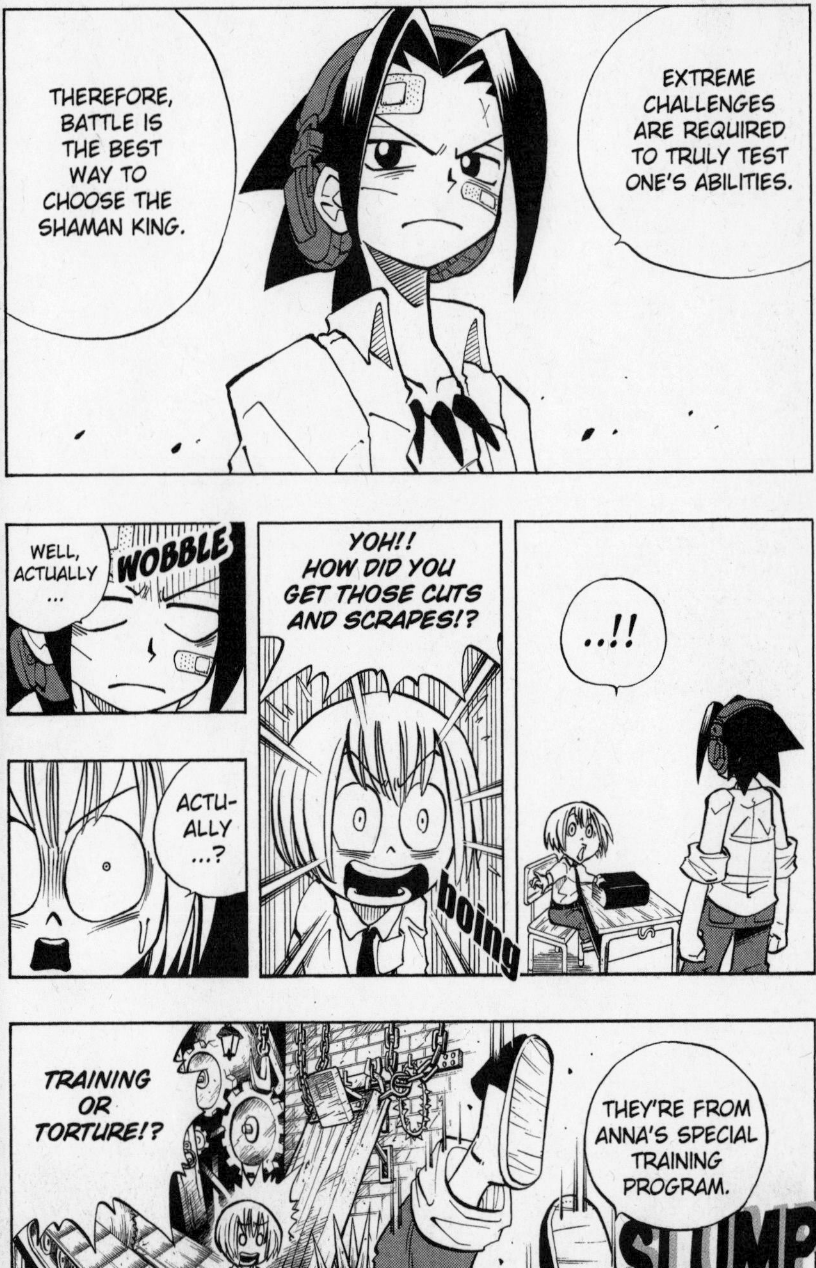

EXTREME CHALLENGES ARE REQUIRED TO TRULY TEST ONE'S ABILITIES.
THEREFORE, BATTLE IS THE BEST WAY TO CHOOSE THE SHAMAN KING.
..!!
YOH!! HOW DID YOU GET THOSE CUTS AND SCRAPES!?
boing
WOBBLE
WELL, ACTUALLY ...
ACTU-ALLY ...?
THEY'RE FROM ANNA'S SPECIAL TRAINING PROGRAM.
SLUMP
TRAINING OR TORTURE!?

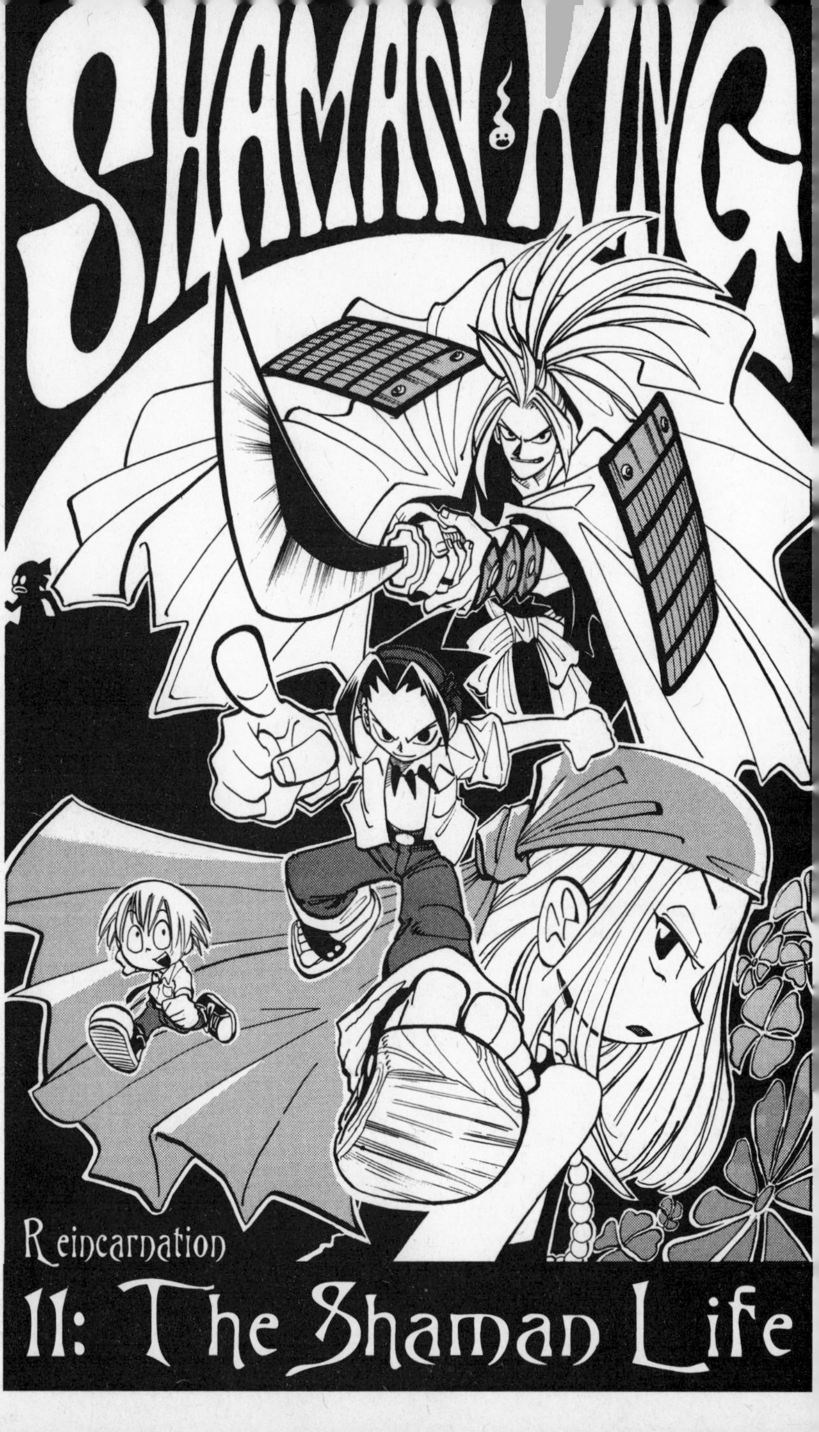
SHAMAN KING
Reincarnation
11: The Shaman Life

READ THIS WAY

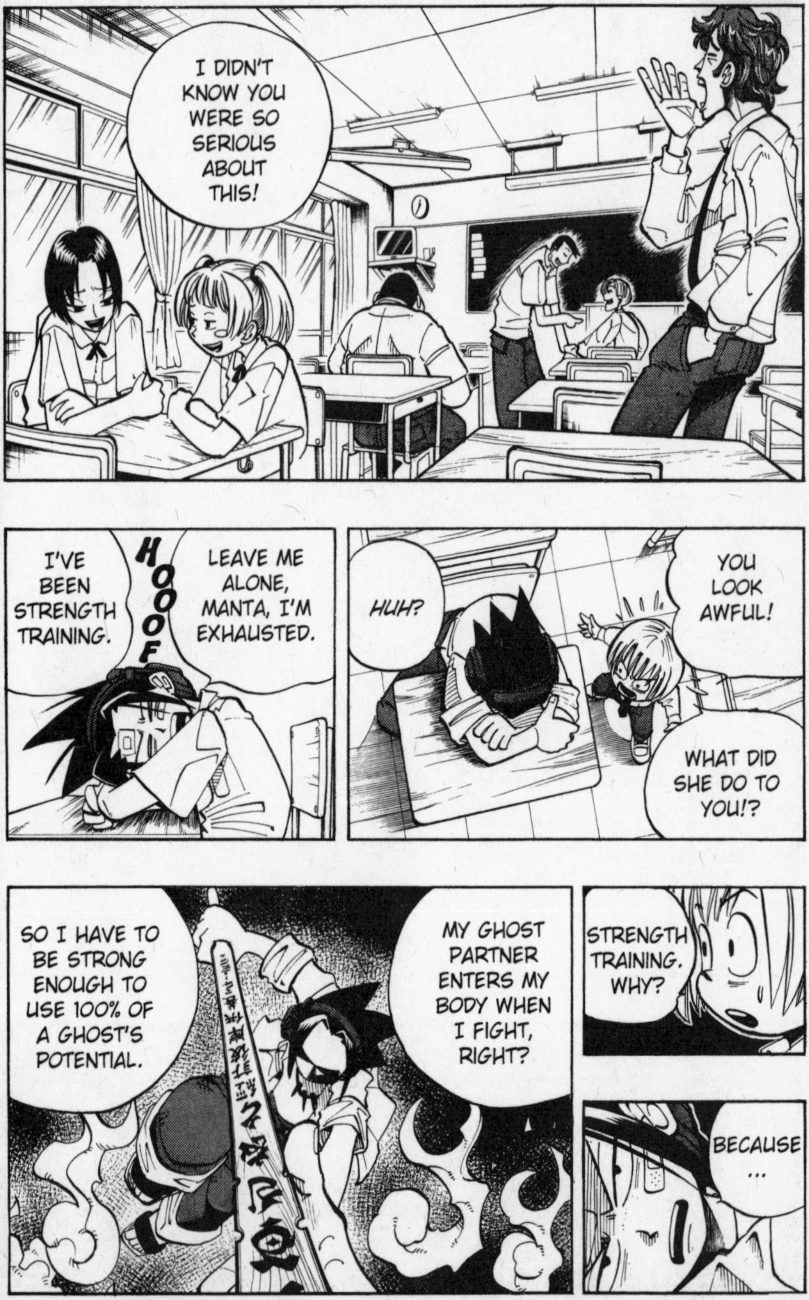
I DIDN'T KNOW YOU WERE SO SERIOUS ABOUT THIS!
YOU LOOK AWFUL!
HUH?
WHAT DID SHE DO TO YOU!?
LEAVE ME ALONE, MANTA, I'M EXHAUSTED.
HOOOF
I'VE BEEN STRENGTH TRAINING.
STRENGTH TRAINING. WHY?
BECAUSE ...
MY GHOST PARTNER ENTERS MY BODY WHEN I FIGHT, RIGHT?
SO I HAVE TO BE STRONG ENOUGH TO USE 100% OF A GHOST'S POTENTIAL.

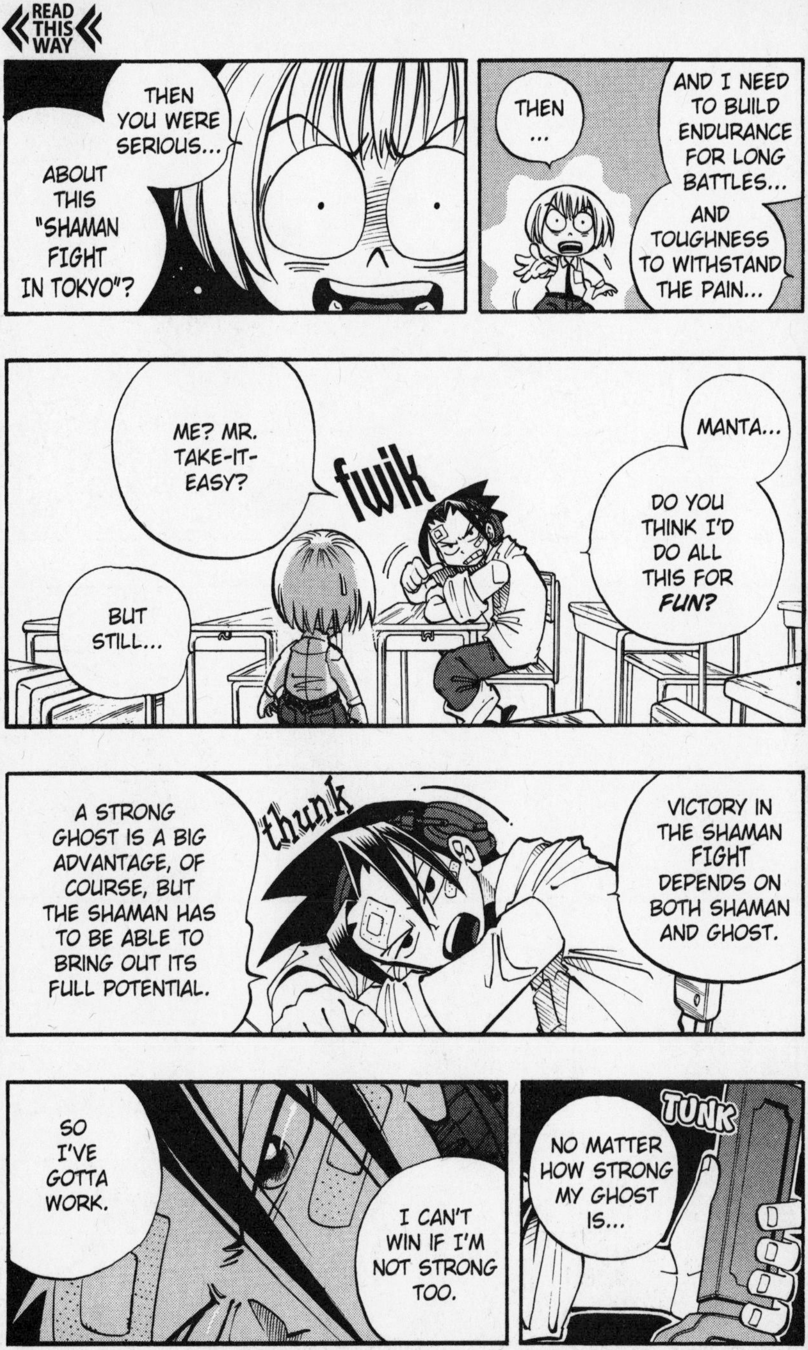
READ THIS WAY
AND I NEED TO BUILD ENDURANCE FOR LONG BATTLES...
AND TOUGHNESS TO WITHSTAND THE PAIN...
THEN ...
THEN YOU WERE SERIOUS...
ABOUT THIS "SHAMAN FIGHT IN TOKYO"?
MANTA...
DO YOU THINK I'D DO ALL THIS FOR *FUN?*
fwik
ME? MR. TAKE-IT-EASY?
BUT STILL...
VICTORY IN THE SHAMAN FIGHT DEPENDS ON BOTH SHAMAN AND GHOST.
thunk
A STRONG GHOST IS A BIG ADVANTAGE, OF COURSE, BUT THE SHAMAN HAS TO BE ABLE TO BRING OUT ITS FULL POTENTIAL.
TUNK
NO MATTER HOW STRONG MY GHOST IS...
I CAN'T WIN IF I'M NOT STRONG TOO.
SO I'VE GOTTA WORK.

READ THIS WAY

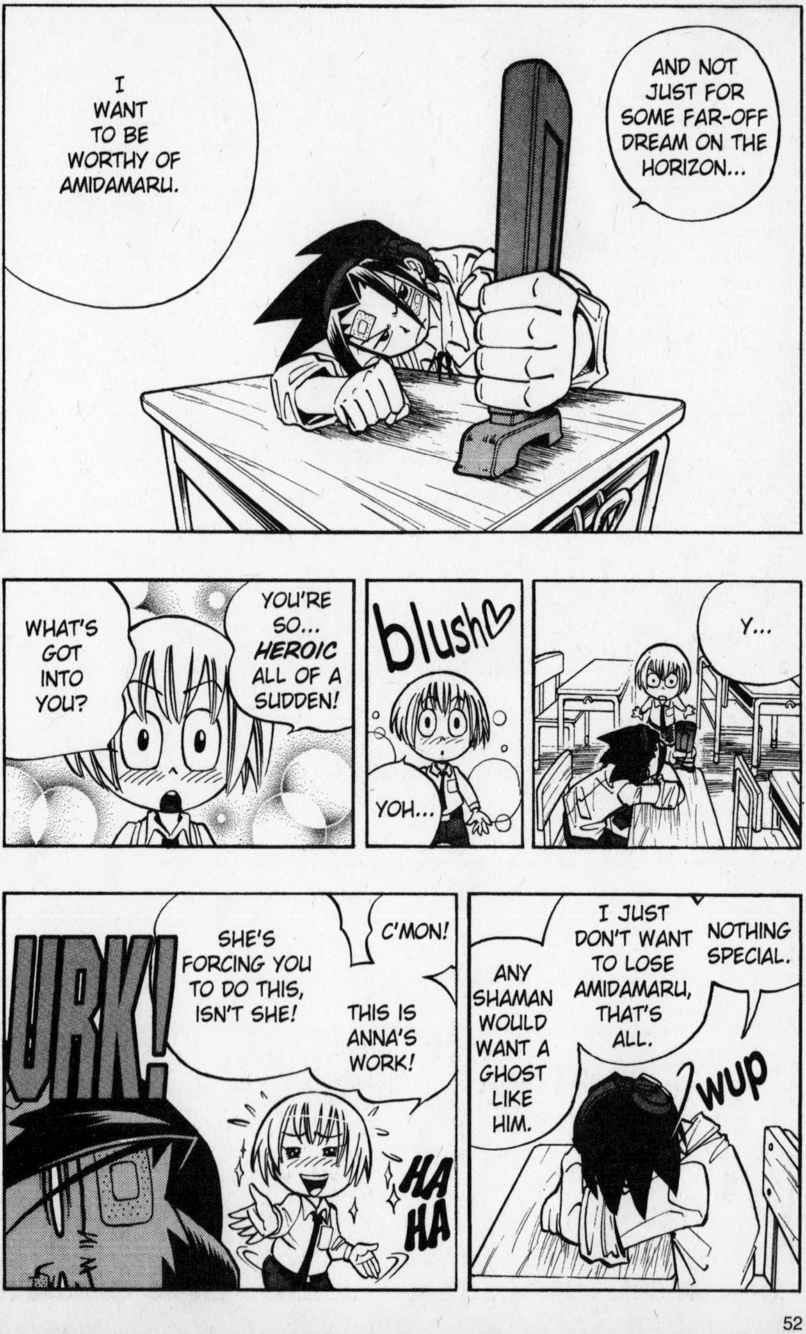
AND NOT JUST FOR SOME FAR-OFF DREAM ON THE HORIZON...
I WANT TO BE WORTHY OF AMIDAMARU.
Y...
blush♡
YOH...
YOU'RE SO... HEROIC ALL OF A SUDDEN!
WHAT'S GOT INTO YOU?
NOTHING SPECIAL.
I JUST DON'T WANT TO LOSE AMIDAMARU, THAT'S ALL.
ANY SHAMAN WOULD WANT A GHOST LIKE HIM.
WUP
C'MON!
SHE'S FORCING YOU TO DO THIS, ISN'T SHE!
THIS IS ANNA'S WORK!
URK!
HA HA

READ THIS WAY

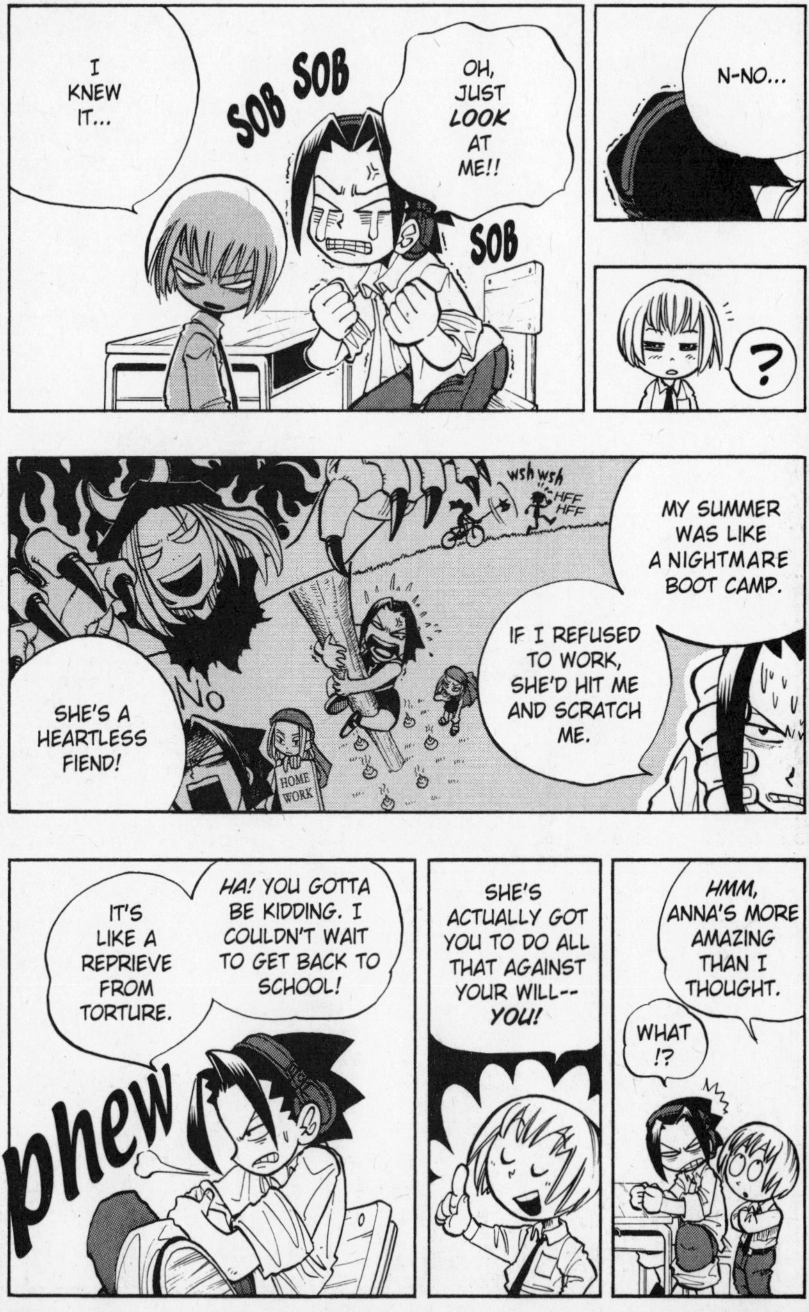

N-NO...
?
OH, JUST LOOK AT ME!!
SOB SOB
SOB
I KNEW IT...
MY SUMMER WAS LIKE A NIGHTMARE BOOT CAMP.
IF I REFUSED TO WORK, SHE'D HIT ME AND SCRATCH ME.
wsh wsh
HFF HFF
SHE'S A HEARTLESS FIEND!
No
HOME WORK
HMM, ANNA'S MORE AMAZING THAN I THOUGHT.
WHAT !?
SHE'S ACTUALLY GOT YOU TO DO ALL THAT AGAINST YOUR WILL-- YOU!
HA! YOU GOTTA BE KIDDING. I COULDN'T WAIT TO GET BACK TO SCHOOL!
IT'S LIKE A REPRIEVE FROM TORTURE.
phew

READ THIS WAY

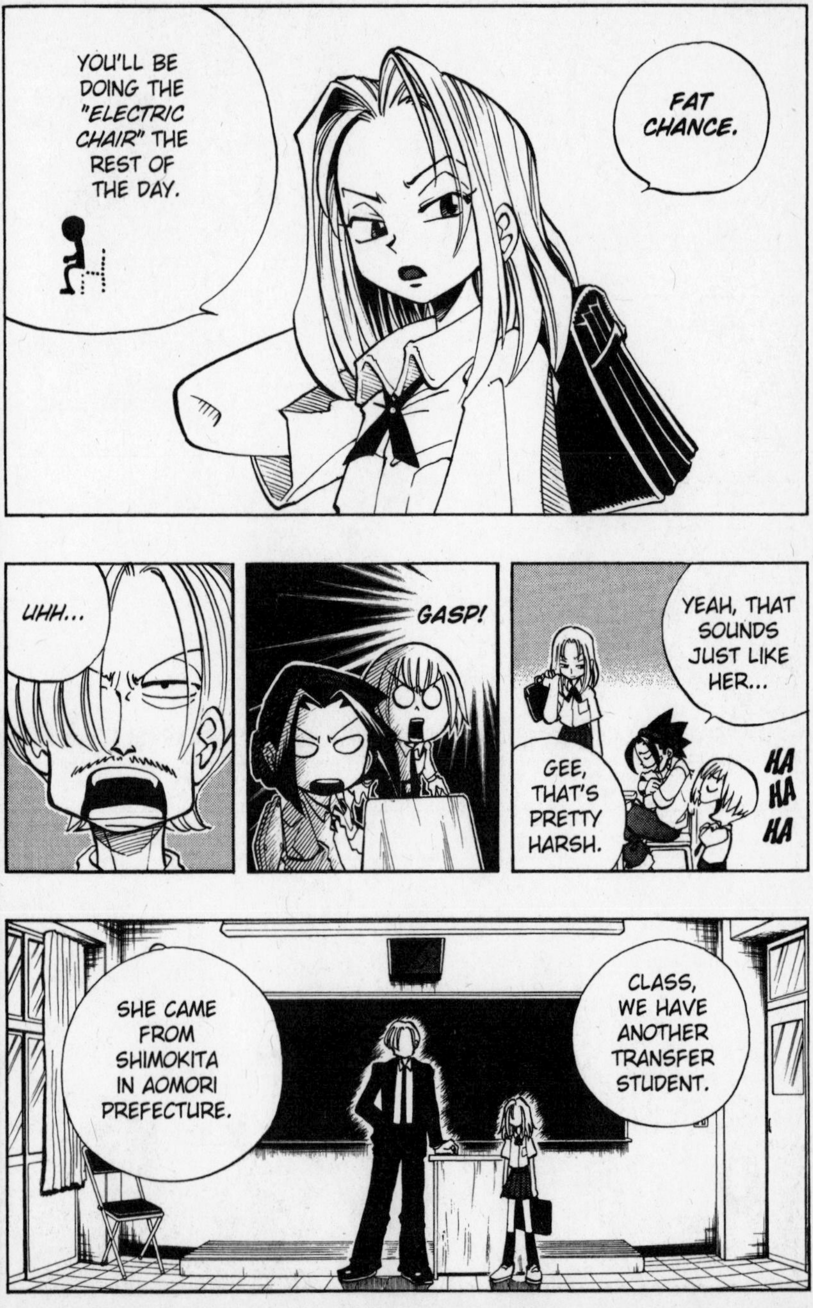
YOU'LL BE DOING THE "ELECTRIC CHAIR" THE REST OF THE DAY.
FAT CHANCE.
YEAH, THAT SOUNDS JUST LIKE HER...
HA HA HA
GEE, THAT'S PRETTY HARSH.
GASP!
UHH...
CLASS, WE HAVE ANOTHER TRANSFER STUDENT.
SHE CAME FROM SHIMOKITA IN AOMORI PREFECTURE.

READ THIS WAY

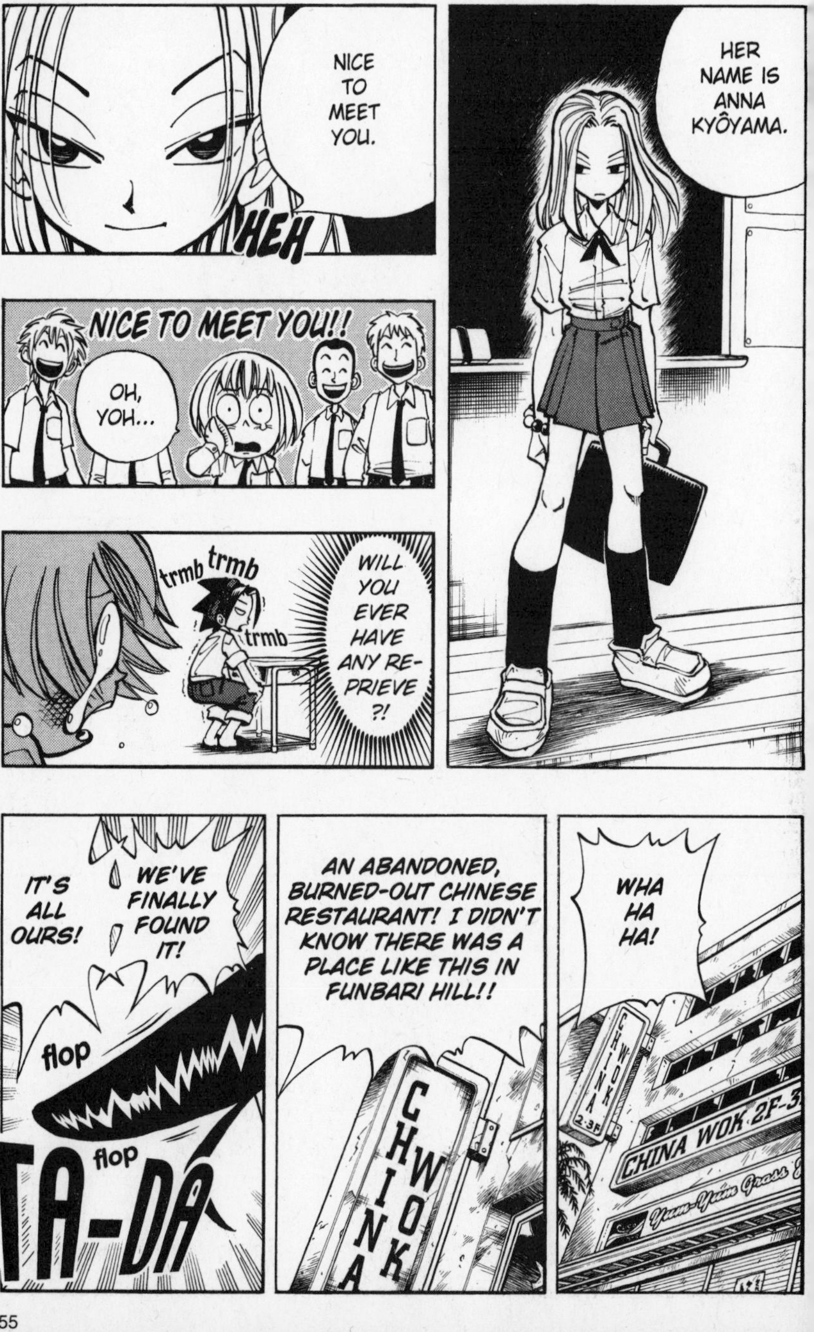

HER NAME IS ANNA KYÔYAMA.
NICE TO MEET YOU.
HEH
NICE TO MEET YOU!!
OH, YOH...
WILL YOU EVER HAVE ANY RE-PRIEVE ?!
trmb trmb
trmb
WHA HA HA!
CHINA WOK 2F-3
Yum-Yum Grass
AN ABANDONED, BURNED-OUT CHINESE RESTAURANT! I DIDN'T KNOW THERE WAS A PLACE LIKE THIS IN FUNBARI HILL!!
WE'VE FINALLY FOUND IT!
IT'S ALL OURS!
flop
flop
TA-DA

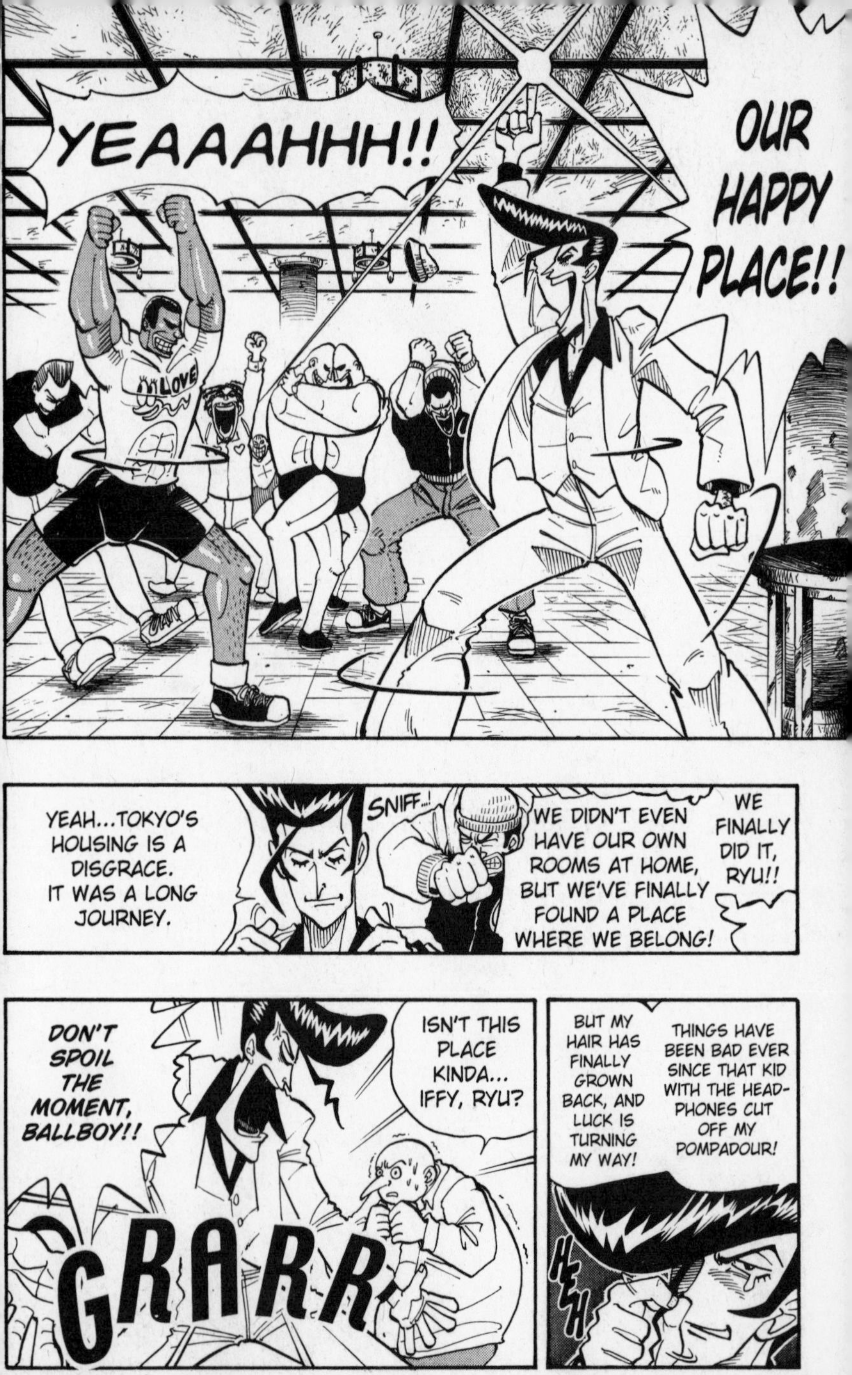
OUR HAPPY PLACE!!
YEAAAAHHH!!
WE FINALLY DID IT, RYU!!
WE DIDN'T EVEN HAVE OUR OWN ROOMS AT HOME, BUT WE'VE FINALLY FOUND A PLACE WHERE WE BELONG!
SNIFF..!
YEAH...TOKYO'S HOUSING IS A DISGRACE. IT WAS A LONG JOURNEY.
THINGS HAVE BEEN BAD EVER SINCE THAT KID WITH THE HEAD-PHONES CUT OFF MY POMPADOUR!
BUT MY HAIR HAS FINALLY GROWN BACK, AND LUCK IS TURNING MY WAY!
HEH
ISN'T THIS PLACE KINDA... IFFY, RYU?
DON'T SPOIL THE MOMENT, BALLBOY!!
GRARR

READ THIS WAY

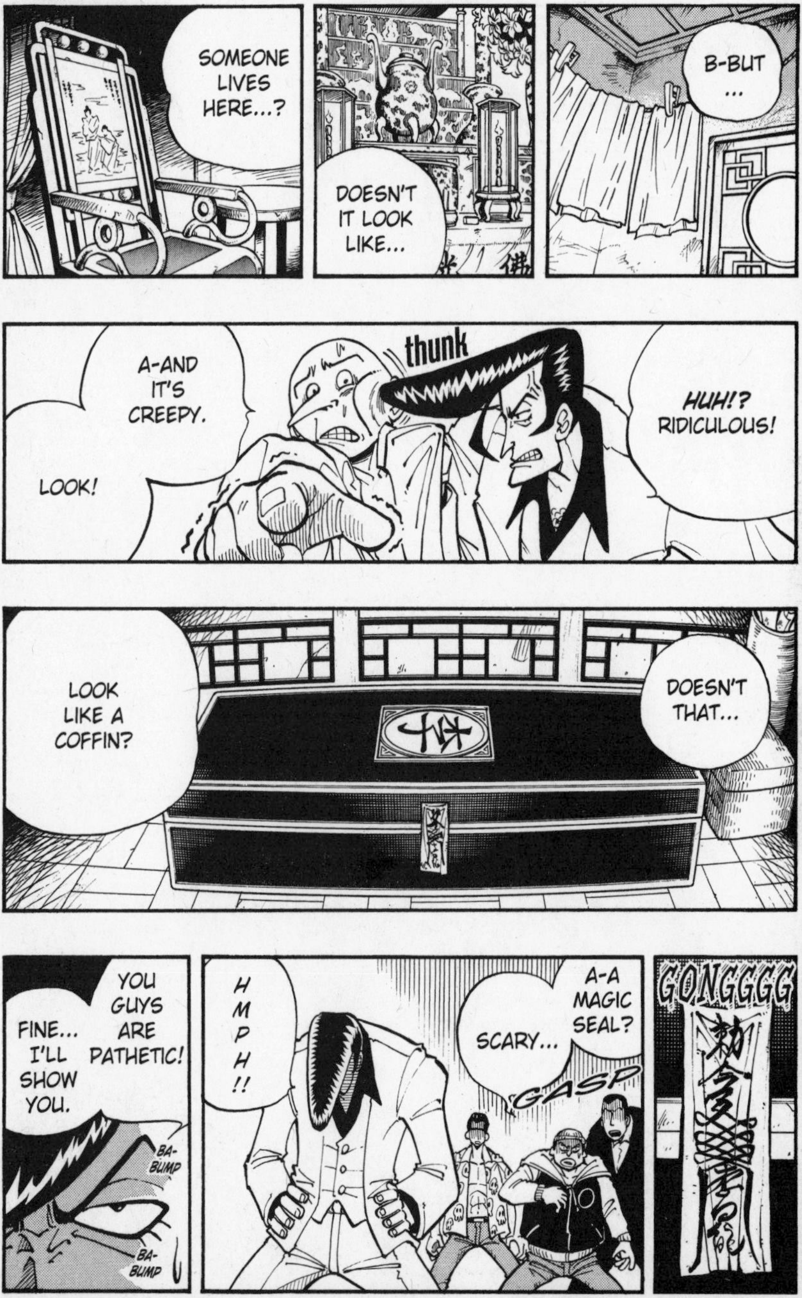

B-BUT ...
DOESN'T IT LOOK LIKE...
SOMEONE LIVES HERE...?
HUH!? RIDICULOUS!
thunk
A-AND IT'S CREEPY.
LOOK!
DOESN'T THAT...
LOOK LIKE A COFFIN?
GONGGGG
A-A MAGIC SEAL?
SCARY...
GASP
HMPH!!
YOU GUYS ARE PATHETIC!
FINE... I'LL SHOW YOU.
BA-BUMP
BA-BUMP

READ THIS WAY

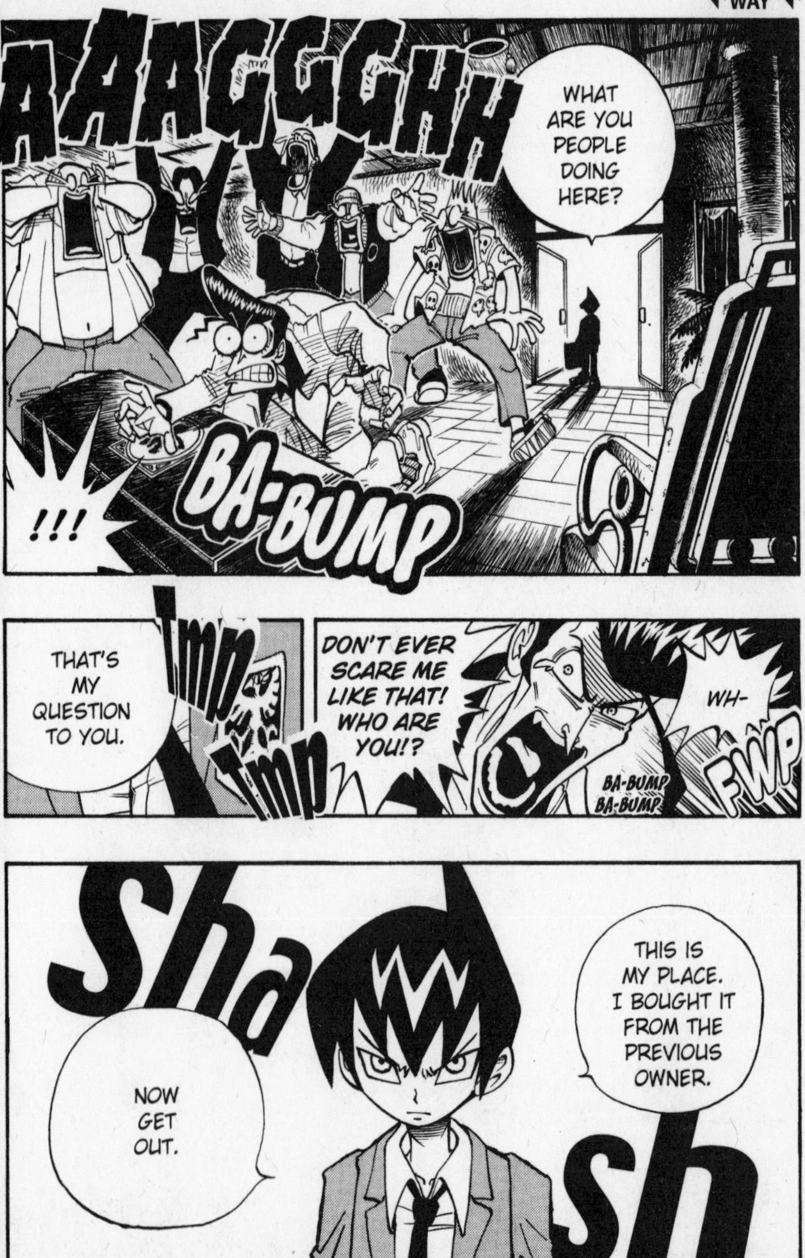

WHAT ARE YOU PEOPLE DOING HERE?
AAAGGGHH
BA-BUMP
!!!
WH-
FWP
BA-BUMP BA-BUMP
DON'T EVER SCARE ME LIKE THAT! WHO ARE YOU!?
Tmp Tmp
THAT'S MY QUESTION TO YOU.
THIS IS MY PLACE. I BOUGHT IT FROM THE PREVIOUS OWNER.
Shash
NOW GET OUT.

READ THIS WAY

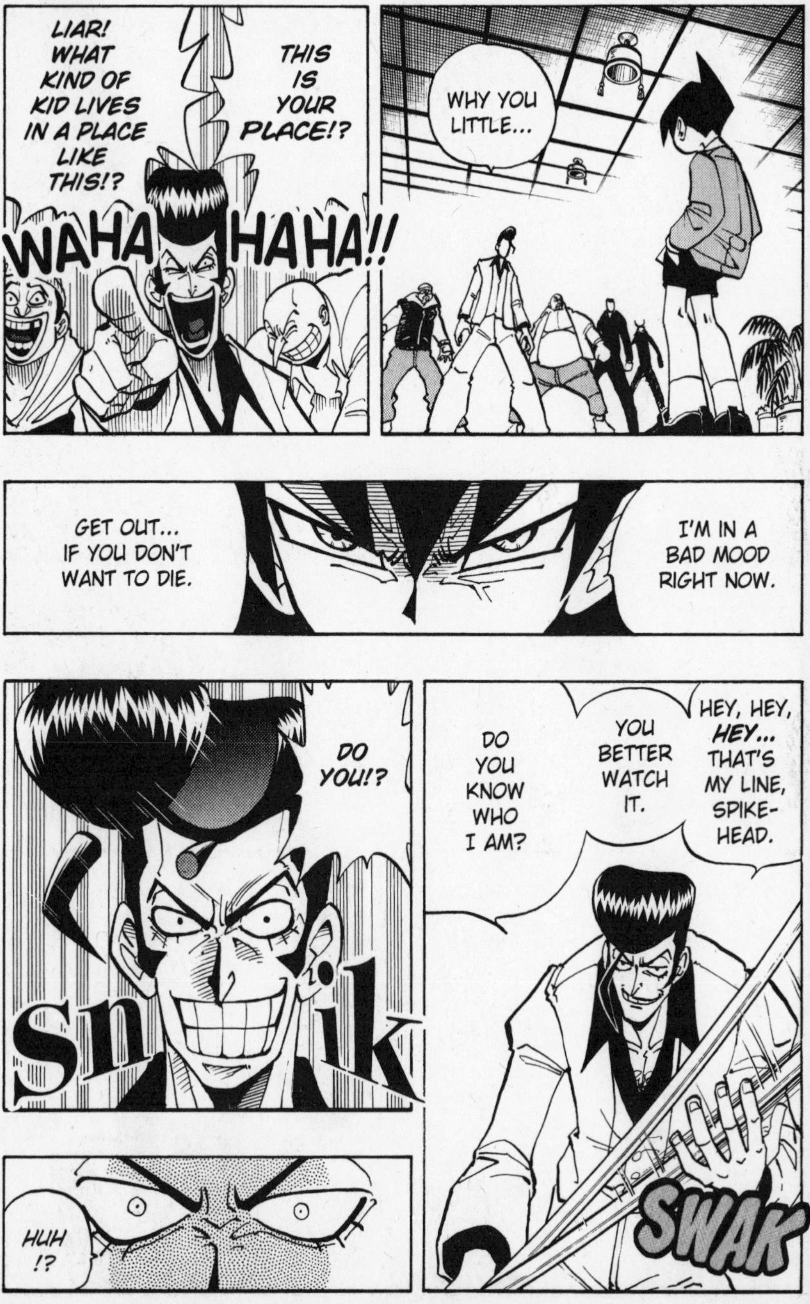
WHY YOU LITTLE...
THIS IS YOUR PLACE!?
LIAR! WHAT KIND OF KID LIVES IN A PLACE LIKE THIS!?
WAHAHAHA!!
I'M IN A BAD MOOD RIGHT NOW.
GET OUT... IF YOU DON'T WANT TO DIE.
HEY, HEY, *HEY*... THAT'S MY LINE, SPIKE-HEAD.
YOU BETTER WATCH IT.
DO YOU KNOW WHO I AM?
SWAK
DO YOU!?
Snik
HUH!?

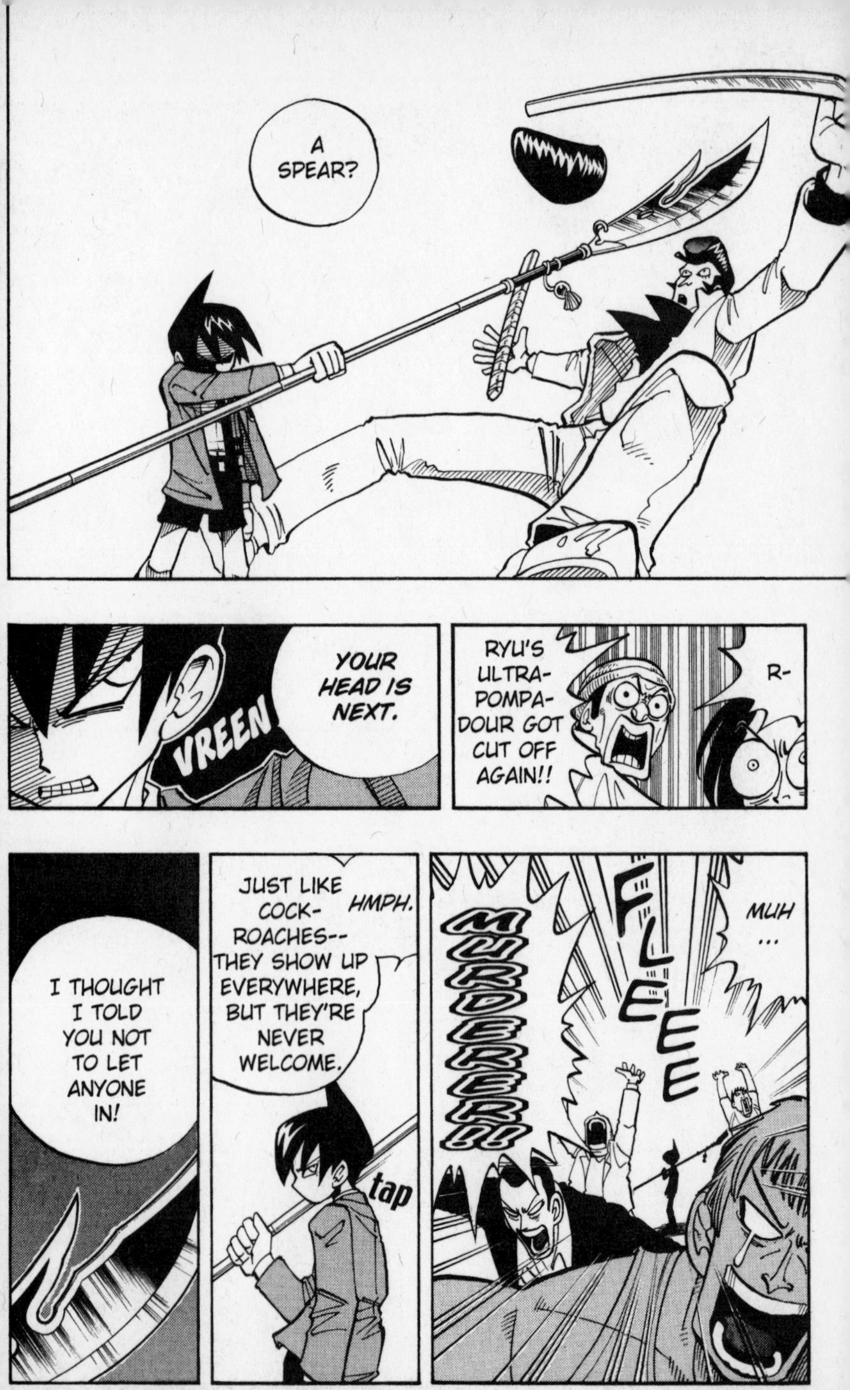
A SPEAR?
R-
RYU'S ULTRA-POMPADOUR GOT CUT OFF AGAIN!!
YOUR HEAD IS NEXT.
VREEN
MUH ...
FLEEE
MURDERER!!
HMPH.
JUST LIKE COCKROACHES-- THEY SHOW UP EVERYWHERE, BUT THEY'RE NEVER WELCOME.
tap
I THOUGHT I TOLD YOU NOT TO LET ANYONE IN!

READ THIS WAY

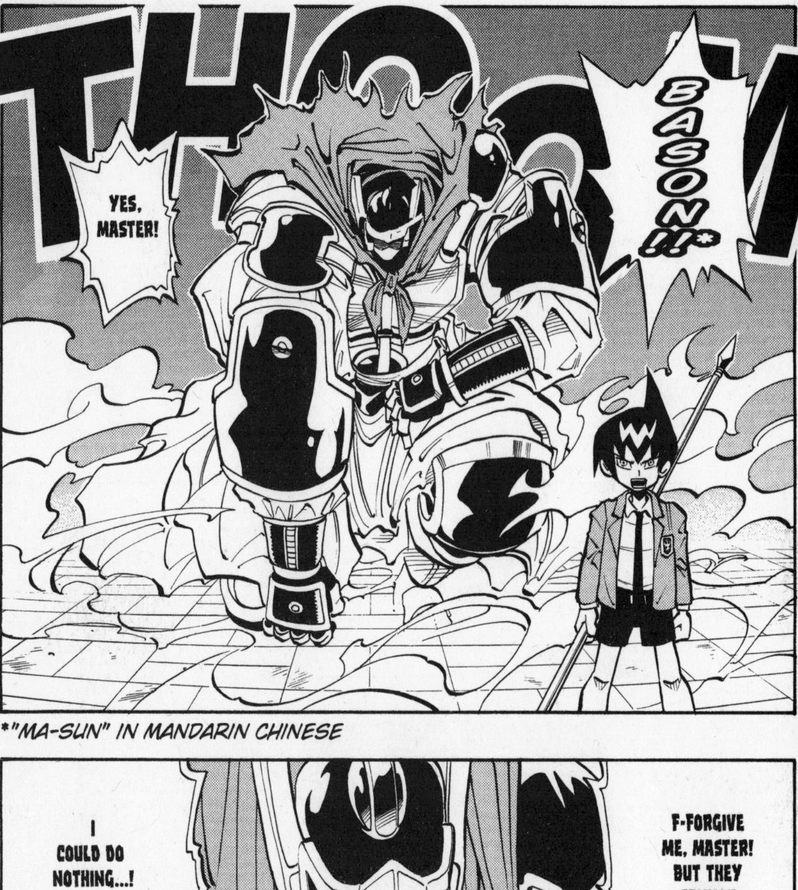
BASON!!*
YES, MASTER!

*"MA-SUN" IN MANDARIN CHINESE

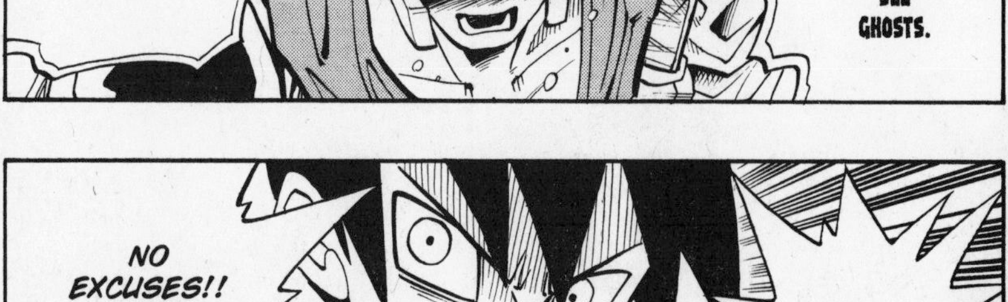
F-FORGIVE ME, MASTER! BUT THEY CANNOT SEE GHOSTS.
I COULD DO NOTHING...!

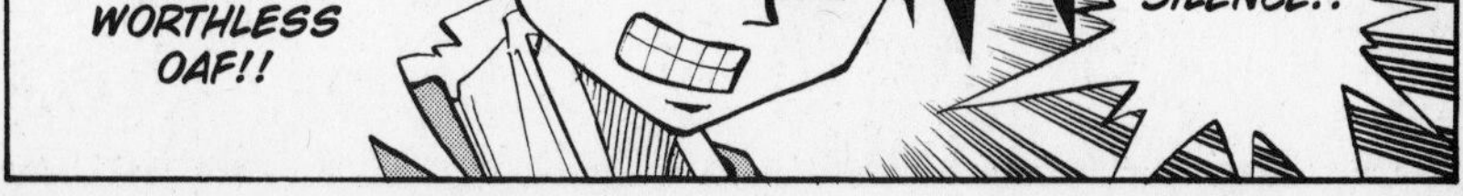
SILENCE!!
NO EXCUSES!! YOU'RE A WORTHLESS OAF!!

READ THIS WAY

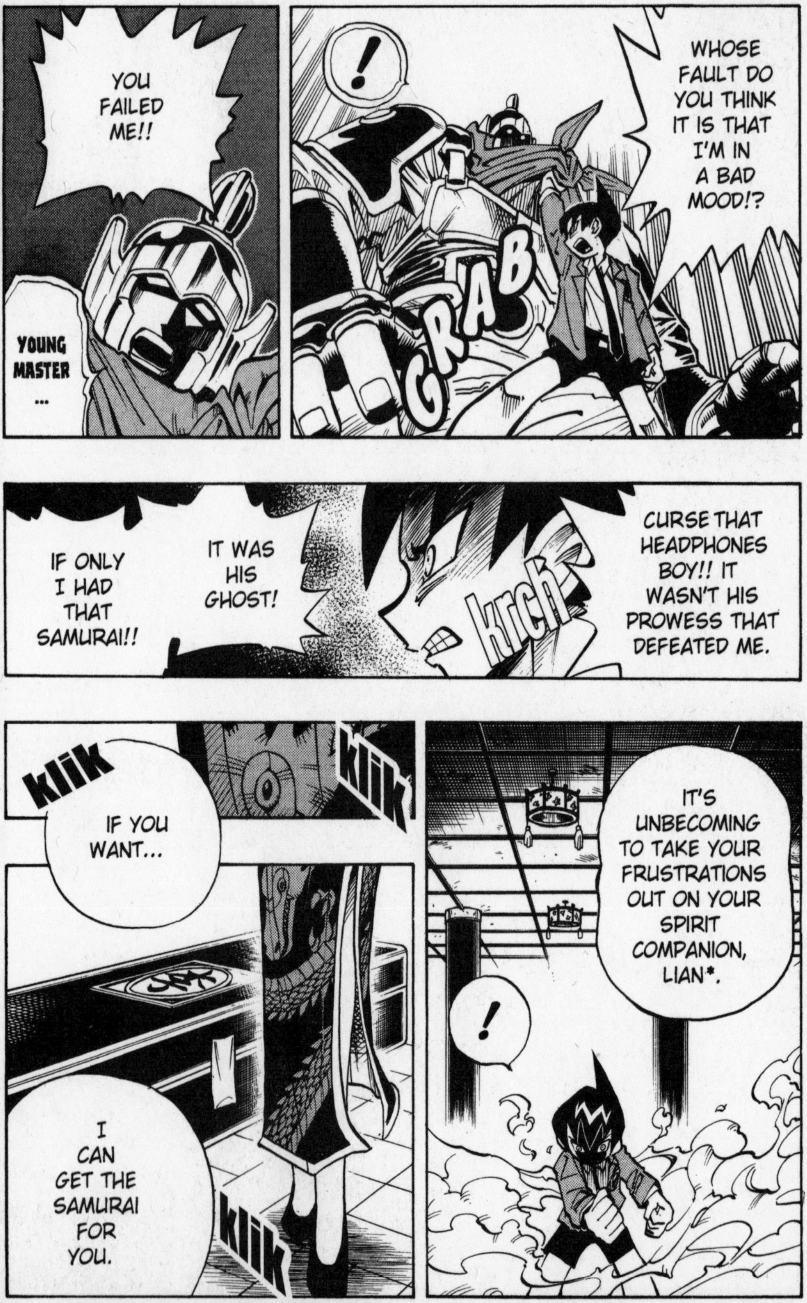
!
WHOSE FAULT DO YOU THINK IT IS THAT I'M IN A BAD MOOD!?
GRAB
YOU FAILED ME!!
YOUNG MASTER ...
CURSE THAT HEADPHONES BOY!! IT WASN'T HIS PROWESS THAT DEFEATED ME.
krch
IT WAS HIS GHOST!
IF ONLY I HAD THAT SAMURAI!!
IT'S UNBECOMING TO TAKE YOUR FRUSTRATIONS OUT ON YOUR SPIRIT COMPANION, LIAN*.
!
klik
klik
IF YOU WANT...
I CAN GET THE SAMURAI FOR YOU.
klik

* MANDARIN CHINESE FOR "REN."

READ THIS WAY

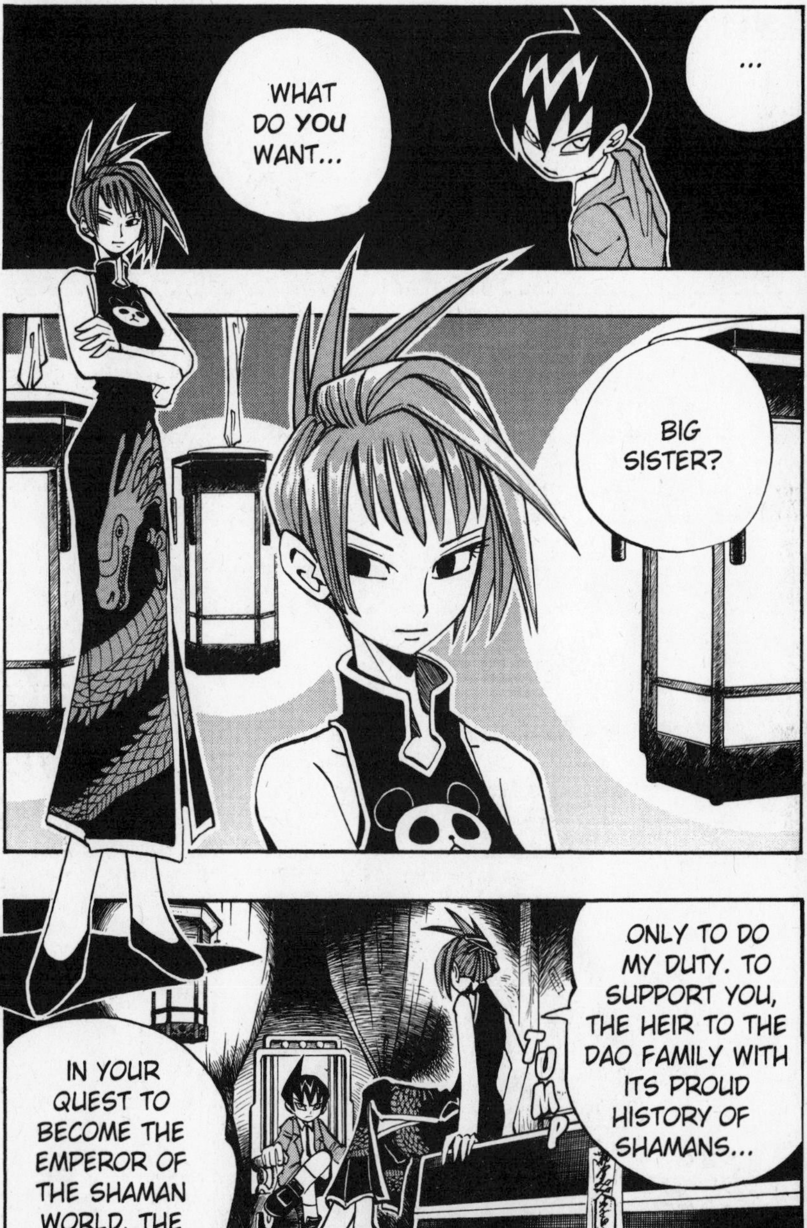
...
WHAT DO YOU WANT...
BIG SISTER?
ONLY TO DO MY DUTY. TO SUPPORT YOU, THE HEIR TO THE DAO FAMILY WITH ITS PROUD HISTORY OF SHAMANS...
TUMP
IN YOUR QUEST TO BECOME THE EMPEROR OF THE SHAMAN WORLD, THE SHAMAN KING.

READ THIS WAY

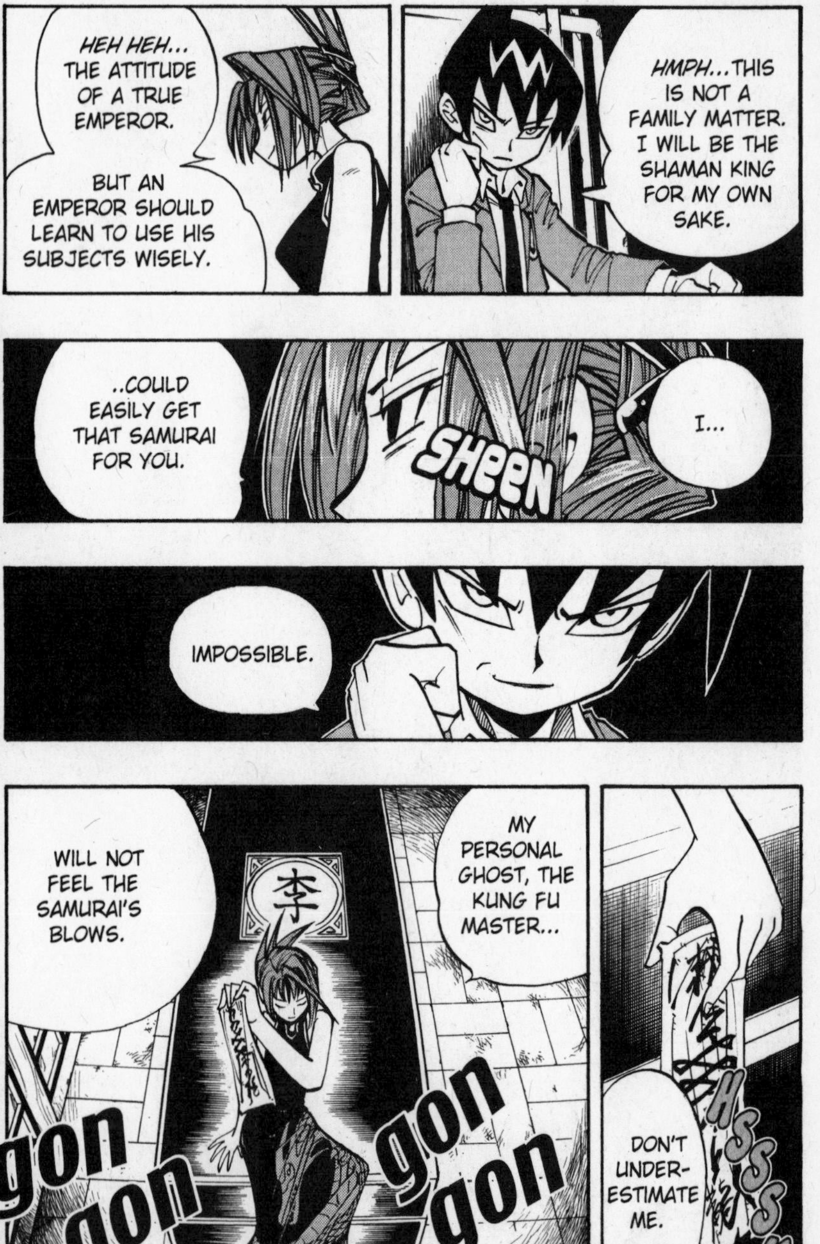
HMPH...THIS IS NOT A FAMILY MATTER. I WILL BE THE SHAMAN KING FOR MY OWN SAKE.
HEH HEH... THE ATTITUDE OF A TRUE EMPEROR.
BUT AN EMPEROR SHOULD LEARN TO USE HIS SUBJECTS WISELY.
I...
SHEEN
..COULD EASILY GET THAT SAMURAI FOR YOU.
IMPOSSIBLE.
HSSSK
DON'T UNDER-ESTIMATE ME.
MY PERSONAL GHOST, THE KUNG FU MASTER...
WILL NOT FEEL THE SAMURAI'S BLOWS.
李
gon gon
gon gon

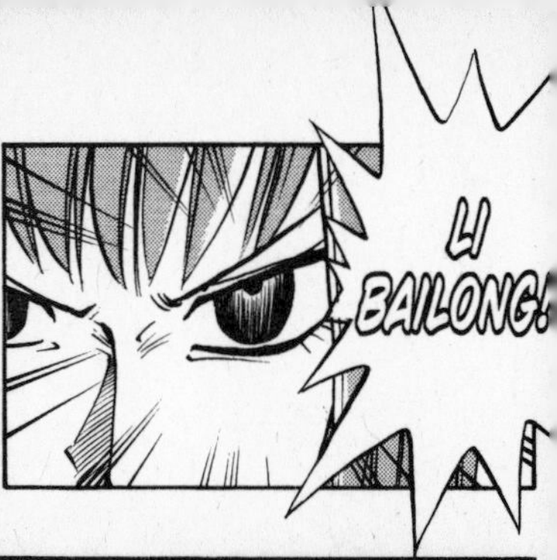
LI BAILONG!
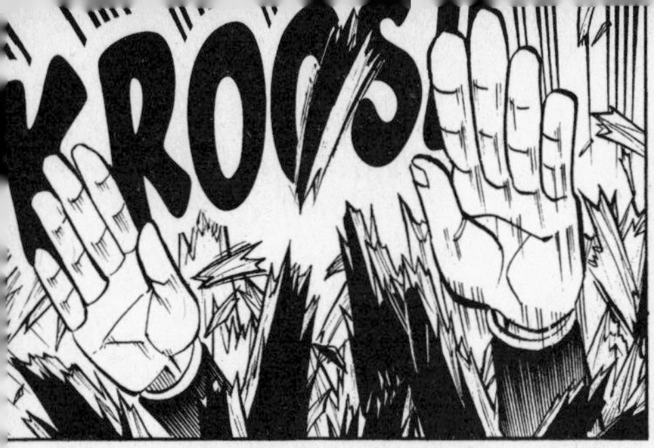
KROOS!
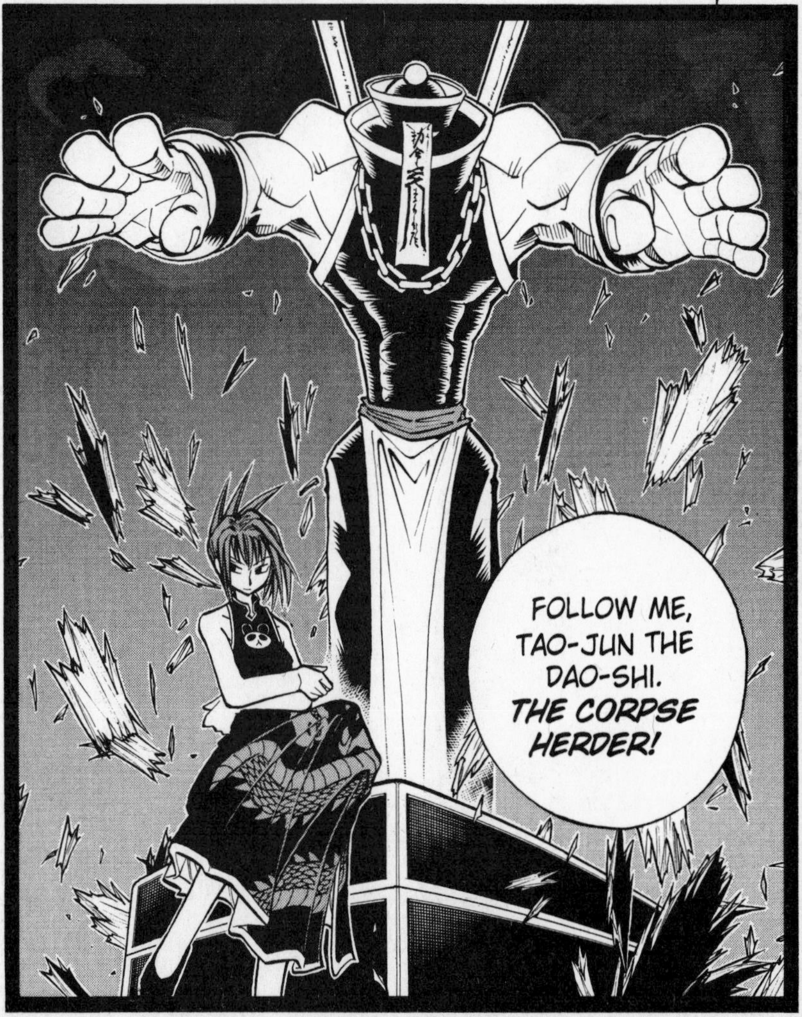
FOLLOW ME, TAO-JUN THE DAO-SHI. THE CORPSE HERDER!

SHAMAN KING CHARACTER FILE No.6

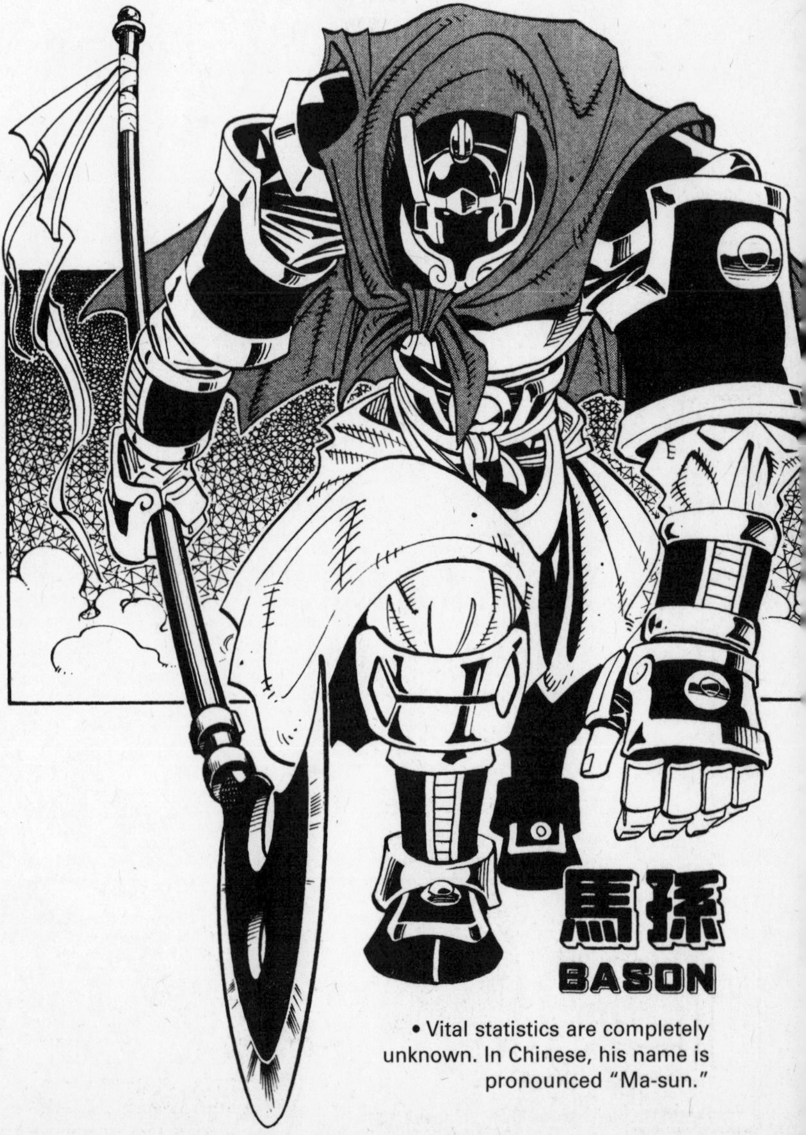

馬孫
BASON

• Vital statistics are completely unknown. In Chinese, his name is pronounced "Ma-sun."

Reincarnation 12: Kung-Fu Master

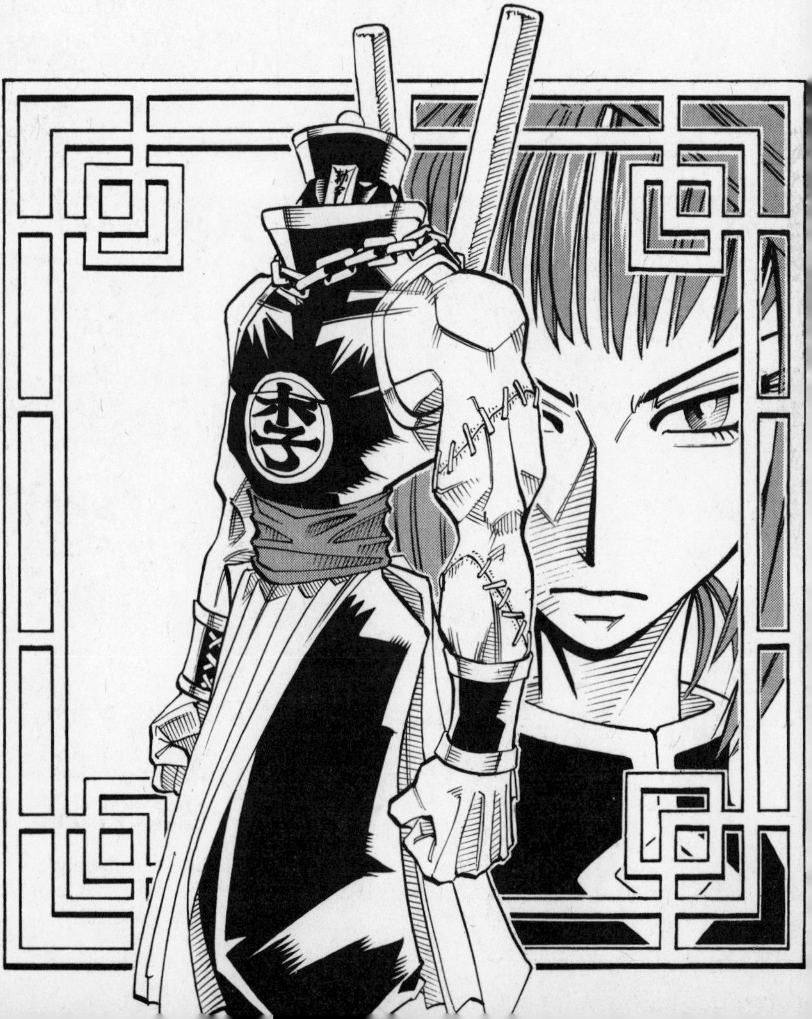

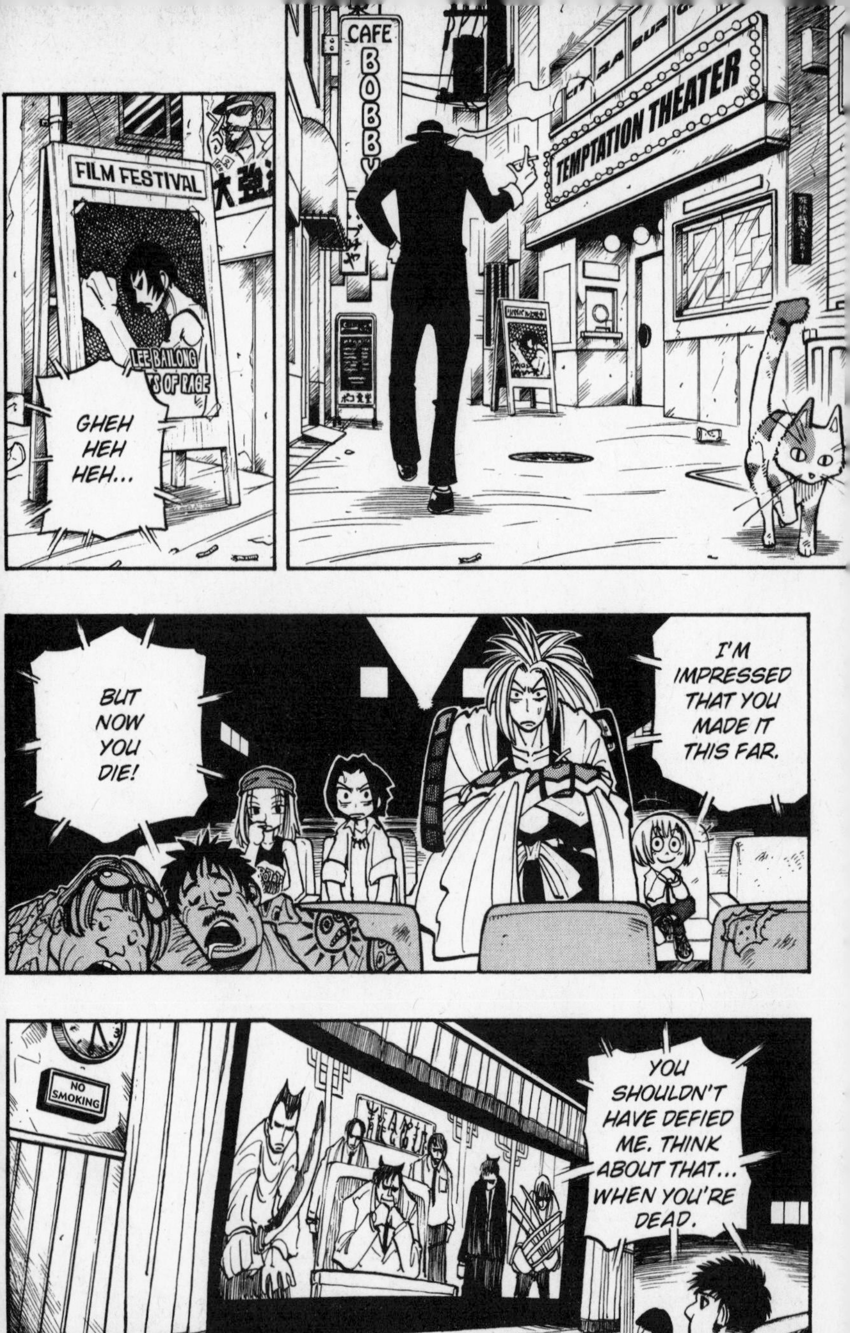
CAFE BOBBY
TEMPTATION THEATER
FILM FESTIVAL
LEE BAILONG
GHEH HEH HEH...
I'M IMPRESSED THAT YOU MADE IT THIS FAR.
BUT NOW YOU DIE!
YOU SHOULDN'T HAVE DEFIED ME. THINK ABOUT THAT... WHEN YOU'RE DEAD.
NO SMOKING

READ THIS WAY

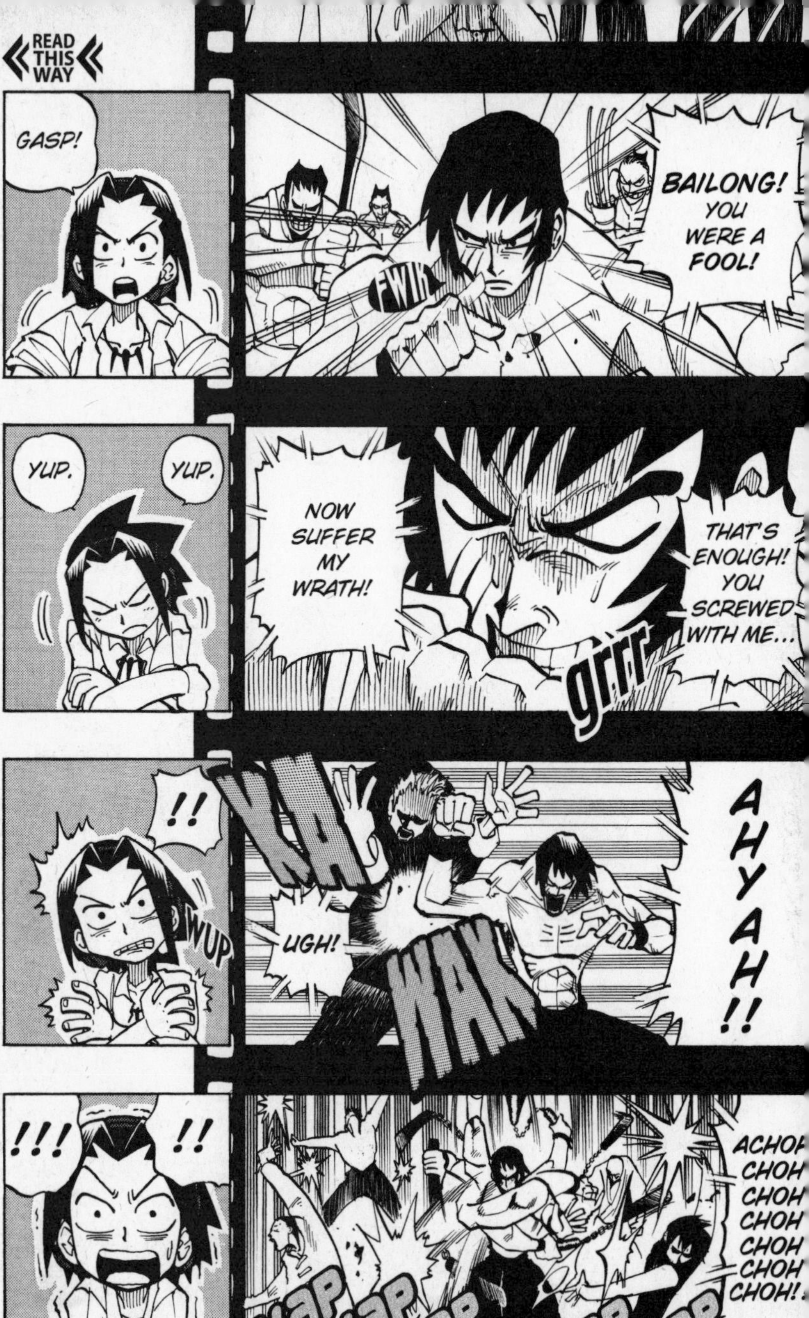

BAILONG! YOU WERE A FOOL!
GASP!
THAT'S ENOUGH! YOU SCREWED WITH ME...
NOW SUFFER MY WRATH!
grrr
YUP.
YUP.
AHYAH!!
WAK
UGH!
WAK
!!
WUP
ACHO CHOH CHOH CHOH CHOH CHOH CHOH!
wap
wap
wap
wap
wap
!!
!!!

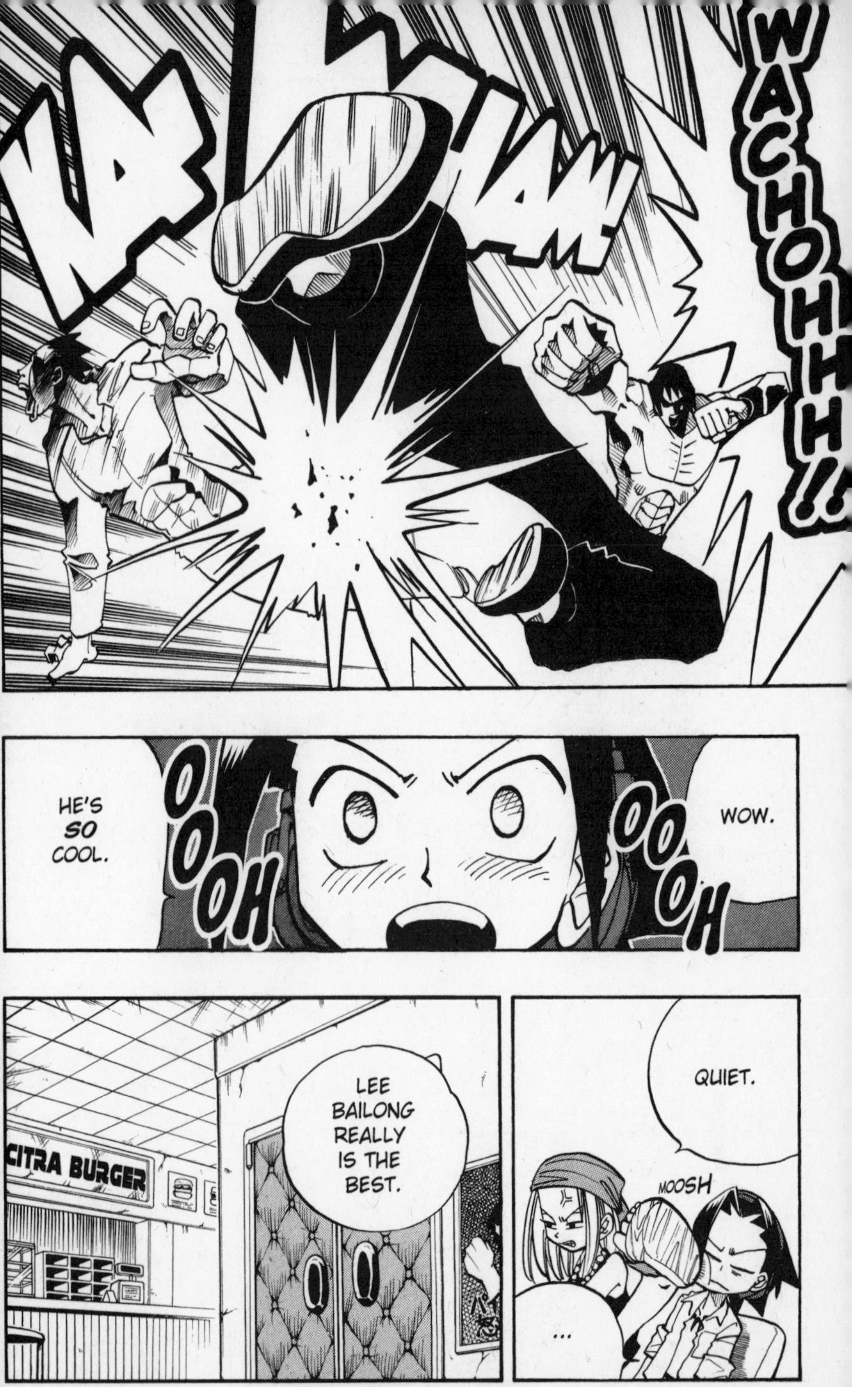
WACHOHHH!!
WOW.
OOOH
HE'S SO COOL.
OOOH
QUIET.
MOOSH
...
LEE BAILONG REALLY IS THE BEST.

READ THIS WAY

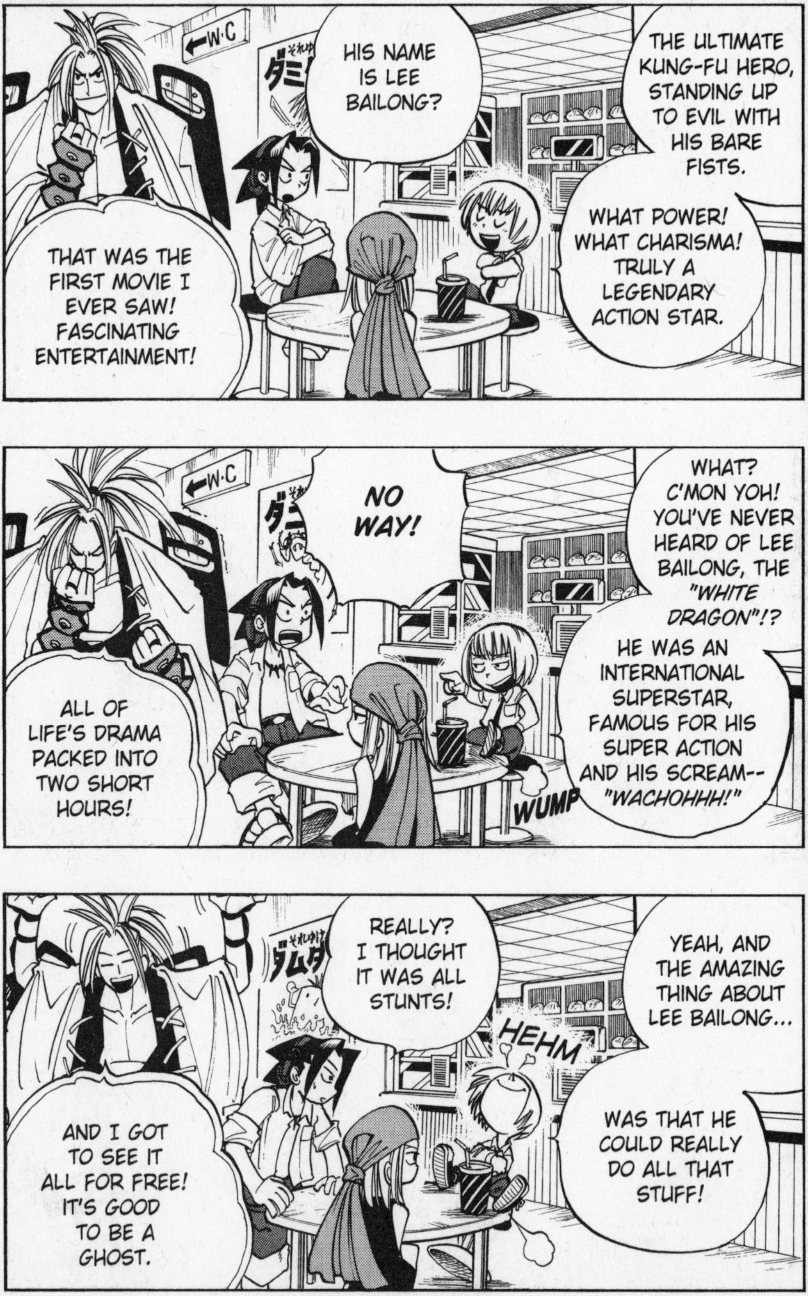

THE ULTIMATE KUNG-FU HERO, STANDING UP TO EVIL WITH HIS BARE FISTS.
HIS NAME IS LEE BAILONG?
WHAT POWER! WHAT CHARISMA! TRULY A LEGENDARY ACTION STAR.
THAT WAS THE FIRST MOVIE I EVER SAW! FASCINATING ENTERTAINMENT!
WHAT? C'MON YOH! YOU'VE NEVER HEARD OF LEE BAILONG, THE "WHITE DRAGON"!?
NO WAY!
HE WAS AN INTERNATIONAL SUPERSTAR, FAMOUS FOR HIS SUPER ACTION AND HIS SCREAM-- "WACHOHHH!"
WUMP
ALL OF LIFE'S DRAMA PACKED INTO TWO SHORT HOURS!
YEAH, AND THE AMAZING THING ABOUT LEE BAILONG...
REALLY? I THOUGHT IT WAS ALL STUNTS!
HEHM
WAS THAT HE COULD REALLY DO ALL THAT STUFF!
AND I GOT TO SEE IT ALL FOR FREE! IT'S GOOD TO BE A GHOST.

READ THIS WAY

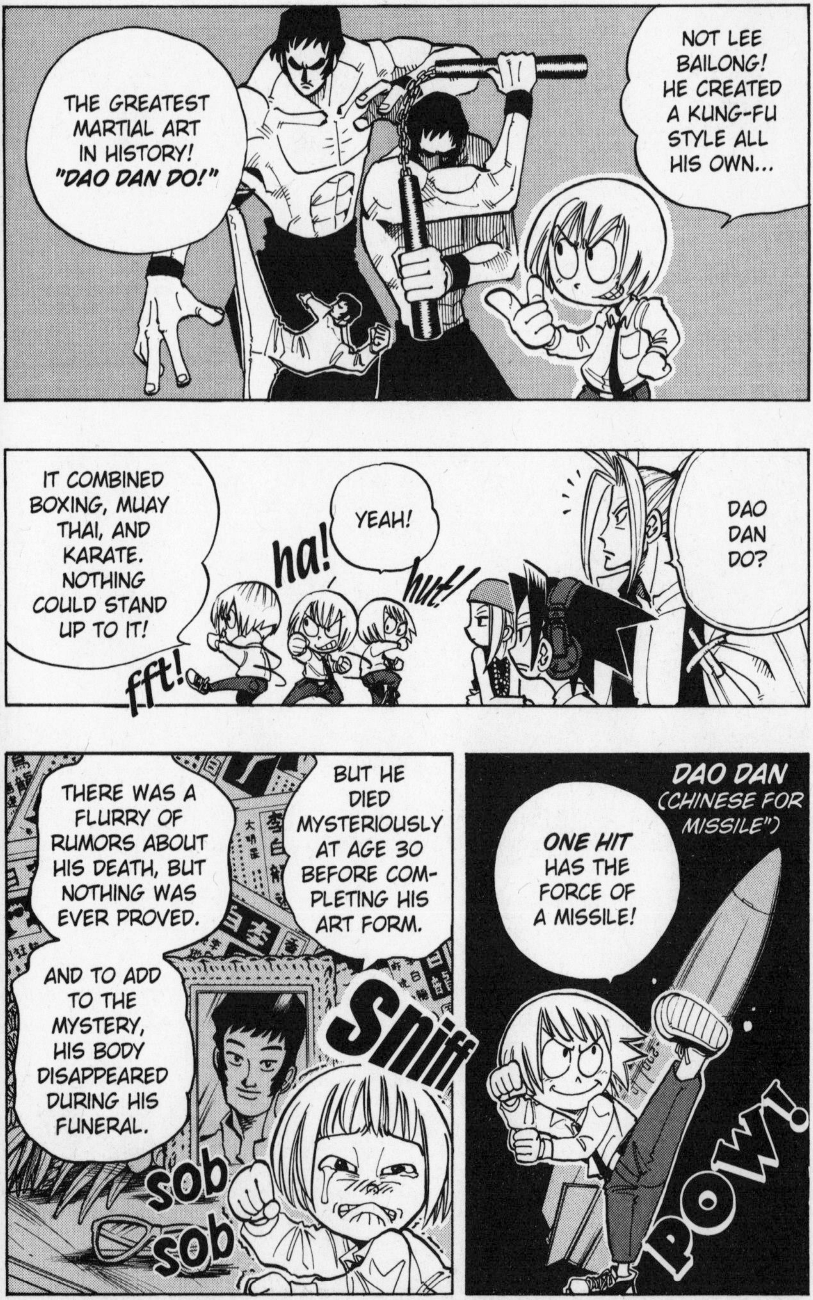

NOT LEE BAILONG! HE CREATED A KUNG-FU STYLE ALL HIS OWN...
THE GREATEST MARTIAL ART IN HISTORY! *"DAO DAN DO!"*
DAO DAN DO?
YEAH!
hut!
ha!
IT COMBINED BOXING, MUAY THAI, AND KARATE. NOTHING COULD STAND UP TO IT!
fft!
DAO DAN (CHINESE FOR MISSILE")
ONE HIT HAS THE FORCE OF A MISSILE!
POW!
BUT HE DIED MYSTERIOUSLY AT AGE 30 BEFORE COM-PLETING HIS ART FORM.
THERE WAS A FLURRY OF RUMORS ABOUT HIS DEATH, BUT NOTHING WAS EVER PROVED.
AND TO ADD TO THE MYSTERY, HIS BODY DISAPPEARED DURING HIS FUNERAL.
Sniff
sob
sob

READ THIS WAY

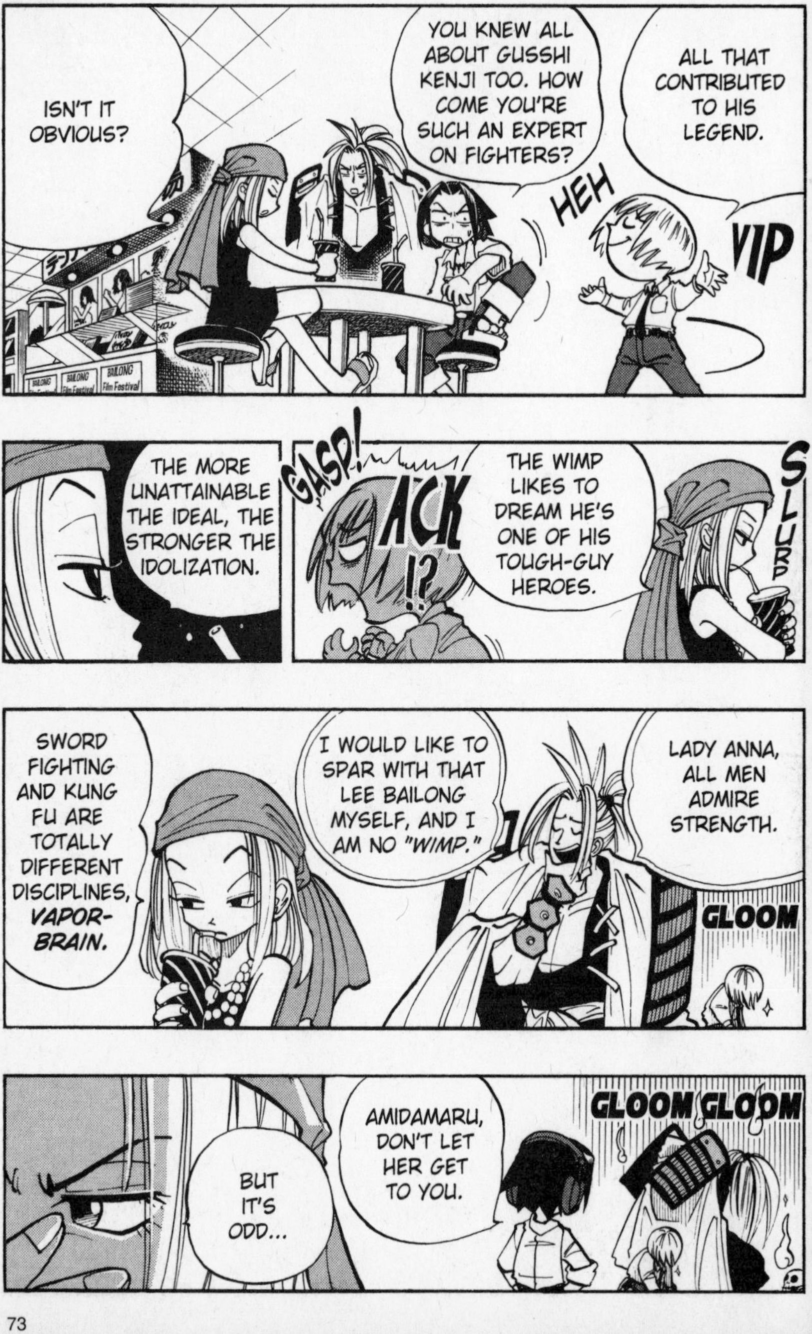

VIP
HEH
ALL THAT CONTRIBUTED TO HIS LEGEND.
YOU KNEW ALL ABOUT GUSSHI KENJI TOO. HOW COME YOU'RE SUCH AN EXPERT ON FIGHTERS?
ISN'T IT OBVIOUS?
BAILONG Film Festival
SLURP
THE WIMP LIKES TO DREAM HE'S ONE OF HIS TOUGH-GUY HEROES.
GASP!
ACK
!?
THE MORE UNATTAINABLE THE IDEAL, THE STRONGER THE IDOLIZATION.
LADY ANNA, ALL MEN ADMIRE STRENGTH.
GLOOM
I WOULD LIKE TO SPAR WITH THAT LEE BAILONG MYSELF, AND I AM NO *"WIMP."*
SWORD FIGHTING AND KUNG FU ARE TOTALLY DIFFERENT DISCIPLINES, ***VAPOR-BRAIN.***
GLOOM GLOOM
AMIDAMARU, DON'T LET HER GET TO YOU.
BUT IT'S ODD...

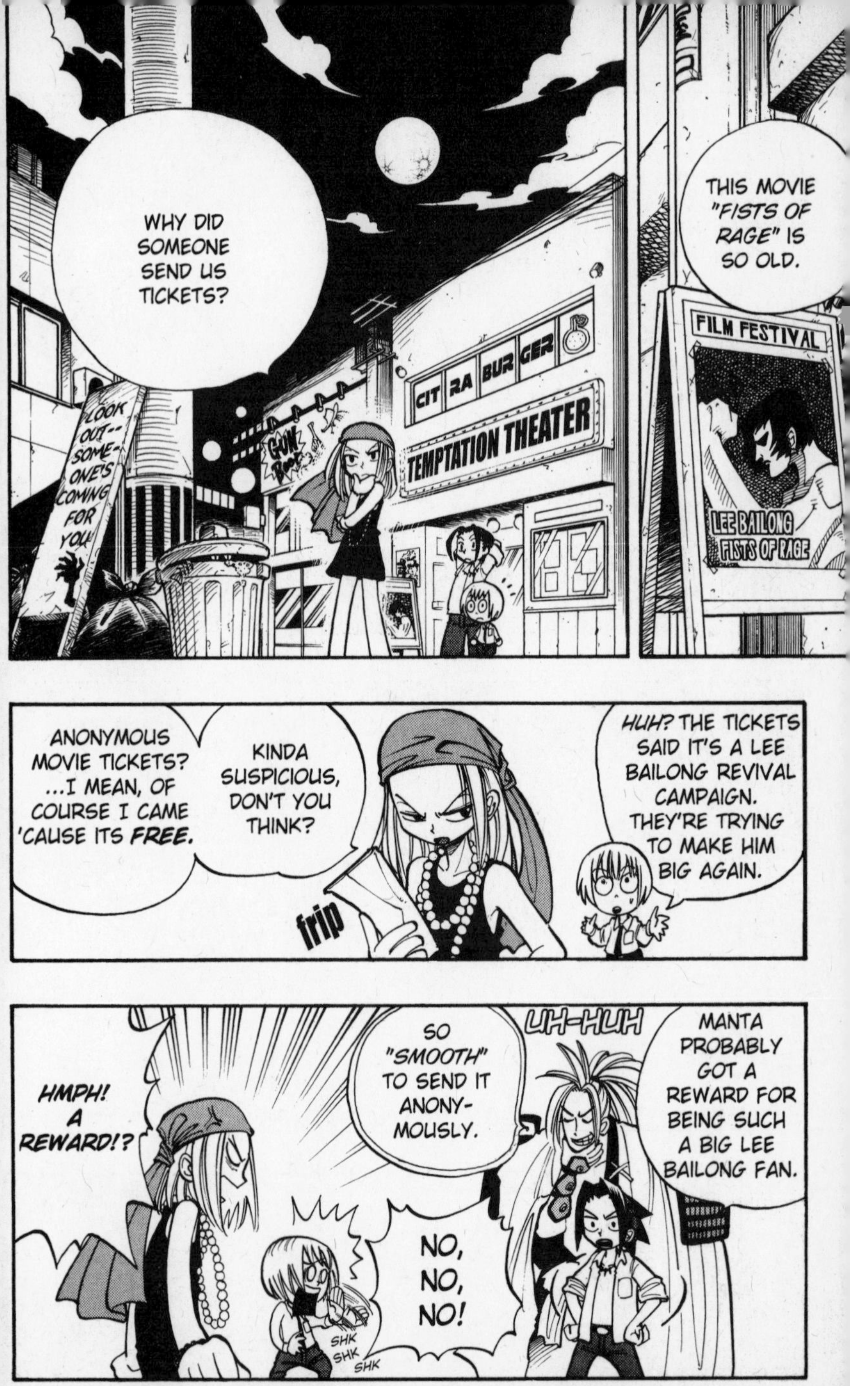
THIS MOVIE "FISTS OF RAGE" IS SO OLD.
FILM FESTIVAL
LEE BAILONG FISTS OF RAGE
WHY DID SOMEONE SEND US TICKETS?
CITRA BURGER
TEMPTATION THEATER
LOOK OUT-- SOME-ONE'S COMING FOR YOU
HUH? THE TICKETS SAID IT'S A LEE BAILONG REVIVAL CAMPAIGN. THEY'RE TRYING TO MAKE HIM BIG AGAIN.
KINDA SUSPICIOUS, DON'T YOU THINK?
ANONYMOUS MOVIE TICKETS? ...I MEAN, OF COURSE I CAME 'CAUSE ITS FREE.
frip
MANTA PROBABLY GOT A REWARD FOR BEING SUCH A BIG LEE BAILONG FAN.
UH-HUH
SO "SMOOTH" TO SEND IT ANONY-MOUSLY.
HMPH! A REWARD!?
NO, NO, NO!
SHK SHK SHK

READ THIS WAY

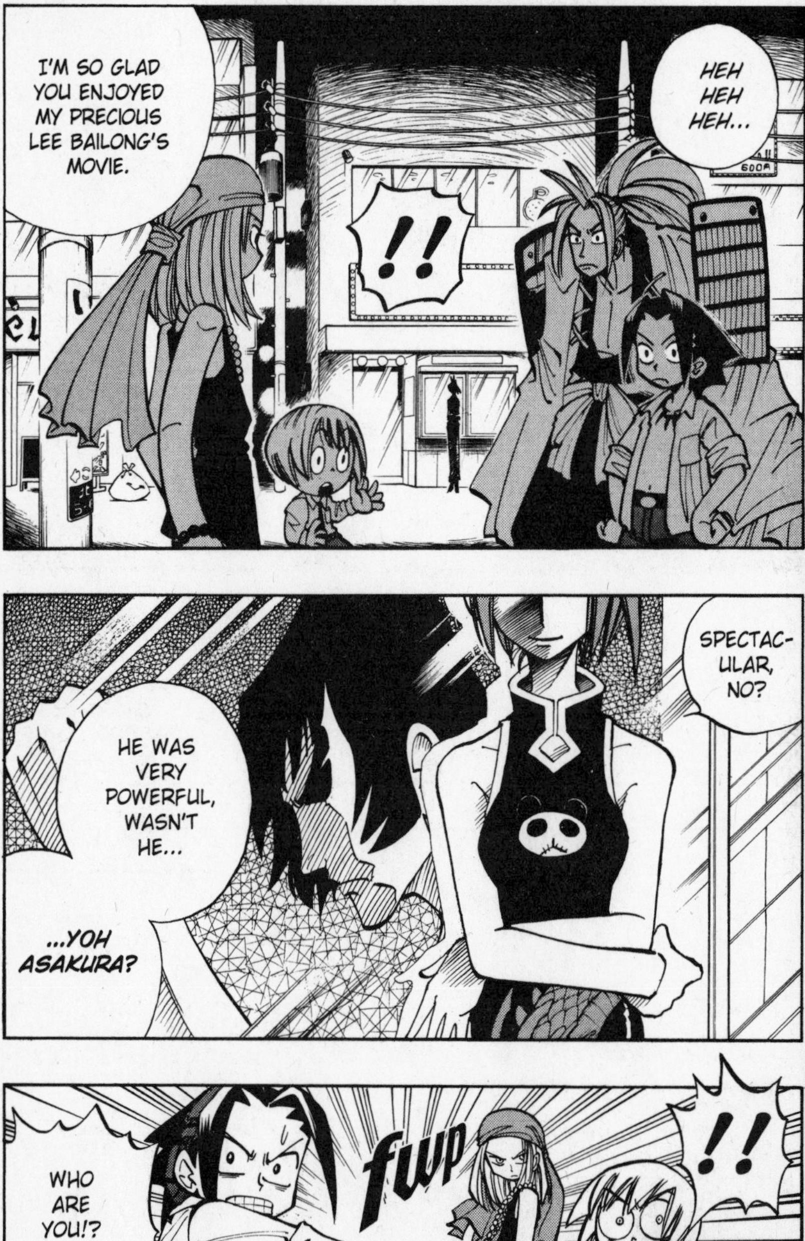

HEH HEH HEH...
I'M SO GLAD YOU ENJOYED MY PRECIOUS LEE BAILONG'S MOVIE.
!!
SPECTAC-ULAR, NO?
HE WAS VERY POWERFUL, WASN'T HE...
...YOH ASAKURA?
!!
fwup
WHO ARE YOU!?

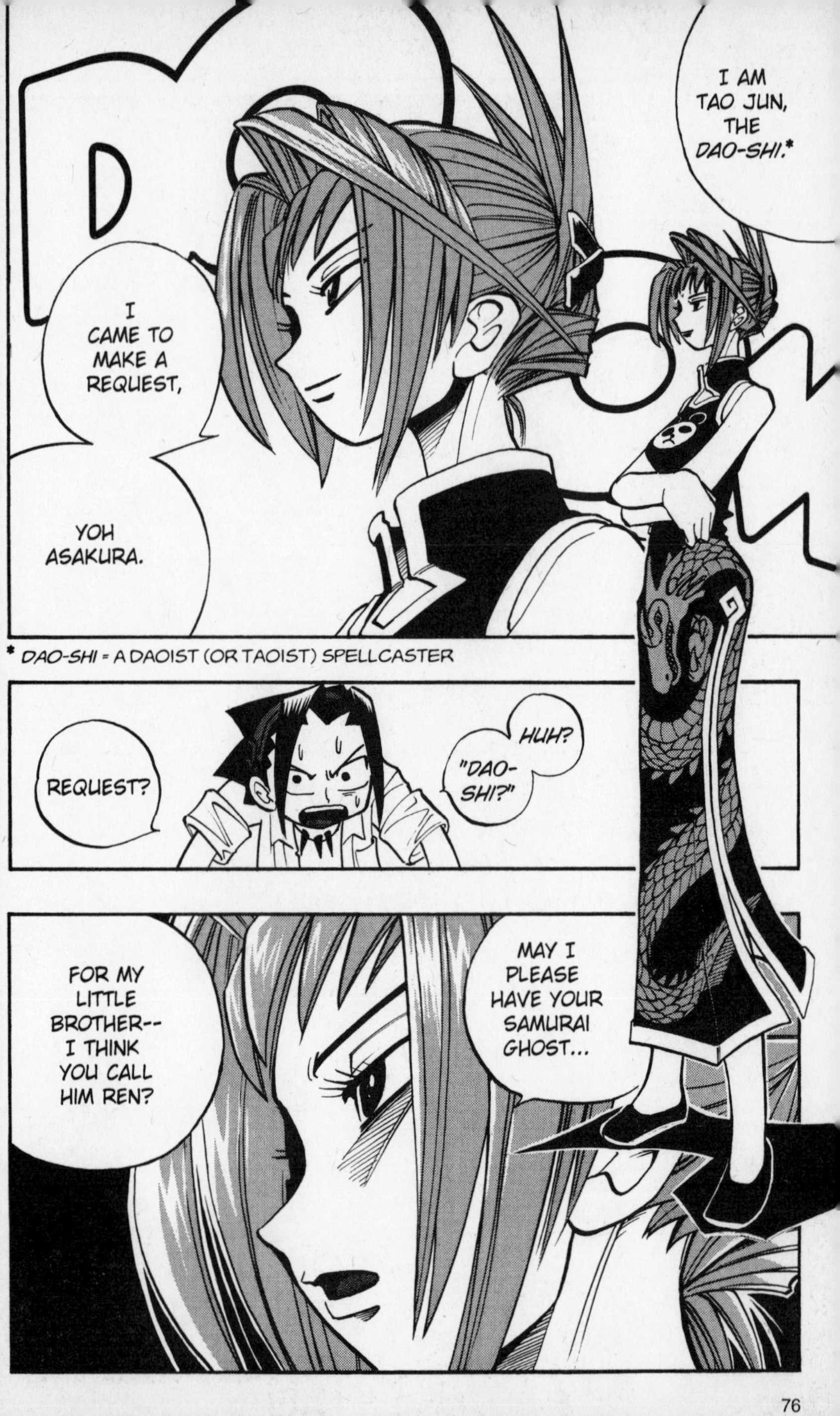
I AM TAO JUN, THE DAO-SHI.*
D
I CAME TO MAKE A REQUEST,
YOH ASAKURA.
HUH? "DAO-SHI?"
REQUEST?
MAY I PLEASE HAVE YOUR SAMURAI GHOST...
FOR MY LITTLE BROTHER-- I THINK YOU CALL HIM REN?

* *DAO-SHI* = A DAOIST (OR TAOIST) SPELLCASTER

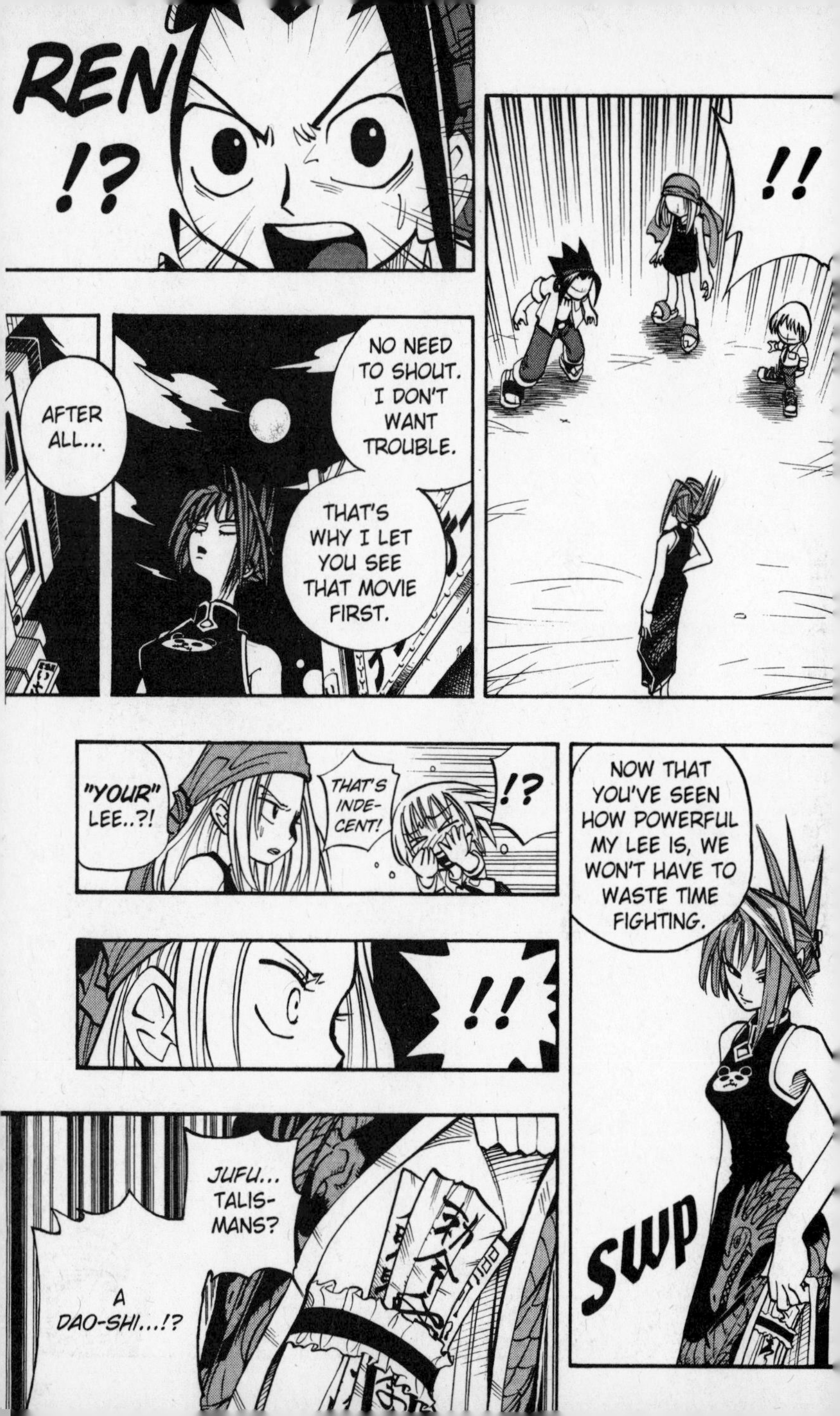
REN
!?
!!
NO NEED TO SHOUT. I DON'T WANT TROUBLE.
THAT'S WHY I LET YOU SEE THAT MOVIE FIRST.
AFTER ALL...
NOW THAT YOU'VE SEEN HOW POWERFUL MY LEE IS, WE WON'T HAVE TO WASTE TIME FIGHTING.
SWP
!?
THAT'S INDE-CENT!
"YOUR" LEE..?!
!!
JUFU... TALIS-MANS?
A DAO-SHI...!?

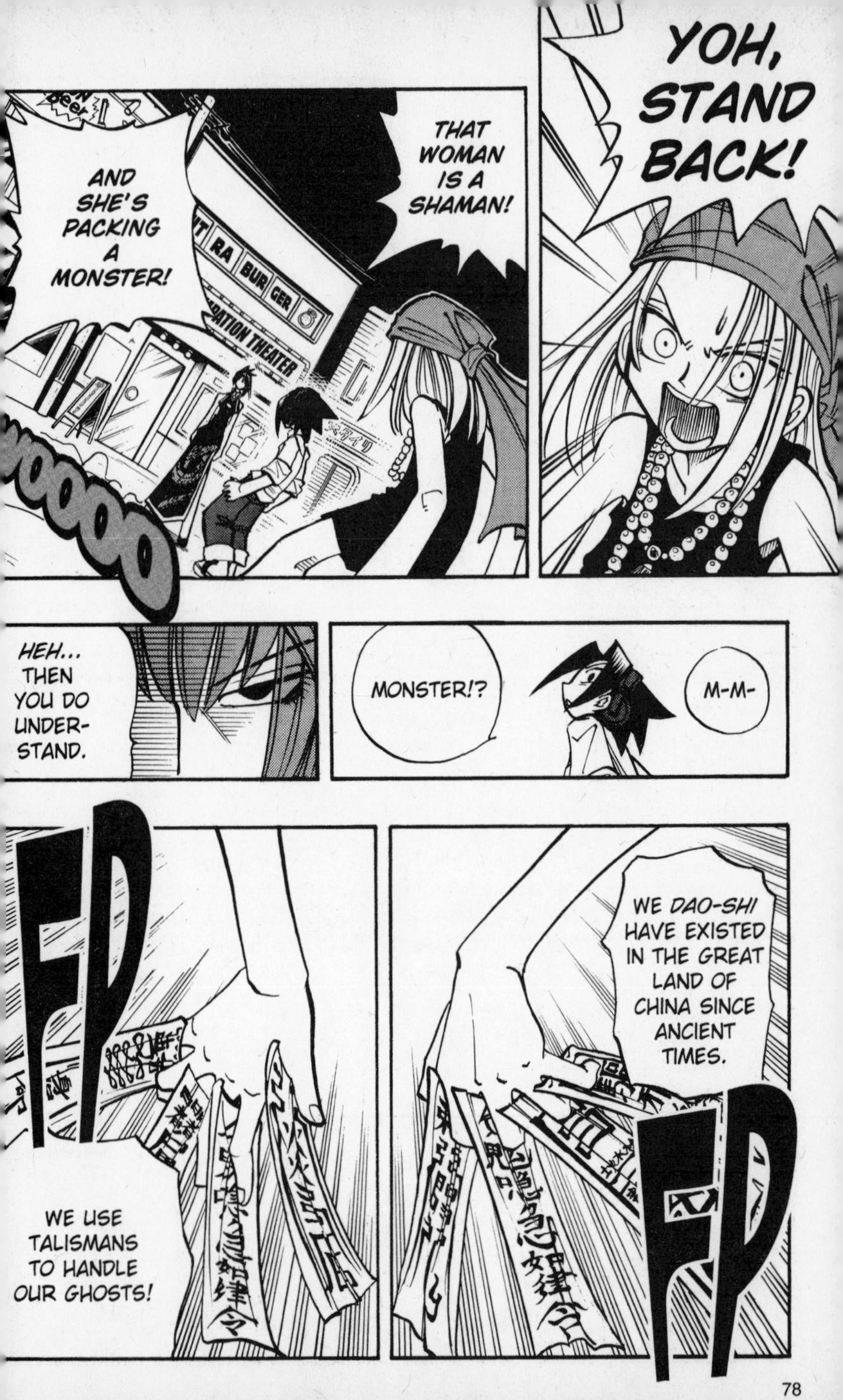
YOH, STAND BACK!
THAT WOMAN IS A SHAMAN!
AND SHE'S PACKING A MONSTER!
M-M-
MONSTER!?
HEH... THEN YOU DO UNDER-STAND.
WE DAO-SHI HAVE EXISTED IN THE GREAT LAND OF CHINA SINCE ANCIENT TIMES.
FP
FP
WE USE TALISMANS TO HANDLE OUR GHOSTS!

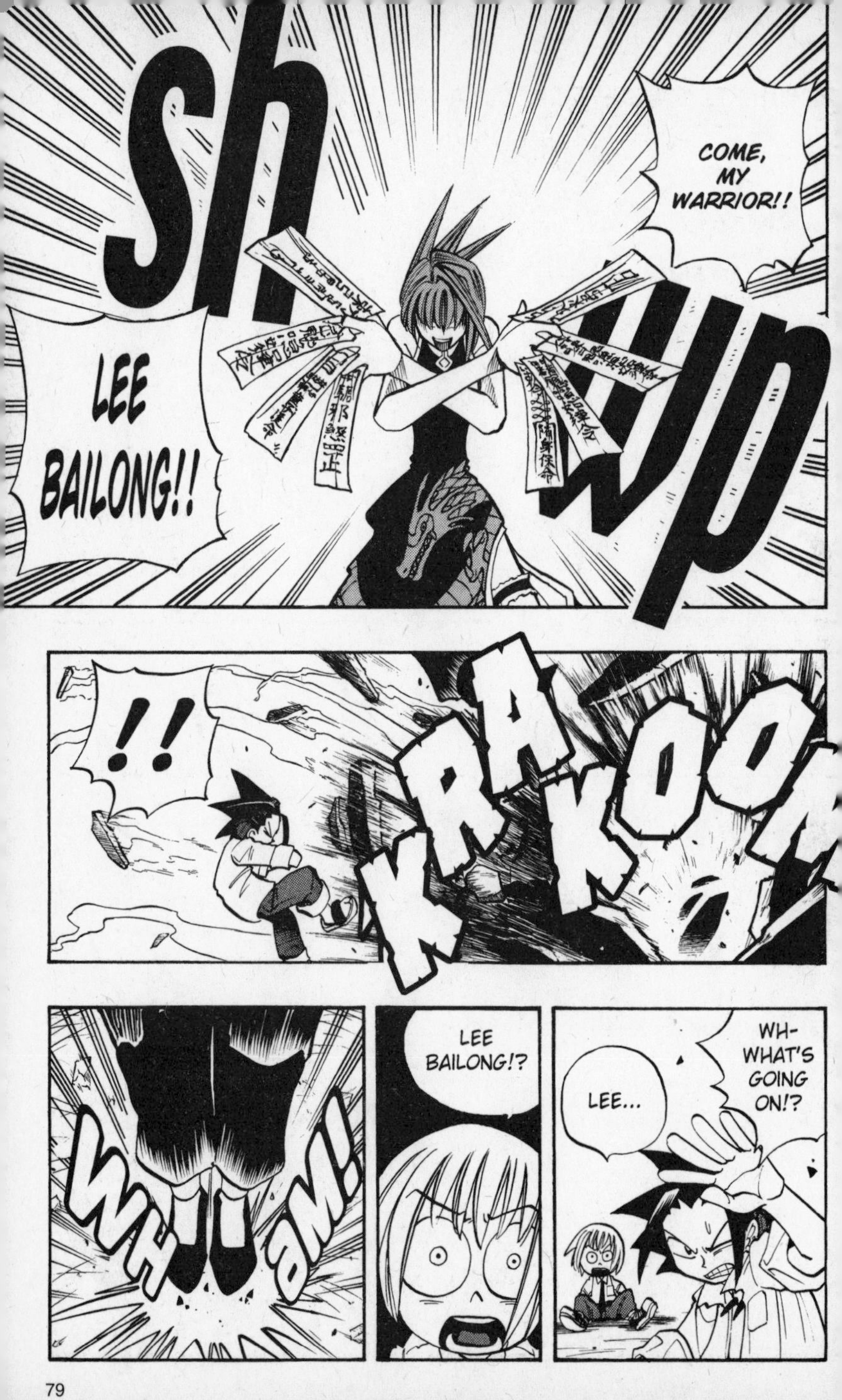
COME, MY WARRIOR!!
SH WHP
LEE BAILONG!!
KRAKOO
!!
WH-WHAT'S GOING ON!?
LEE...
LEE BAILONG!?
WHAM!!

IT'S REALLY HIM!!

DADA DOOM

...NO WAY...

...

80

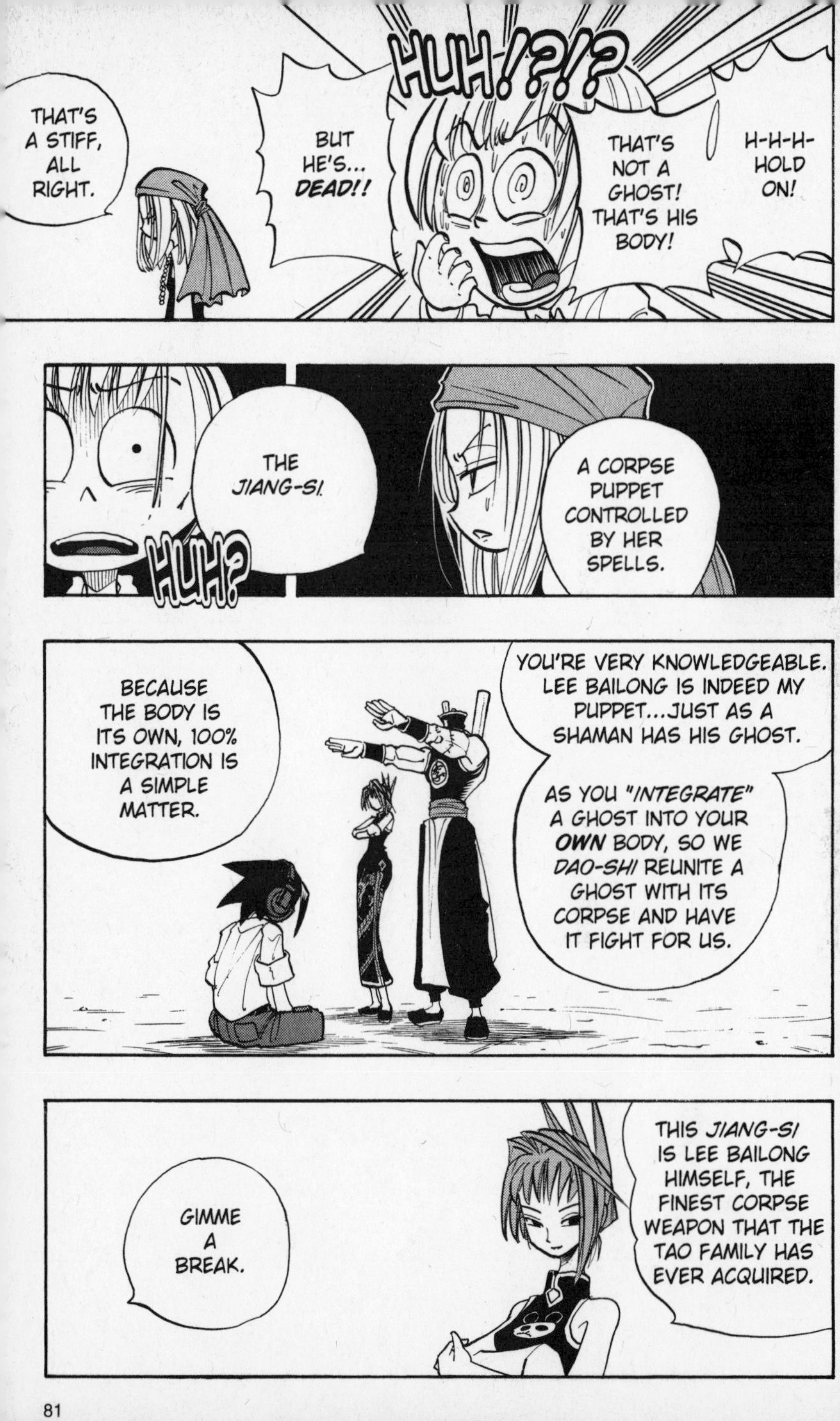
H-H-H-HOLD ON!
HUH!?!?
THAT'S NOT A GHOST! THAT'S HIS BODY!
BUT HE'S... DEAD!!
THAT'S A STIFF, ALL RIGHT.
A CORPSE PUPPET CONTROLLED BY HER SPELLS.
THE JIANG-SI.
HUH?
YOU'RE VERY KNOWLEDGEABLE. LEE BAILONG IS INDEED MY PUPPET...JUST AS A SHAMAN HAS HIS GHOST.
AS YOU "INTEGRATE" A GHOST INTO YOUR OWN BODY, SO WE DAO-SHI REUNITE A GHOST WITH ITS CORPSE AND HAVE IT FIGHT FOR US.
BECAUSE THE BODY IS ITS OWN, 100% INTEGRATION IS A SIMPLE MATTER.
THIS JIANG-SI IS LEE BAILONG HIMSELF, THE FINEST CORPSE WEAPON THAT THE TAO FAMILY HAS EVER ACQUIRED.
GIMME A BREAK.

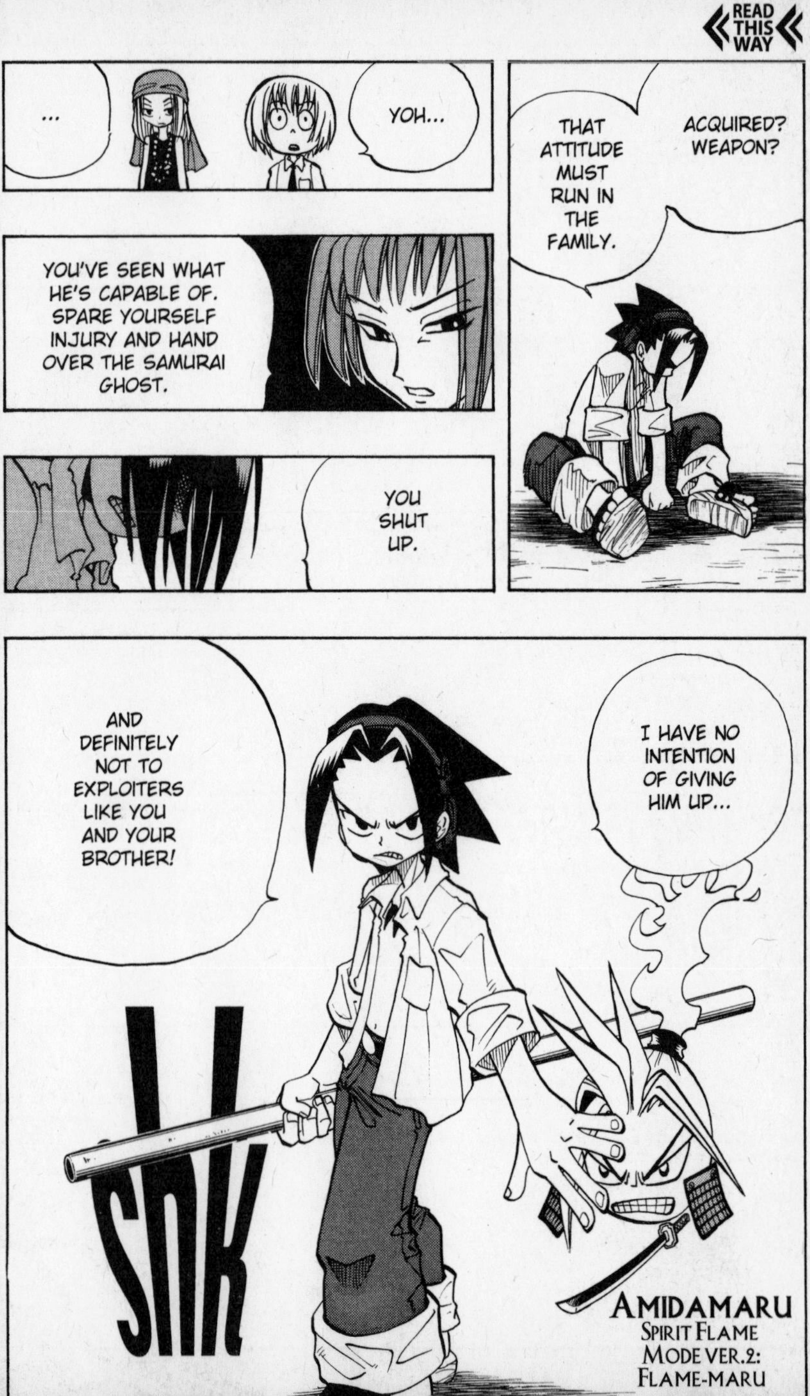
READ THIS WAY
ACQUIRED? WEAPON?
THAT ATTITUDE MUST RUN IN THE FAMILY.
YOH...
...
YOU'VE SEEN WHAT HE'S CAPABLE OF. SPARE YOURSELF INJURY AND HAND OVER THE SAMURAI GHOST.
YOU SHUT UP.
I HAVE NO INTENTION OF GIVING HIM UP...
AND DEFINITELY NOT TO EXPLOITERS LIKE YOU AND YOUR BROTHER!
SHK
AMIDAMARU
SPIRIT FLAME MODE VER.2: FLAME-MARU

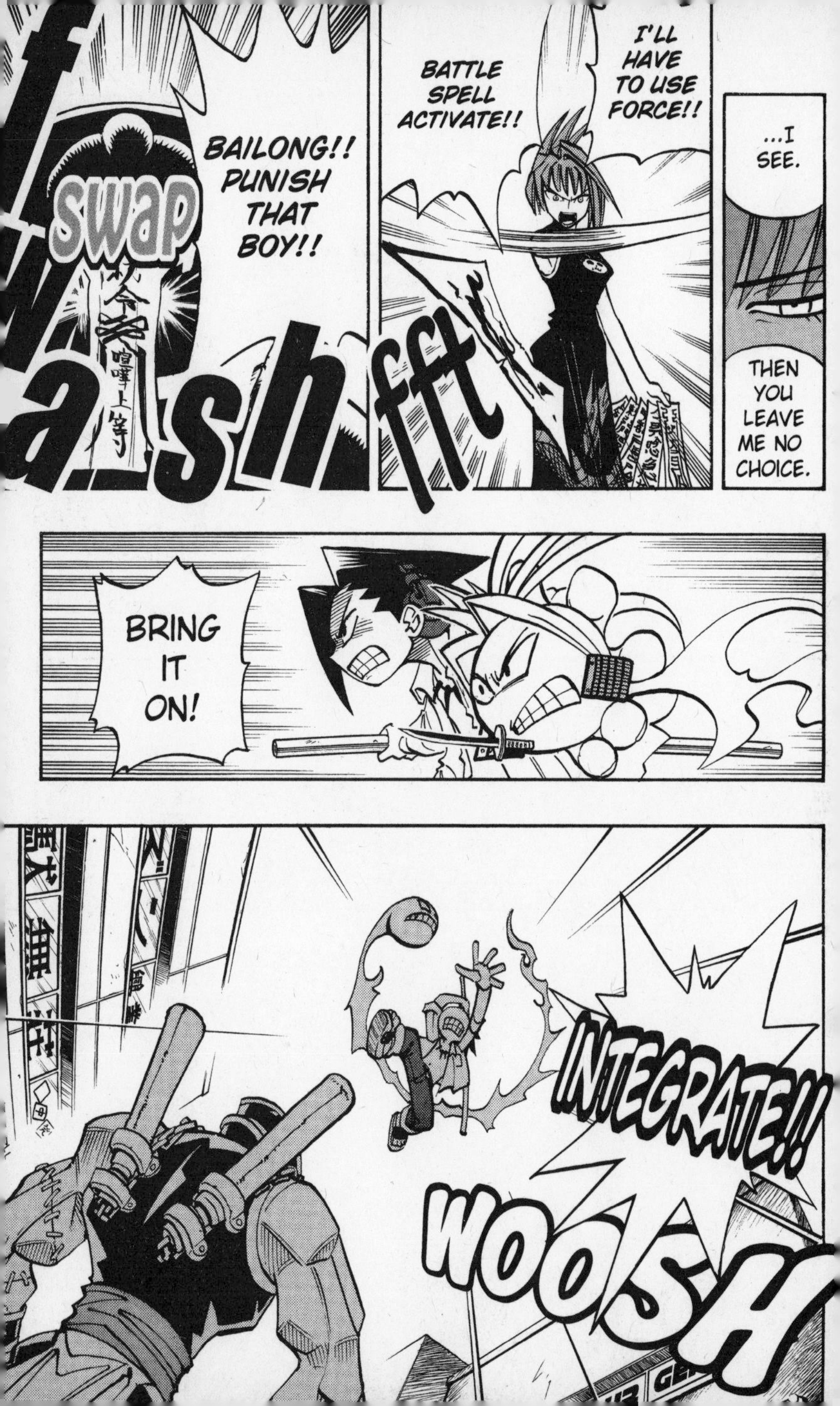
...I SEE.
THEN YOU LEAVE ME NO CHOICE.
I'LL HAVE TO USE FORCE!!
BATTLE SPELL ACTIVATE!!
fft
BAILONG!! PUNISH THAT BOY!!
swap
BRING IT ON!
INTEGRATE!!
WOOSH

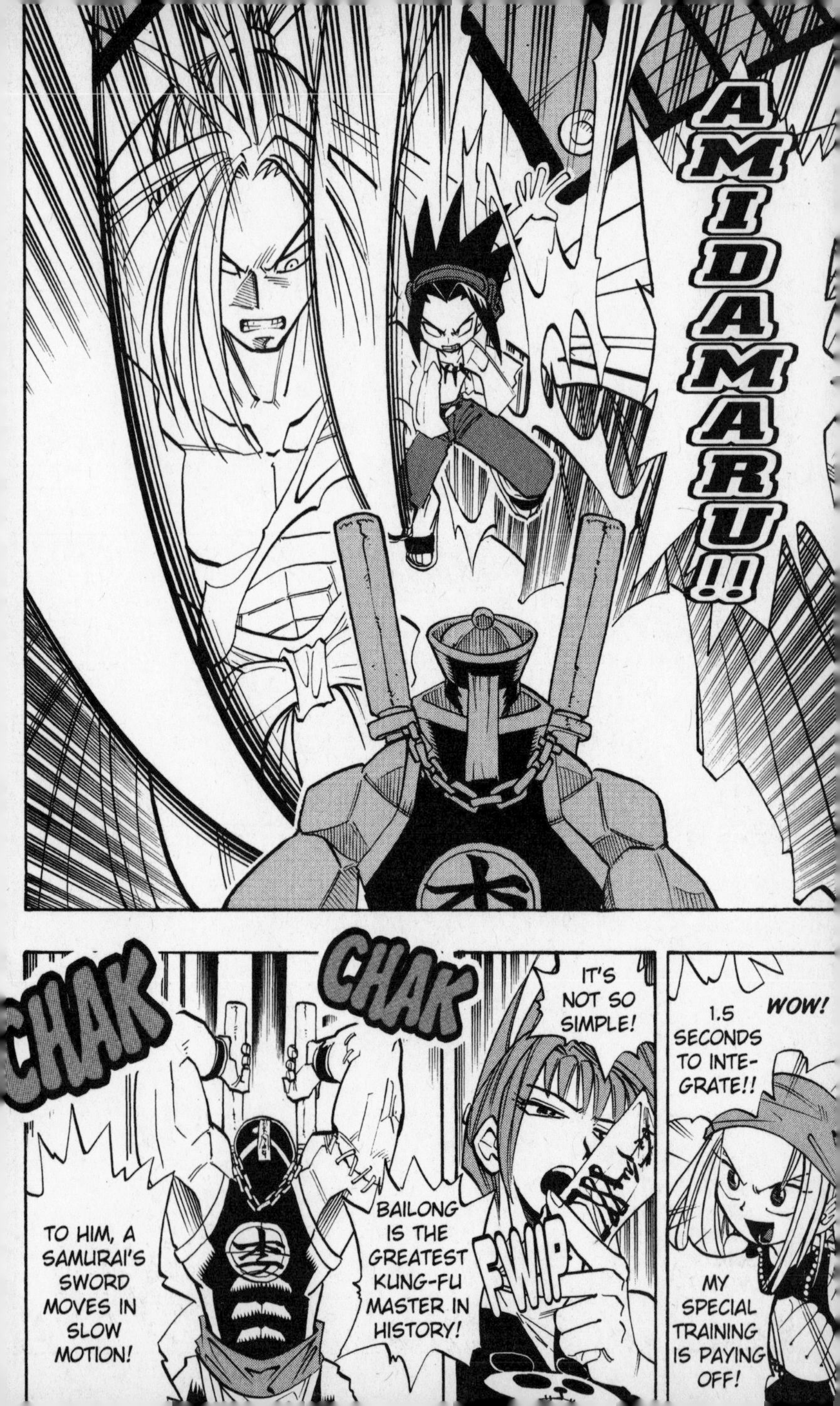
AMIDAMARU!!
WOW!
1.5 SECONDS TO INTEGRATE!!
MY SPECIAL TRAINING IS PAYING OFF!
IT'S NOT SO SIMPLE!
BAILONG IS THE GREATEST KUNG-FU MASTER IN HISTORY!
FWIP
CHAK
CHAK
TO HIM, A SAMURAI'S SWORD MOVES IN SLOW MOTION!

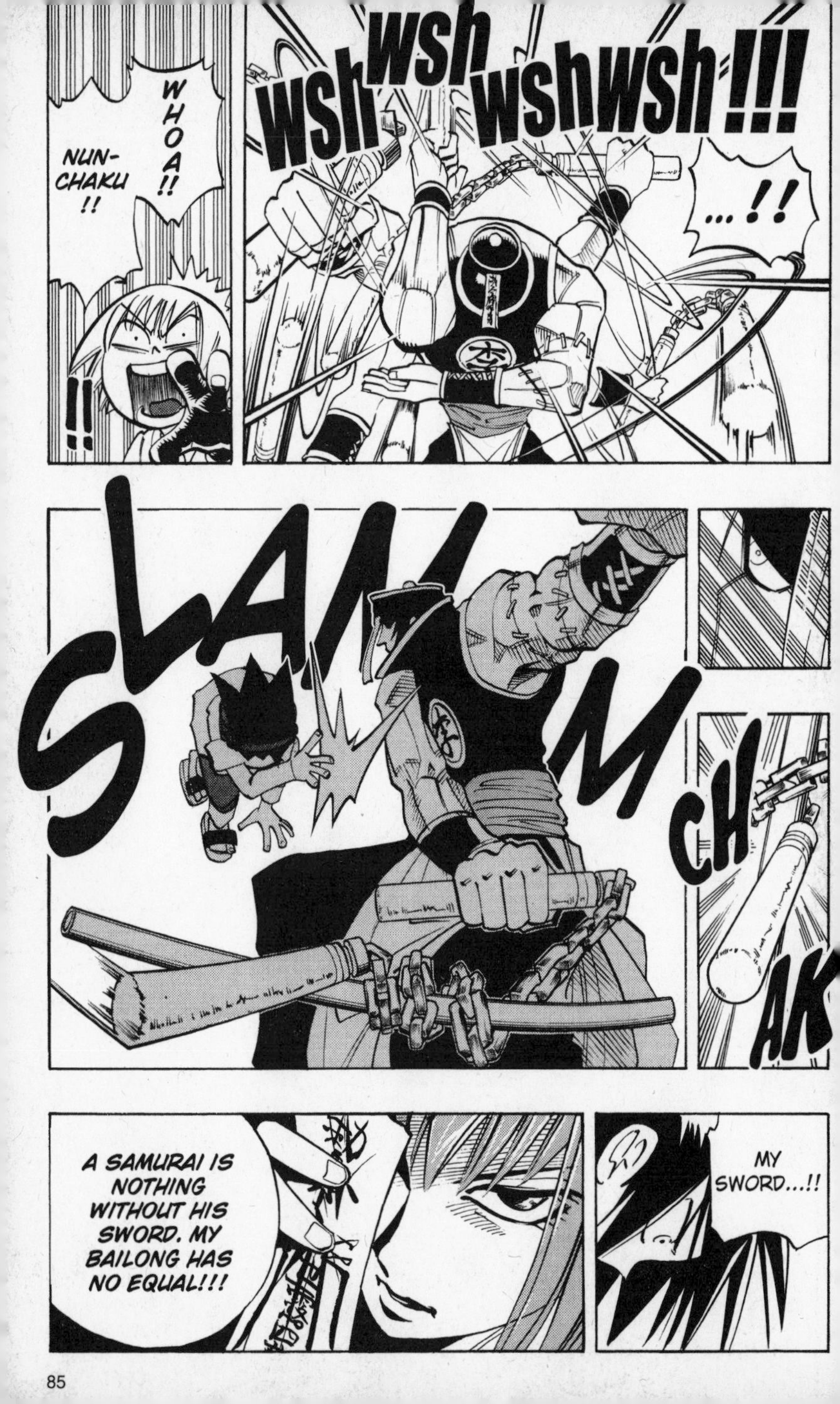

wsh wsh wshwsh!!!
...!!
WHOA!!
NUN-CHAKU!!
!!
CH
AK
SLAM
MY SWORD...!!
A SAMURAI IS NOTHING WITHOUT HIS SWORD. MY BAILONG HAS NO EQUAL!!!

SHAMAN
KING
2

TRUNK

REINCARNATION 13: THE CORPSE PUPPET

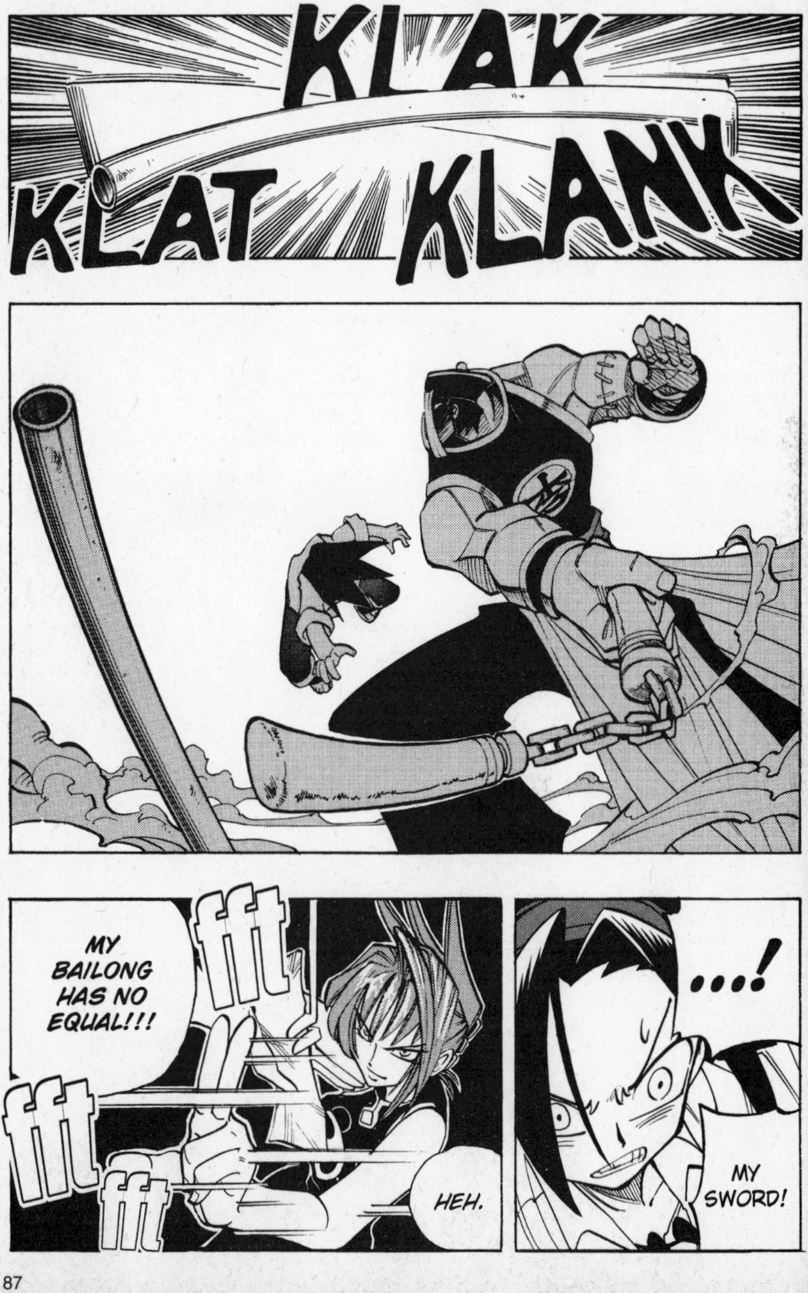
KLAK
KLANK
KLAT
...!
MY SWORD!
fft
MY BAILONG HAS NO EQUAL!!!
fft
HEH.
fft

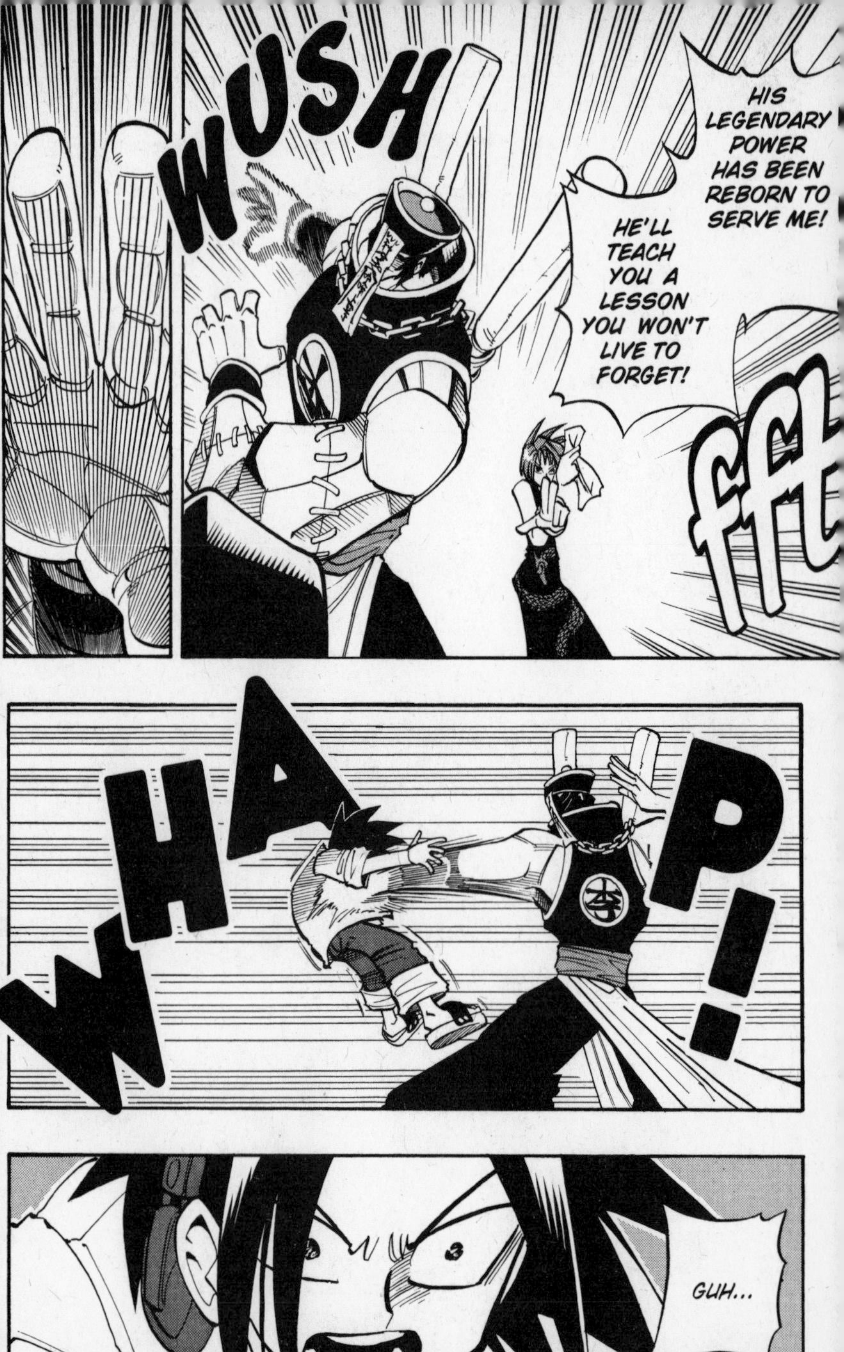
HIS LEGENDARY POWER HAS BEEN REBORN TO SERVE ME!
HE'LL TEACH YOU A LESSON YOU WON'T LIVE TO FORGET!
WUSH
fft
WHAP!!
GUH...

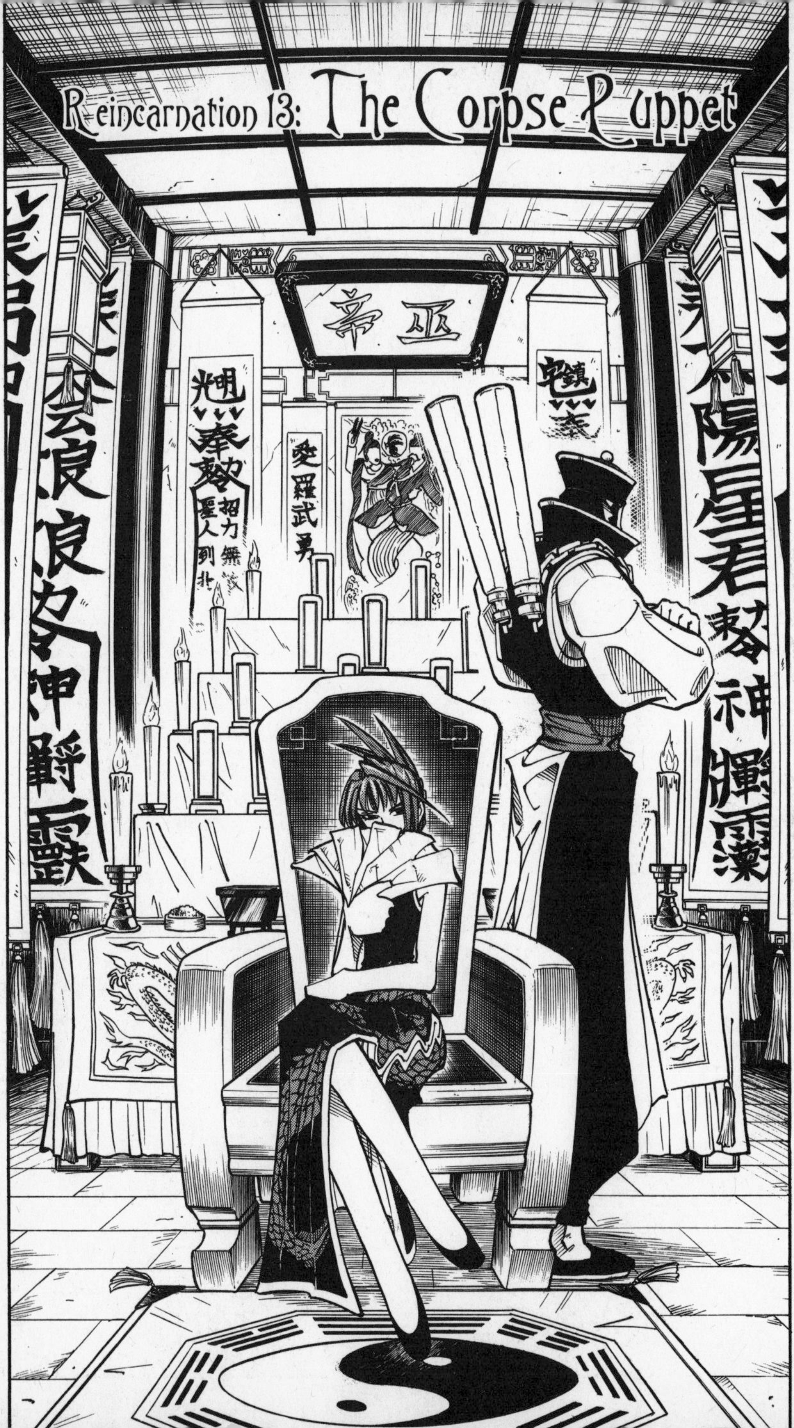
Reincarnation 13: The Corpse Puppet

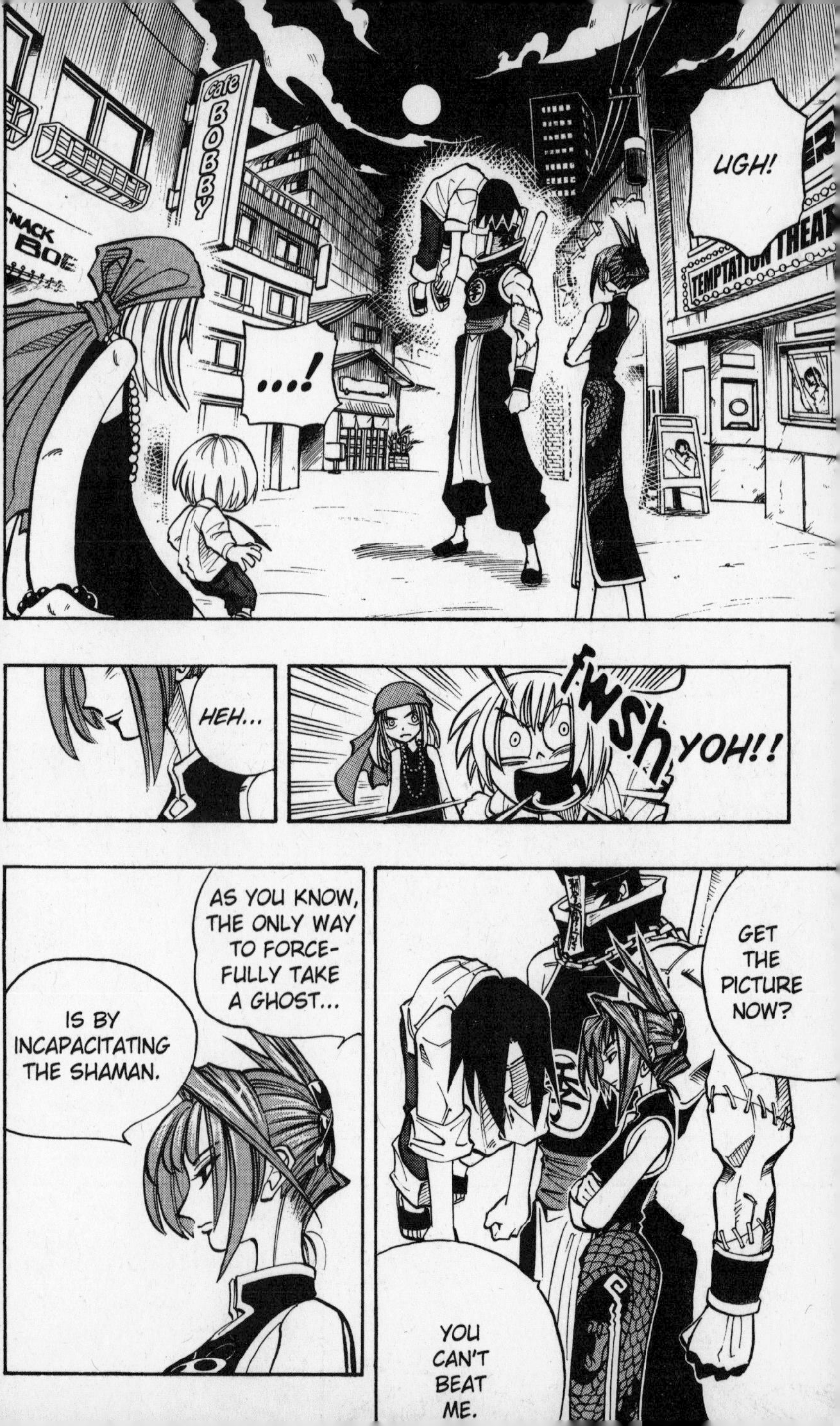
UGH!
TEMPTATION THEAT
Cafe BOBBY
SNACK BOE
...!
fwsh
YOH!!
HEH...
GET THE PICTURE NOW?
YOU CAN'T BEAT ME.
AS YOU KNOW, THE ONLY WAY TO FORCE-FULLY TAKE A GHOST...
IS BY INCAPACITATING THE SHAMAN.

READ THIS WAY

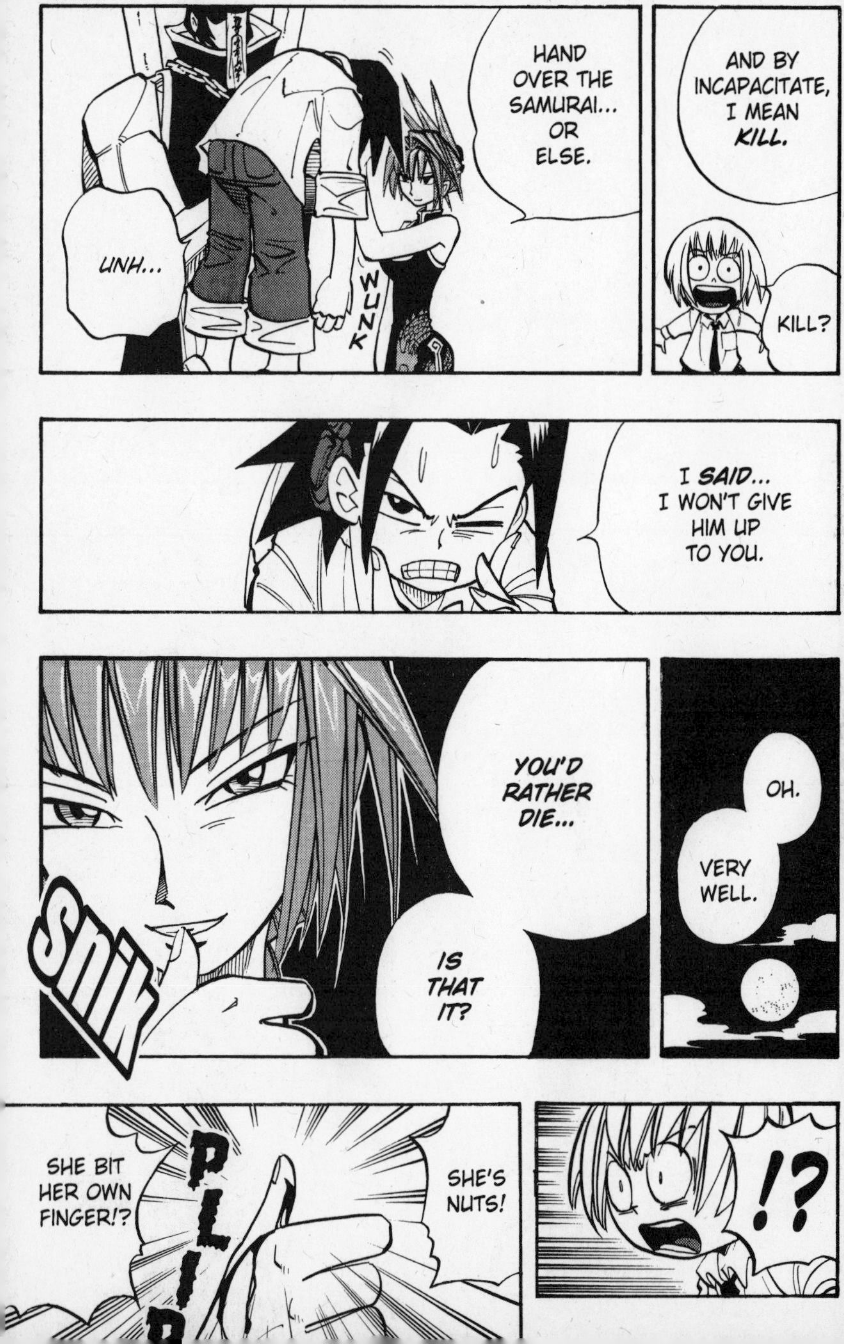
AND BY INCAPACITATE, I MEAN KILL.
KILL?
HAND OVER THE SAMURAI... OR ELSE.
WUNK
UNH...
I SAID... I WON'T GIVE HIM UP TO YOU.
OH.
VERY WELL.
YOU'D RATHER DIE...
IS THAT IT?
SNIK
!?
SHE'S NUTS!
SHE BIT HER OWN FINGER!?
PLI

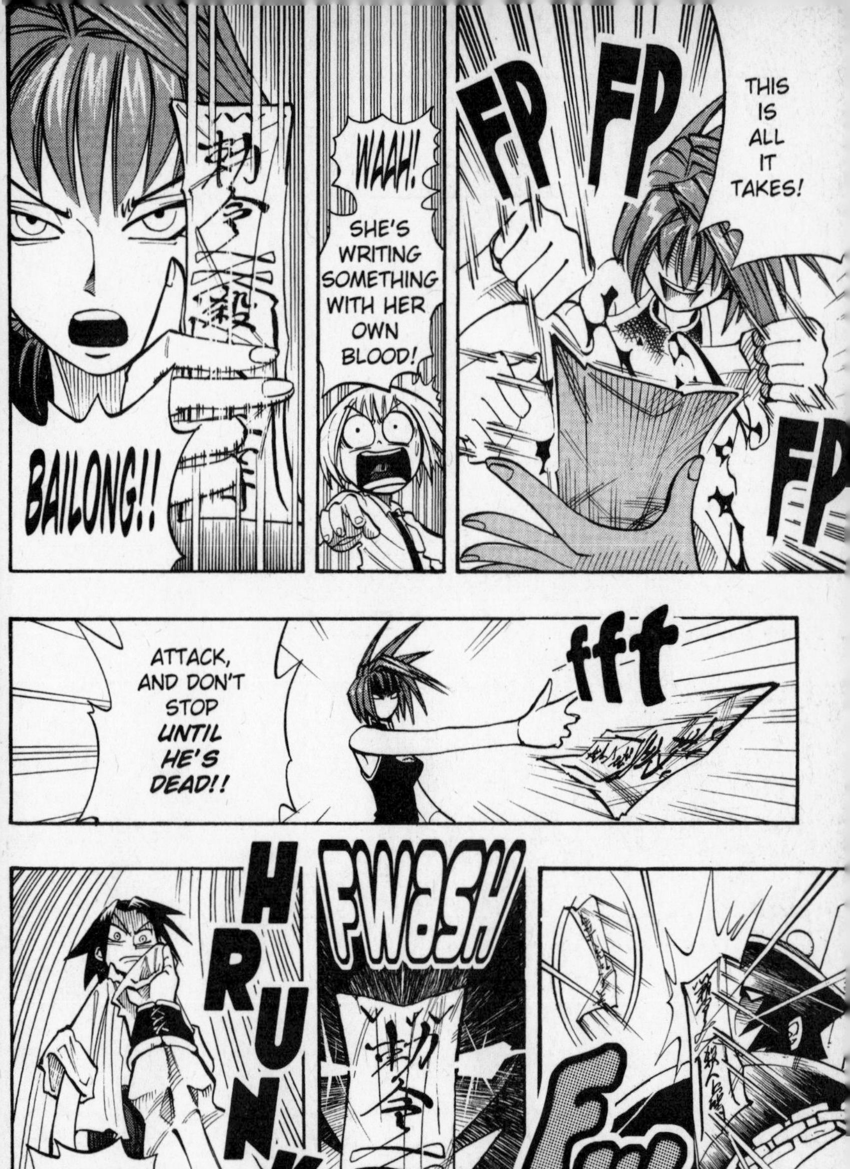
THIS IS ALL IT TAKES!
FP FP
FP
WAAH!
SHE'S WRITING SOMETHING WITH HER OWN BLOOD!
BAILONG!!
fff
ATTACK, AND DON'T STOP *UNTIL HE'S DEAD!!*
FWAP
FWASH
HRUNK
!!

(SLIP READS:
"IMPERIAL DECREE: ***EXECUTION***")

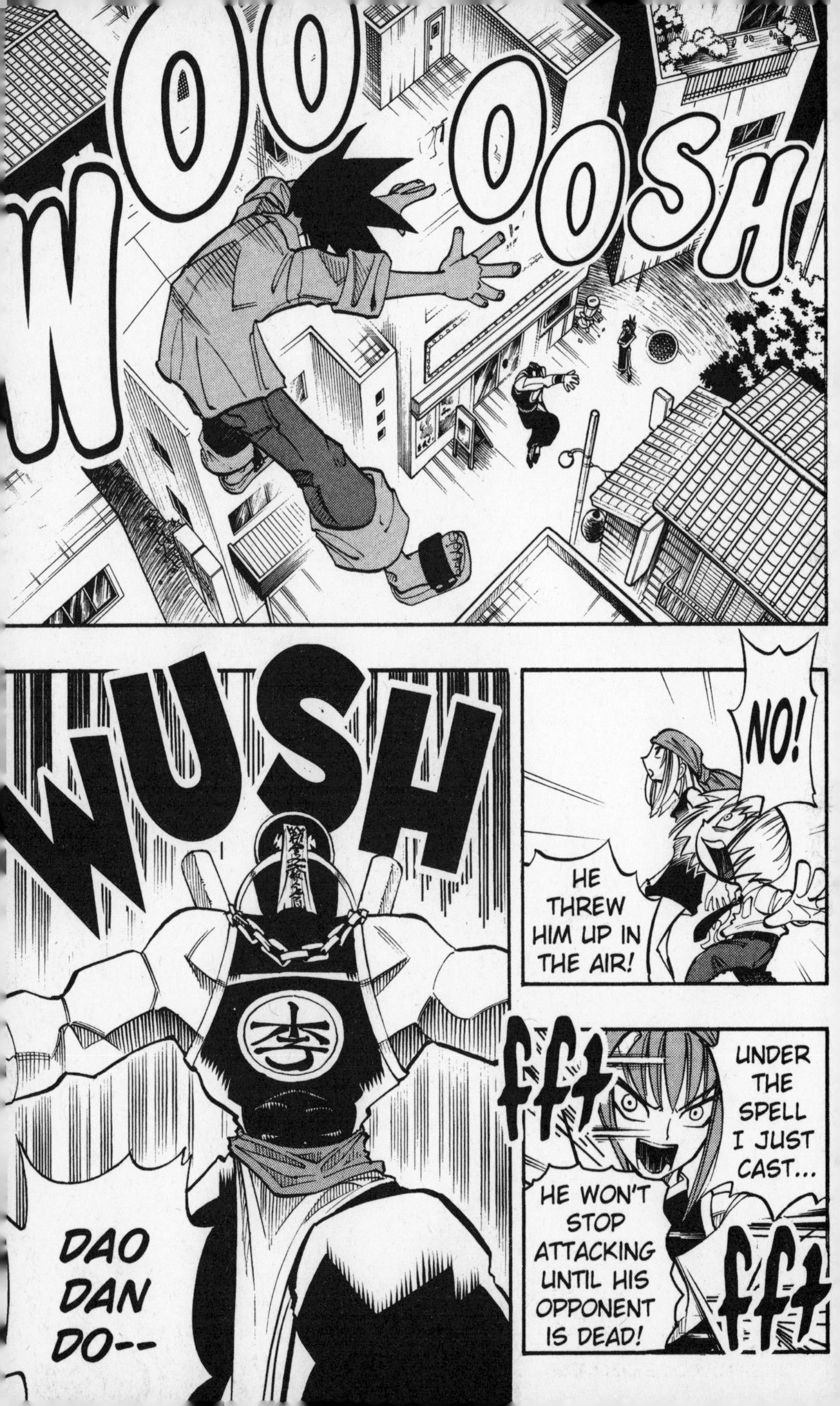
WOOOOOSH
NO!
HE THREW HIM UP IN THE AIR!
fft
UNDER THE SPELL I JUST CAST...
HE WON'T STOP ATTACKING UNTIL HIS OPPONENT IS DEAD!
fft
WUSH
DAO DAN DO--

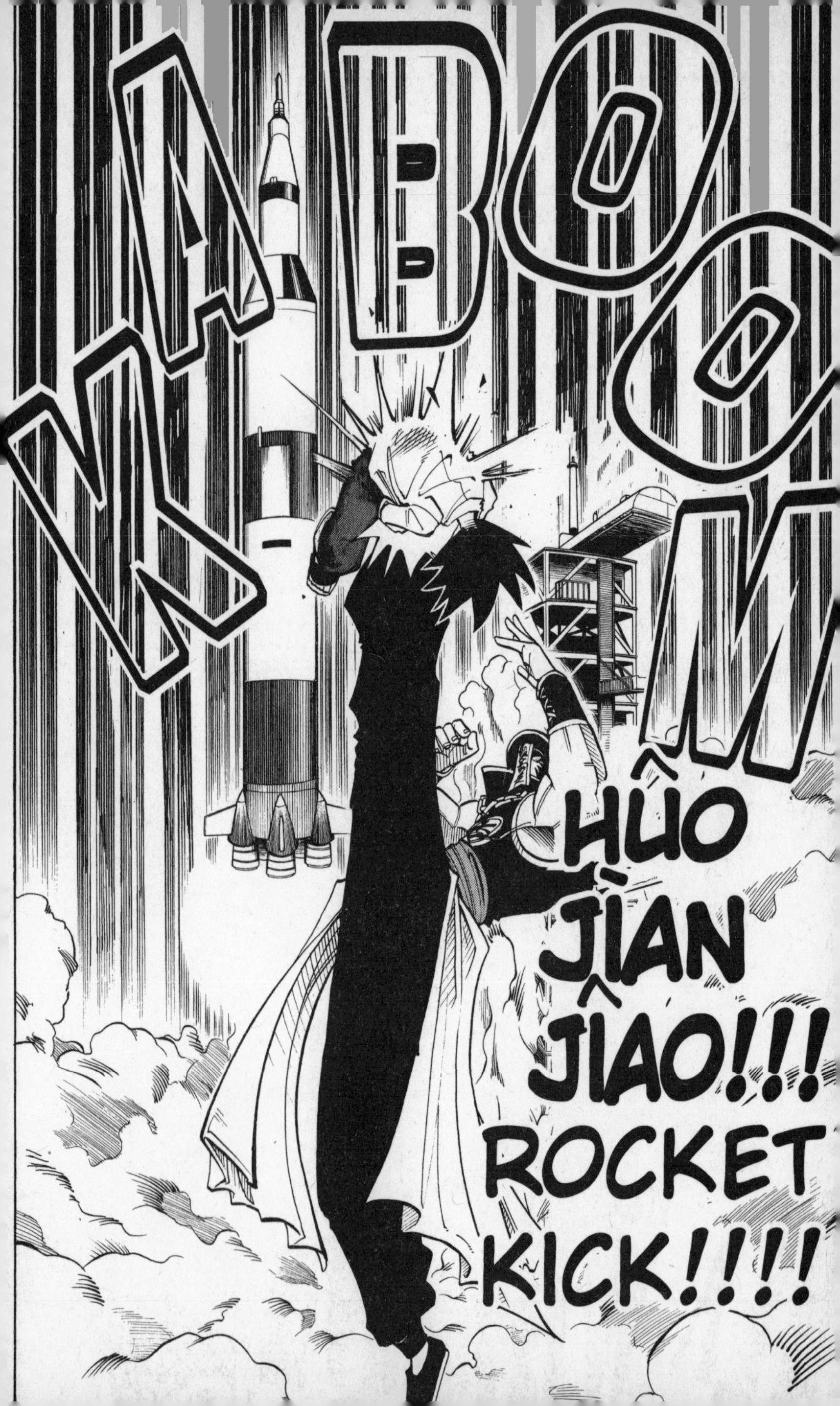
KABOOM
HÛO JÌAN JÎAO!!! ROCKET KICK!!!!

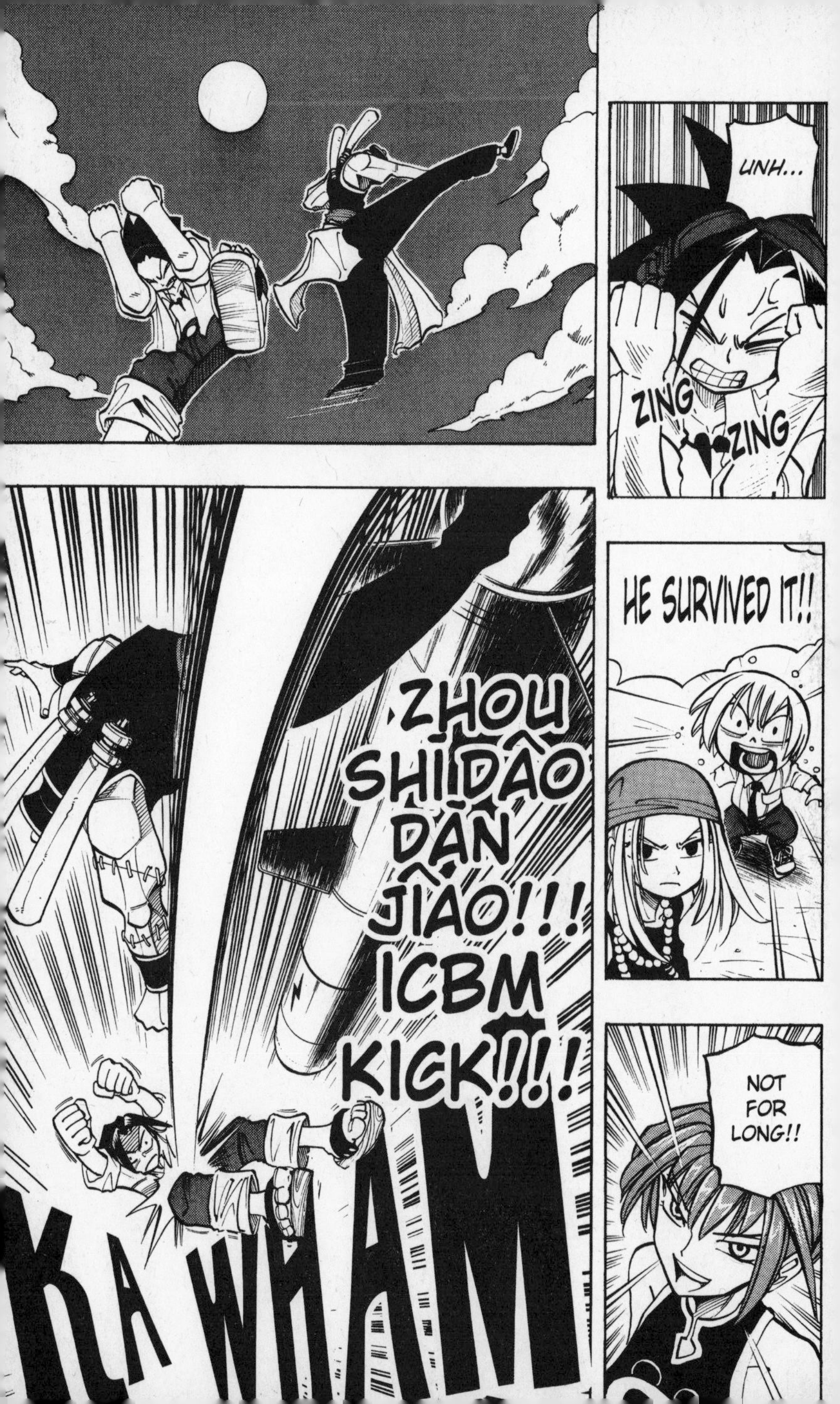
UNH...
ZING
ZING
HE SURVIVED IT!!
NOT FOR LONG!!
ZHOU SHĪDÂO DĀN JÎAO!!! ICBM KICK!!!
KA WHAM

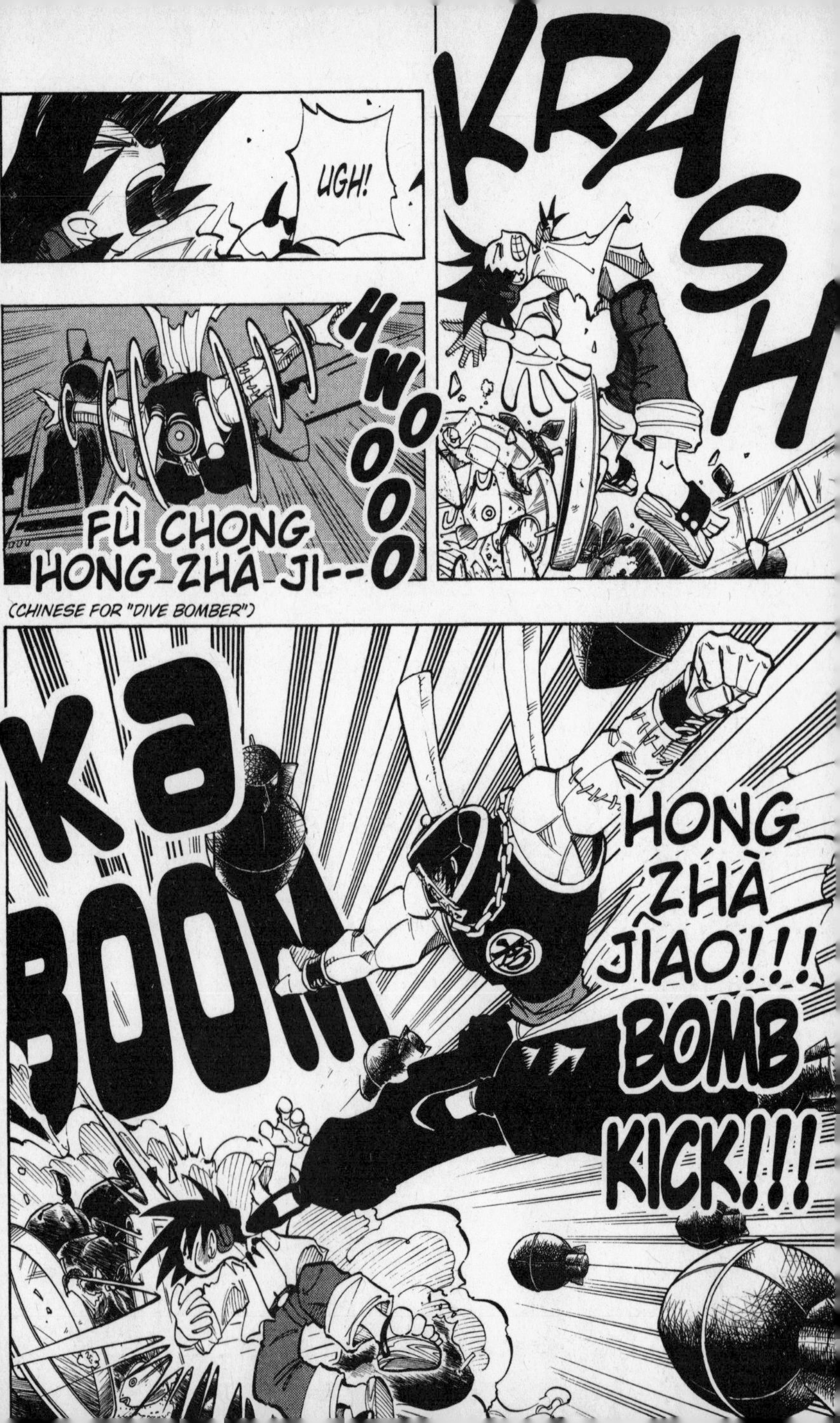
KRASH
UGH!
HWOOOOOO
FÛ CHONG HONG ZHÁ JI--
(CHINESE FOR "DIVE BOMBER")
HONG ZHÀ JÎAO!!!
BOMB KICK!!!
Ka BOOM

READ THIS WAY

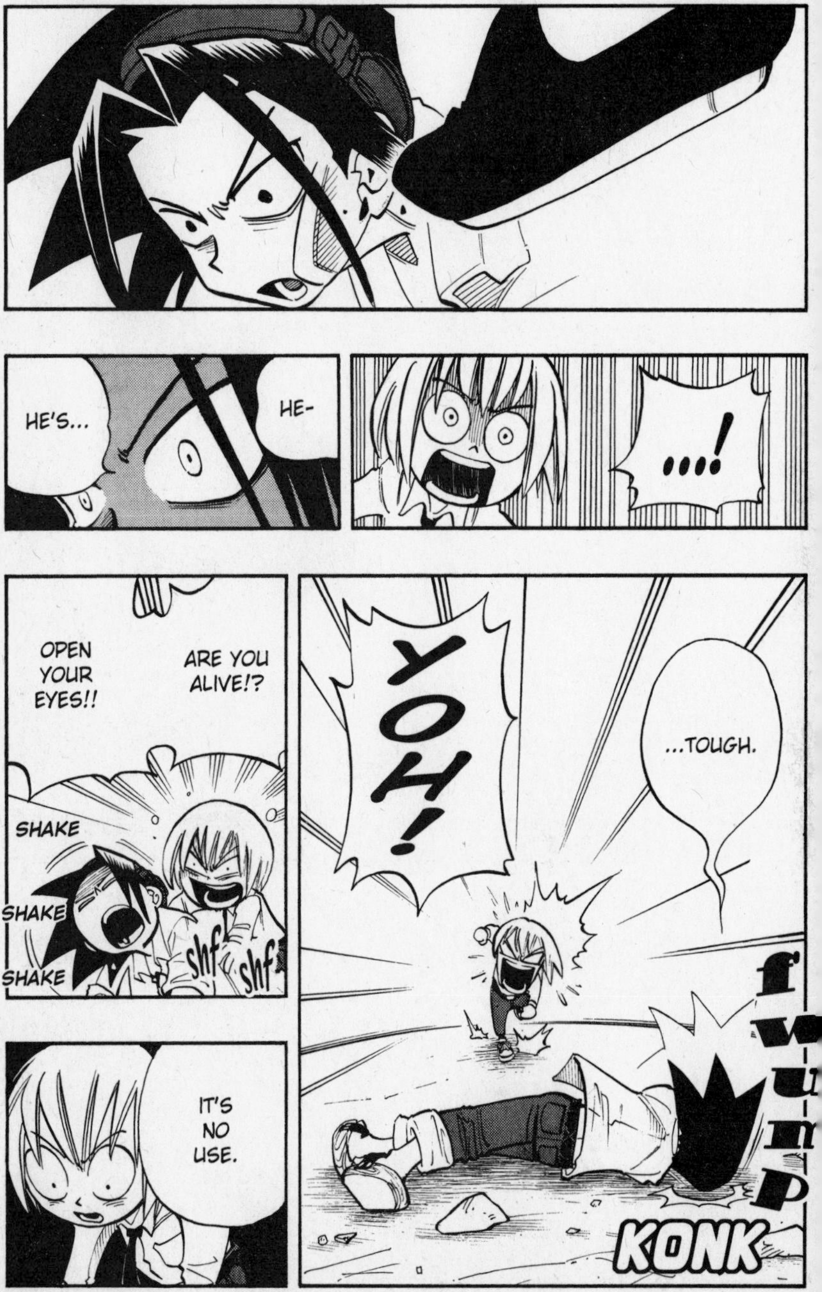
...!
HE-
HE'S...
YOH!
...TOUGH.
fwump
KONK
ARE YOU ALIVE!?
OPEN YOUR EYES!!
SHAKE
SHAKE
SHAKE
shf
shf
IT'S NO USE.

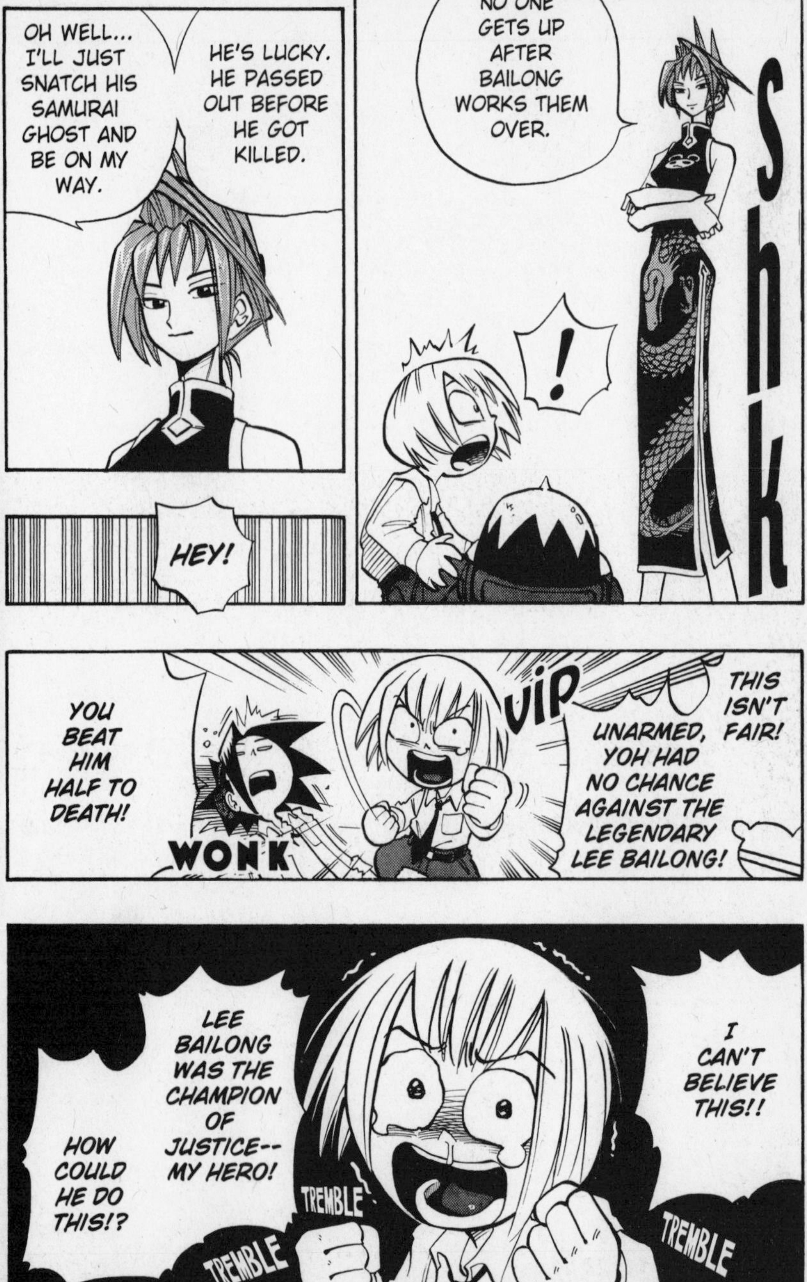

NO ONE GETS UP AFTER BAILONG WORKS THEM OVER.
!
Shk
HE'S LUCKY. HE PASSED OUT BEFORE HE GOT KILLED.
OH WELL... I'LL JUST SNATCH HIS SAMURAI GHOST AND BE ON MY WAY.
HEY!
THIS ISN'T FAIR!
UIP
UNARMED, YOH HAD NO CHANCE AGAINST THE LEGENDARY LEE BAILONG!
YOU BEAT HIM HALF TO DEATH!
WONK
I CAN'T BELIEVE THIS!!
LEE BAILONG WAS THE CHAMPION OF JUSTICE-- MY HERO!
HOW COULD HE DO THIS!?
TREMBLE
TREMBLE
TREMBLE

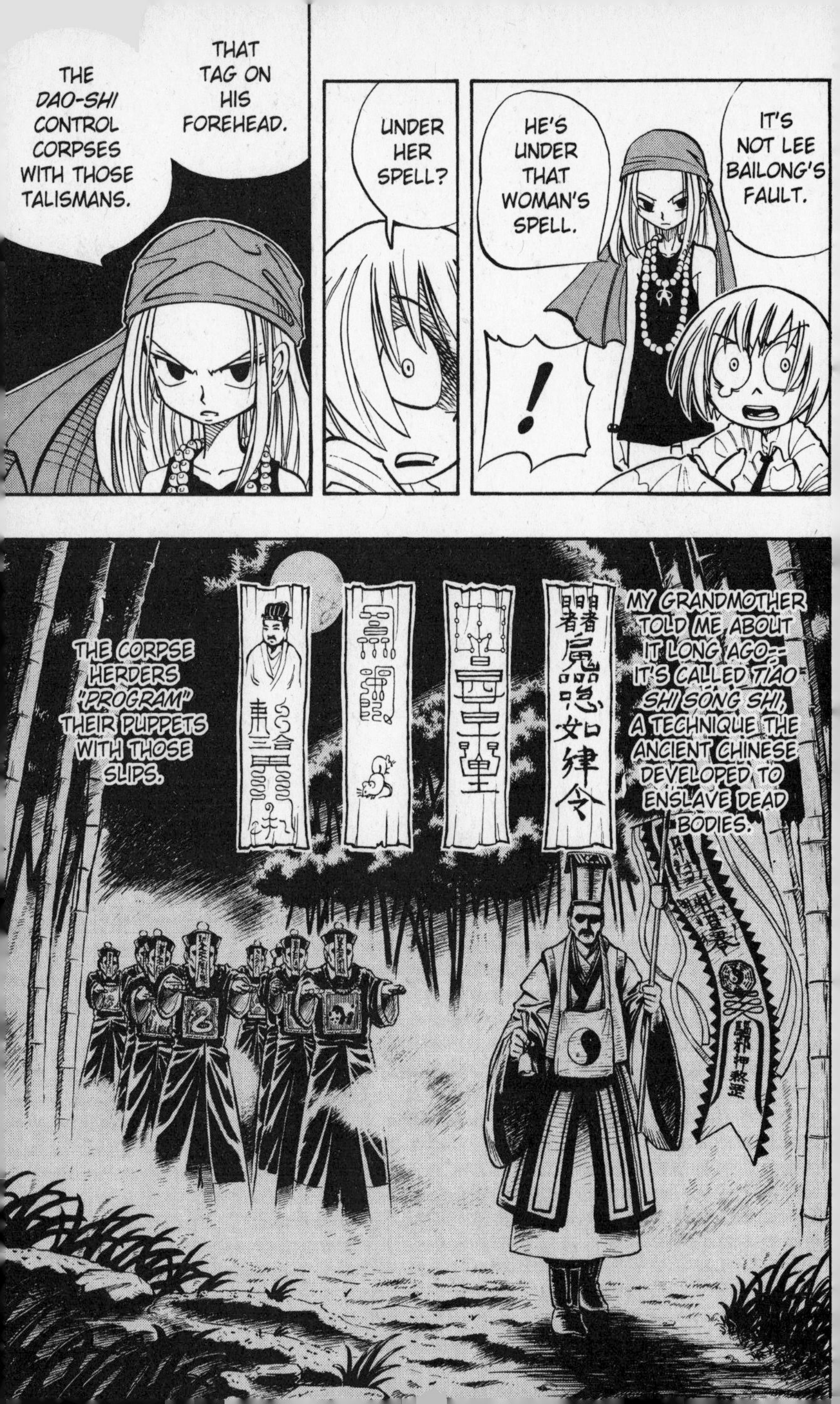

IT'S NOT LEE BAILONG'S FAULT.
HE'S UNDER THAT WOMAN'S SPELL.
!
UNDER HER SPELL?
THAT TAG ON HIS FOREHEAD.
THE *DAO-SHI* CONTROL CORPSES WITH THOSE TALISMANS.
MY GRANDMOTHER TOLD ME ABOUT IT LONG AGO-- IT'S CALLED *TIAO SHI SONG SHI*, A TECHNIQUE THE ANCIENT CHINESE DEVELOPED TO ENSLAVE DEAD BODIES.
THE CORPSE HERDERS *"PROGRAM"* THEIR PUPPETS WITH THOSE SLIPS.

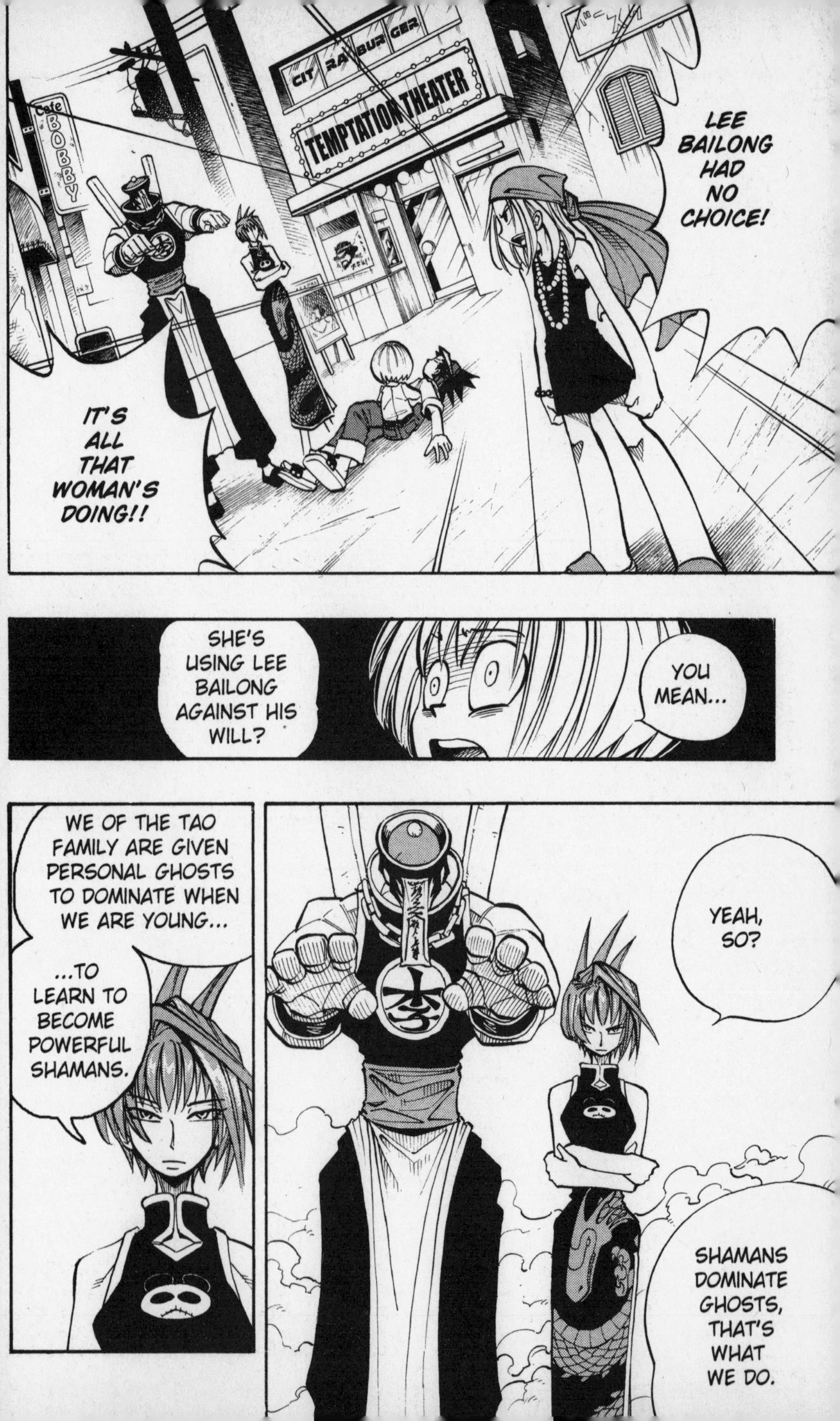

CIT RA BUR GER
TEMPTATION THEATER
Cafe BOBBY
LEE BAILONG HAD NO CHOICE!
IT'S ALL THAT WOMAN'S DOING!!
YOU MEAN...
SHE'S USING LEE BAILONG AGAINST HIS WILL?
YEAH, SO?
SHAMANS DOMINATE GHOSTS, THAT'S WHAT WE DO.
WE OF THE TAO FAMILY ARE GIVEN PERSONAL GHOSTS TO DOMINATE WHEN WE ARE YOUNG...
...TO LEARN TO BECOME POWERFUL SHAMANS.

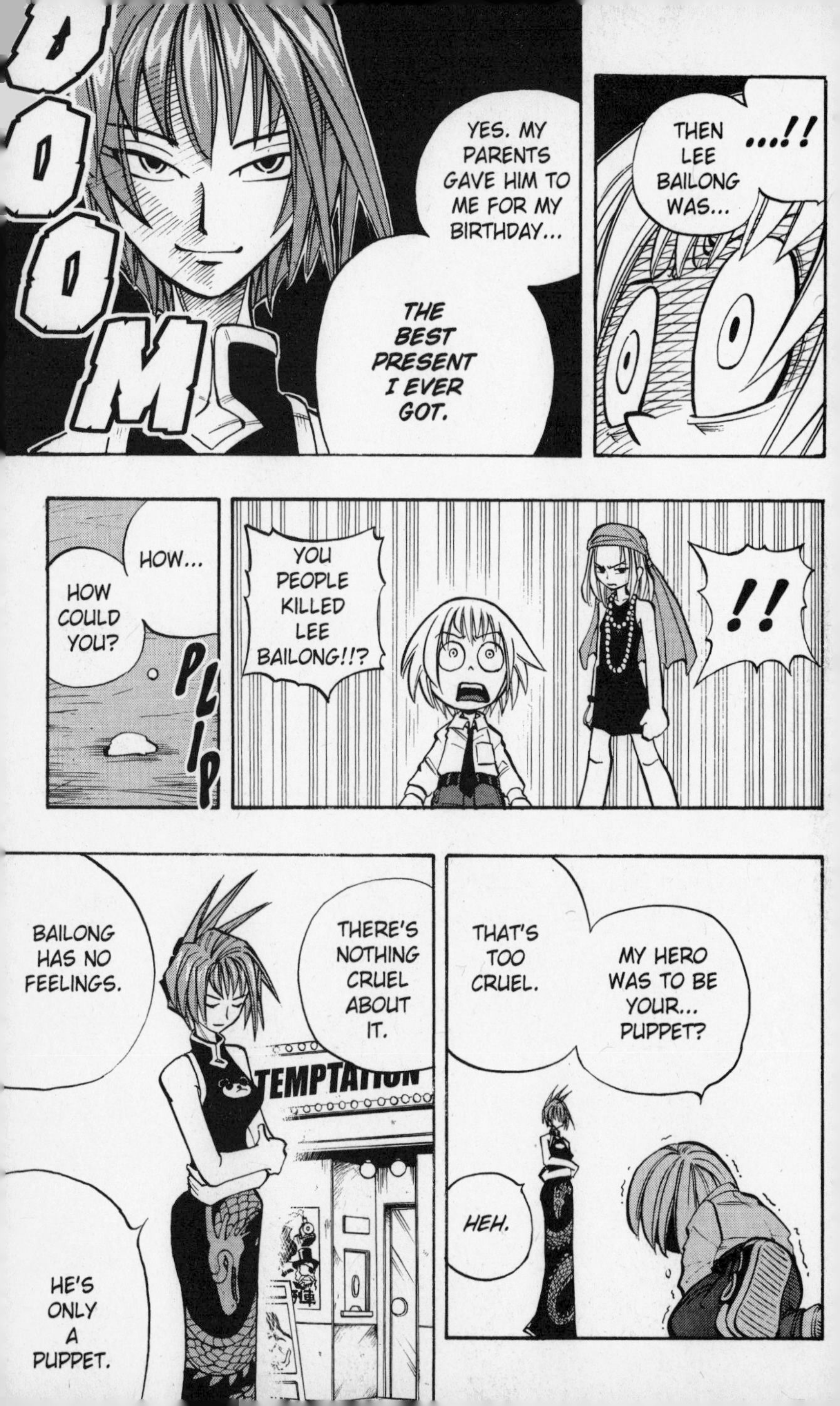
THEN LEE BAILONG WAS...
...!!
YES. MY PARENTS GAVE HIM TO ME FOR MY BIRTHDAY...
DOOOM
THE BEST PRESENT I EVER GOT.
!!
YOU PEOPLE KILLED LEE BAILONG!!?
HOW...
HOW COULD YOU?
PLIP
MY HERO WAS TO BE YOUR... PUPPET?
THAT'S TOO CRUEL.
HEH.
THERE'S NOTHING CRUEL ABOUT IT.
BAILONG HAS NO FEELINGS.
TEMPTATION
HE'S ONLY A PUPPET.

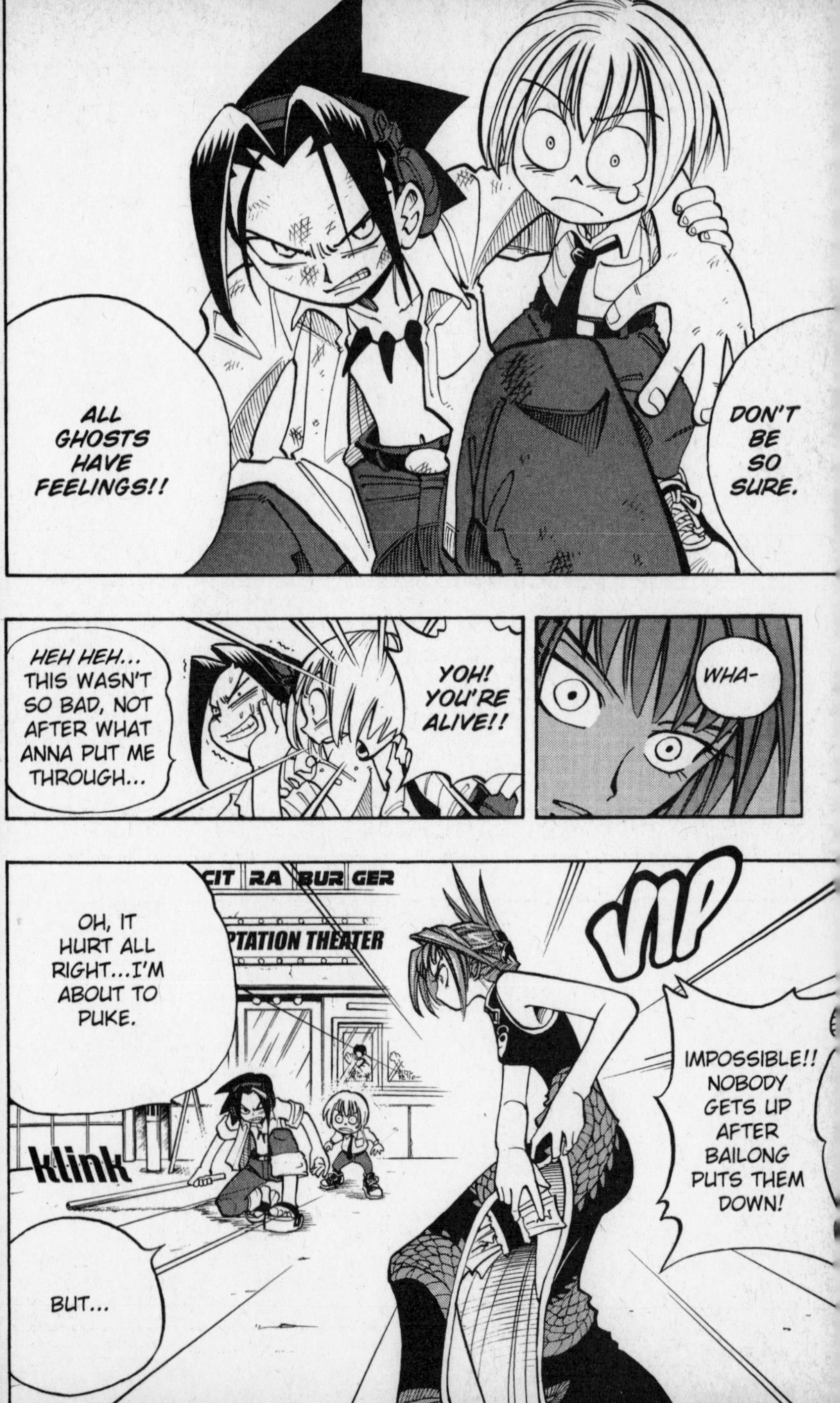
ALL GHOSTS HAVE FEELINGS!!
DON'T BE SO SURE.
WHA-
YOH! YOU'RE ALIVE!!
HEH HEH... THIS WASN'T SO BAD, NOT AFTER WHAT ANNA PUT ME THROUGH...
VIP
IMPOSSIBLE!! NOBODY GETS UP AFTER BAILONG PUTS THEM DOWN!
CIT RA BUR GER
PTATION THEATER
klink
OH, IT HURT ALL RIGHT...I'M ABOUT TO PUKE.
BUT...

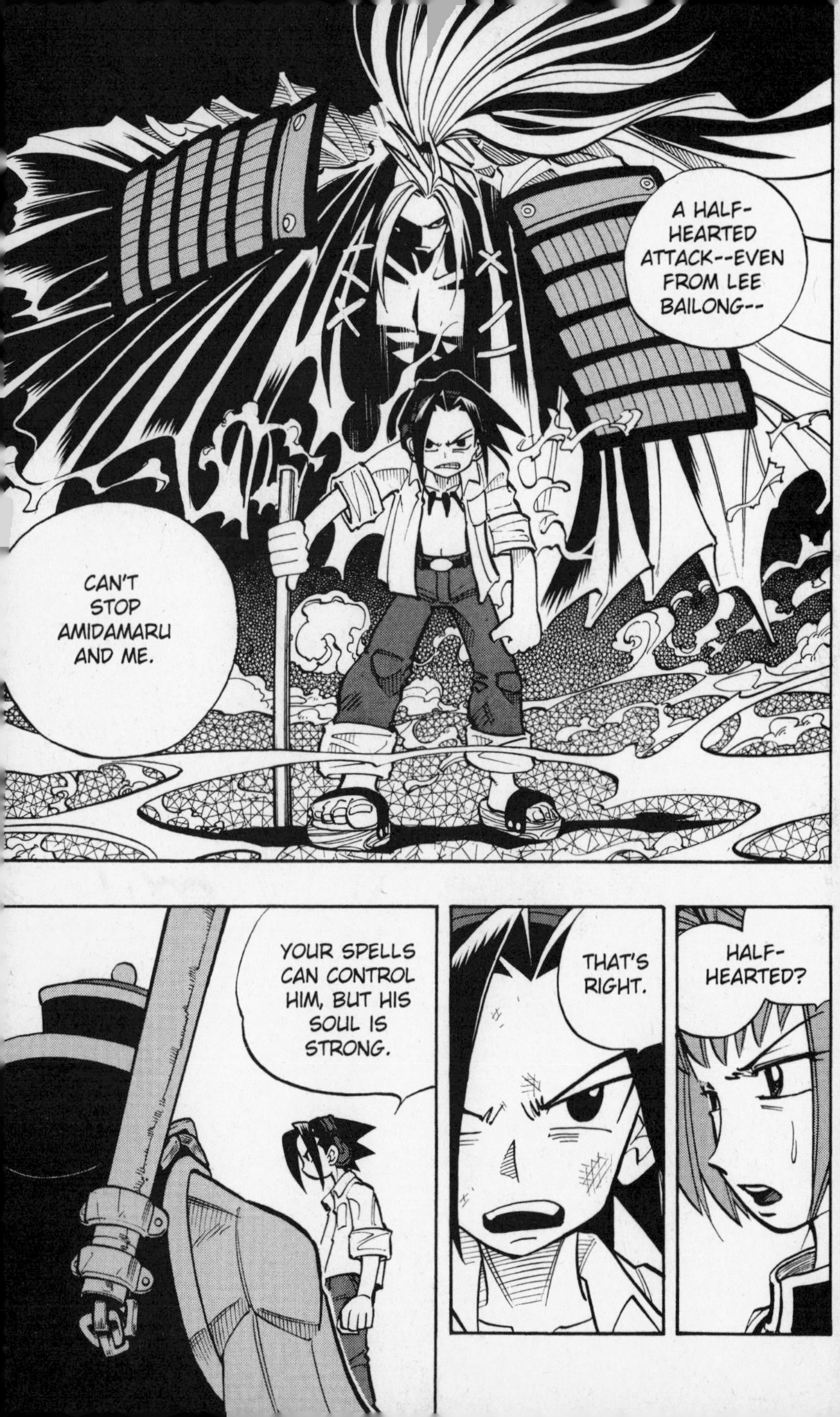
A HALF-HEARTED ATTACK--EVEN FROM LEE BAILONG--
CAN'T STOP AMIDAMARU AND ME.
HALF-HEARTED?
THAT'S RIGHT.
YOUR SPELLS CAN CONTROL HIM, BUT HIS SOUL IS STRONG.

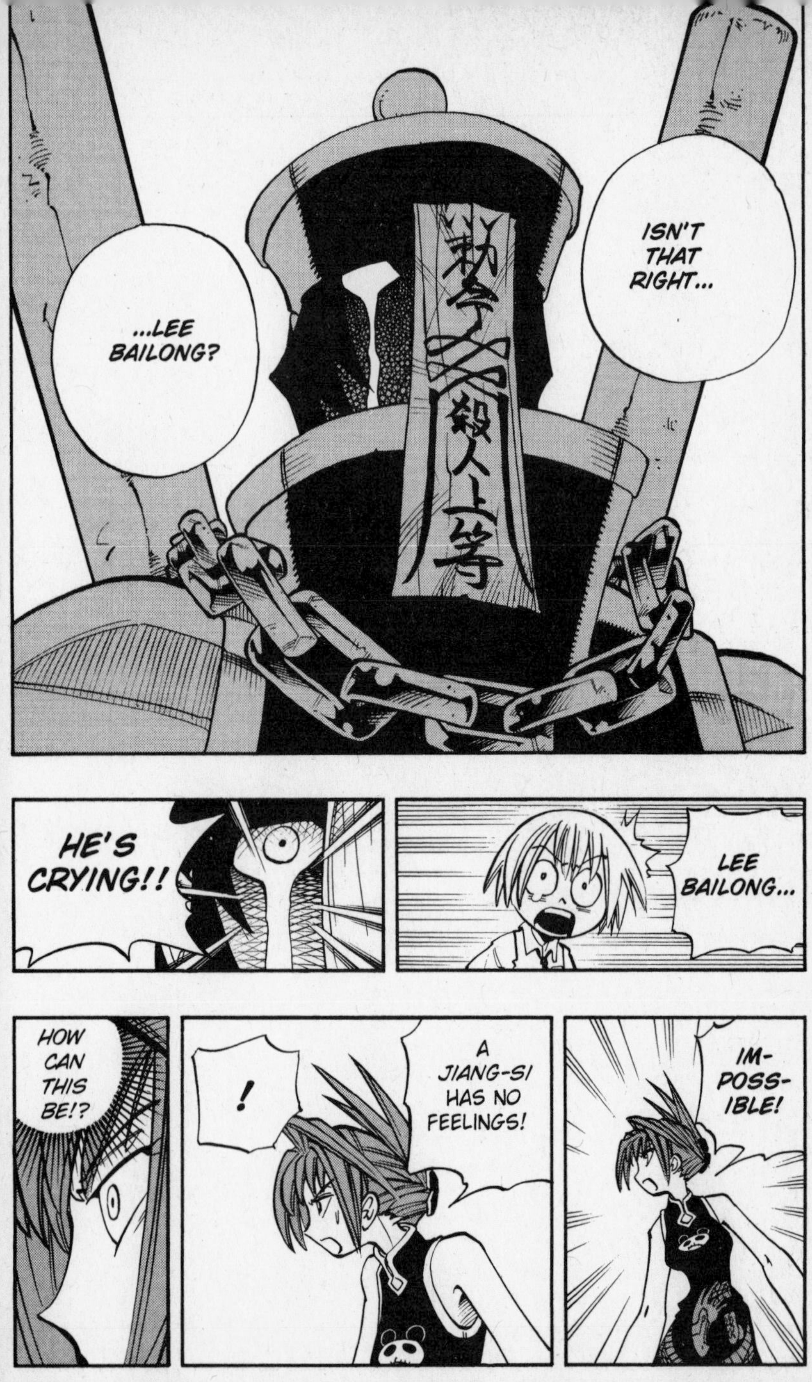
ISN'T THAT RIGHT...
...LEE BAILONG?
殺人上等
LEE BAILONG...
HE'S CRYING!!
IM-POSS-IBLE!
A JIANG-SI HAS NO FEELINGS!
!
HOW CAN THIS BE!?

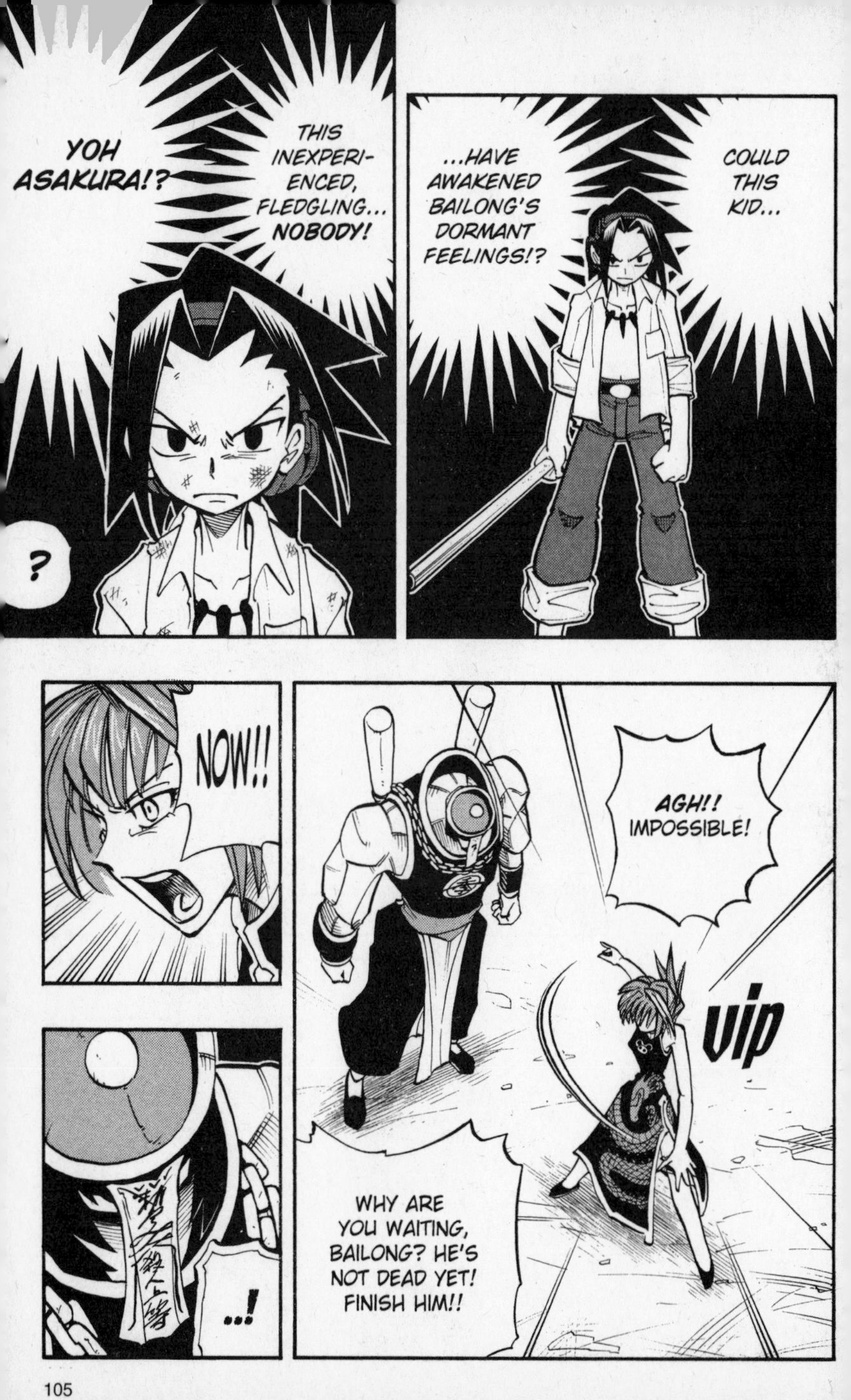
COULD THIS KID...
...HAVE AWAKENED BAILONG'S DORMANT FEELINGS!?
THIS INEXPERI-ENCED, FLEDGLING... NOBODY!
YOH ASAKURA!?
?
AGH!! IMPOSSIBLE!
vip
WHY ARE YOU WAITING, BAILONG? HE'S NOT DEAD YET! FINISH HIM!!
NOW!!
..!

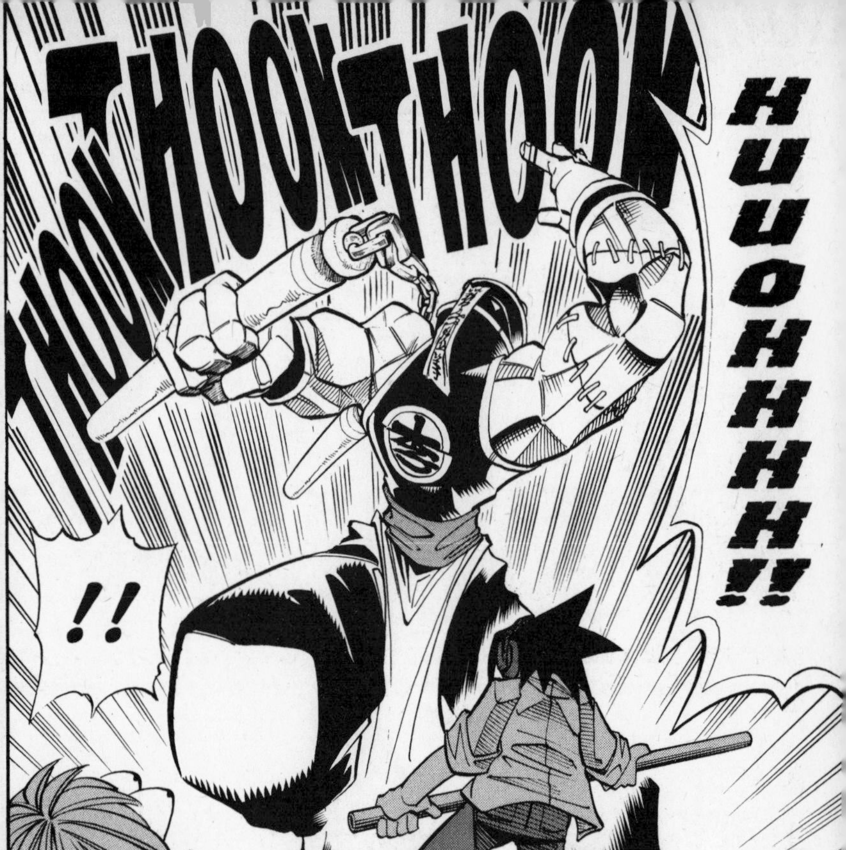
THOOK THOOK THOOK
HUUOHHHHH!!
!!

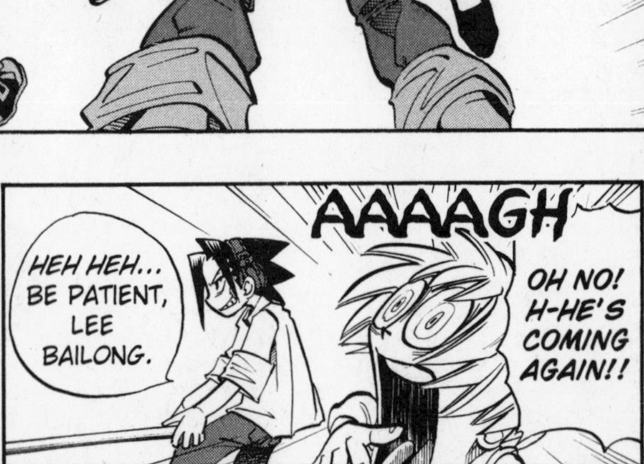
AAAAGH
OH NO! H-HE'S COMING AGAIN!!
HEH HEH... BE PATIENT, LEE BAILONG.

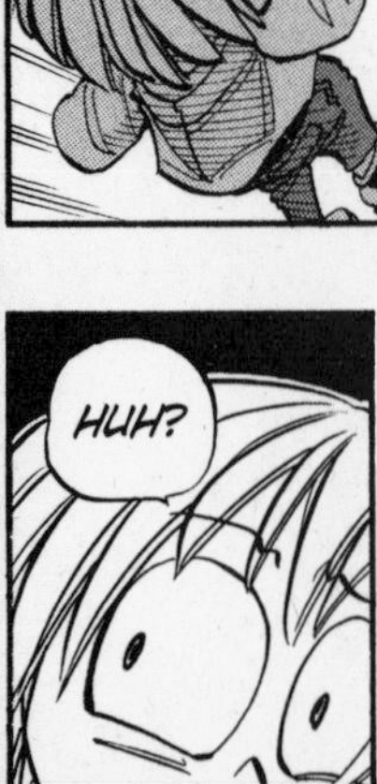
HUH?

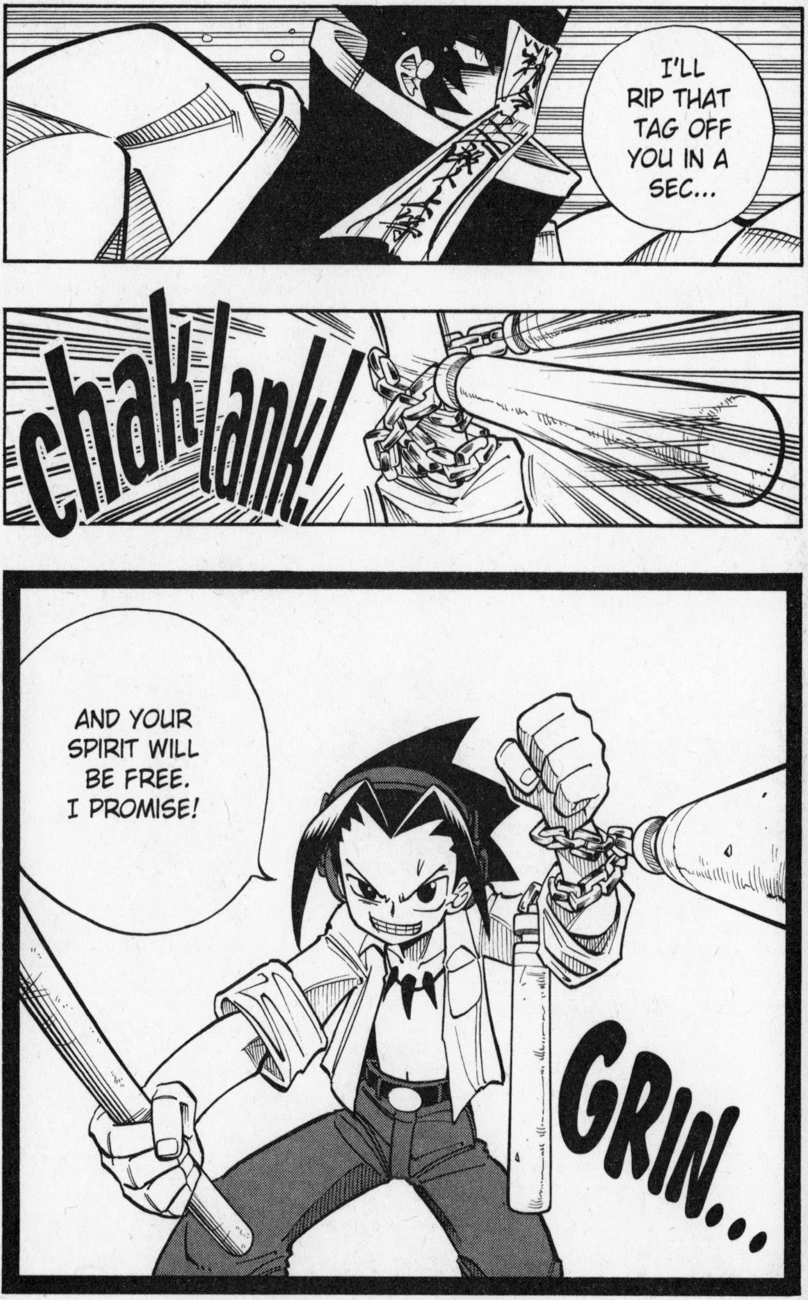
READ THIS WAY
I'LL RIP THAT TAG OFF YOU IN A SEC...
chaklank!
AND YOUR SPIRIT WILL BE FREE. I PROMISE!
GRIN...

SHAMAN KING CHARACTER FILE No.7

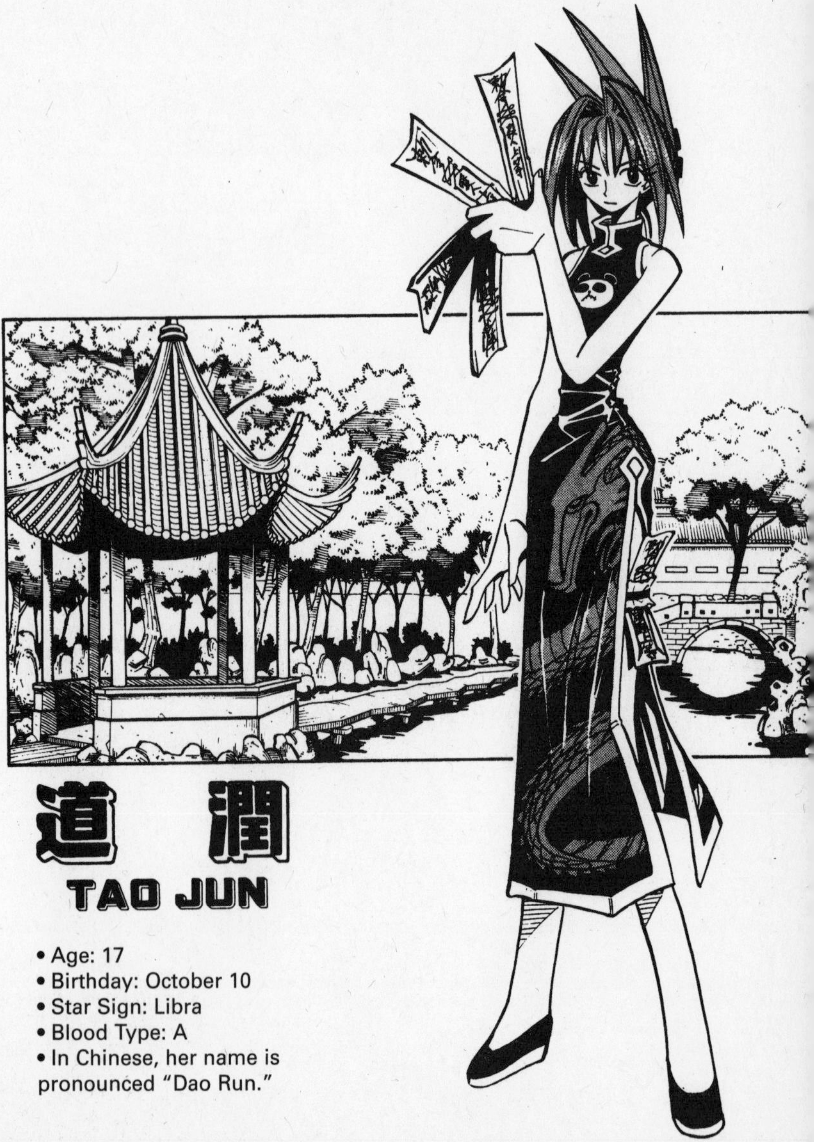

道　潤

TAO JUN

- Age: 17
- Birthday: October 10
- Star Sign: Libra
- Blood Type: A
- In Chinese, her name is pronounced "Dao Run."

Reincarnation 14: Run, Manta, Run

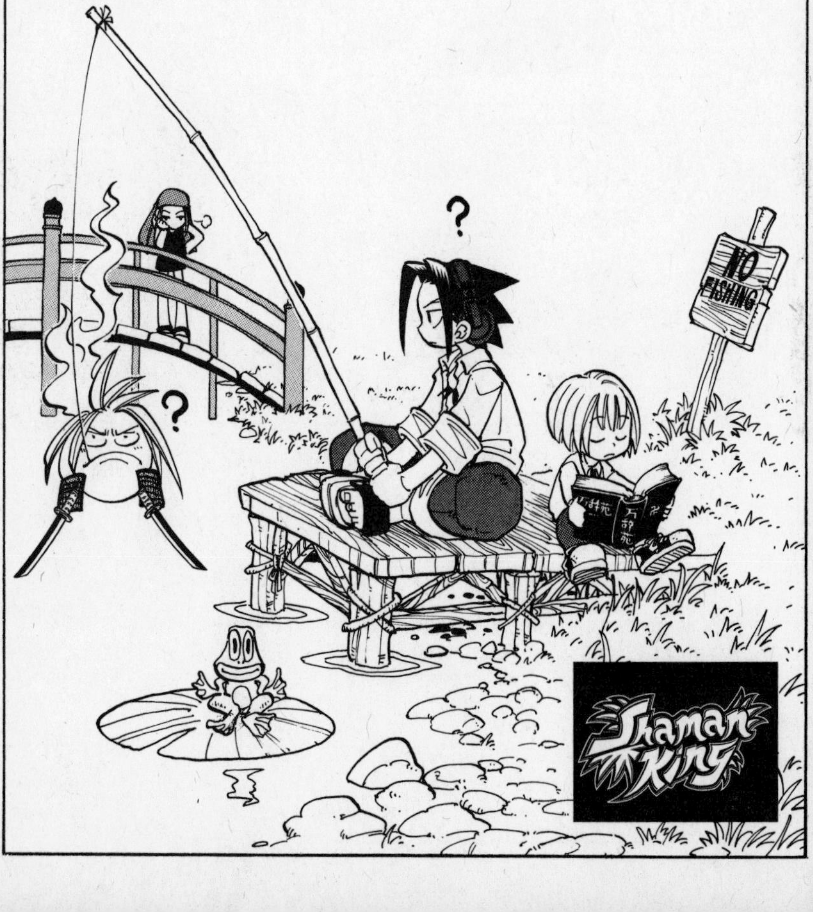
?
?
NO FISHING
Shaman King

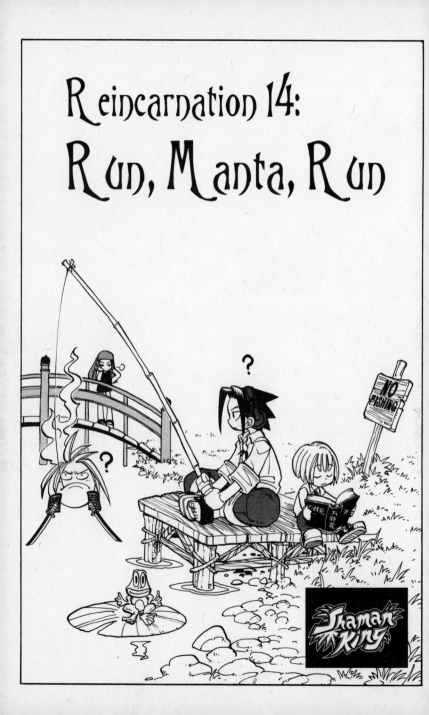

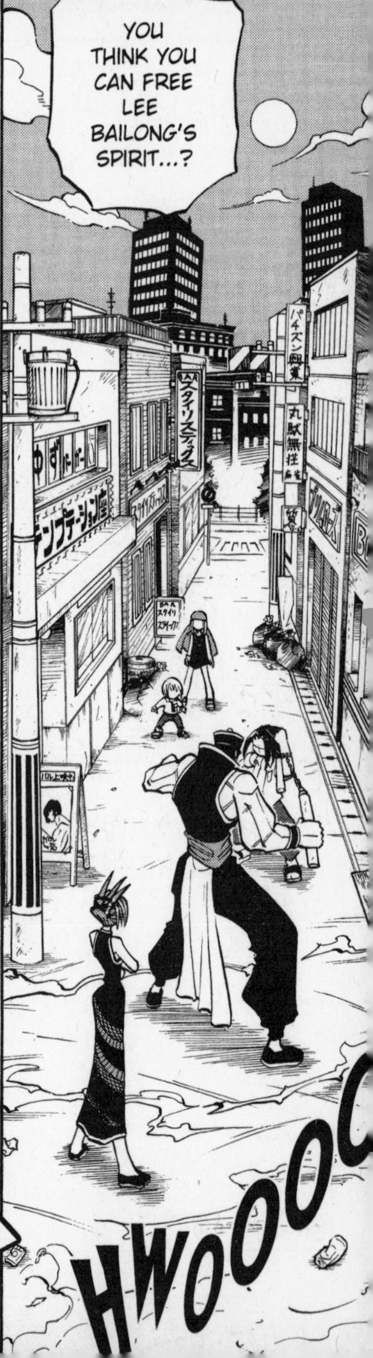
YOU THINK YOU CAN FREE LEE BAILONG'S SPIRIT...?
HWOOOO

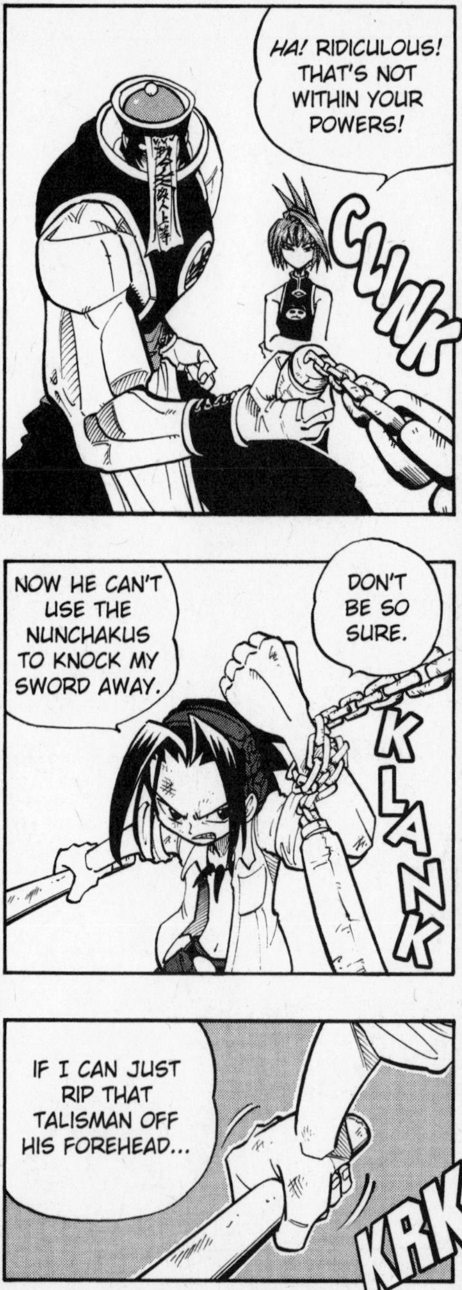
HA! RIDICULOUS! THAT'S NOT WITHIN YOUR POWERS!
CLINK
DON'T BE SO SURE.
NOW HE CAN'T USE THE NUNCHAKUS TO KNOCK MY SWORD AWAY.
KLANK
IF I CAN JUST RIP THAT TALISMAN OFF HIS FOREHEAD...
KRK

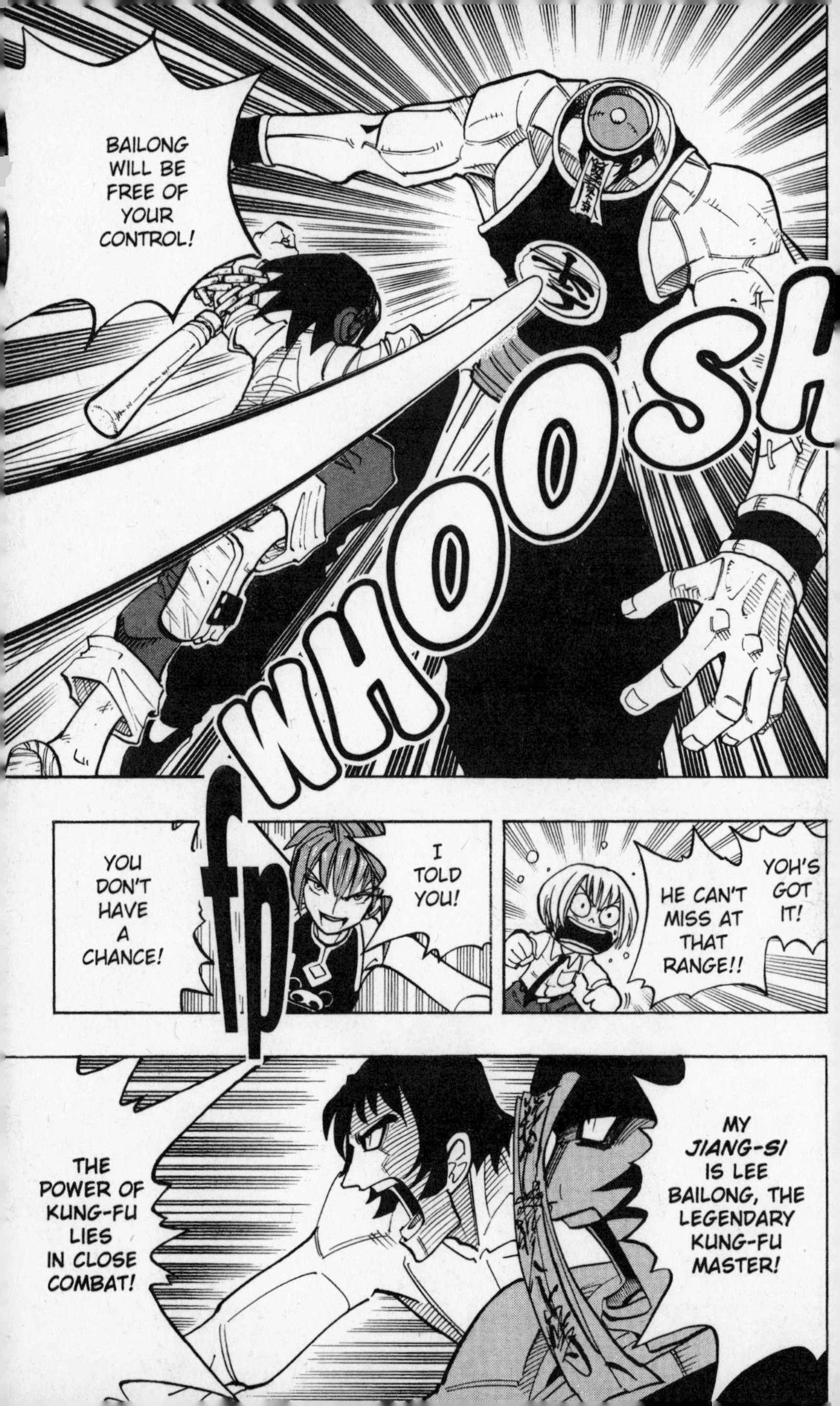
BAILONG WILL BE FREE OF YOUR CONTROL!
WHOOOSH
YOH'S GOT IT!
HE CAN'T MISS AT THAT RANGE!!
I TOLD YOU!
YOU DON'T HAVE A CHANCE!
fp
MY JIANG-SI IS LEE BAILONG, THE LEGENDARY KUNG-FU MASTER!
THE POWER OF KUNG-FU LIES IN CLOSE COMBAT!

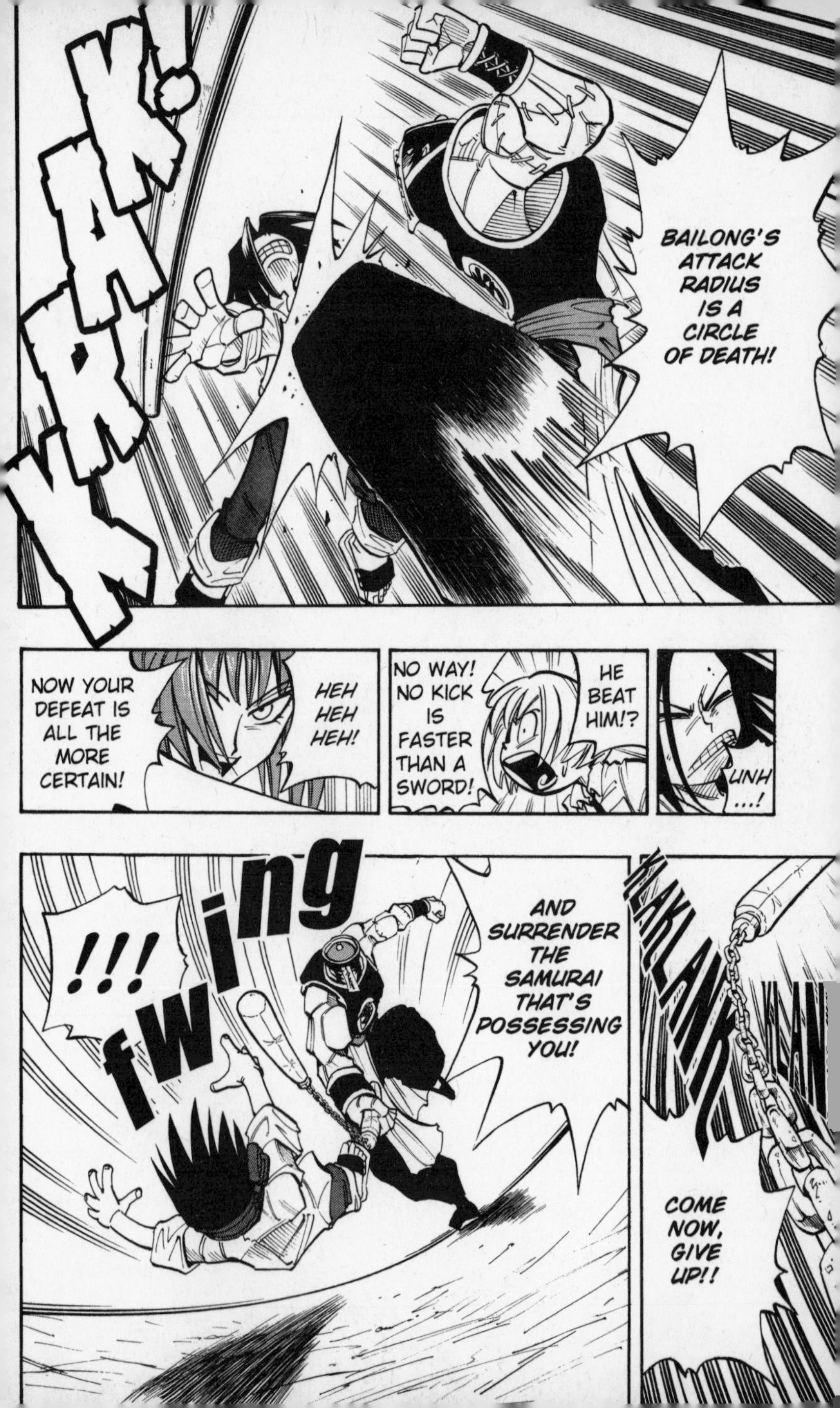
BAILONG'S ATTACK RADIUS IS A CIRCLE OF DEATH!
KAK!
UNH ...!
HE BEAT HIM!?
NO WAY! NO KICK IS FASTER THAN A SWORD!
HEH HEH HEH!
NOW YOUR DEFEAT IS ALL THE MORE CERTAIN!
KLAKLANK
COME NOW, GIVE UP!!
AND SURRENDER THE SAMURAI THAT'S POSSESSING YOU!
!!!
fwing

READ THIS WAY

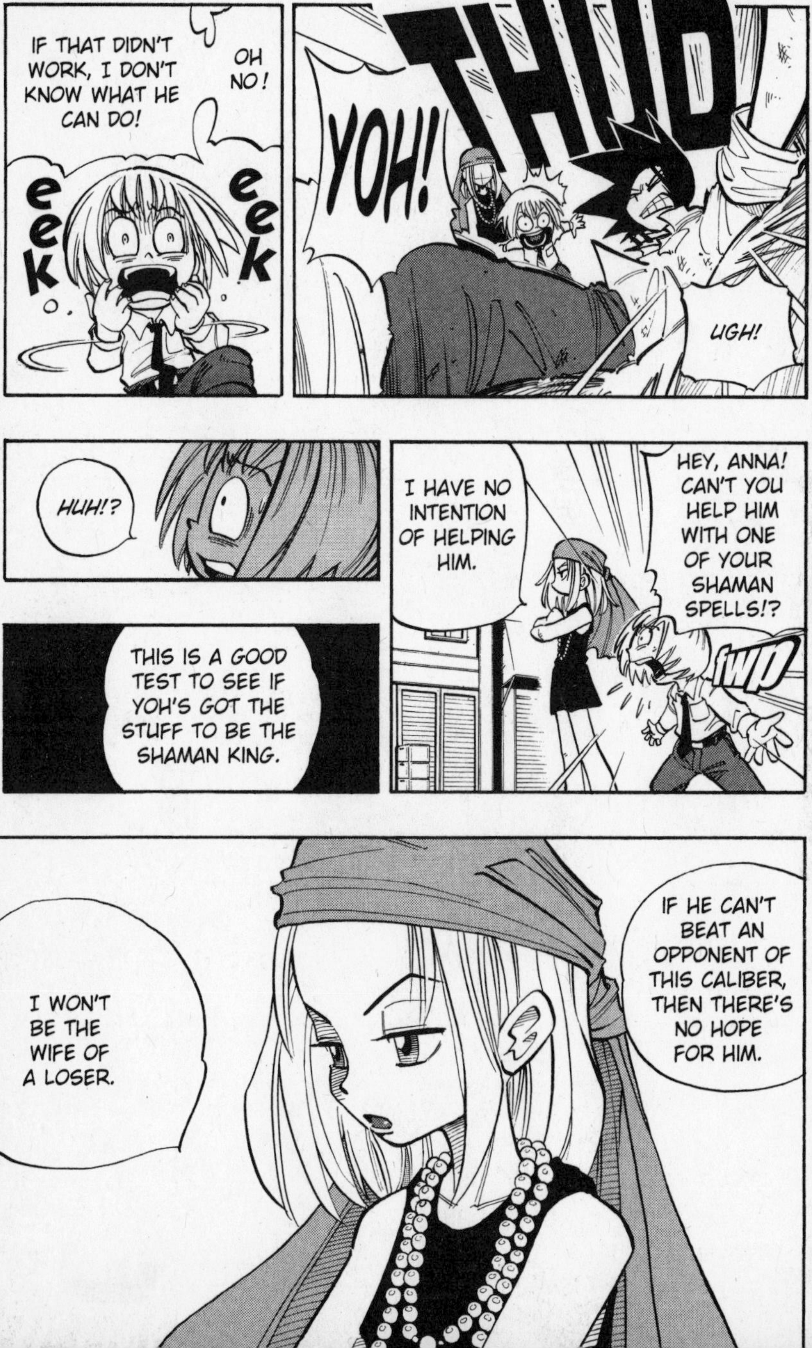

THUD
YOH!
UGH!
OH NO!
IF THAT DIDN'T WORK, I DON'T KNOW WHAT HE CAN DO!
eeek
eeek
HEY, ANNA! CAN'T YOU HELP HIM WITH ONE OF YOUR SHAMAN SPELLS!?
I HAVE NO INTENTION OF HELPING HIM.
fwp
HUH!?
THIS IS A GOOD TEST TO SEE IF YOH'S GOT THE STUFF TO BE THE SHAMAN KING.
IF HE CAN'T BEAT AN OPPONENT OF THIS CALIBER, THEN THERE'S NO HOPE FOR HIM.
I WON'T BE THE WIFE OF A LOSER.

READ THIS WAY

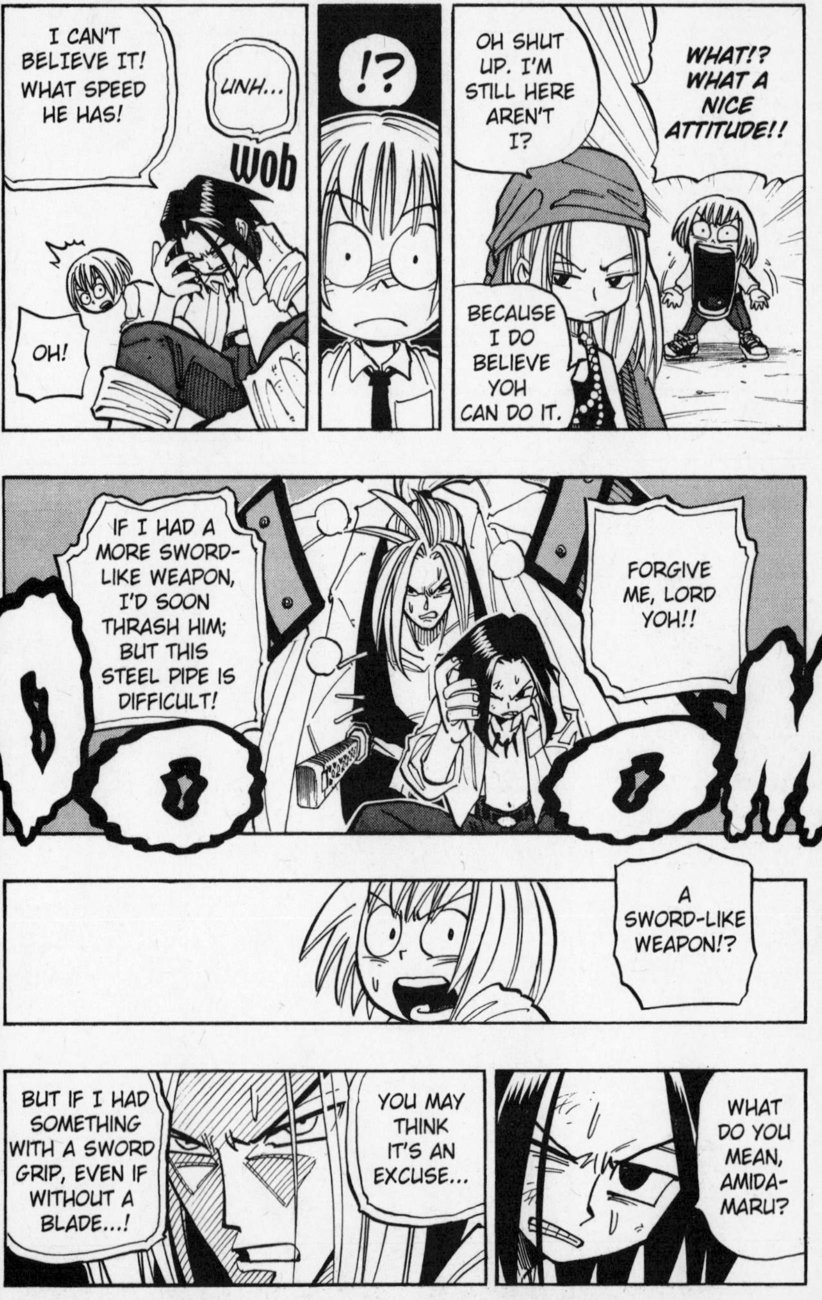
WHAT!? WHAT A NICE ATTITUDE!!
OH SHUT UP. I'M STILL HERE AREN'T I?
BECAUSE I DO BELIEVE YOH CAN DO IT.
!?
I CAN'T BELIEVE IT! WHAT SPEED HE HAS!
UNH...
Wob
OH!
FORGIVE ME, LORD YOH!!
IF I HAD A MORE SWORD-LIKE WEAPON, I'D SOON THRASH HIM; BUT THIS STEEL PIPE IS DIFFICULT!
DOOM
A SWORD-LIKE WEAPON!?
WHAT DO YOU MEAN, AMIDA-MARU?
YOU MAY THINK IT'S AN EXCUSE...
BUT IF I HAD SOMETHING WITH A SWORD GRIP, EVEN IF WITHOUT A BLADE...!

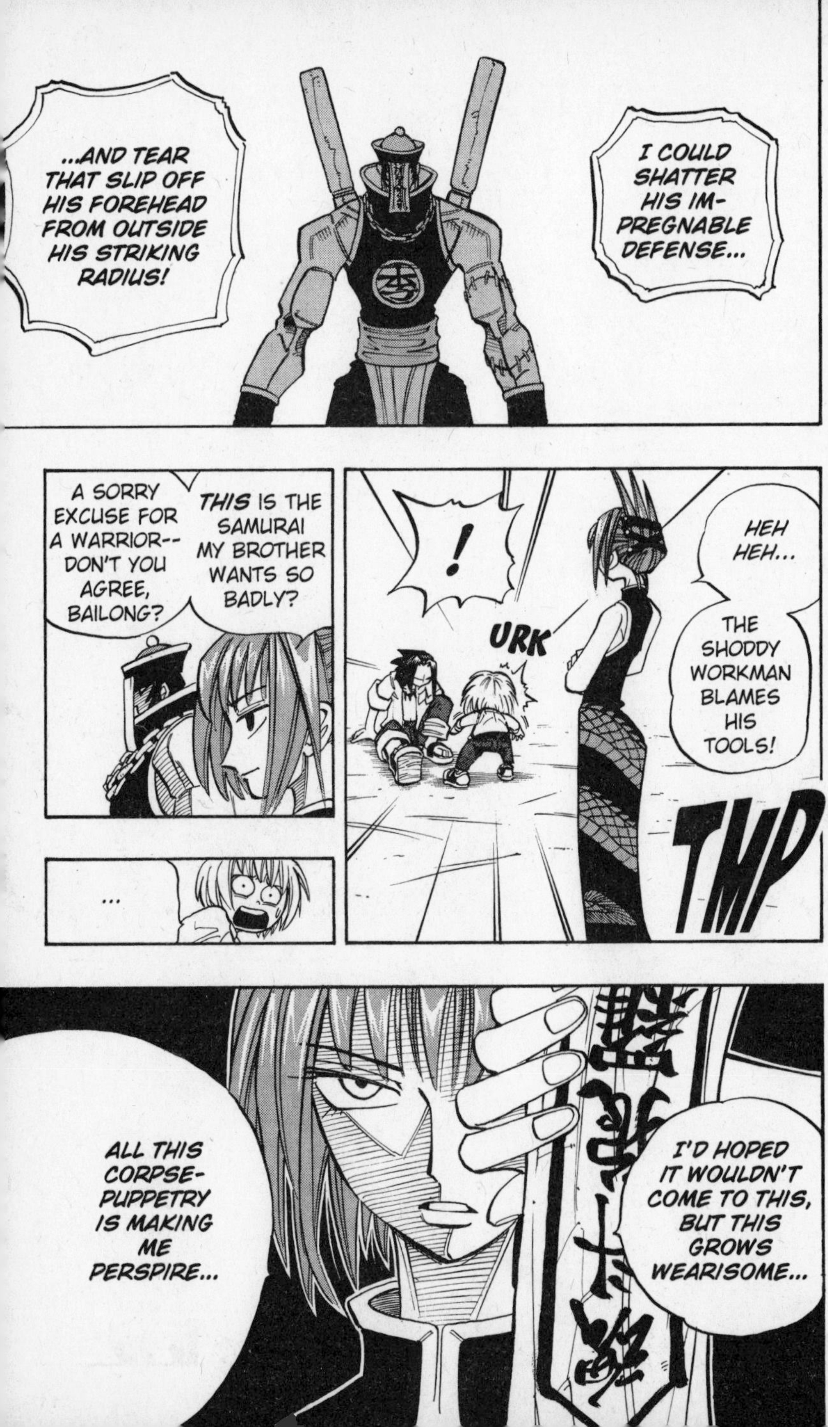
I COULD SHATTER HIS IM-PREGNABLE DEFENSE...
...AND TEAR THAT SLIP OFF HIS FOREHEAD FROM OUTSIDE HIS STRIKING RADIUS!
HEH HEH...
!
THE SHODDY WORKMAN BLAMES HIS TOOLS!
URK
TMP
THIS IS THE SAMURAI MY BROTHER WANTS SO BADLY?
A SORRY EXCUSE FOR A WARRIOR--DON'T YOU AGREE, BAILONG?
...
I'D HOPED IT WOULDN'T COME TO THIS, BUT THIS GROWS WEARISOME...
ALL THIS CORPSE-PUPPETRY IS MAKING ME PERSPIRE...

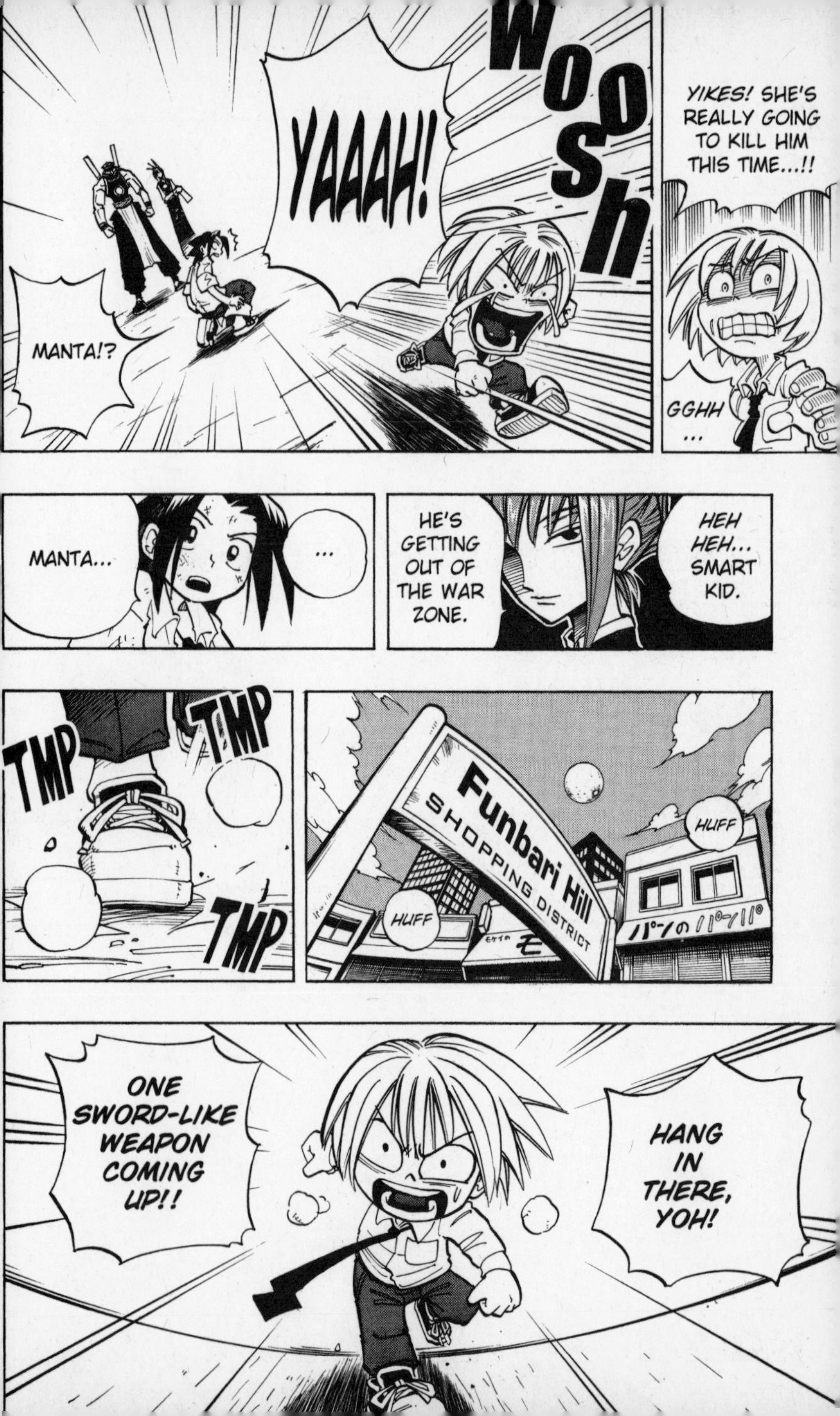
YIKES! SHE'S REALLY GOING TO KILL HIM THIS TIME...!!
GGHH ...
WOOSH
YAAAH!
MANTA!?
HEH HEH... SMART KID.
HE'S GETTING OUT OF THE WAR ZONE.
...
MANTA...
Funbari Hill
SHOPPING DISTRICT
HUFF
HUFF
TMP
TMP
TMP
HANG IN THERE, YOH!
ONE SWORD-LIKE WEAPON COMING UP!!

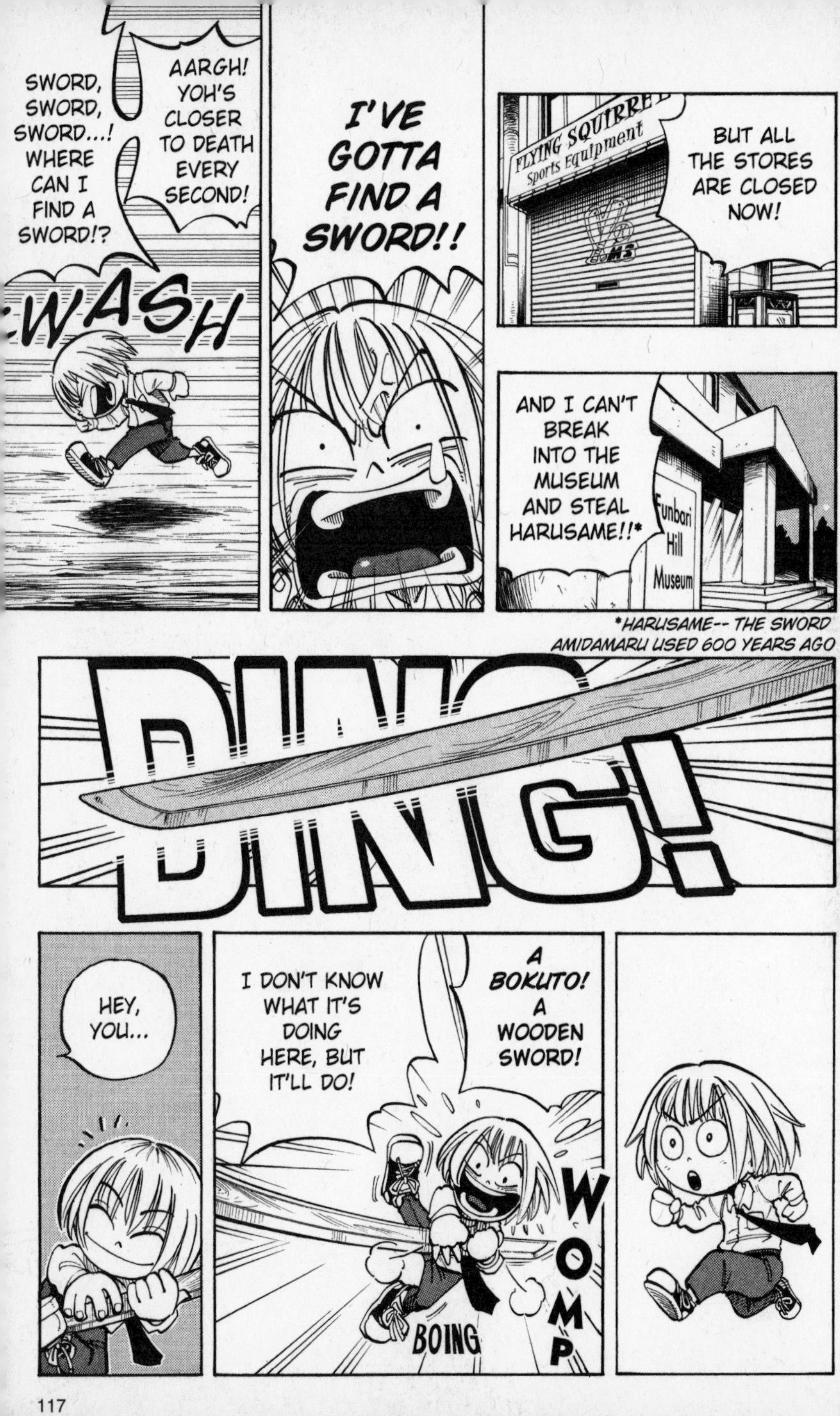
BUT ALL THE STORES ARE CLOSED NOW!
FLYING SQUIRREL Sports Equipment
AND I CAN'T BREAK INTO THE MUSEUM AND STEAL HARUSAME!!*
Funbari Hill Museum
*HARUSAME-- THE SWORD AMIDAMARU USED 600 YEARS AGO
I'VE GOTTA FIND A SWORD!!
AARGH! YOH'S CLOSER TO DEATH EVERY SECOND!
SWORD, SWORD, SWORD...! WHERE CAN I FIND A SWORD!?
WASH
DING!
A BOKUTO! A WOODEN SWORD!
I DON'T KNOW WHAT IT'S DOING HERE, BUT IT'LL DO!
WOMP
BOING
HEY, YOU...

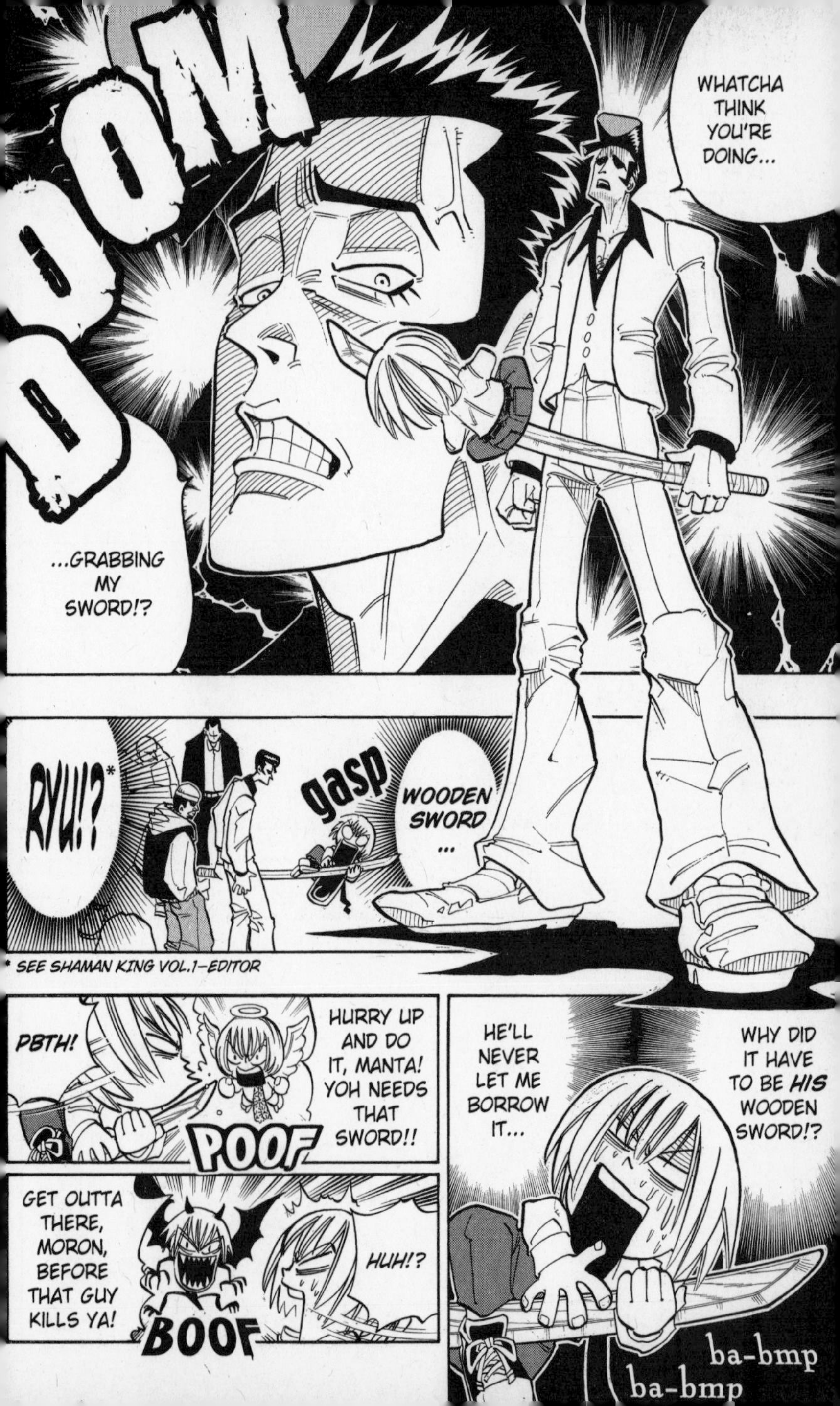
WHATCHA THINK YOU'RE DOING...
DOOM
...GRABBING MY SWORD!?
WOODEN SWORD ...
gasp
RYU!?*
WHY DID IT HAVE TO BE HIS WOODEN SWORD!?
HE'LL NEVER LET ME BORROW IT...
ba-bmp
ba-bmp
HURRY UP AND DO IT, MANTA! YOH NEEDS THAT SWORD!!
POOF
PBTH!
HUH!?
GET OUTTA THERE, MORON, BEFORE THAT GUY KILLS YA!
BOOF

* SEE SHAMAN KING VOL.1—EDITOR

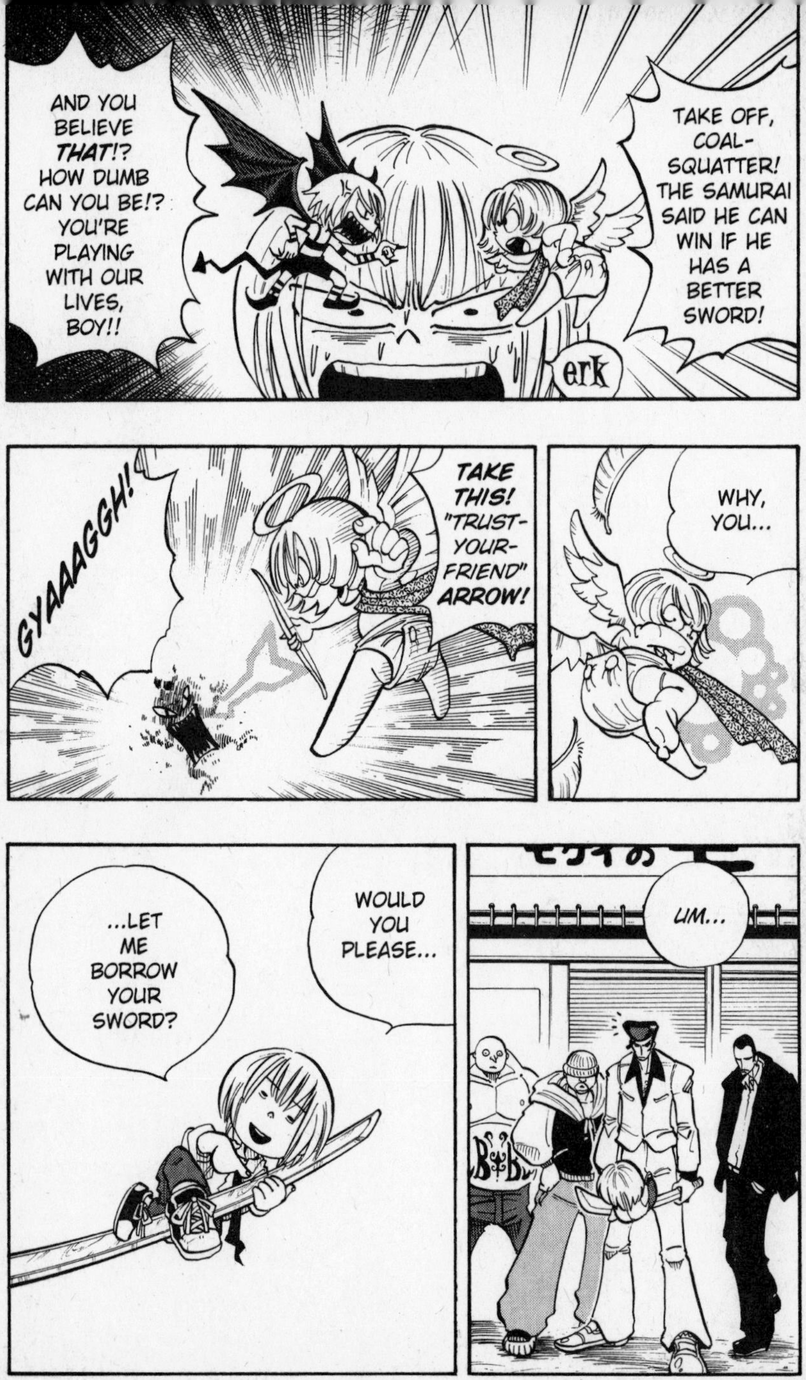
TAKE OFF, COAL-SQUATTER! THE SAMURAI SAID HE CAN WIN IF HE HAS A BETTER SWORD!
AND YOU BELIEVE THAT!? HOW DUMB CAN YOU BE!? YOU'RE PLAYING WITH OUR LIVES, BOY!!
erk
WHY, YOU...
TAKE THIS! "TRUST-YOUR-FRIEND" ARROW!
GYAAAGGH!
UM...
WOULD YOU PLEASE...
...LET ME BORROW YOUR SWORD?

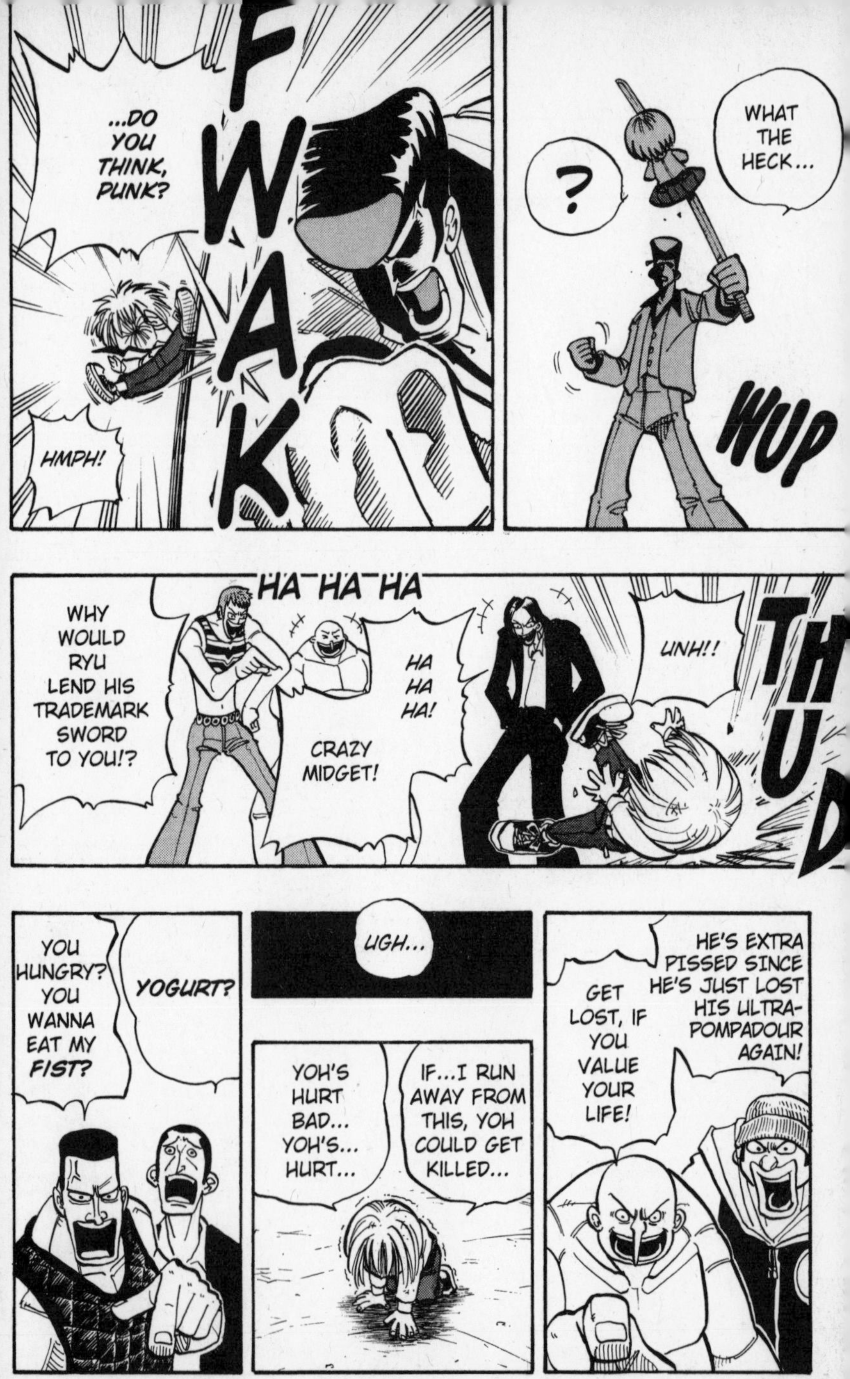

WHAT THE HECK...
?
WUP
...DO YOU THINK, PUNK?
FWAK
HMPH!
THUD
UNH!!
HA HA HA
HA HA HA!
CRAZY MIDGET!
WHY WOULD RYU LEND HIS TRADEMARK SWORD TO YOU!?
HE'S EXTRA PISSED SINCE HE'S JUST LOST HIS ULTRA-POMPADOUR AGAIN!
GET LOST, IF YOU VALUE YOUR LIFE!
UGH...
IF...I RUN AWAY FROM THIS, YOH COULD GET KILLED...
YOH'S HURT BAD... YOH'S... HURT...
YOGURT?
YOU HUNGRY? YOU WANNA EAT MY FIST?

READ THIS WAY

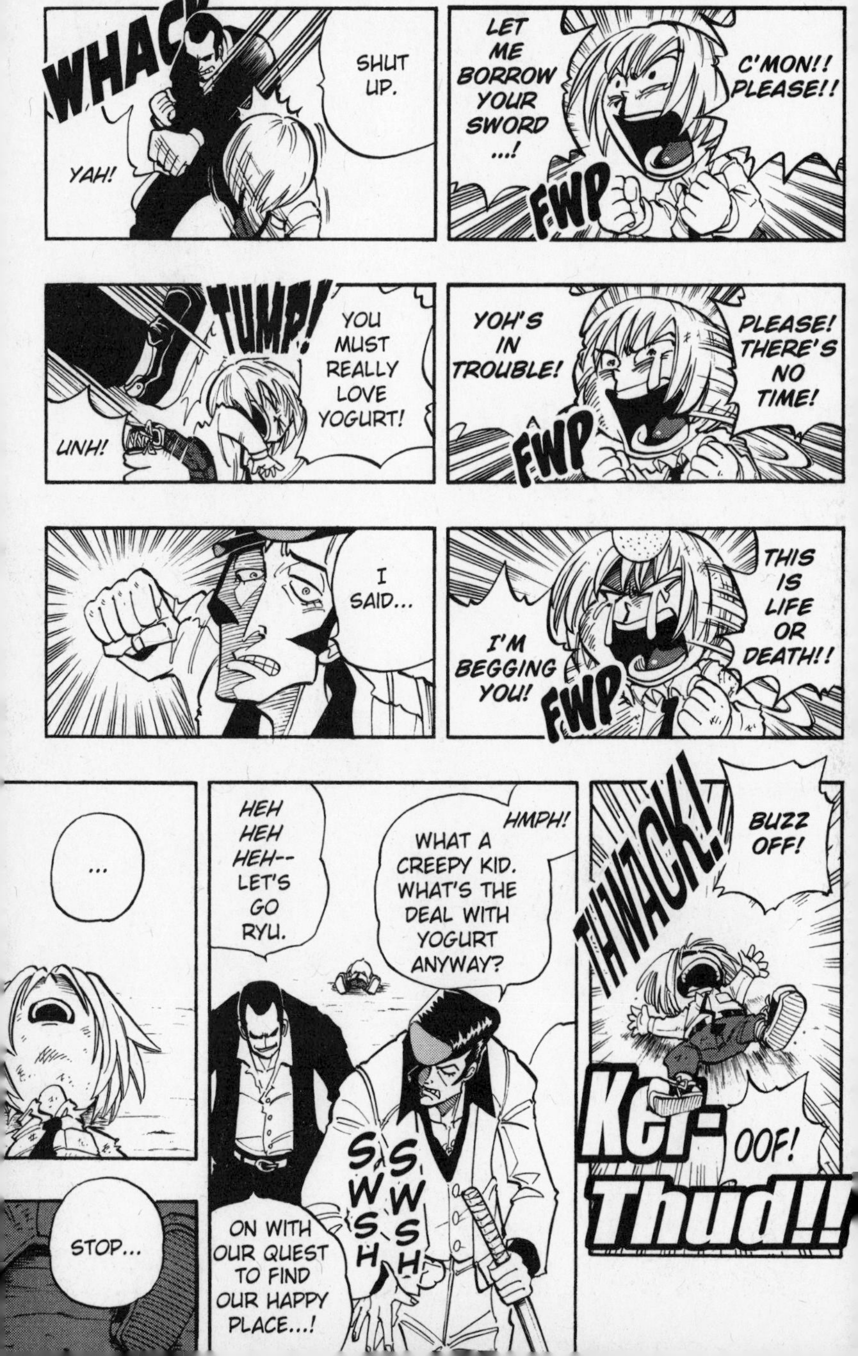

LET ME BORROW YOUR SWORD ...!
C'MON!! PLEASE!!
FWP
WHACK
SHUT UP.
YAH!
YOH'S IN TROUBLE!
PLEASE! THERE'S NO TIME!
FWP
TUMP!
YOU MUST REALLY LOVE YOGURT!
UNH!
THIS IS LIFE OR DEATH!!
I'M BEGGING YOU!
FWP
I SAID...
BUZZ OFF!
THWACK!
OOF!
Ker-Thud!!
HMPH!
WHAT A CREEPY KID. WHAT'S THE DEAL WITH YOGURT ANYWAY?
HEH HEH HEH-- LET'S GO RYU.
SWSH SWSH
ON WITH OUR QUEST TO FIND OUR HAPPY PLACE...!
...
STOP...

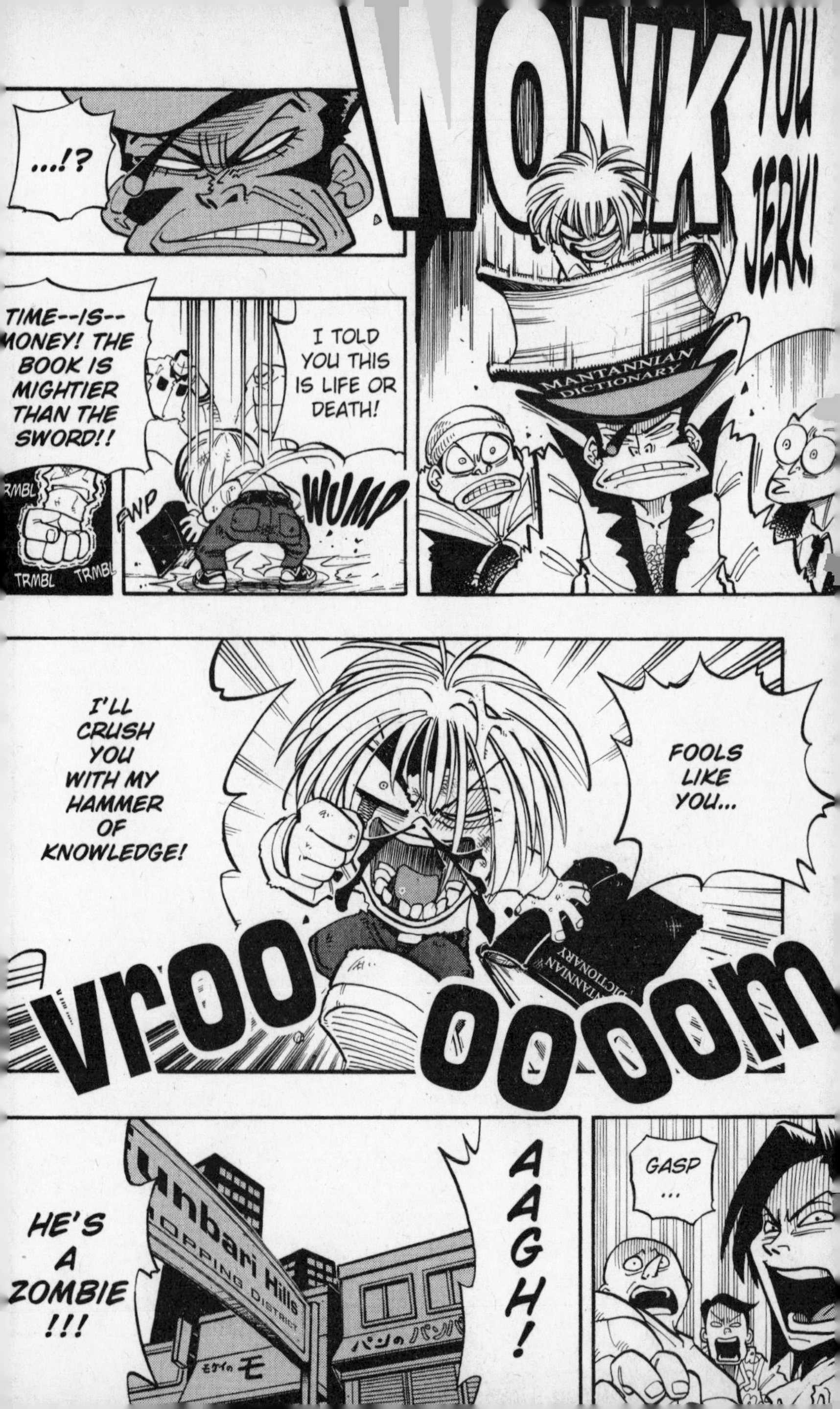
WONK
YOU JERK!
MANTANNIAN DICTIONARY
...!?
I TOLD YOU THIS IS LIFE OR DEATH!
WUMP
FWP
TIME--IS--MONEY! THE BOOK IS MIGHTIER THAN THE SWORD!!
TRMBL
TRMBL
TRMBL
FOOLS LIKE YOU...
I'LL CRUSH YOU WITH MY HAMMER OF KNOWLEDGE!
MANTANNIAN DICTIONARY
vrooooooom
GASP ...
AAGH!
HE'S A ZOMBIE !!!

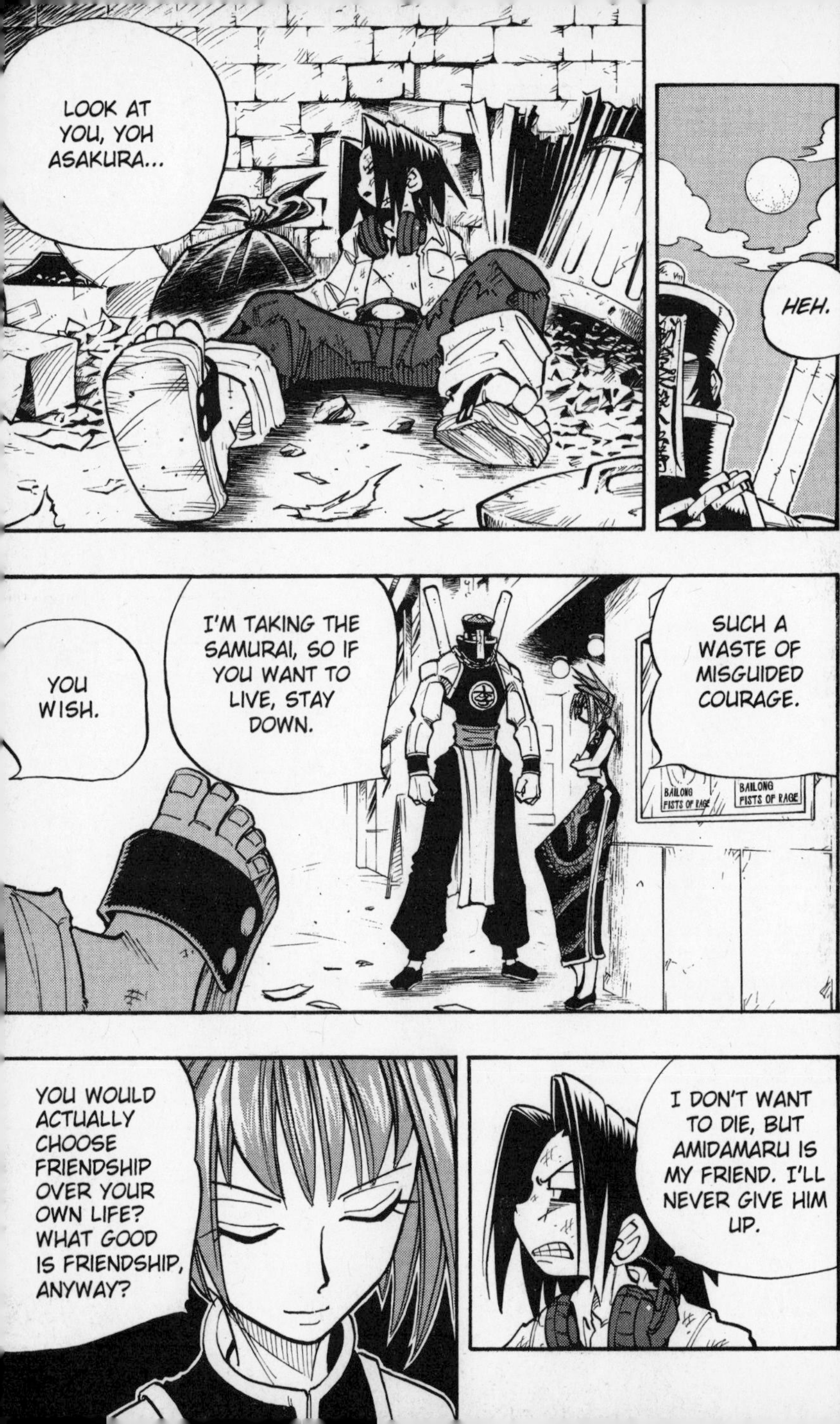
HEH.
LOOK AT YOU, YOH ASAKURA...
SUCH A WASTE OF MISGUIDED COURAGE.
BAILONG FISTS OF RAGE
BAILONG FISTS OF RAGE
I'M TAKING THE SAMURAI, SO IF YOU WANT TO LIVE, STAY DOWN.
YOU WISH.
I DON'T WANT TO DIE, BUT AMIDAMARU IS MY FRIEND. I'LL NEVER GIVE HIM UP.
YOU WOULD ACTUALLY CHOOSE FRIENDSHIP OVER YOUR OWN LIFE? WHAT GOOD IS FRIENDSHIP, ANYWAY?

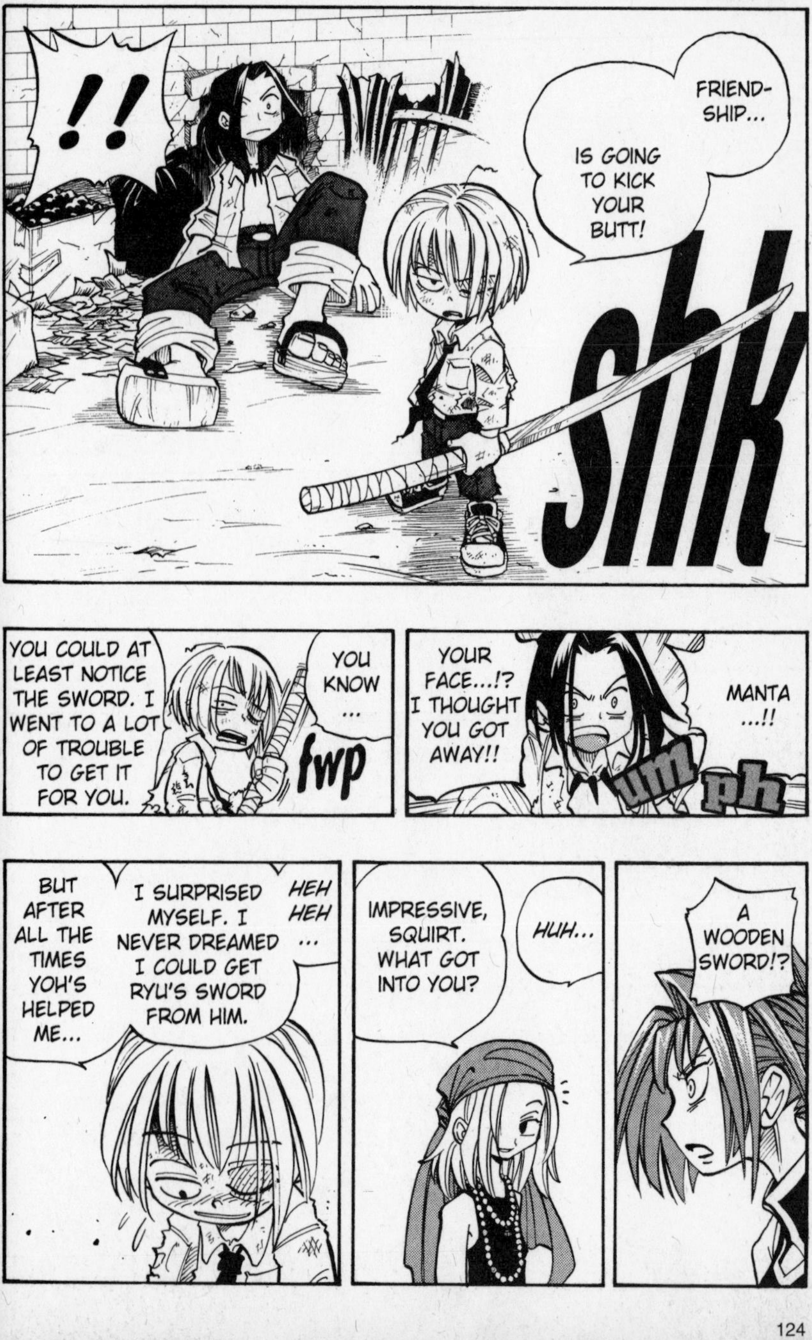
FRIEND-SHIP... IS GOING TO KICK YOUR BUTT!
SHK
!!
MANTA ...!!
YOUR FACE...!? I THOUGHT YOU GOT AWAY!!
umph
YOU KNOW ...
fwp
YOU COULD AT LEAST NOTICE THE SWORD. I WENT TO A LOT OF TROUBLE TO GET IT FOR YOU.
A WOODEN SWORD!?
HUH...
IMPRESSIVE, SQUIRT. WHAT GOT INTO YOU?
HEH HEH ...
I SURPRISED MYSELF. I NEVER DREAMED I COULD GET RYU'S SWORD FROM HIM.
BUT AFTER ALL THE TIMES YOH'S HELPED ME...

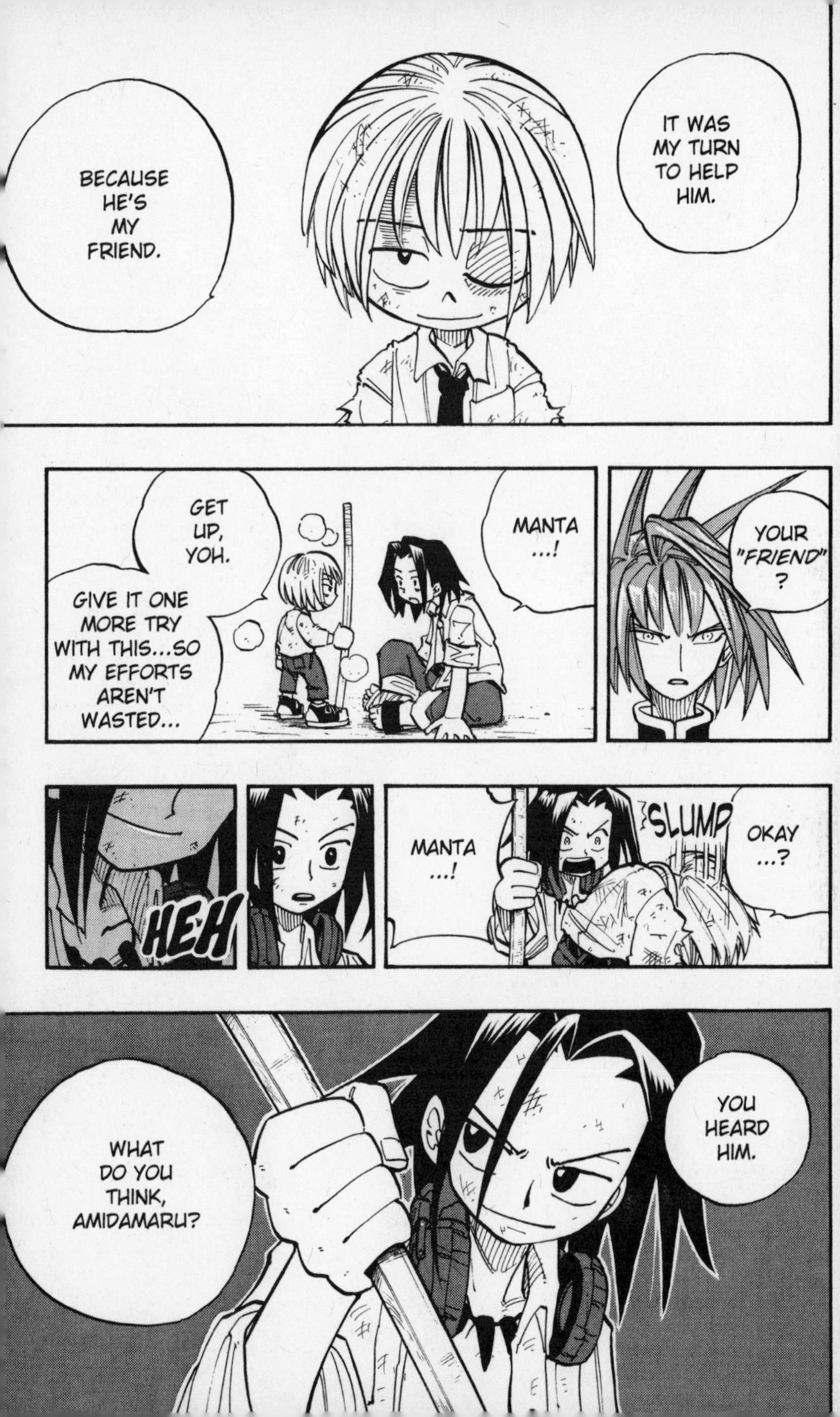
IT WAS MY TURN TO HELP HIM.
BECAUSE HE'S MY FRIEND.
YOUR "FRIEND"?
MANTA ...!
GET UP, YOH.
GIVE IT ONE MORE TRY WITH THIS...SO MY EFFORTS AREN'T WASTED...
OKAY ...?
SLUMP
MANTA ...!
HEH
YOU HEARD HIM.
WHAT DO YOU THINK, AMIDAMARU?

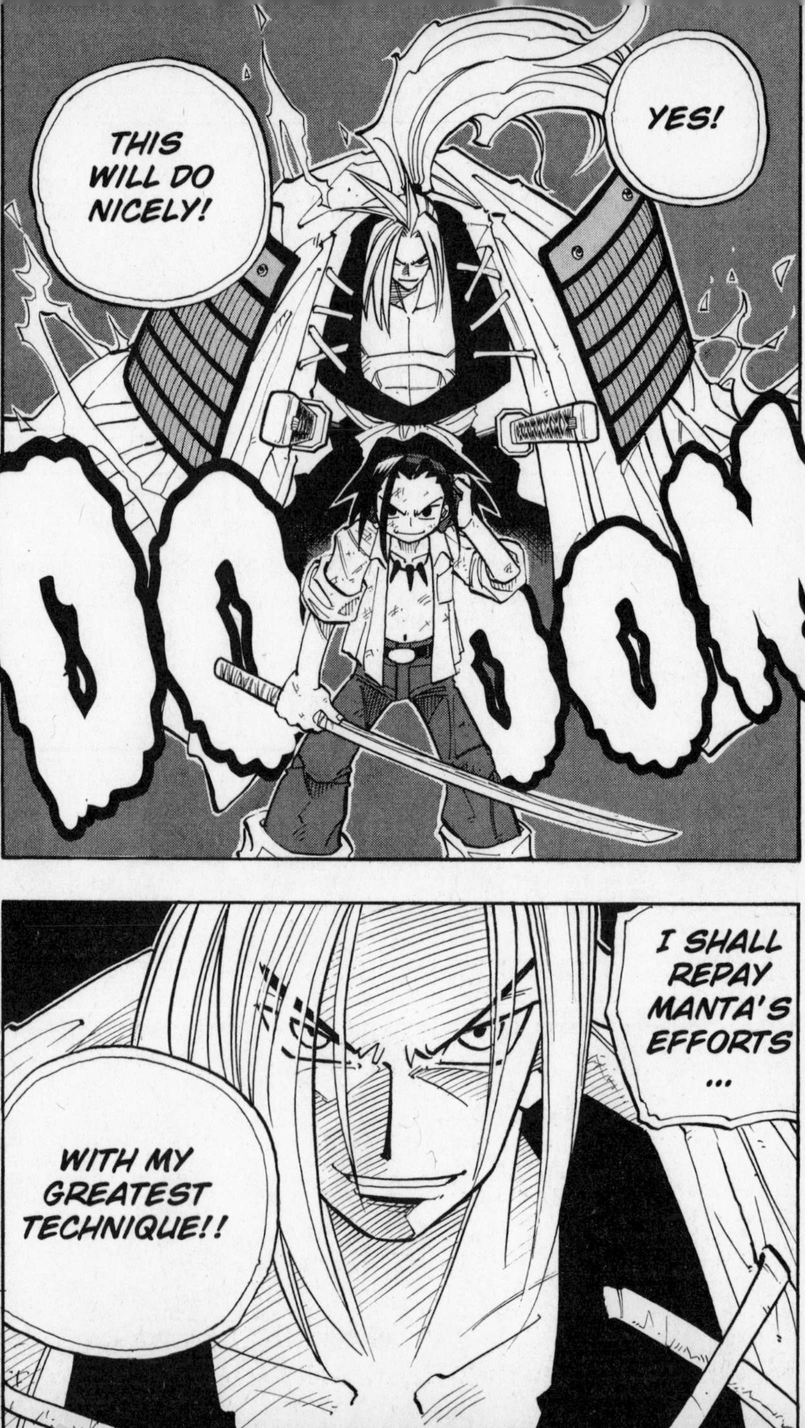
YES!
THIS WILL DO NICELY!
DOOM
I SHALL REPAY MANTA'S EFFORTS ...
WITH MY GREATEST TECHNIQUE!!

READ THIS WAY

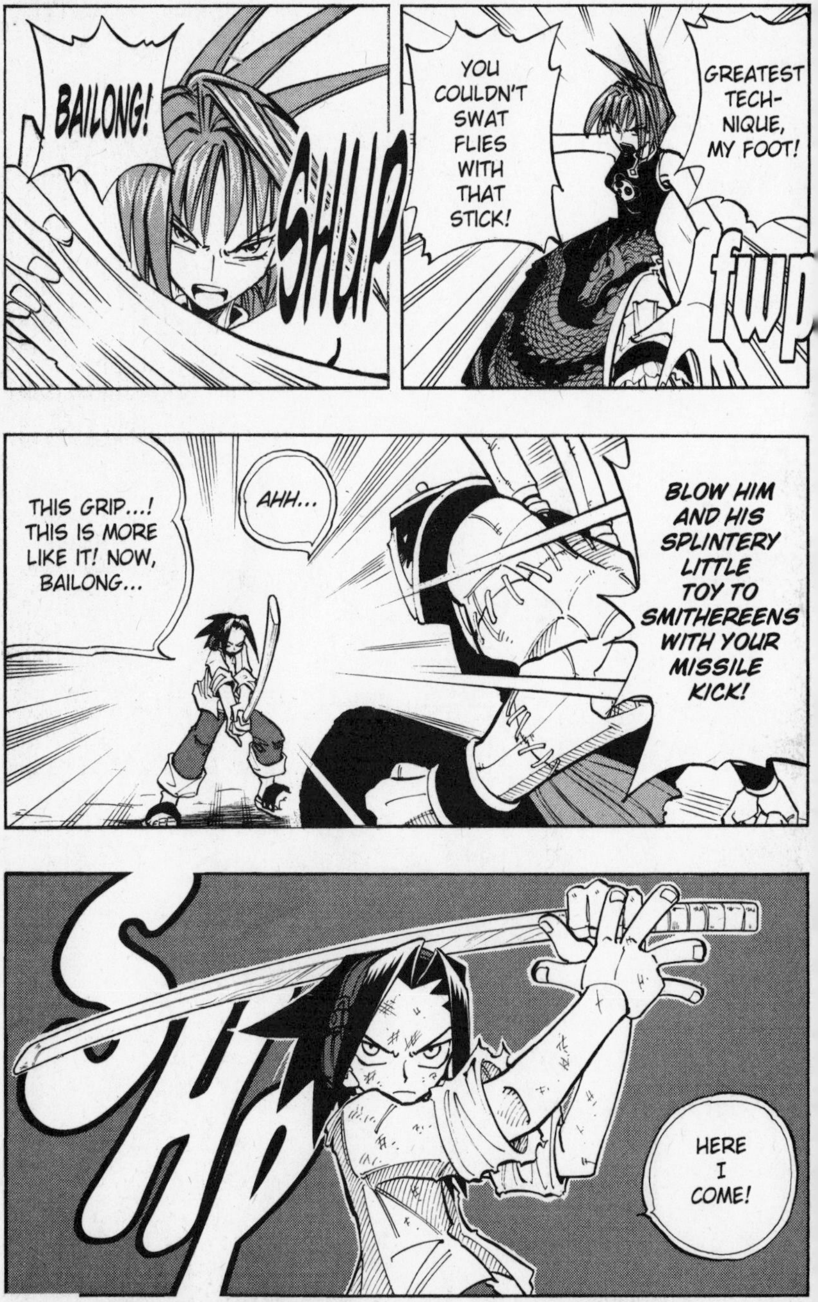
GREATEST TECH- NIQUE, MY FOOT!
YOU COULDN'T SWAT FLIES WITH THAT STICK!
fwp
SHUP
BAILONG!
BLOW HIM AND HIS SPLINTERY LITTLE TOY TO SMITHEREENS WITH YOUR MISSILE KICK!
AHH...
THIS GRIP...! THIS IS MORE LIKE IT! NOW, BAILONG...
HERE I COME!
SHP

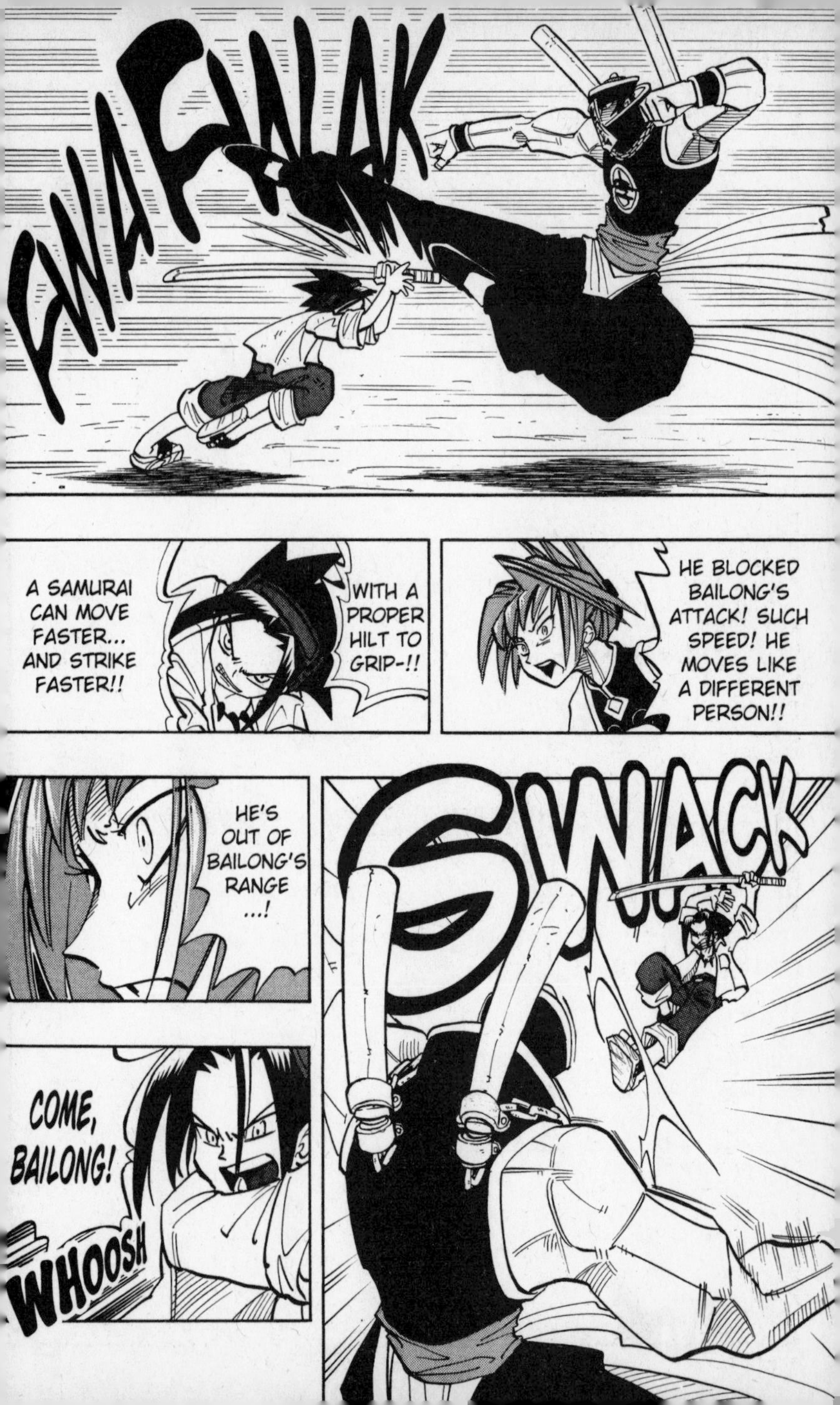
FWA FWAK
HE BLOCKED BAILONG'S ATTACK! SUCH SPEED! HE MOVES LIKE A DIFFERENT PERSON!!
WITH A PROPER HILT TO GRIP-!!
A SAMURAI CAN MOVE FASTER... AND STRIKE FASTER!!
SWACK
HE'S OUT OF BAILONG'S RANGE ...!
COME, BAILONG!
WHOOSH

READ THIS WAY

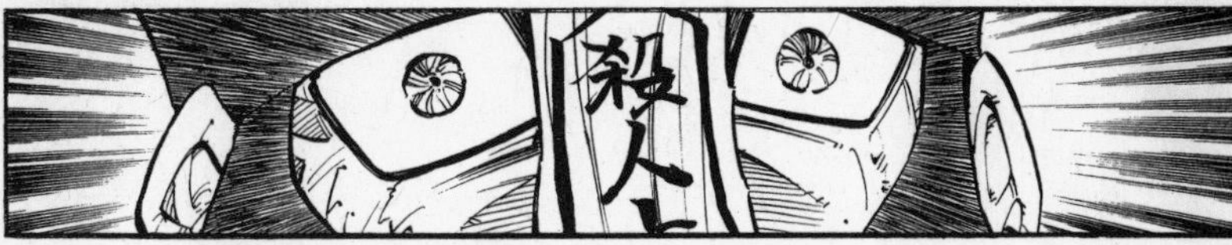
殺人

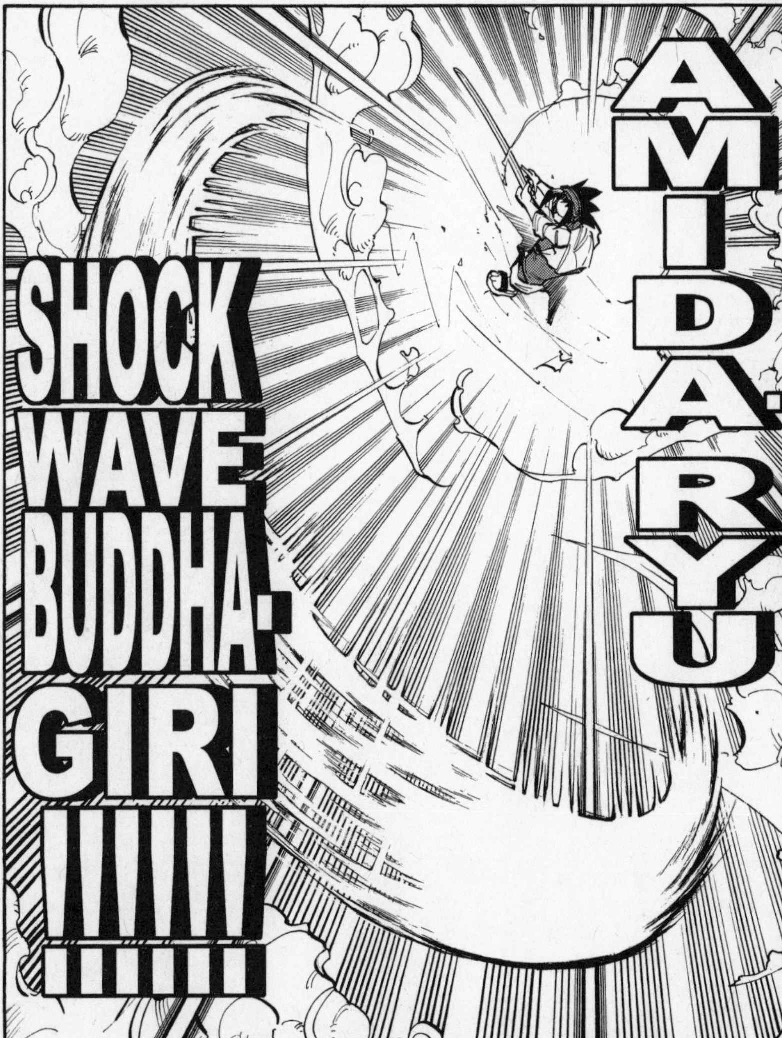
AMIDA-RYU
SHOCKWAVE BUDDHA-GIRI!!!!!!

*BUDDHA-GIRI=BUDDHA SLASH, OR "TO CLEAVE OR CHOP"

SHAMAN
KING
2

O-FUDA
(Also called *jufu*, these
sacred slips of paper are
often inscribed with charms
or curses.)

REINCARNATION 15: FISTS OF RAGE

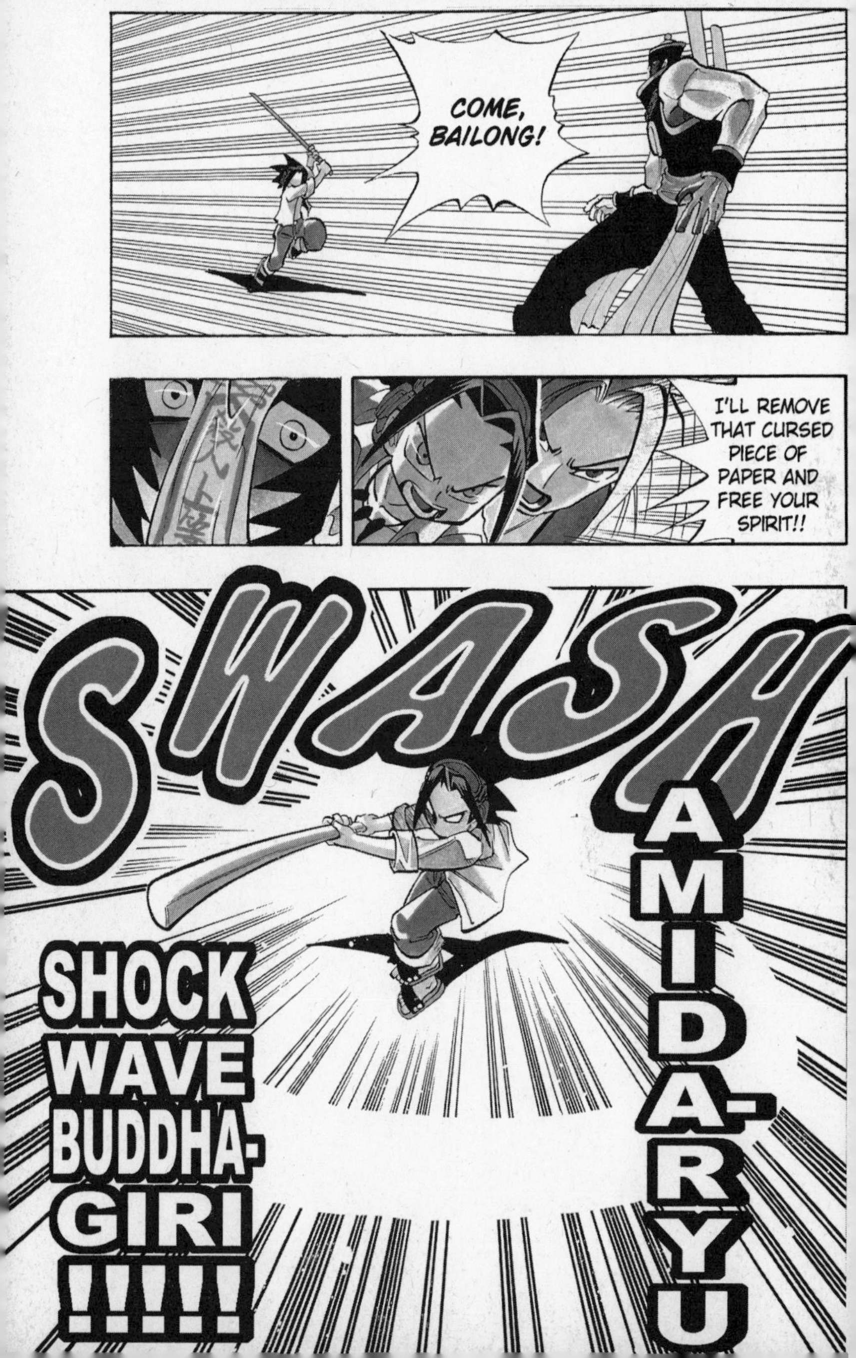
COME, BAILONG!
I'LL REMOVE THAT CURSED PIECE OF PAPER AND FREE YOUR SPIRIT!!
SWASH
AMIDA-RYU
SHOCK WAVE BUDDHA-GIRI !!!!!

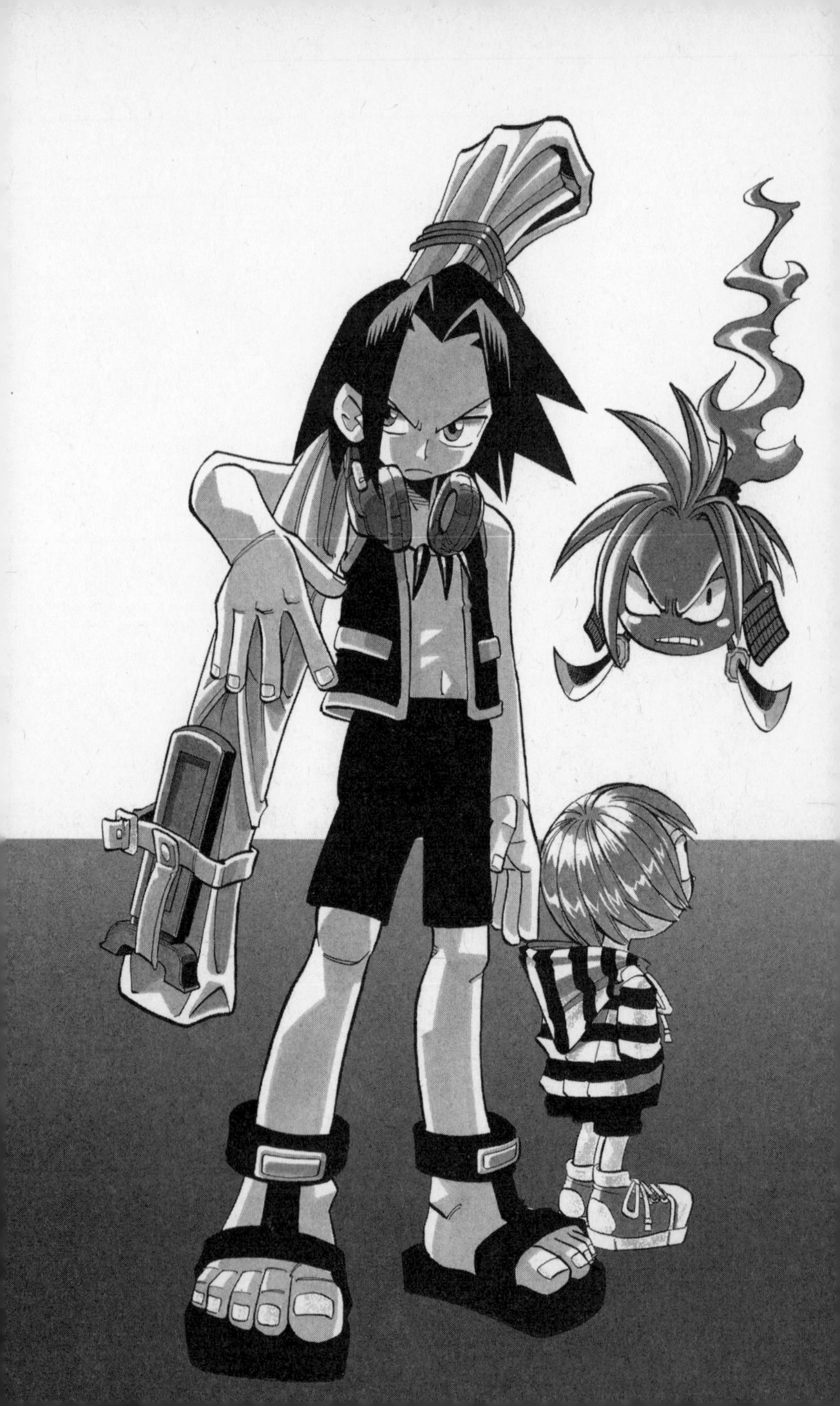

Reincarnation 15: Fists of Rage

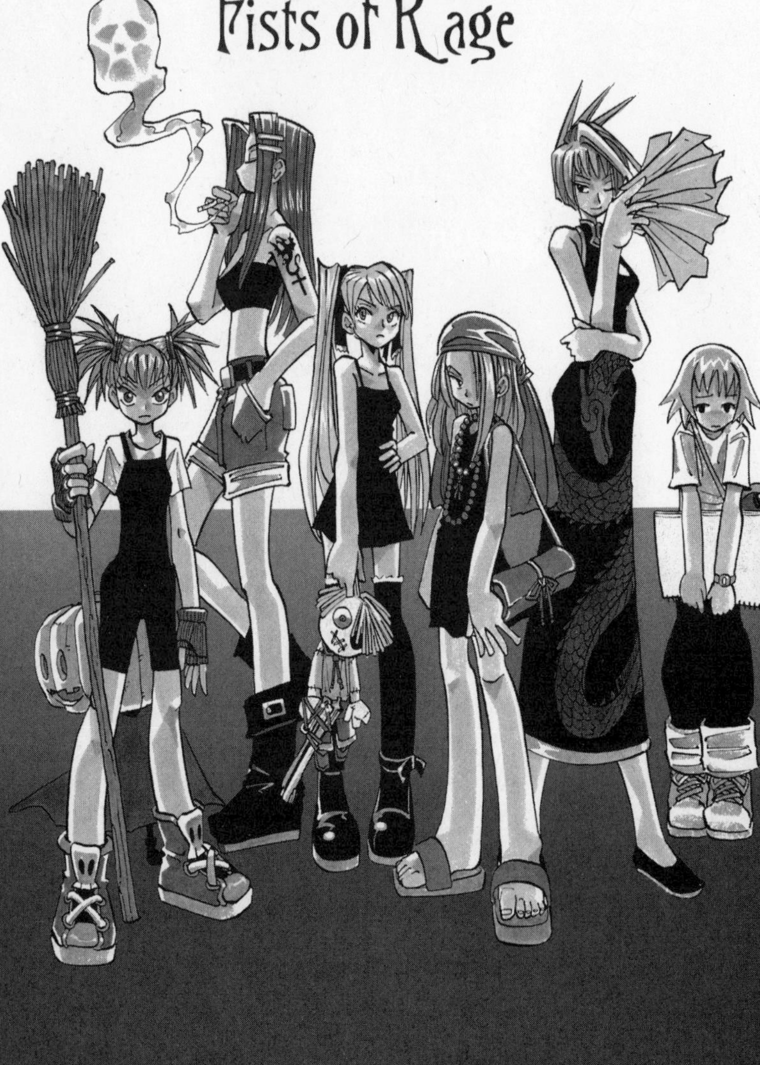

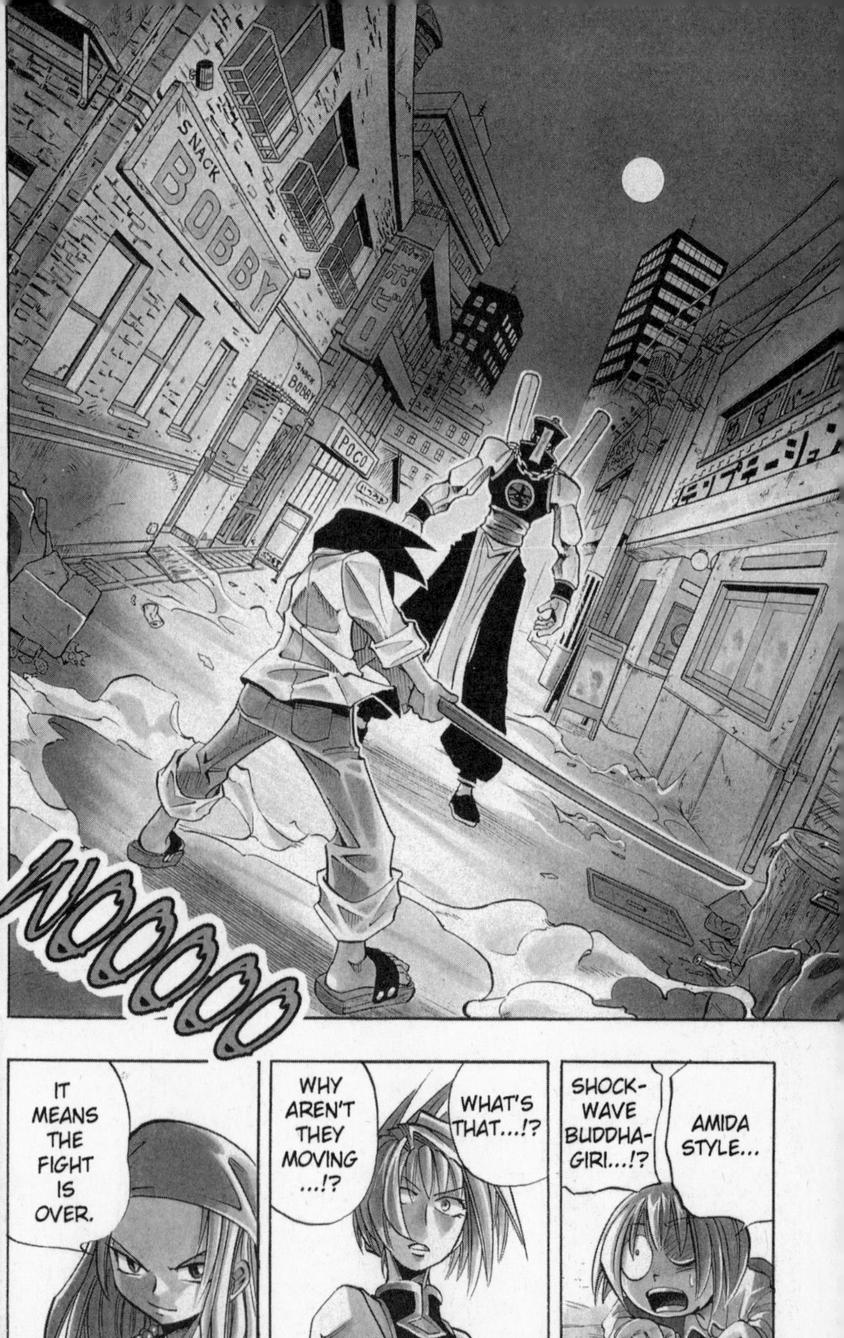
SNACK BOBBY
SNACK BOBBY
POCO
WOOOOO
AMIDA STYLE...
SHOCK-WAVE BUDDHA-GIRI...!?
WHAT'S THAT...!?
WHY AREN'T THEY MOVING ...!?
IT MEANS THE FIGHT IS OVER.

READ THIS WAY

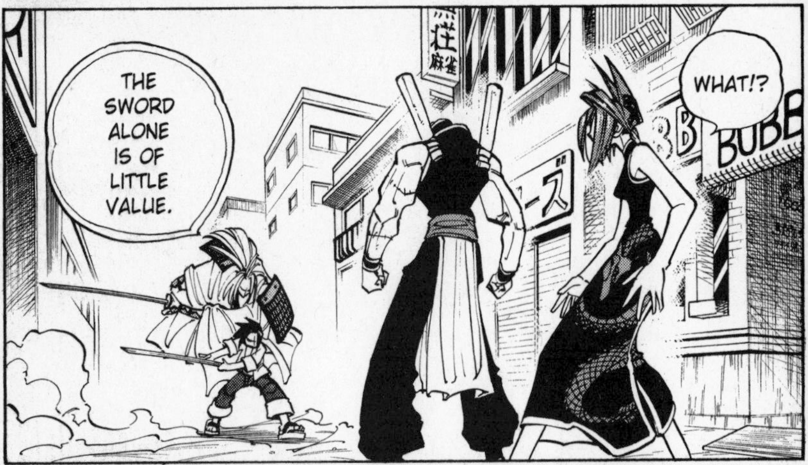

WHAT!?
BUBB
THE SWORD ALONE IS OF LITTLE VALUE.

*PROVERB-THE **SWORD** CAN ONLY STRIKE ONE ENEMY AT A TIME, BUT **TACTICS** CAN DEFEAT TEN THOUSAND MEN AT ONCE.

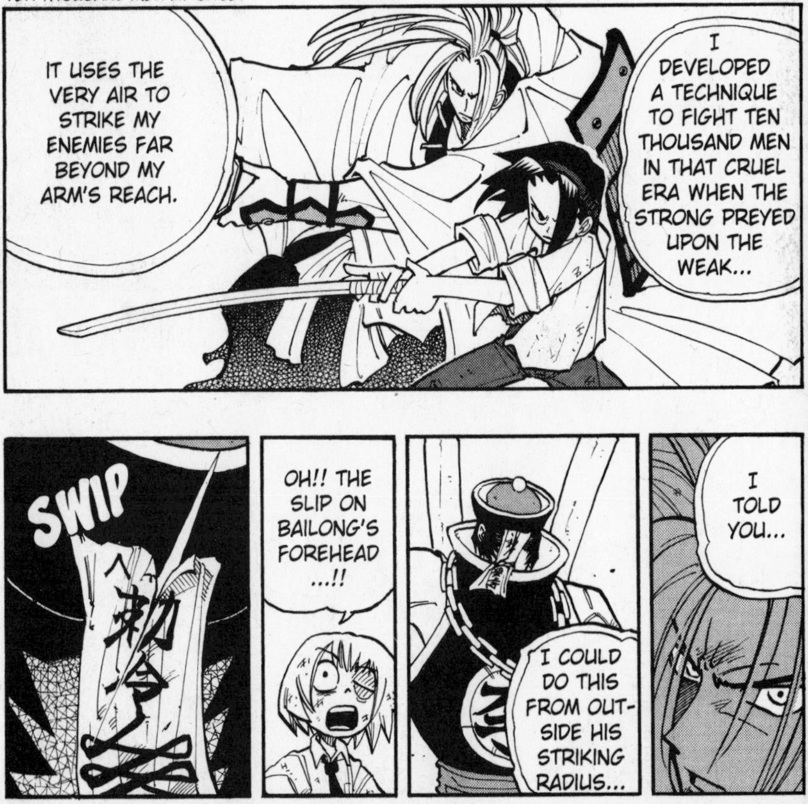

I DEVELOPED A TECHNIQUE TO FIGHT TEN THOUSAND MEN IN THAT CRUEL ERA WHEN THE STRONG PREYED UPON THE WEAK...
IT USES THE VERY AIR TO STRIKE MY ENEMIES FAR BEYOND MY ARM'S REACH.
I TOLD YOU...
I COULD DO THIS FROM OUT-SIDE HIS STRIKING RADIUS...
OH!! THE SLIP ON BAILONG'S FOREHEAD ...!!
SWIP

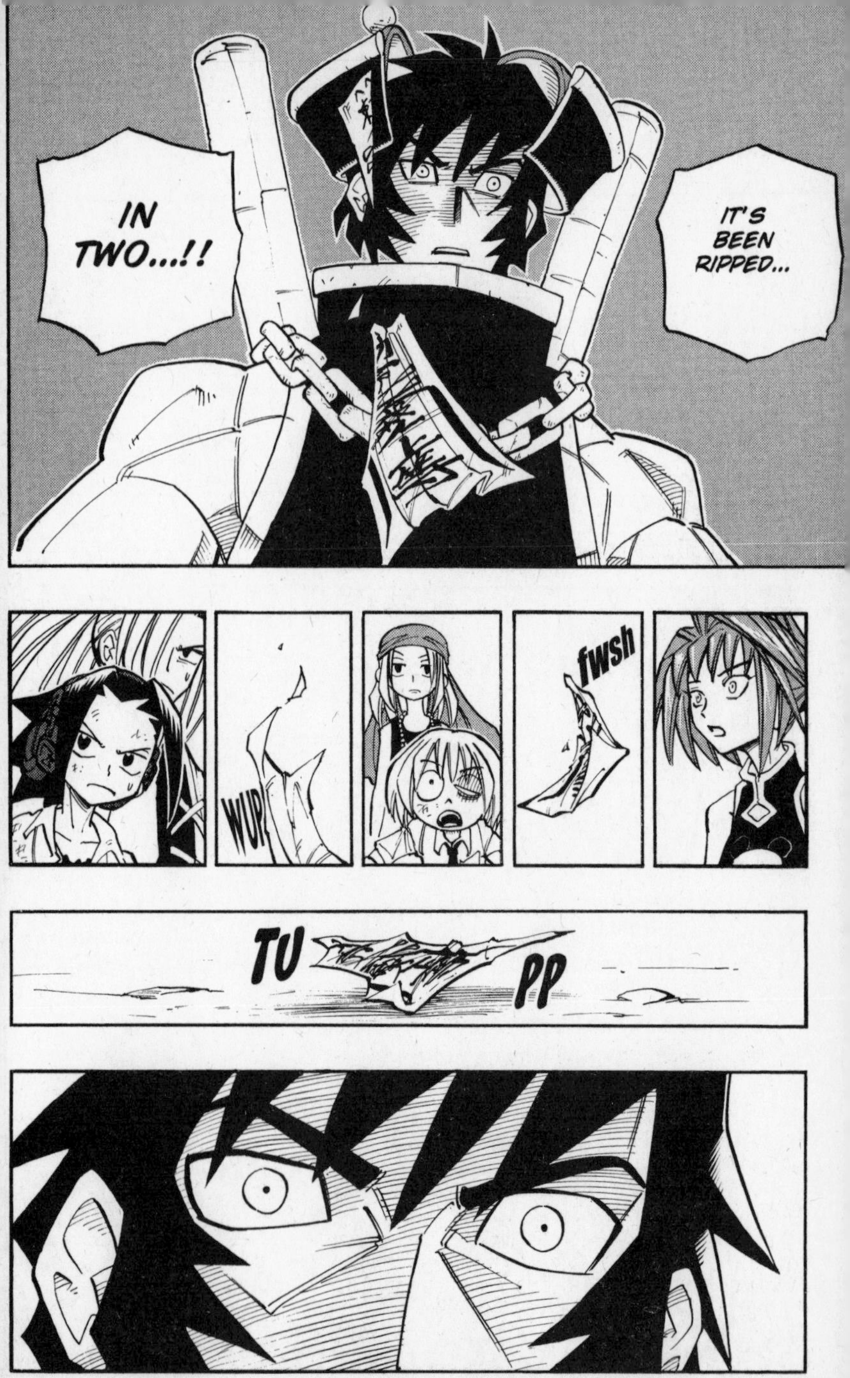
IT'S BEEN RIPPED...
IN TWO...!!
fwsh
WUP
TUPP

READ THIS WAY

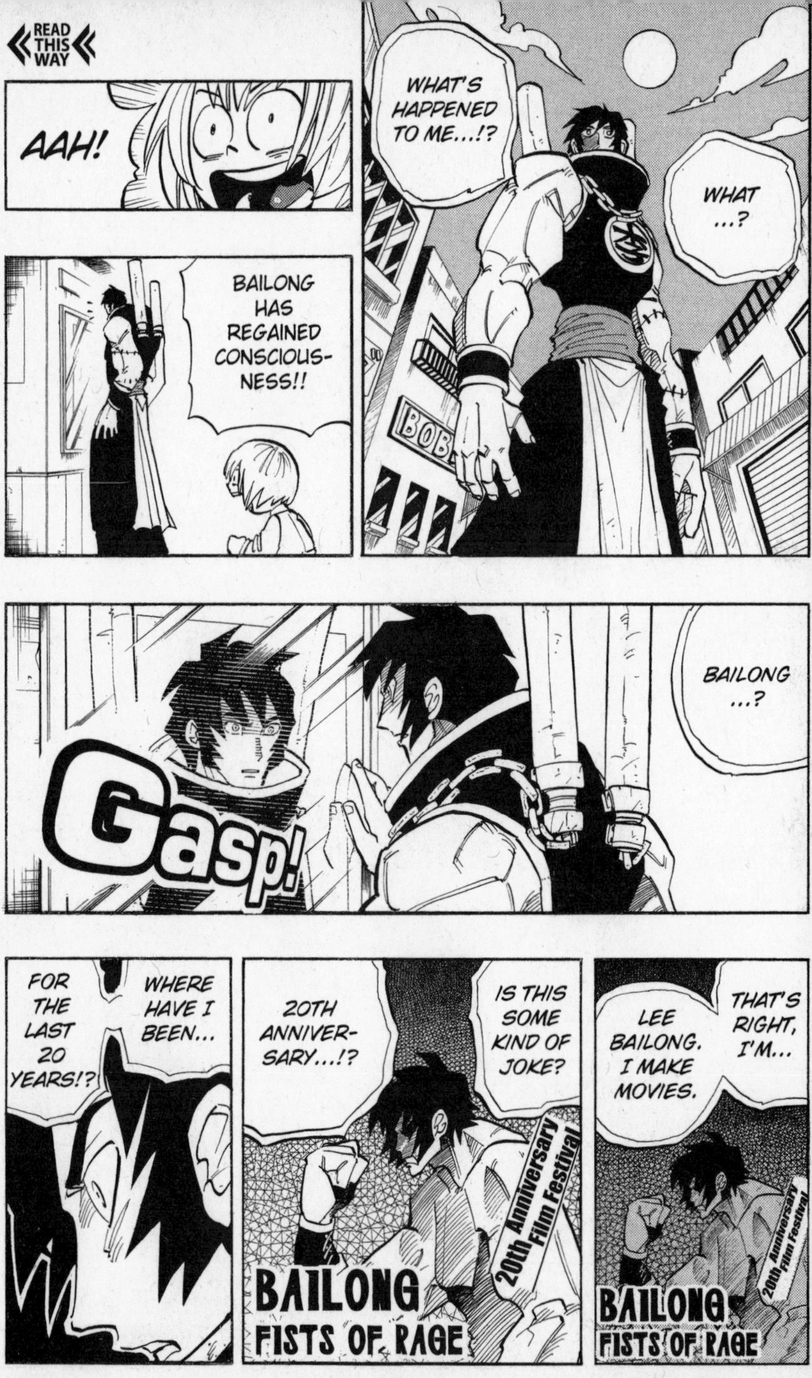

WHAT ...?
WHAT'S HAPPENED TO ME...!?
AAH!
BAILONG HAS REGAINED CONSCIOUS-NESS!!
BAILONG ...?
Gasp!
THAT'S RIGHT, I'M...
LEE BAILONG. I MAKE MOVIES.
20th Anniversary Film Festival
BAILONG FISTS OF RAGE
IS THIS SOME KIND OF JOKE?
20TH ANNIVER-SARY...!?
20th Anniversary Film Festival
BAILONG FISTS OF RAGE
WHERE HAVE I BEEN...
FOR THE LAST 20 YEARS!?

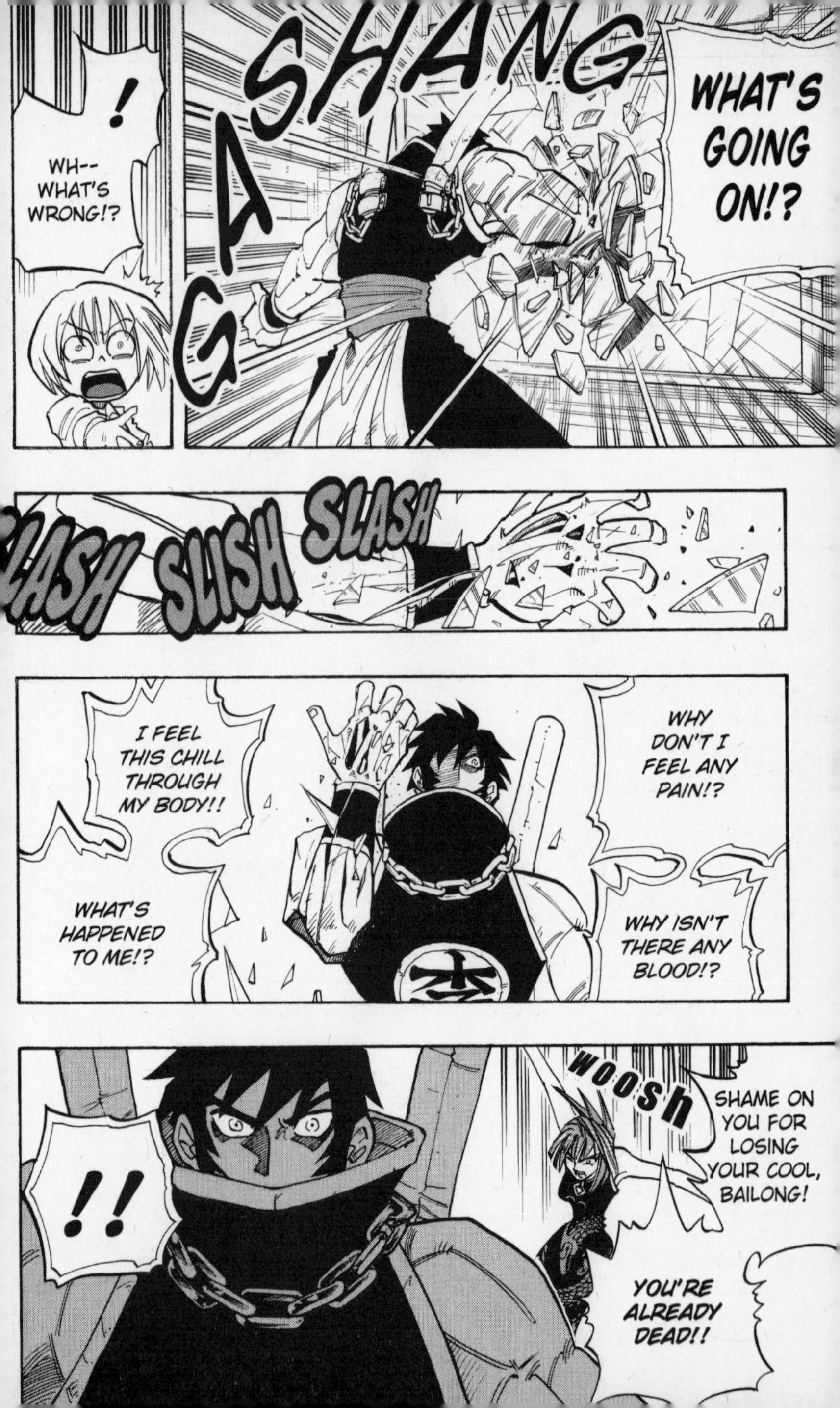
GASHANG
WHAT'S GOING ON!?
!
WH-- WHAT'S WRONG!?
SLASH
SLISH
SLASH
WHY DON'T I FEEL ANY PAIN!?
WHY ISN'T THERE ANY BLOOD!?
I FEEL THIS CHILL THROUGH MY BODY!!
WHAT'S HAPPENED TO ME!?
WOOSH
SHAME ON YOU FOR LOSING YOUR COOL, BAILONG!
YOU'RE ALREADY DEAD!!
!!

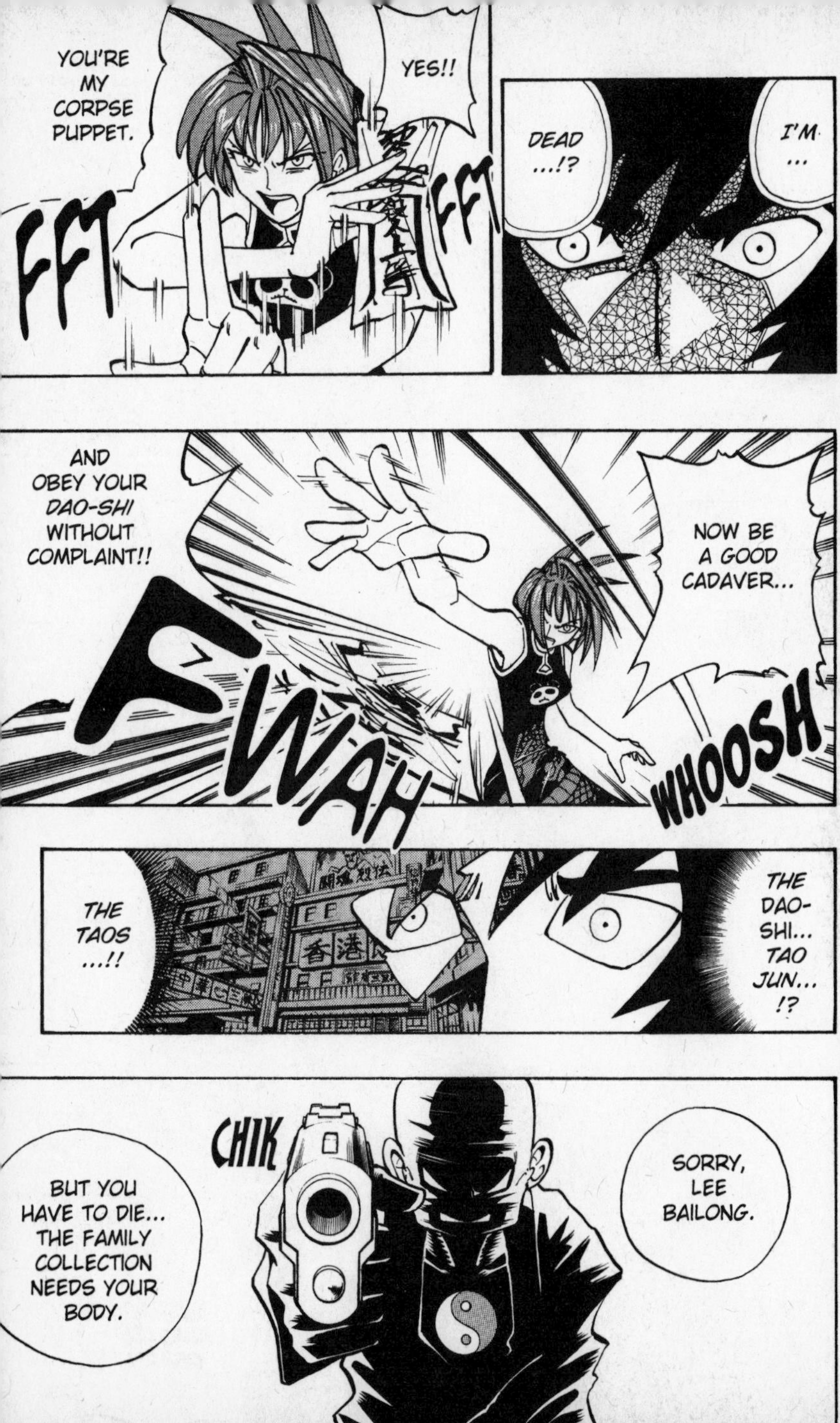
I'M ...
DEAD ...!?
YES!!
YOU'RE MY CORPSE PUPPET.
FFT
FFT
NOW BE A GOOD CADAVER...
AND OBEY YOUR *DAO-SHI* WITHOUT COMPLAINT!!
WHOOSH
SWAH
THE DAO-SHI... TAO JUN... !?
THE TAOS ...!!
SORRY, LEE BAILONG.
CHIK
BUT YOU HAVE TO DIE... THE FAMILY COLLECTION NEEDS YOUR BODY.

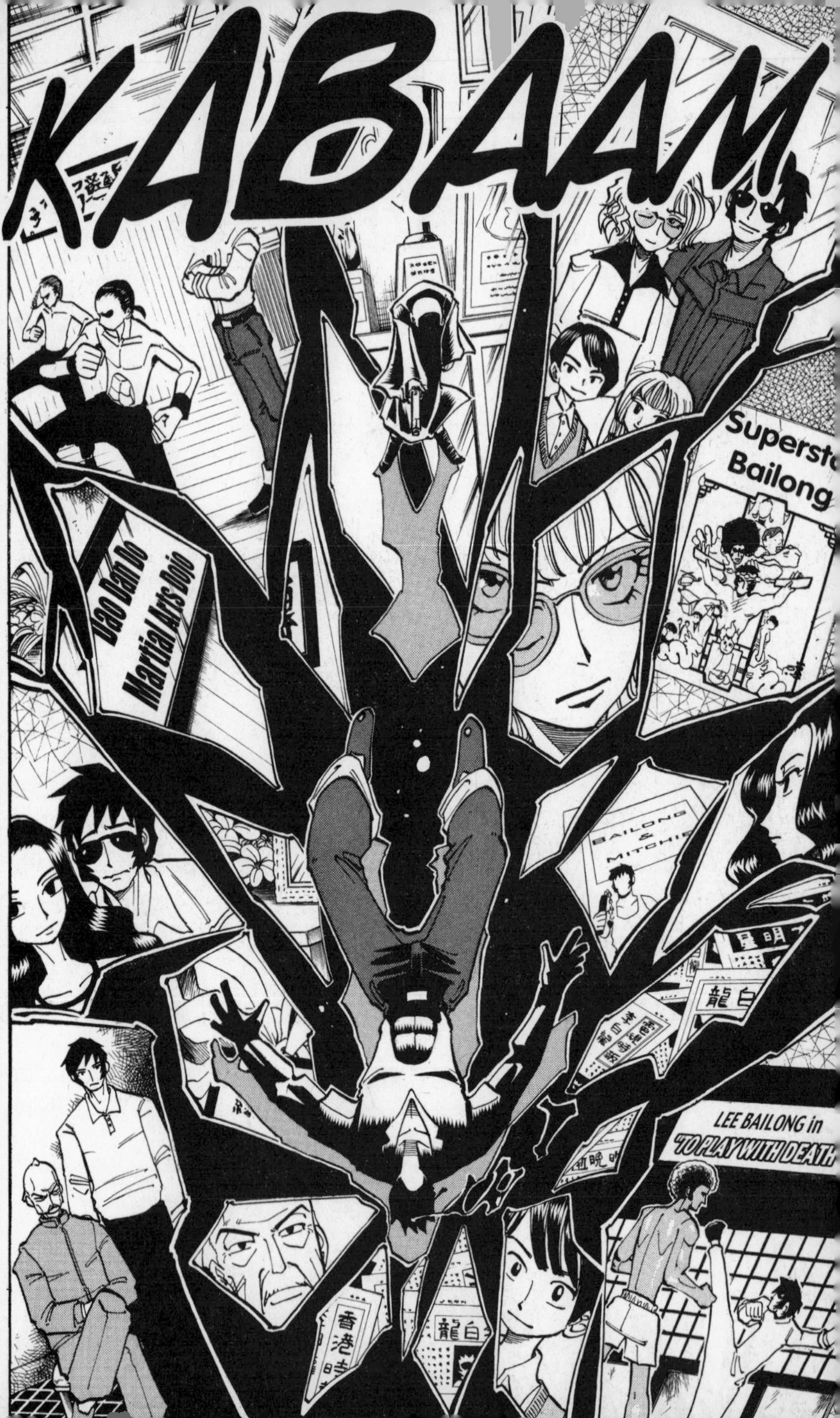
KABAAM
Superst
Bailong
Dao Dan Do
Martial Arts Dojo
BAILONG & MITCHIE
龍白
LEE BAILONG in
"TO PLAY WITH DEATH"
香港時
龍白

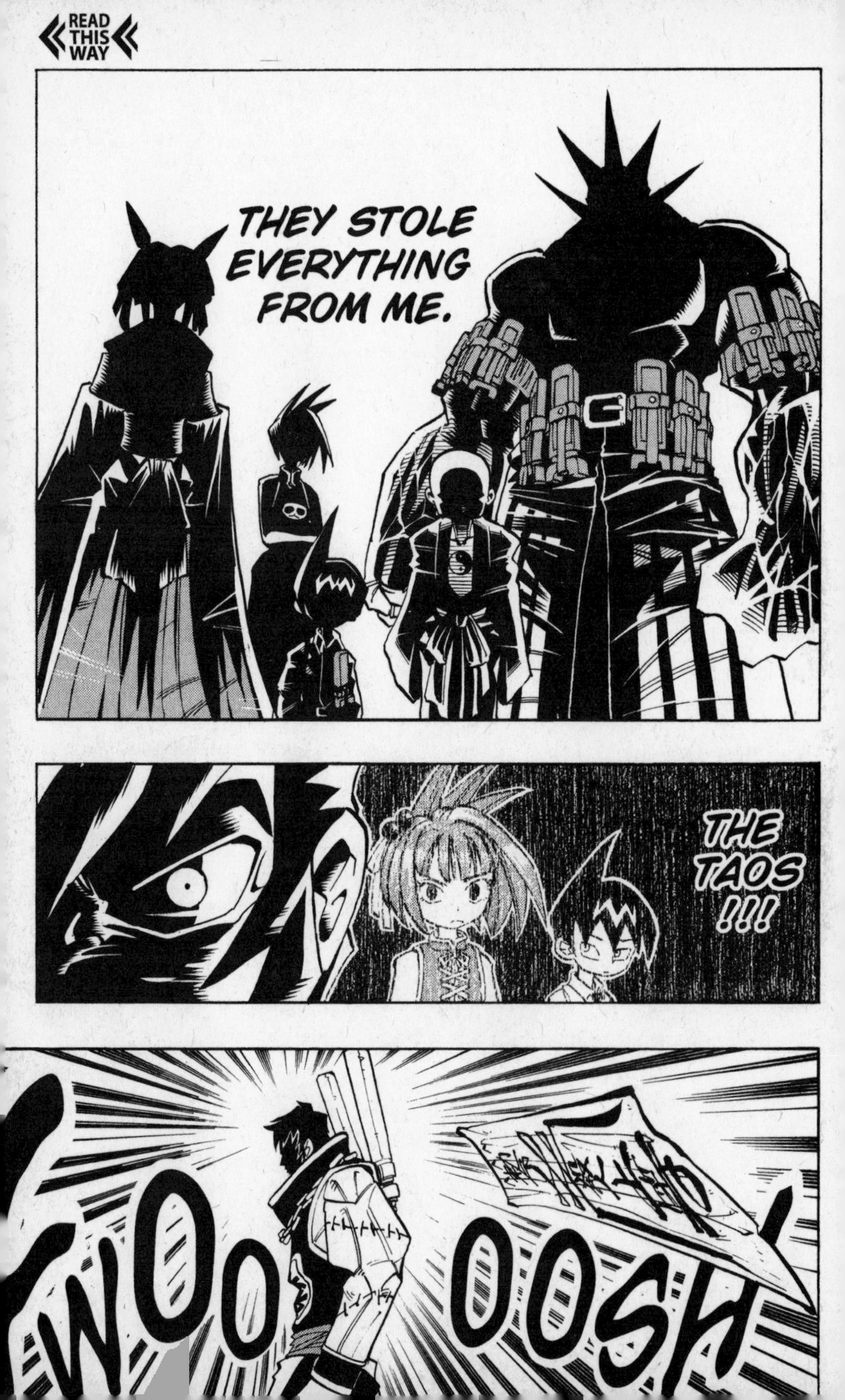
READ THIS WAY
THEY STOLE EVERYTHING FROM ME.
THE TAOS !!!
WOOOOOSH

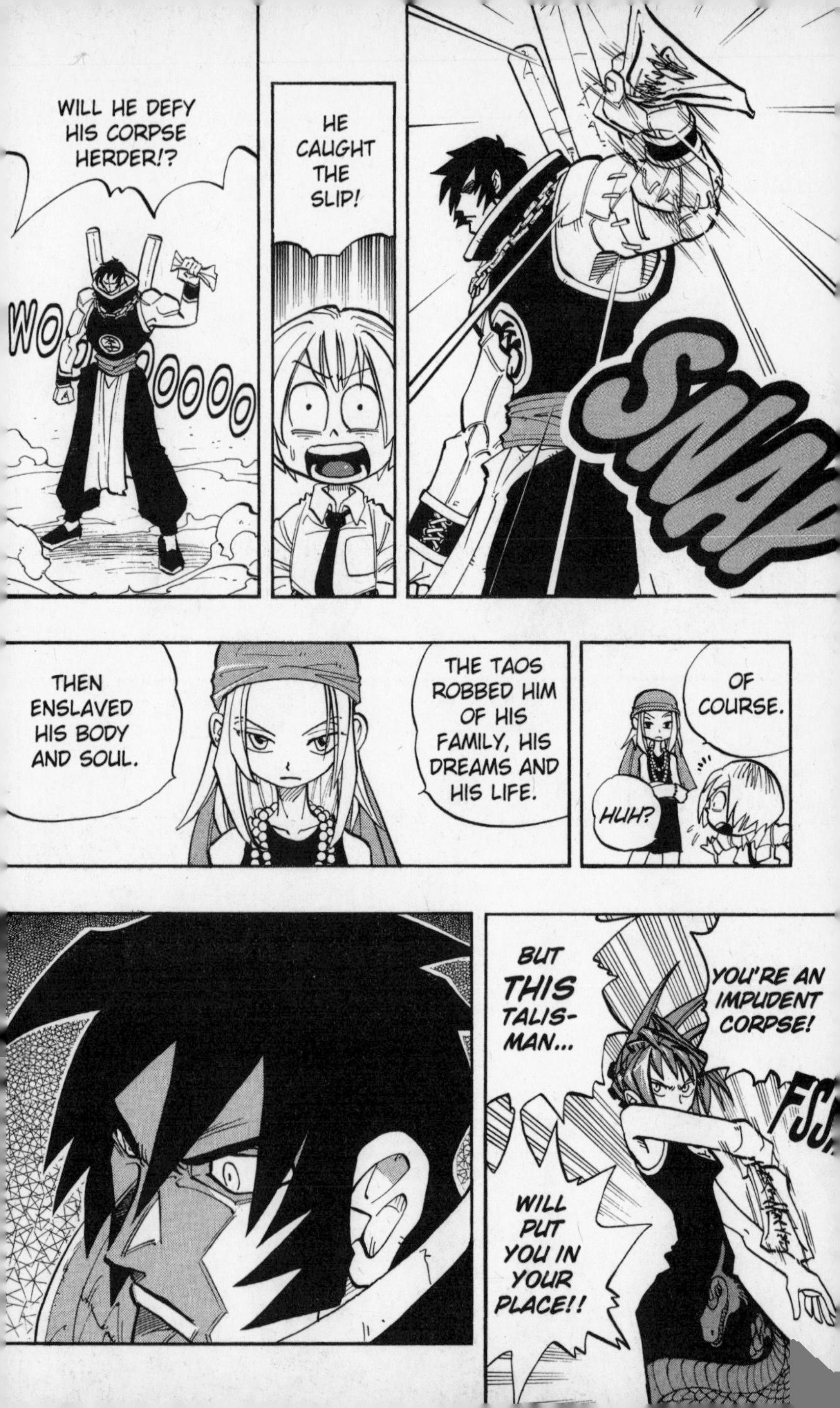
SNAP
HE CAUGHT THE SLIP!
WILL HE DEFY HIS CORPSE HERDER!?
WOOOOOOO
OF COURSE.
HUH?
THE TAOS ROBBED HIM OF HIS FAMILY, HIS DREAMS AND HIS LIFE.
THEN ENSLAVED HIS BODY AND SOUL.
BUT THIS TALIS-MAN...
YOU'RE AN IMPUDENT CORPSE!
FSS
WILL PUT YOU IN YOUR PLACE!!

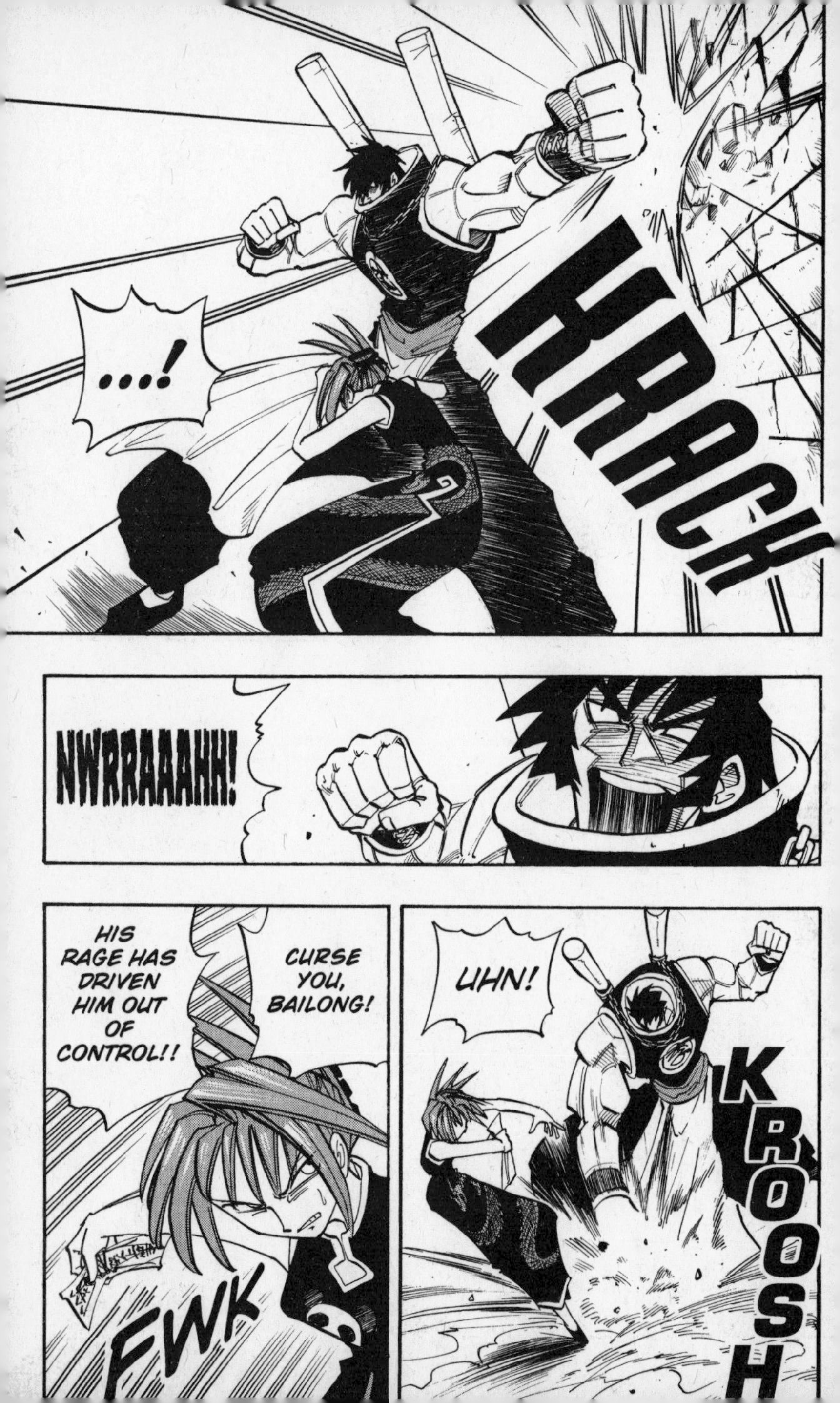
...!
KRACK
NWRRAAAHH!
UHN!
KROOSH
CURSE YOU, BAILONG!
HIS RAGE HAS DRIVEN HIM OUT OF CONTROL!!
FWK

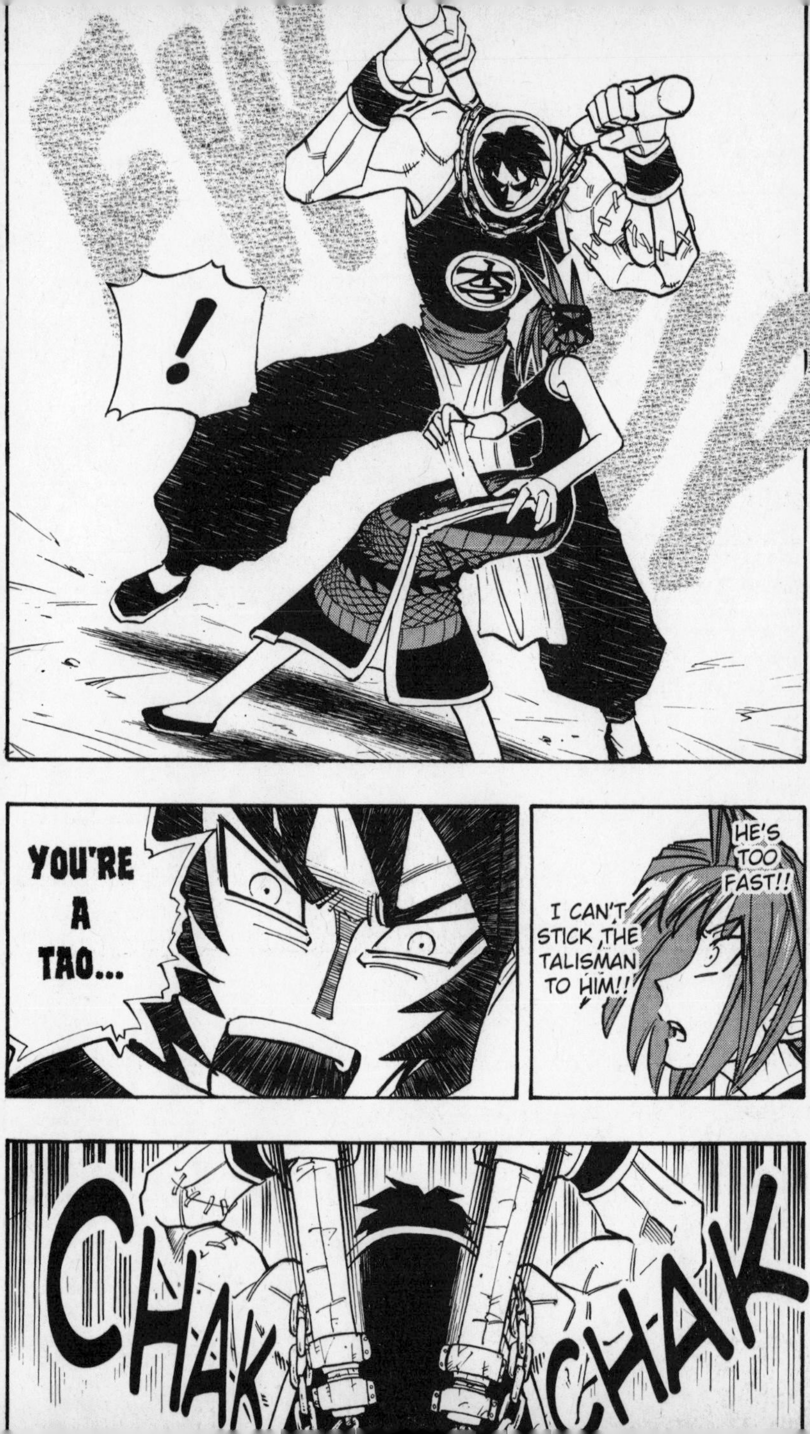
!
HE'S TOO FAST!!
I CAN'T STICK THE TALISMAN TO HIM!!
YOU'RE A TAO...
CHAK
CHAK

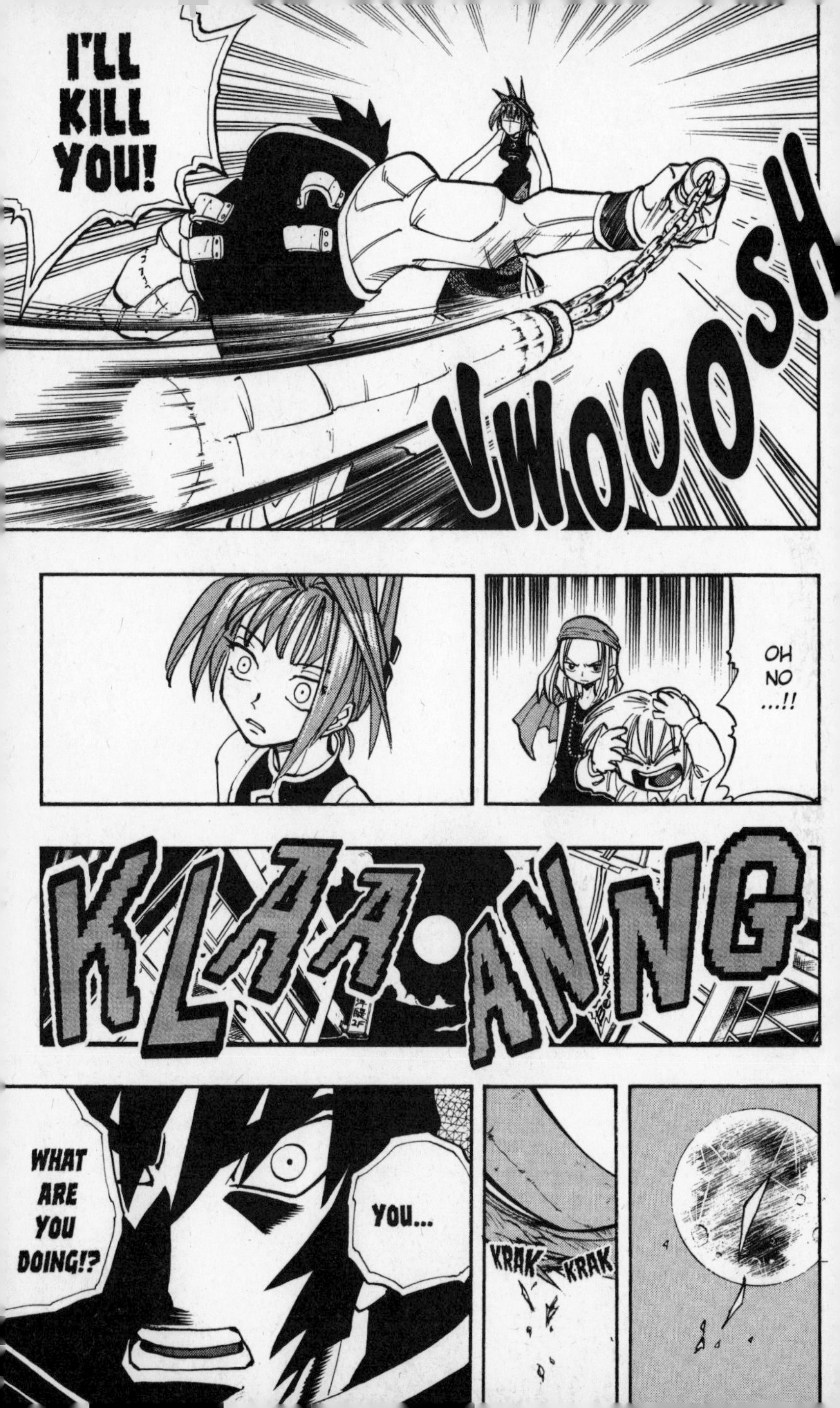
I'LL KILL YOU!
VWOOOSH
OH NO ...!!
KLAA-ANNG
KRAK KRAK
YOU...
WHAT ARE YOU DOING!?

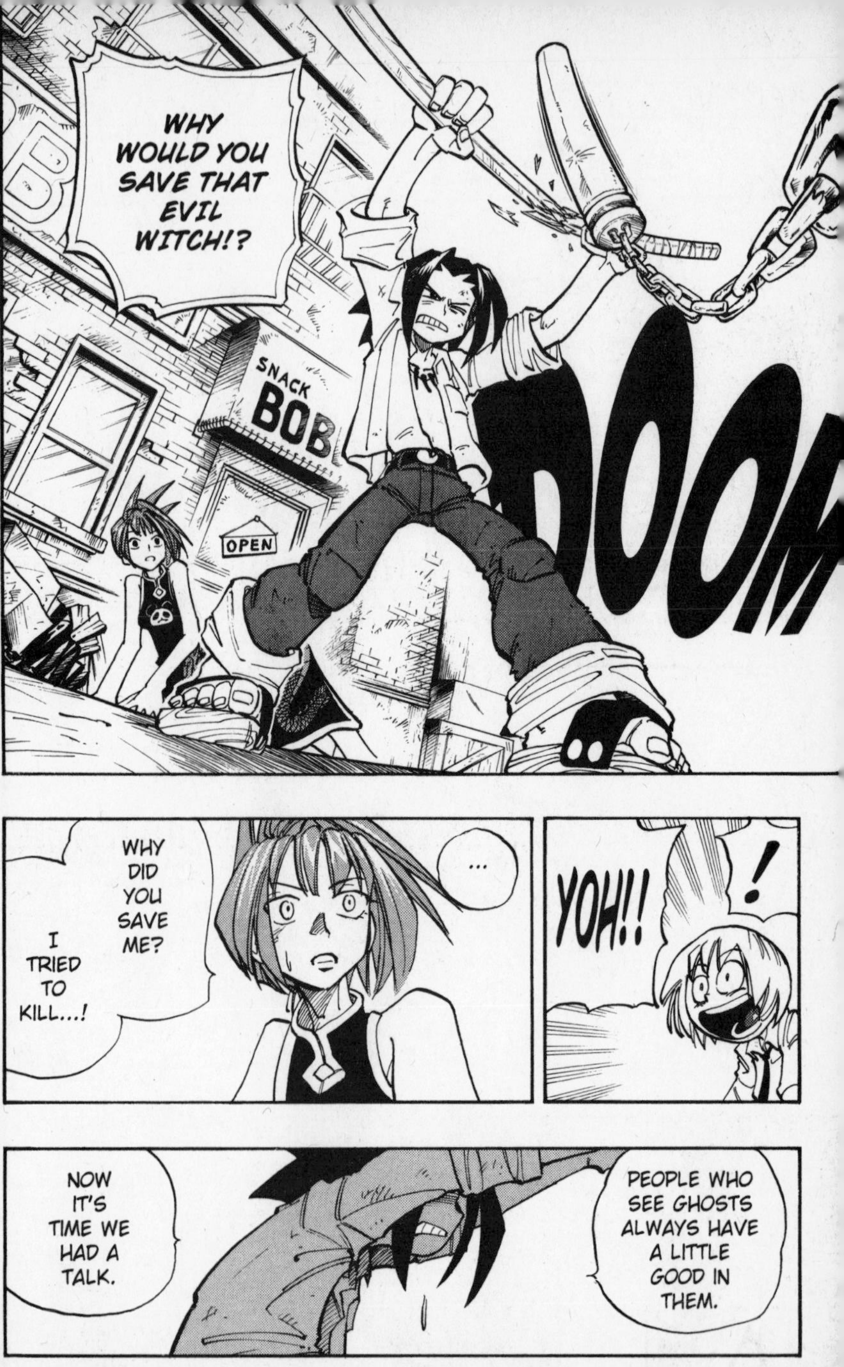
WHY WOULD YOU SAVE THAT EVIL WITCH!?
SNACK BOB
OPEN
DOOM
YOH!!
!
...
WHY DID YOU SAVE ME?
I TRIED TO KILL...!
PEOPLE WHO SEE GHOSTS ALWAYS HAVE A LITTLE GOOD IN THEM.
NOW IT'S TIME WE HAD A TALK.

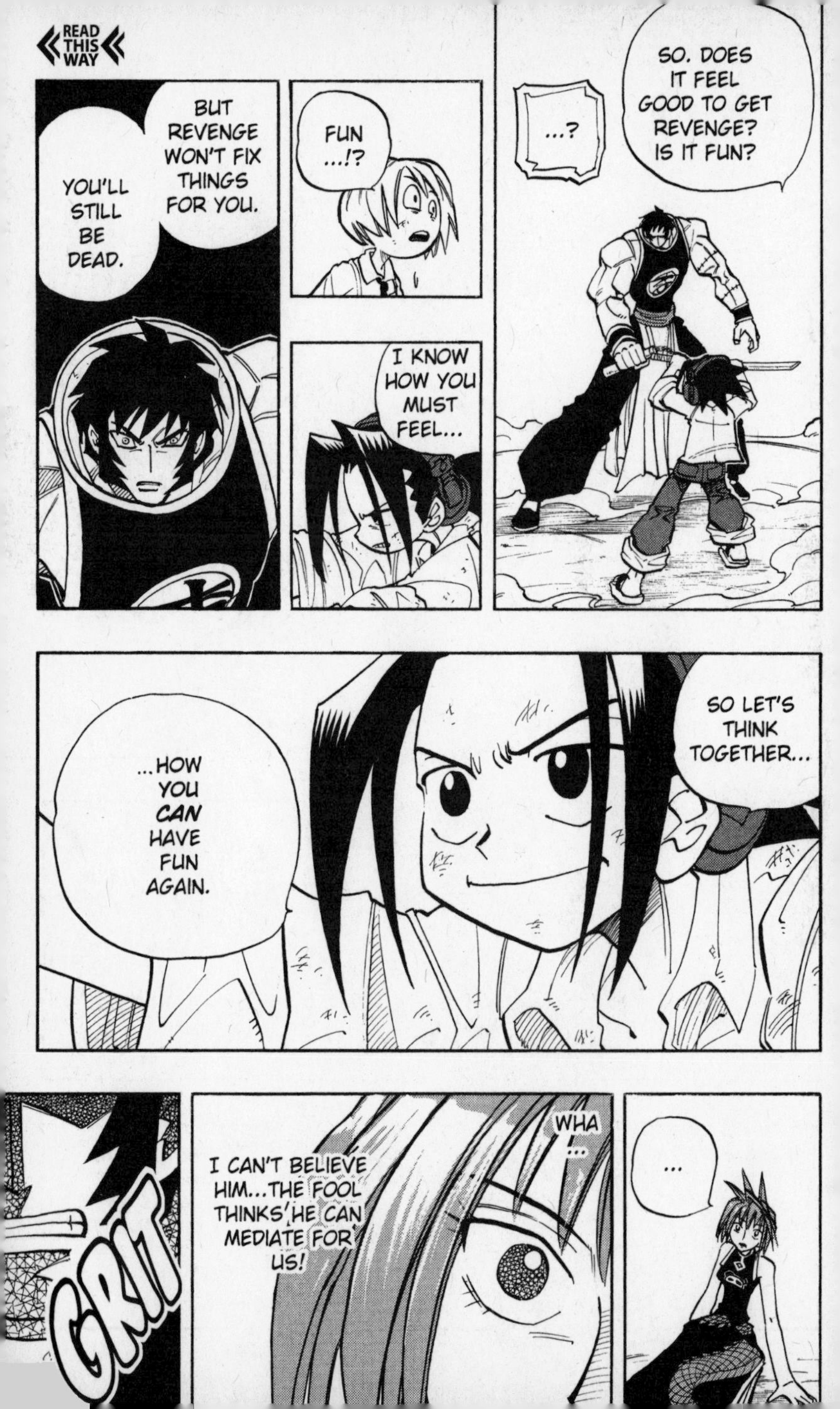
READ THIS WAY
SO. DOES IT FEEL GOOD TO GET REVENGE? IS IT FUN?
...?
FUN ...!?
I KNOW HOW YOU MUST FEEL...
BUT REVENGE WON'T FIX THINGS FOR YOU.
YOU'LL STILL BE DEAD.
SO LET'S THINK TOGETHER...
...HOW YOU *CAN* HAVE FUN AGAIN.
...
WHA ...
I CAN'T BELIEVE HIM...THE FOOL THINKS HE CAN MEDIATE FOR US!
GRIT

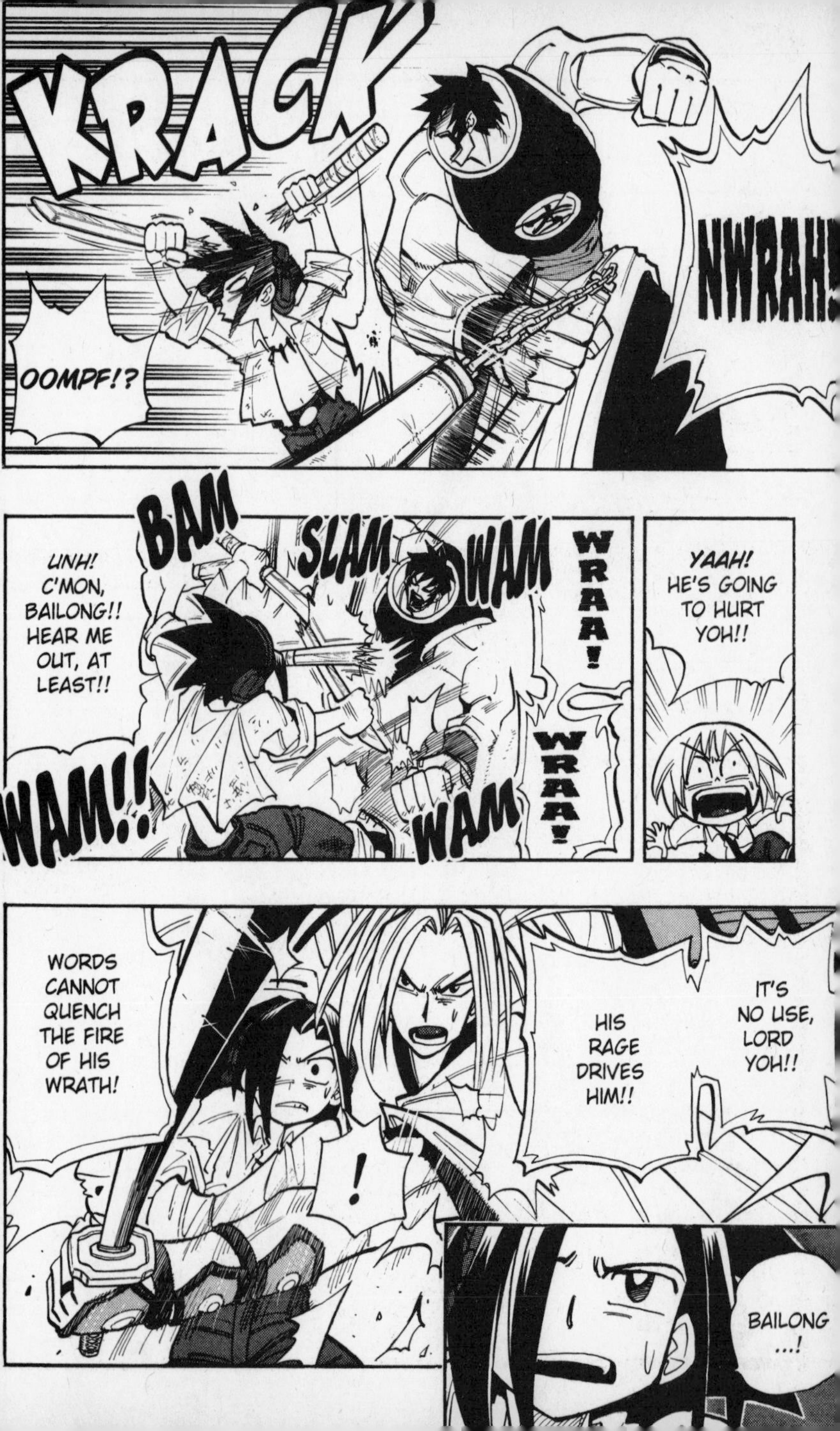
KRACK
NWRAH!
OOMPF!?
YAAH! HE'S GOING TO HURT YOH!!
WRAAA!
WAM
SLAM
BAM
UNH! C'MON, BAILONG!! HEAR ME OUT, AT LEAST!!
WRAAA!
WAM
WAM!!
IT'S NO USE, LORD YOH!!
HIS RAGE DRIVES HIM!!
WORDS CANNOT QUENCH THE FIRE OF HIS WRATH!
!
BAILONG ...!

READ THIS WAY

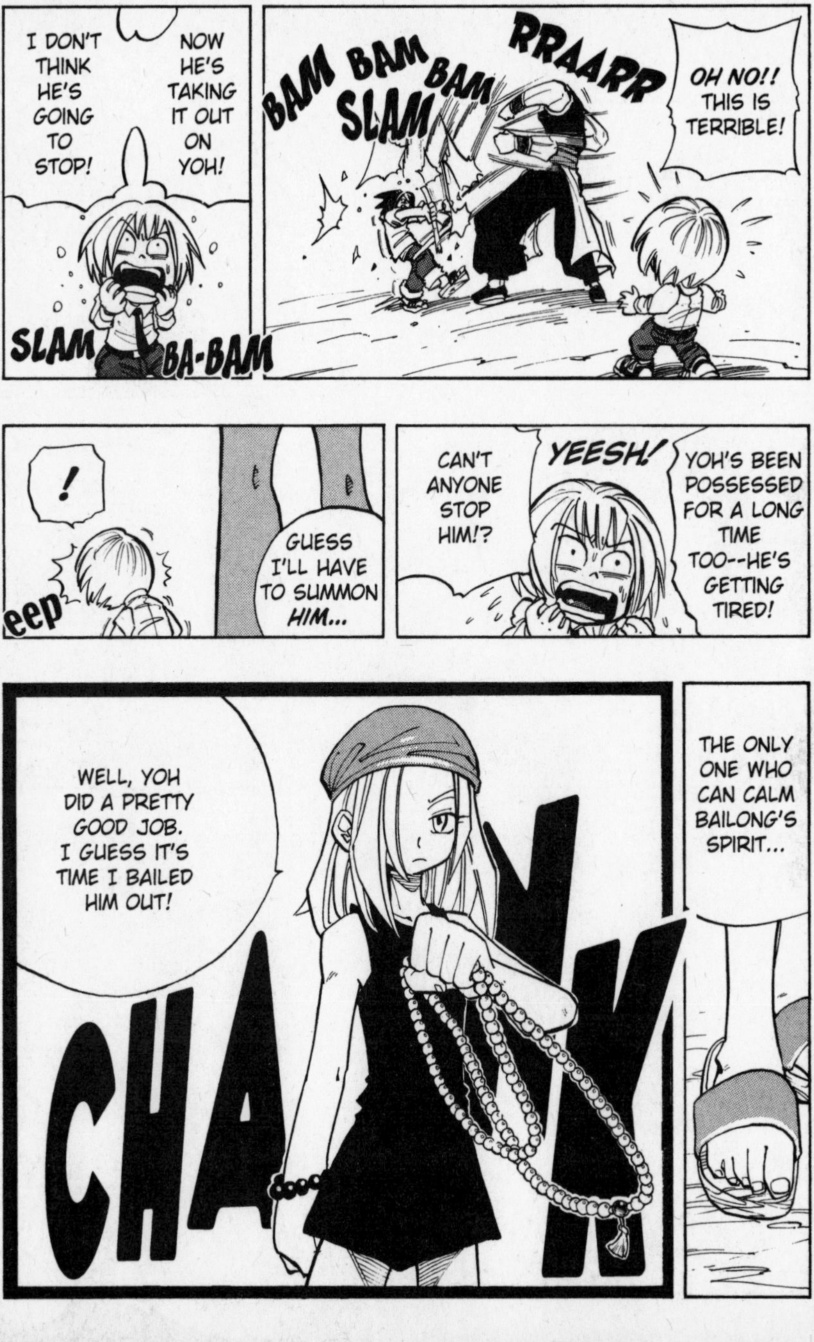
RRAARR
BAM BAM BAM
SLAM
OH NO!! THIS IS TERRIBLE!
NOW HE'S TAKING IT OUT ON YOH!
I DON'T THINK HE'S GOING TO STOP!
SLAM
BA-BAM
YOH'S BEEN POSSESSED FOR A LONG TIME TOO--HE'S GETTING TIRED!
YEESH!
CAN'T ANYONE STOP HIM!?
GUESS I'LL HAVE TO SUMMON HIM...
!
eep
THE ONLY ONE WHO CAN CALM BAILONG'S SPIRIT...
WELL, YOH DID A PRETTY GOOD JOB. I GUESS IT'S TIME I BAILED HIM OUT!
CHAK

SHAMAN KING CHARACTER FILE No.8

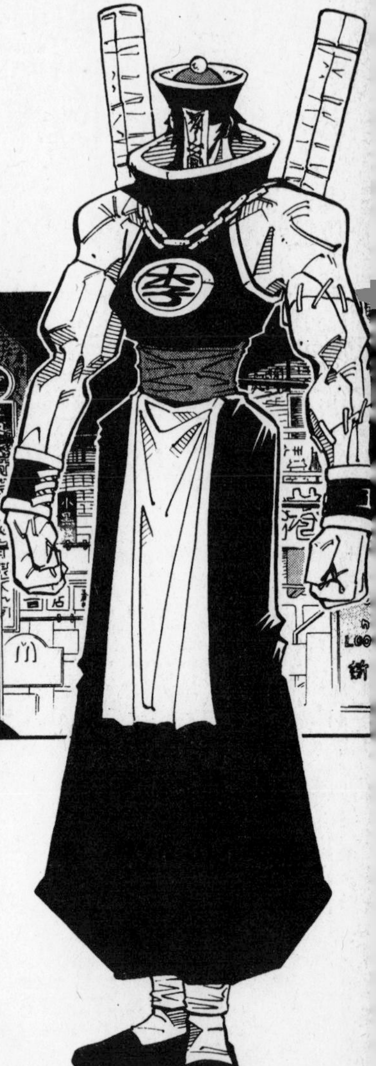

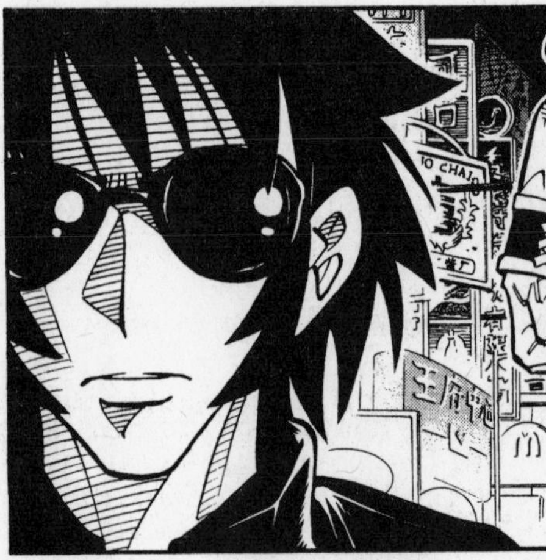

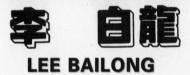

李 白龍

LEE BAILONG

- Age (at time of death): 30
- Birthdate: November 29, 1948
- Star Sign: Sagittarius
- Blood Type: B
- In Chinese, "Bailong" means "white dragon." In Japanese, his name is pronounced "Pairon" or "Pyron."

Reincarnation 16:
Raising the Dead

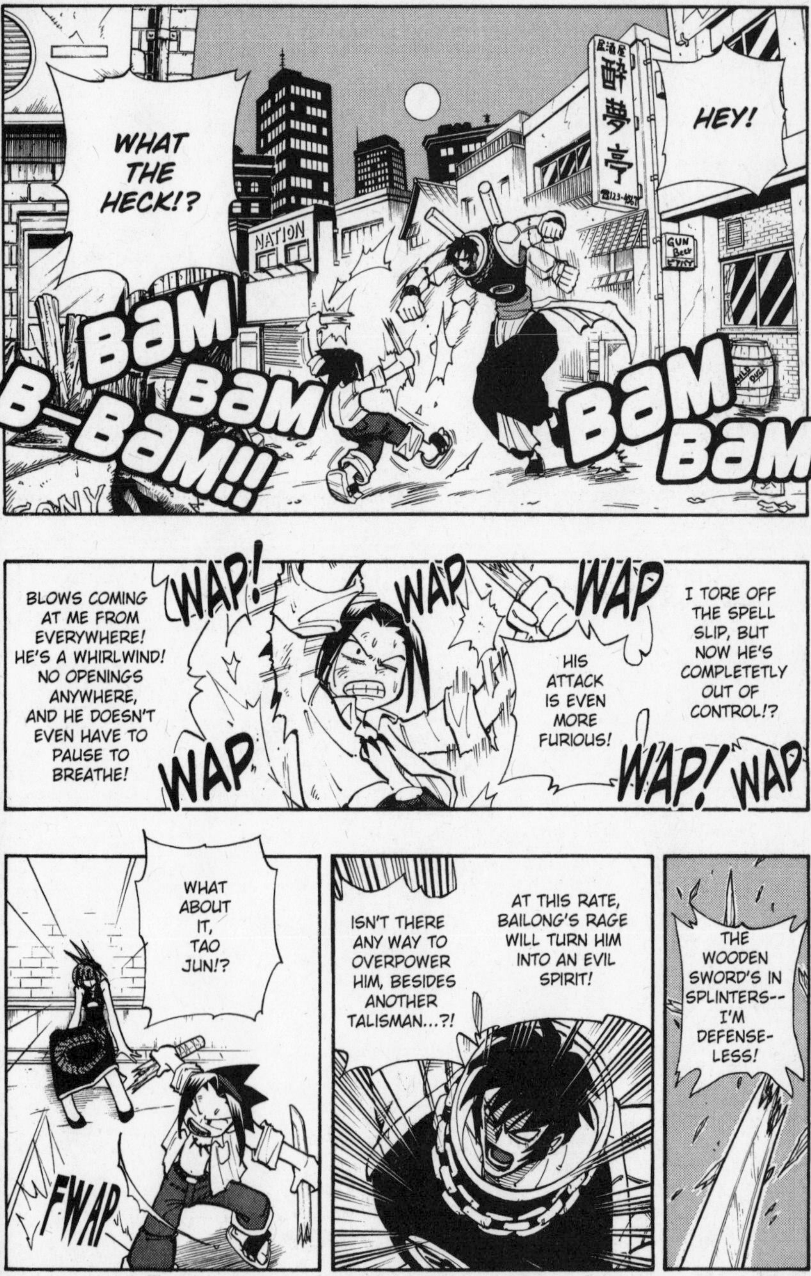
HEY!
WHAT THE HECK!?
BAM BAM
BAM BAM B-BAM!!
I TORE OFF THE SPELL SLIP, BUT NOW HE'S COMPLETETLY OUT OF CONTROL!?
WAP! WAP
WAP
HIS ATTACK IS EVEN MORE FURIOUS!
WAP
WAP!
BLOWS COMING AT ME FROM EVERYWHERE! HE'S A WHIRLWIND! NO OPENINGS ANYWHERE, AND HE DOESN'T EVEN HAVE TO PAUSE TO BREATHE!
WAP
THE WOODEN SWORD'S IN SPLINTERS-- I'M DEFENSE-LESS!
AT THIS RATE, BAILONG'S RAGE WILL TURN HIM INTO AN EVIL SPIRIT!
ISN'T THERE ANY WAY TO OVERPOWER HIM, BESIDES ANOTHER TALISMAN...?!
WHAT ABOUT IT, TAO JUN!?
FWAP

READ THIS WAY

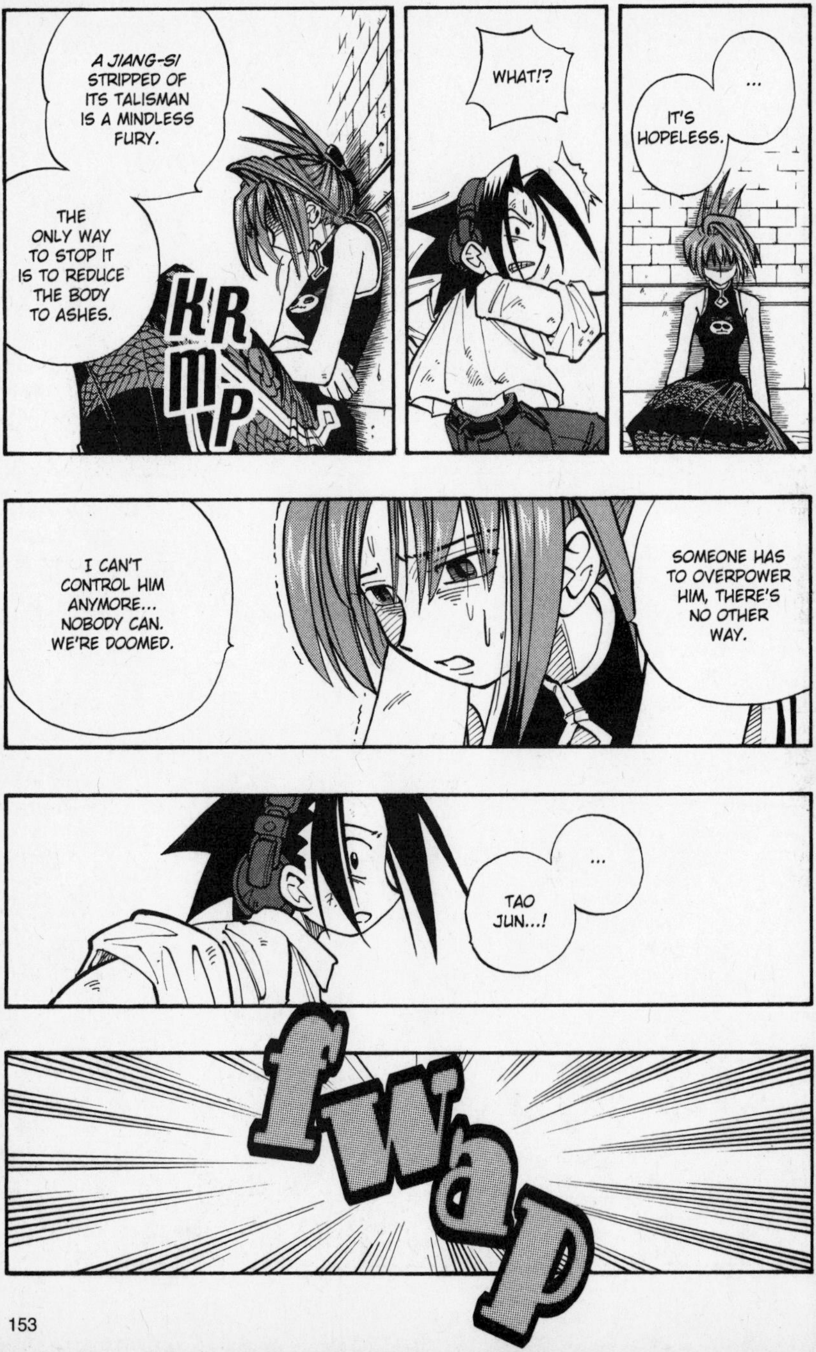
...
IT'S HOPELESS.
WHAT!?
A JIANG-SI STRIPPED OF ITS TALISMAN IS A MINDLESS FURY.
THE ONLY WAY TO STOP IT IS TO REDUCE THE BODY TO ASHES.
KRmP
SOMEONE HAS TO OVERPOWER HIM, THERE'S NO OTHER WAY.
I CAN'T CONTROL HIM ANYMORE... NOBODY CAN. WE'RE DOOMED.
...
TAO JUN...!
fwap

READ THIS WAY

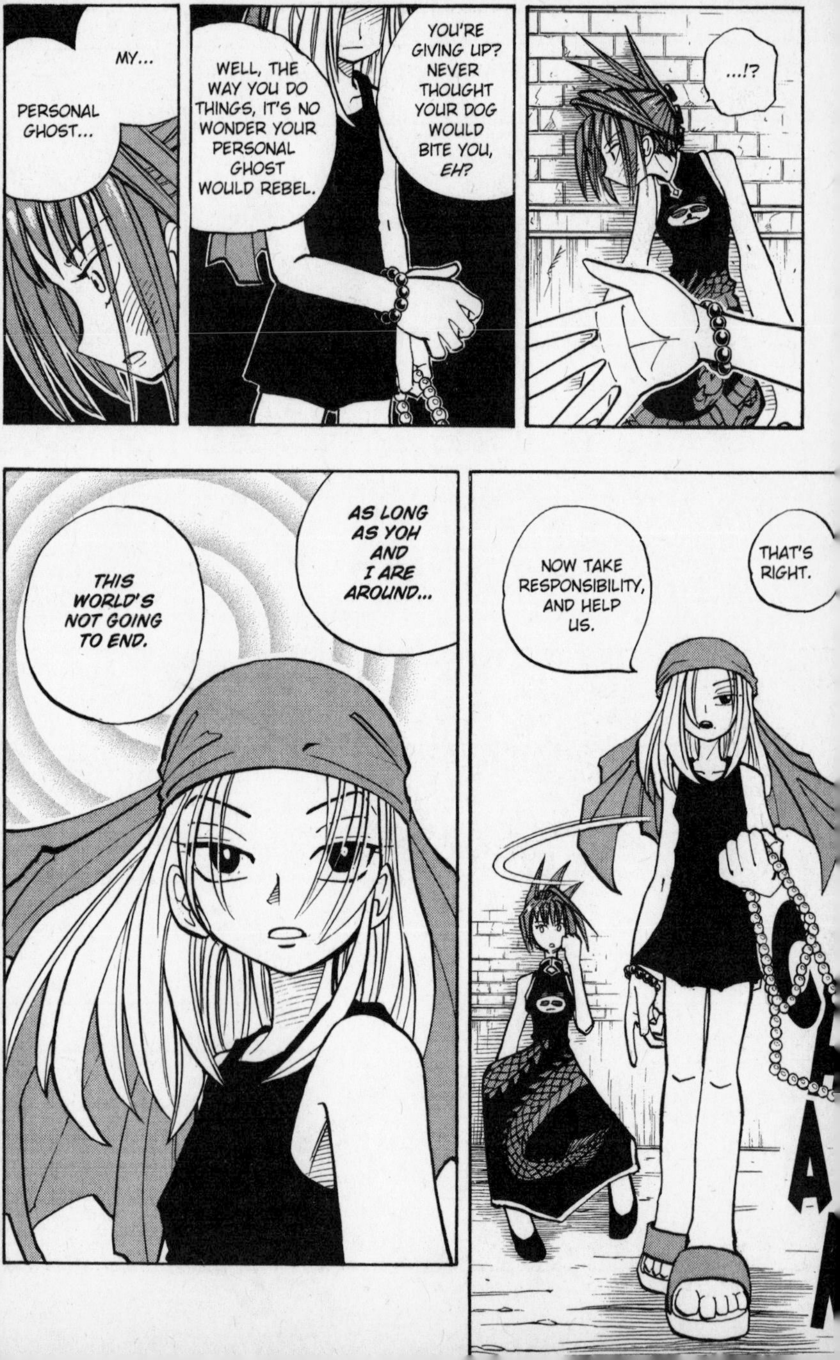
...!?
YOU'RE GIVING UP? NEVER THOUGHT YOUR DOG WOULD BITE YOU, EH?
WELL, THE WAY YOU DO THINGS, IT'S NO WONDER YOUR PERSONAL GHOST WOULD REBEL.
MY...
PERSONAL GHOST...
THAT'S RIGHT.
NOW TAKE RESPONSIBILITY, AND HELP US.
AS LONG AS YOH AND I ARE AROUND...
THIS WORLD'S NOT GOING TO END.

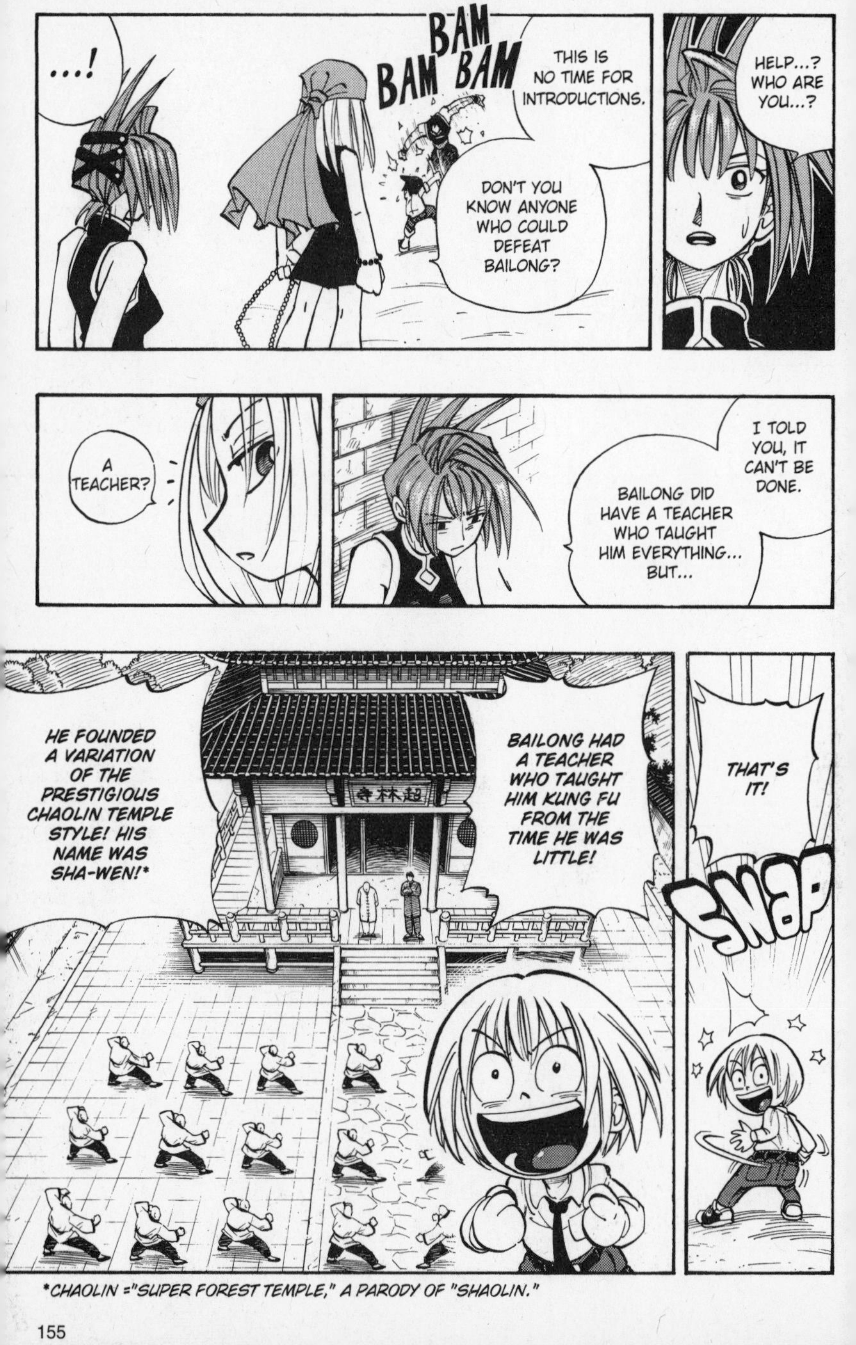
HELP...? WHO ARE YOU...?
BAM BAM BAM
THIS IS NO TIME FOR INTRODUCTIONS.
DON'T YOU KNOW ANYONE WHO COULD DEFEAT BAILONG?
...!
I TOLD YOU, IT CAN'T BE DONE.
BAILONG DID HAVE A TEACHER WHO TAUGHT HIM EVERYTHING... BUT...
A TEACHER?
THAT'S IT!
SNAP
BAILONG HAD A TEACHER WHO TAUGHT HIM KUNG FU FROM THE TIME HE WAS LITTLE!
超林寺
HE FOUNDED A VARIATION OF THE PRESTIGIOUS CHAOLIN TEMPLE STYLE! HIS NAME WAS SHA-WEN!*

*CHAOLIN ="SUPER FOREST TEMPLE," A PARODY OF "SHAOLIN."

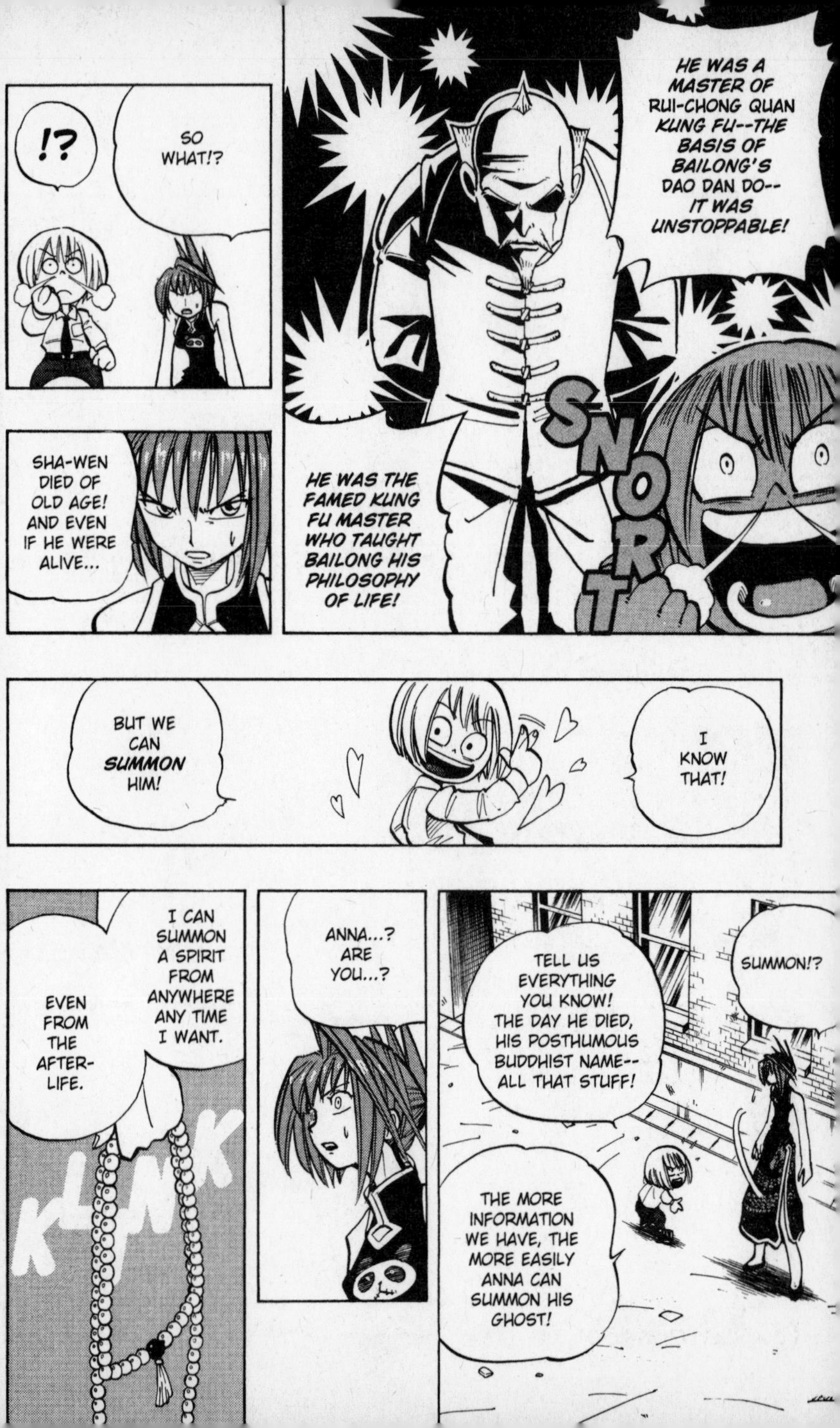
HE WAS A MASTER OF RUI-CHONG QUAN KUNG FU--THE BASIS OF BAILONG'S DAO DAN DO--IT WAS UNSTOPPABLE!
SNORT
HE WAS THE FAMED KUNG FU MASTER WHO TAUGHT BAILONG HIS PHILOSOPHY OF LIFE!
SO WHAT!?
!?
SHA-WEN DIED OF OLD AGE! AND EVEN IF HE WERE ALIVE...
I KNOW THAT!
BUT WE CAN SUMMON HIM!
SUMMON!?
TELL US EVERYTHING YOU KNOW! THE DAY HE DIED, HIS POSTHUMOUS BUDDHIST NAME--ALL THAT STUFF!
THE MORE INFORMATION WE HAVE, THE MORE EASILY ANNA CAN SUMMON HIS GHOST!
ANNA...? ARE YOU...?
I CAN SUMMON A SPIRIT FROM ANYWHERE ANY TIME I WANT.
EVEN FROM THE AFTER-LIFE.
KLINK

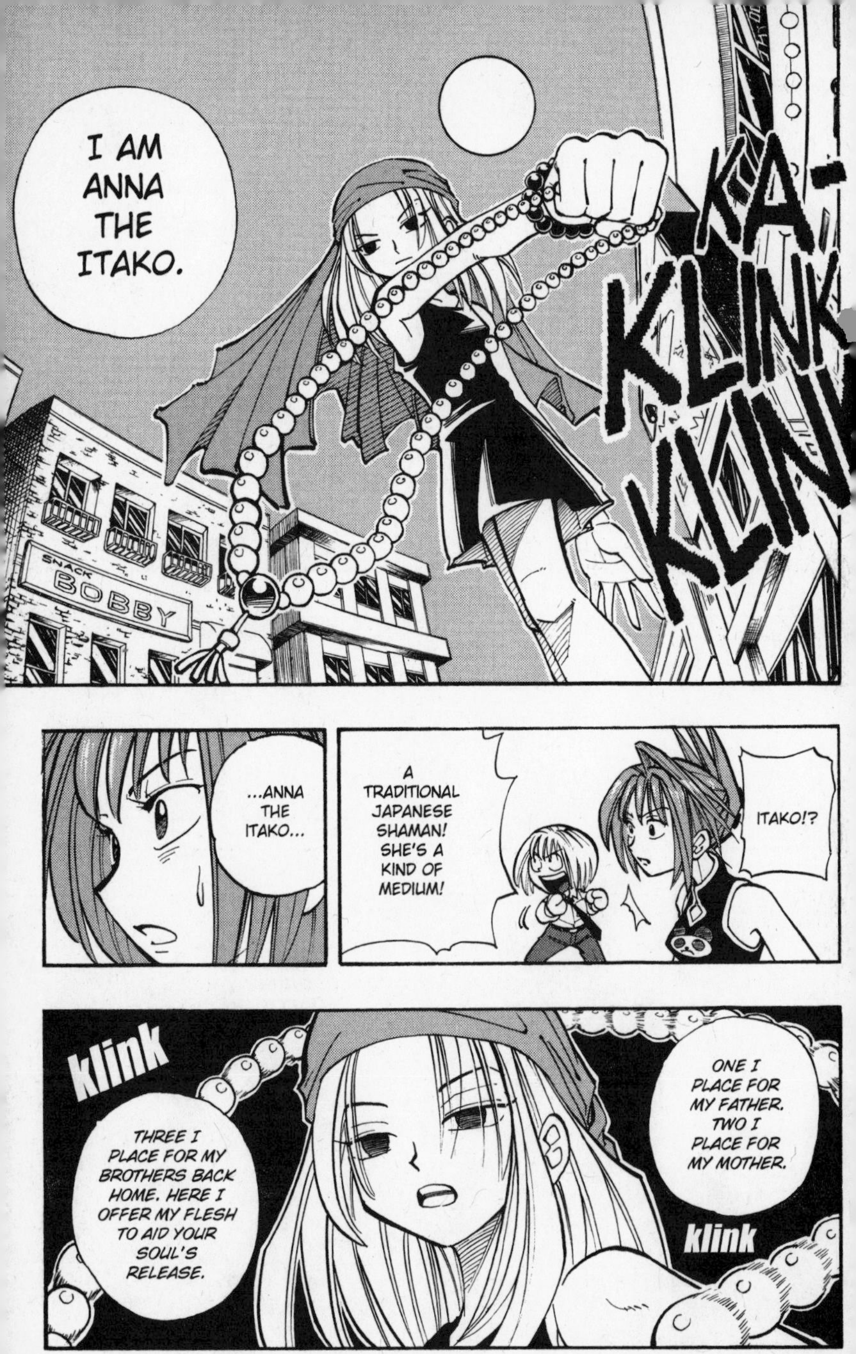

KA-KLINK KLINK
I AM ANNA THE ITAKO.
ITAKO!?
A TRADITIONAL JAPANESE SHAMAN! SHE'S A KIND OF MEDIUM!
...ANNA THE ITAKO...
klink
ONE I PLACE FOR MY FATHER. TWO I PLACE FOR MY MOTHER.
klink
THREE I PLACE FOR MY BROTHERS BACK HOME. HERE I OFFER MY FLESH TO AID YOUR SOUL'S RELEASE.
SNACK BOBBY

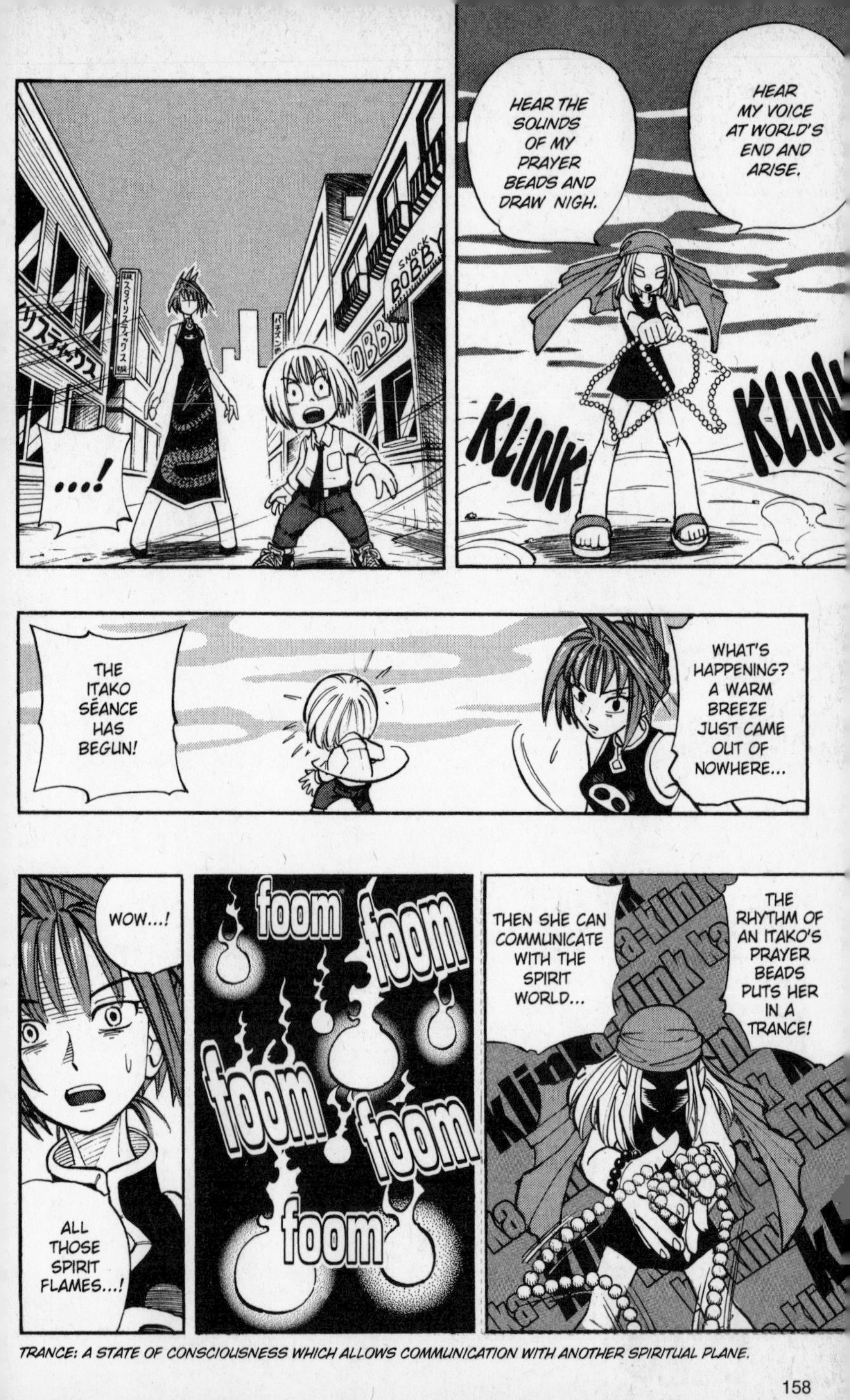
HEAR MY VOICE AT WORLD'S END AND ARISE.
HEAR THE SOUNDS OF MY PRAYER BEADS AND DRAW NIGH.
KLINK
KLINK
SNACK BOBBY
...!
WHAT'S HAPPENING? A WARM BREEZE JUST CAME OUT OF NOWHERE...
THE ITAKO SÉANCE HAS BEGUN!
THE RHYTHM OF AN ITAKO'S PRAYER BEADS PUTS HER IN A TRANCE!
THEN SHE CAN COMMUNICATE WITH THE SPIRIT WORLD...
ka-klink
foom
foom
foom
foom
foom
WOW...!
ALL THOSE SPIRIT FLAMES...!

TRANCE: A STATE OF CONSCIOUSNESS WHICH ALLOWS COMMUNICATION WITH ANOTHER SPIRITUAL PLANE.

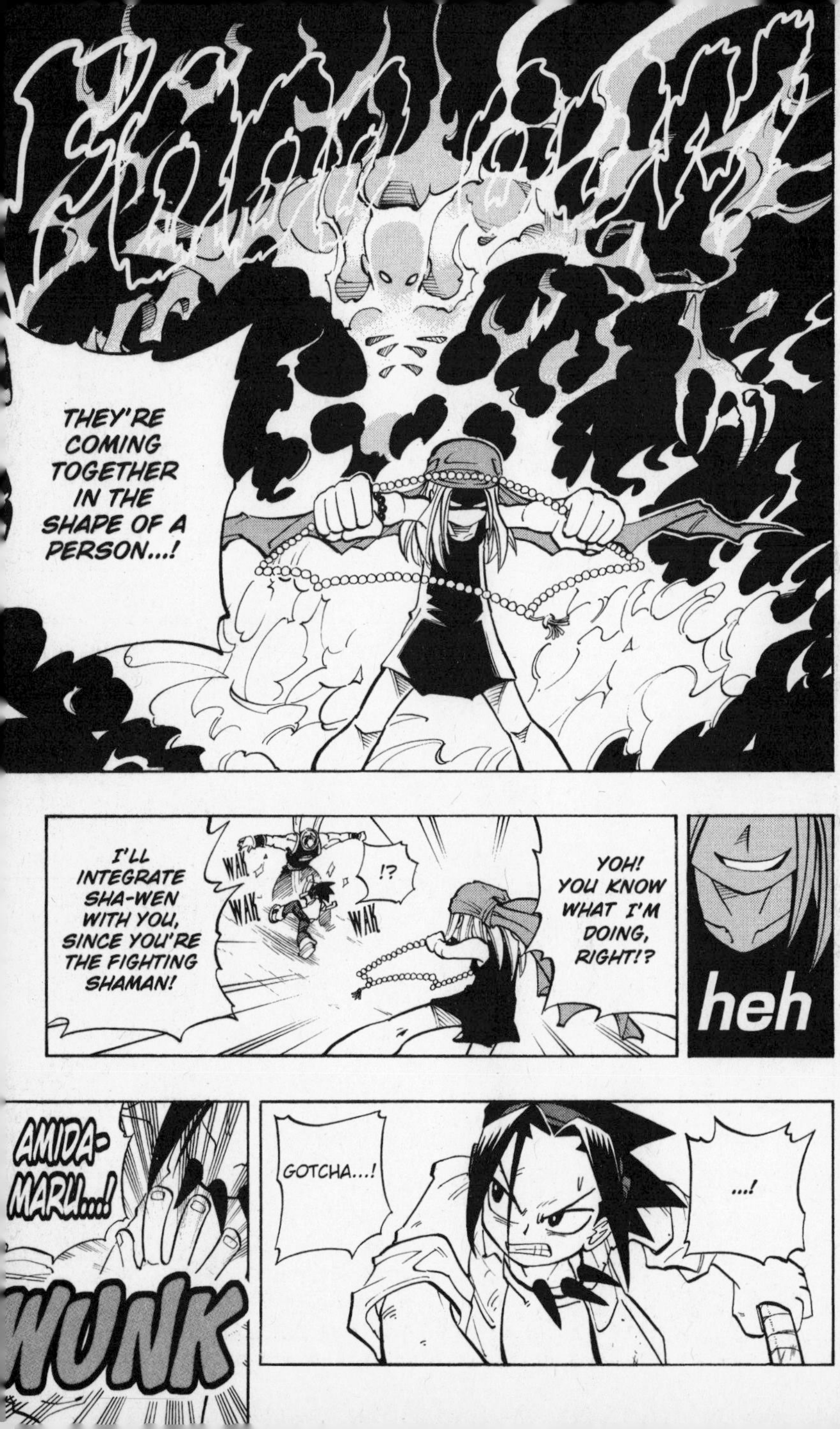
THEY'RE COMING TOGETHER IN THE SHAPE OF A PERSON...!
heh
YOH! YOU KNOW WHAT I'M DOING, RIGHT!?
!?
WAK
WAK
WAK
I'LL INTEGRATE SHA-WEN WITH YOU, SINCE YOU'RE THE FIGHTING SHAMAN!
...!
GOTCHA...!
AMIDA-MARU...!
WUNK

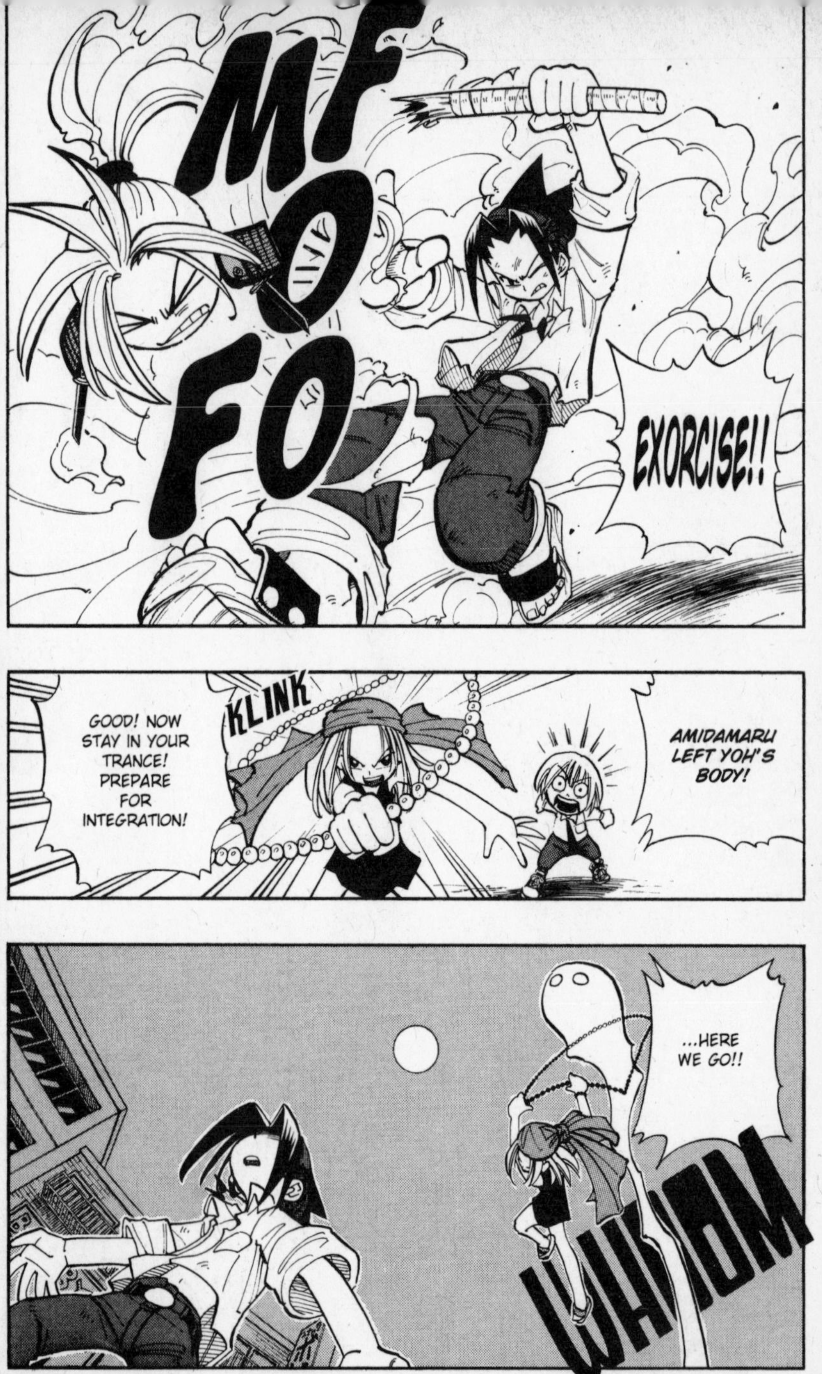
MF
O
FO
EXORCISE!!
AMIDAMARU LEFT YOH'S BODY!
KLINK
GOOD! NOW STAY IN YOUR TRANCE! PREPARE FOR INTEGRATION!
...HERE WE GO!!
WHOOM

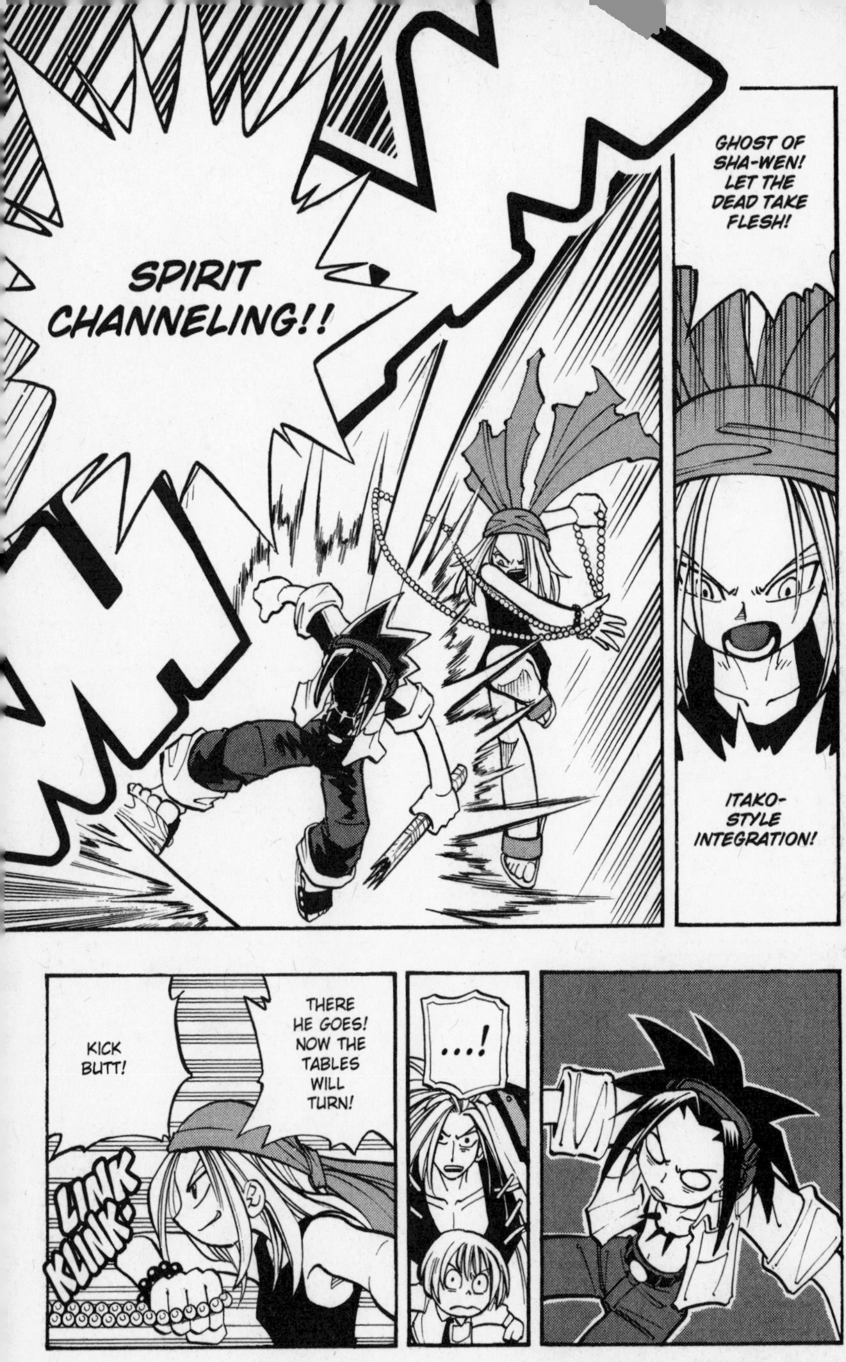
GHOST OF SHA-WEN! LET THE DEAD TAKE FLESH!
ITAKO-STYLE INTEGRATION!
SPIRIT CHANNELING!!
...!
THERE HE GOES! NOW THE TABLES WILL TURN!
KICK BUTT!
CLINK KLINK!

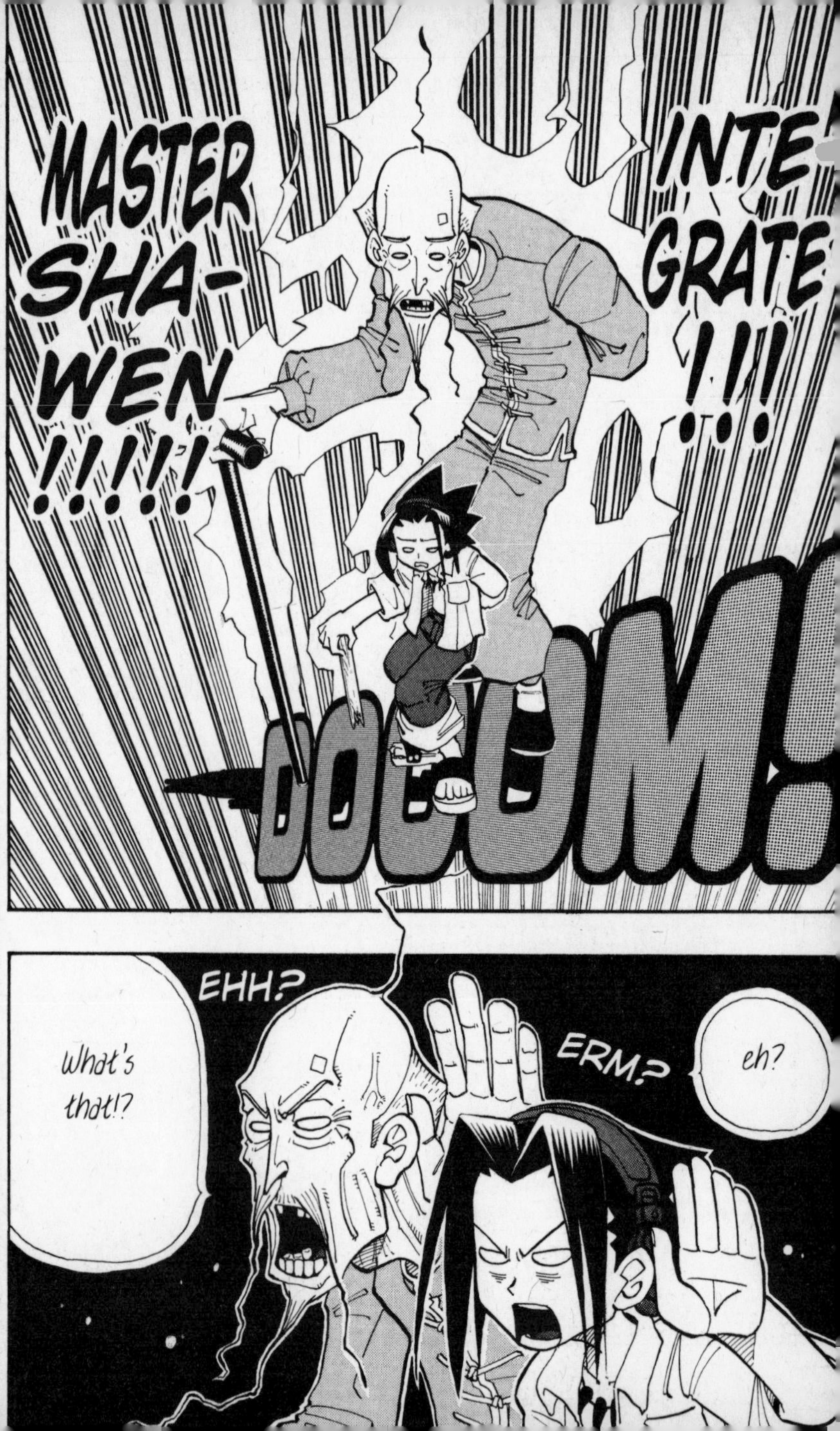
INTE-GRATE!!!
MASTER SHA-WEN!!!!!
DOOOM!!
eh?
ERM?
EHH?
What's that!?

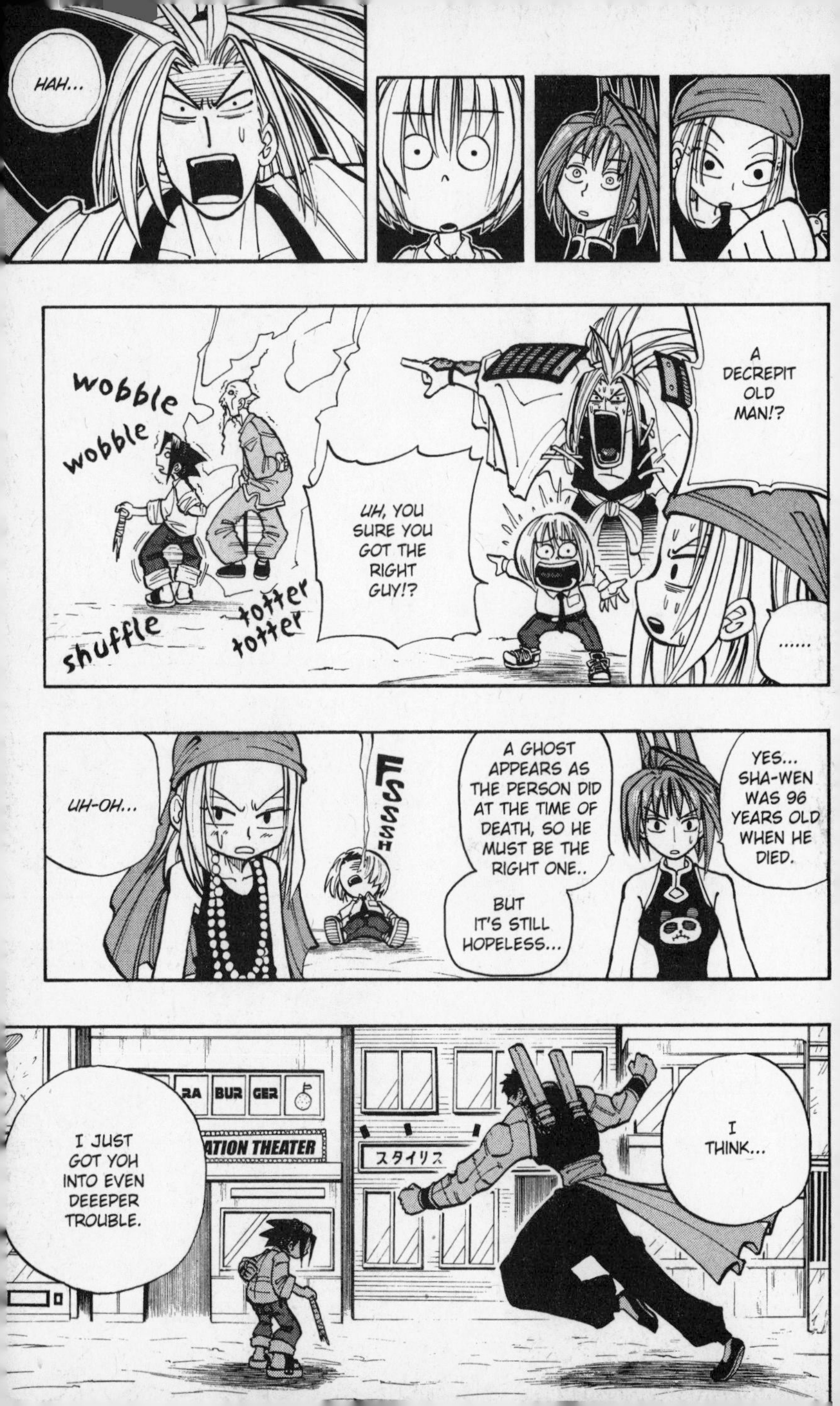
HAH...
A DECREPIT OLD MAN!?
......
UH, YOU SURE YOU GOT THE RIGHT GUY!?
totter totter
wobble wobble
shuffle
YES... SHA-WEN WAS 96 YEARS OLD WHEN HE DIED.
A GHOST APPEARS AS THE PERSON DID AT THE TIME OF DEATH, SO HE MUST BE THE RIGHT ONE..
BUT IT'S STILL HOPELESS...
FSSSH
UH-OH...
I THINK...
スタイリス
RA BUR GER
ATION THEATER
I JUST GOT YOH INTO EVEN DEEEPER TROUBLE.

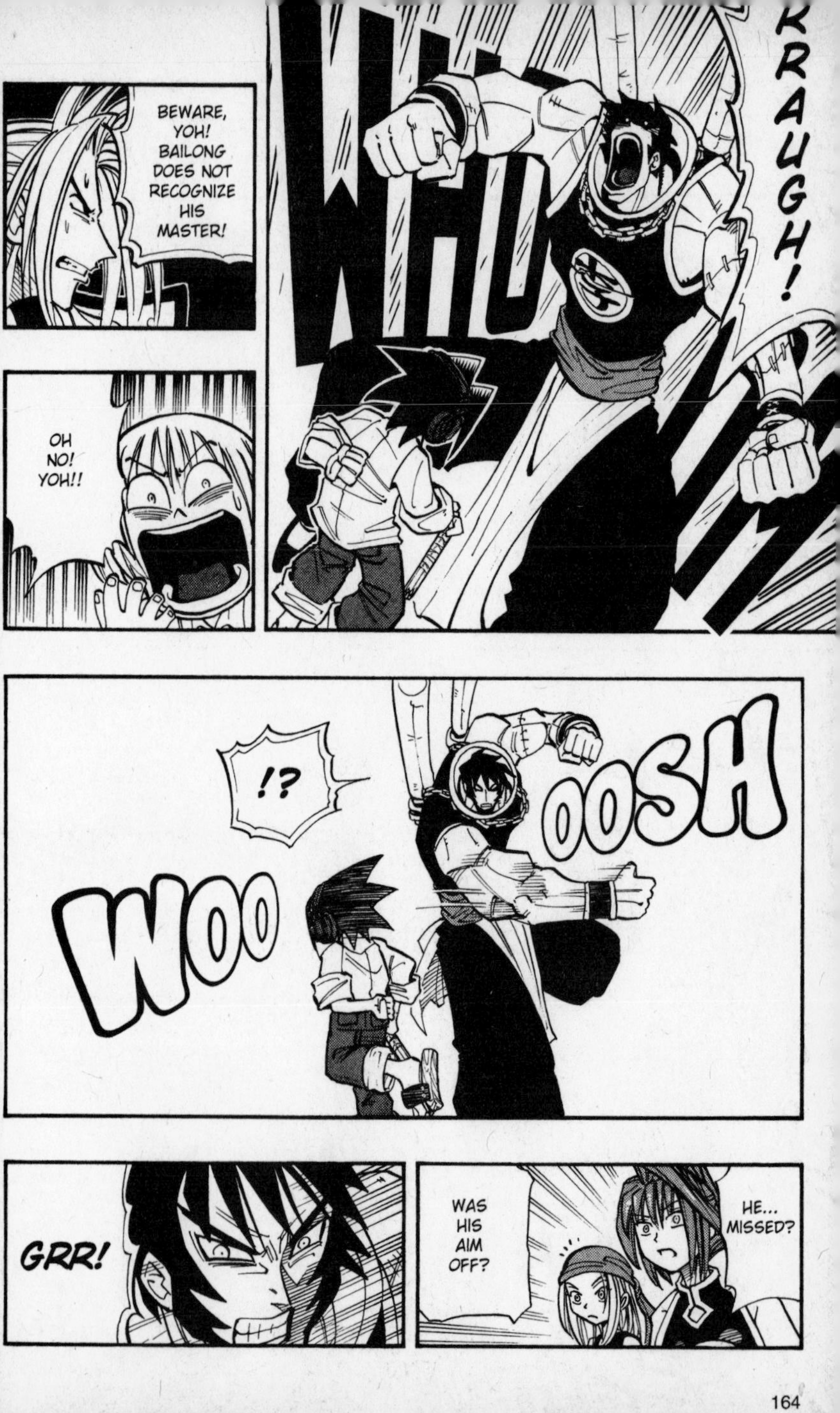
KRAUGH!
BEWARE, YOH! BAILONG DOES NOT RECOGNIZE HIS MASTER!
OH NO! YOH!!
!?
WOO
OOSH
HE... MISSED?
WAS HIS AIM OFF?
GRR!

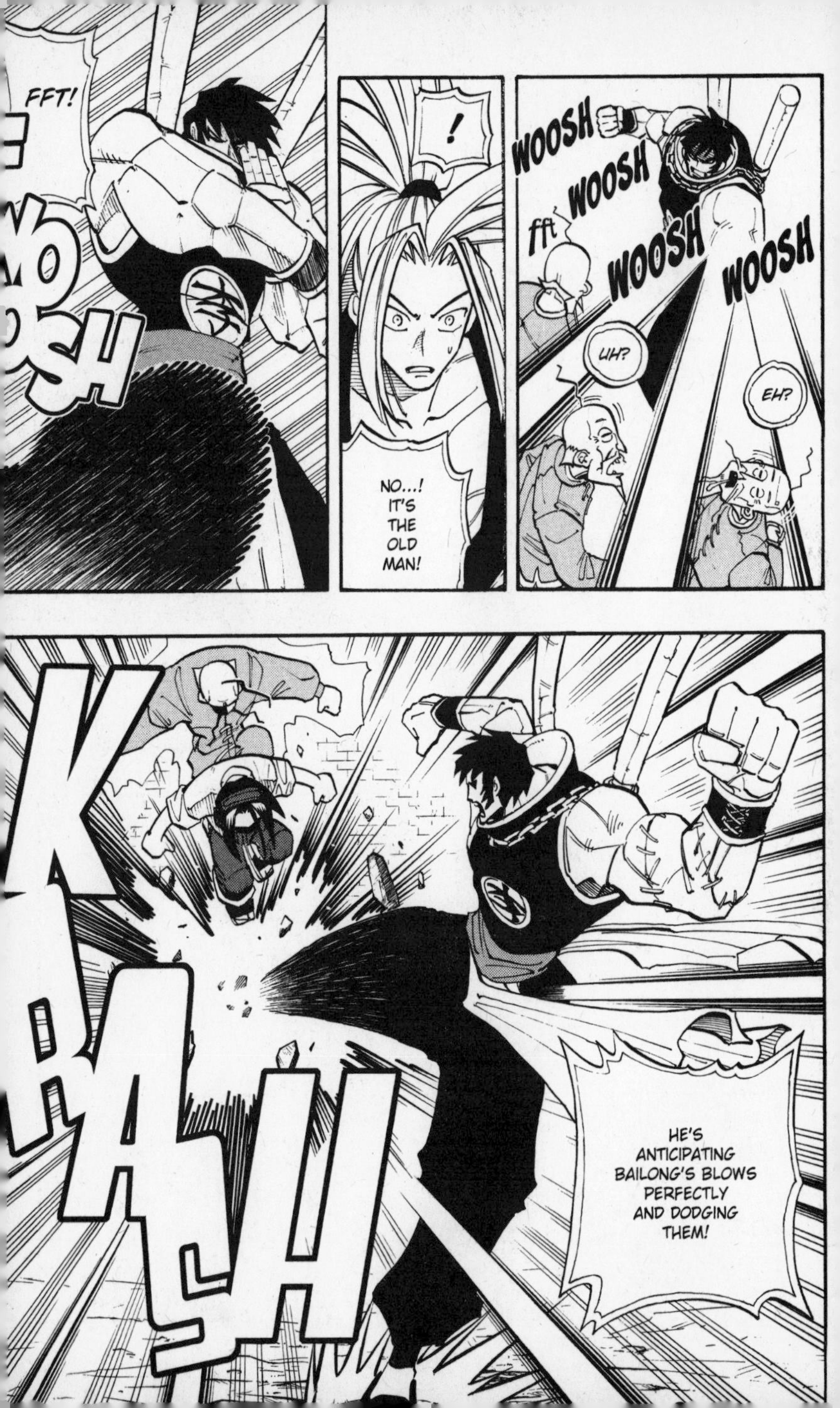
WOOSH
WOOSH
fft
WOOSH
WOOSH
UH?
EH?
!
NO...! IT'S THE OLD MAN!
FFT!
KRASH
HE'S ANTICIPATING BAILONG'S BLOWS PERFECTLY AND DODGING THEM!

READ THIS WAY

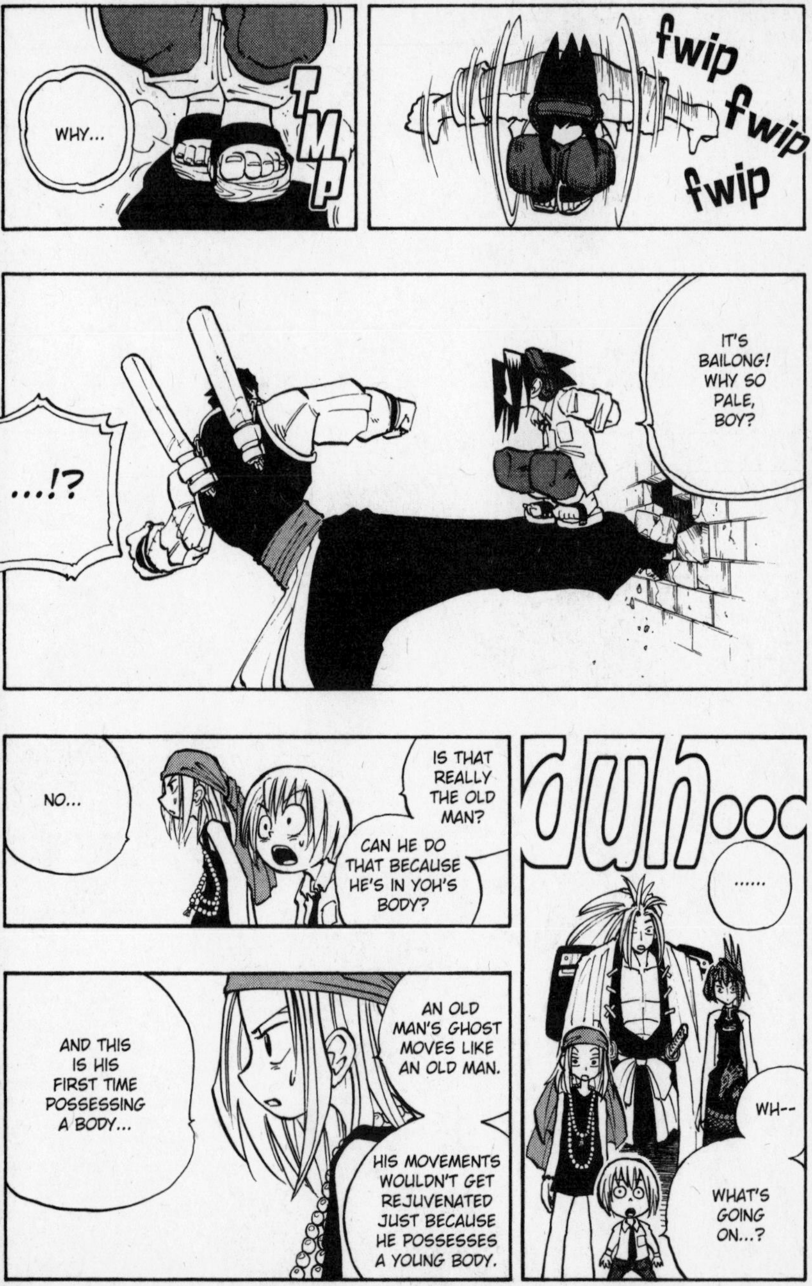
fwip
fwip
fwip
TMP
WHY...
IT'S BAILONG! WHY SO PALE, BOY?
...!?
duhooo
......
WH--
WHAT'S GOING ON...?
IS THAT REALLY THE OLD MAN?
CAN HE DO THAT BECAUSE HE'S IN YOH'S BODY?
NO...
AN OLD MAN'S GHOST MOVES LIKE AN OLD MAN.
HIS MOVEMENTS WOULDN'T GET REJUVENATED JUST BECAUSE HE POSSESSES A YOUNG BODY.
AND THIS IS HIS FIRST TIME POSSESSING A BODY...

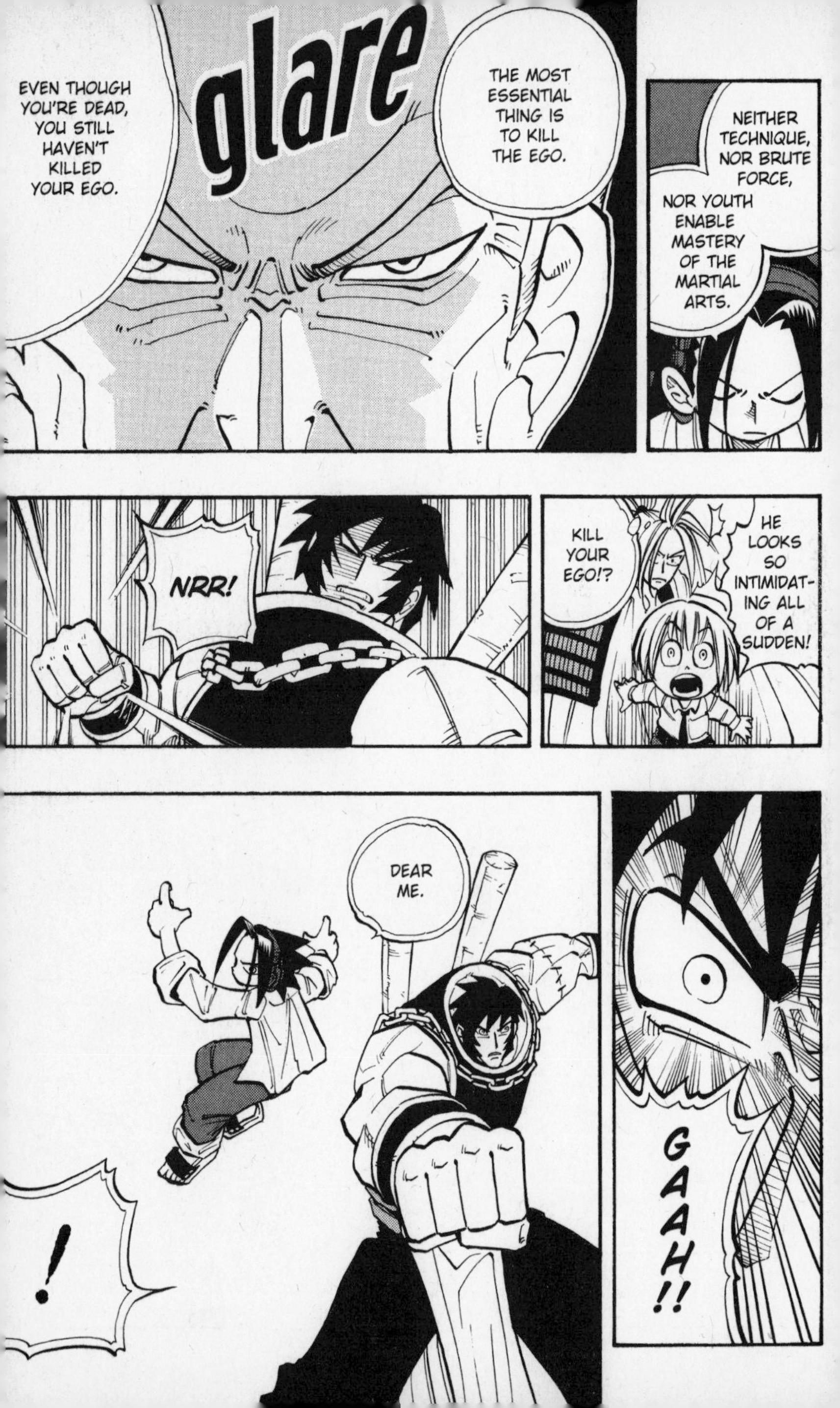
NEITHER TECHNIQUE, NOR BRUTE FORCE,
NOR YOUTH ENABLE MASTERY OF THE MARTIAL ARTS.
THE MOST ESSENTIAL THING IS TO KILL THE EGO.
glare
EVEN THOUGH YOU'RE DEAD, YOU STILL HAVEN'T KILLED YOUR EGO.
HE LOOKS SO INTIMIDATING ALL OF A SUDDEN!
KILL YOUR EGO!?
NRR!
GAAH!!
DEAR ME.
!

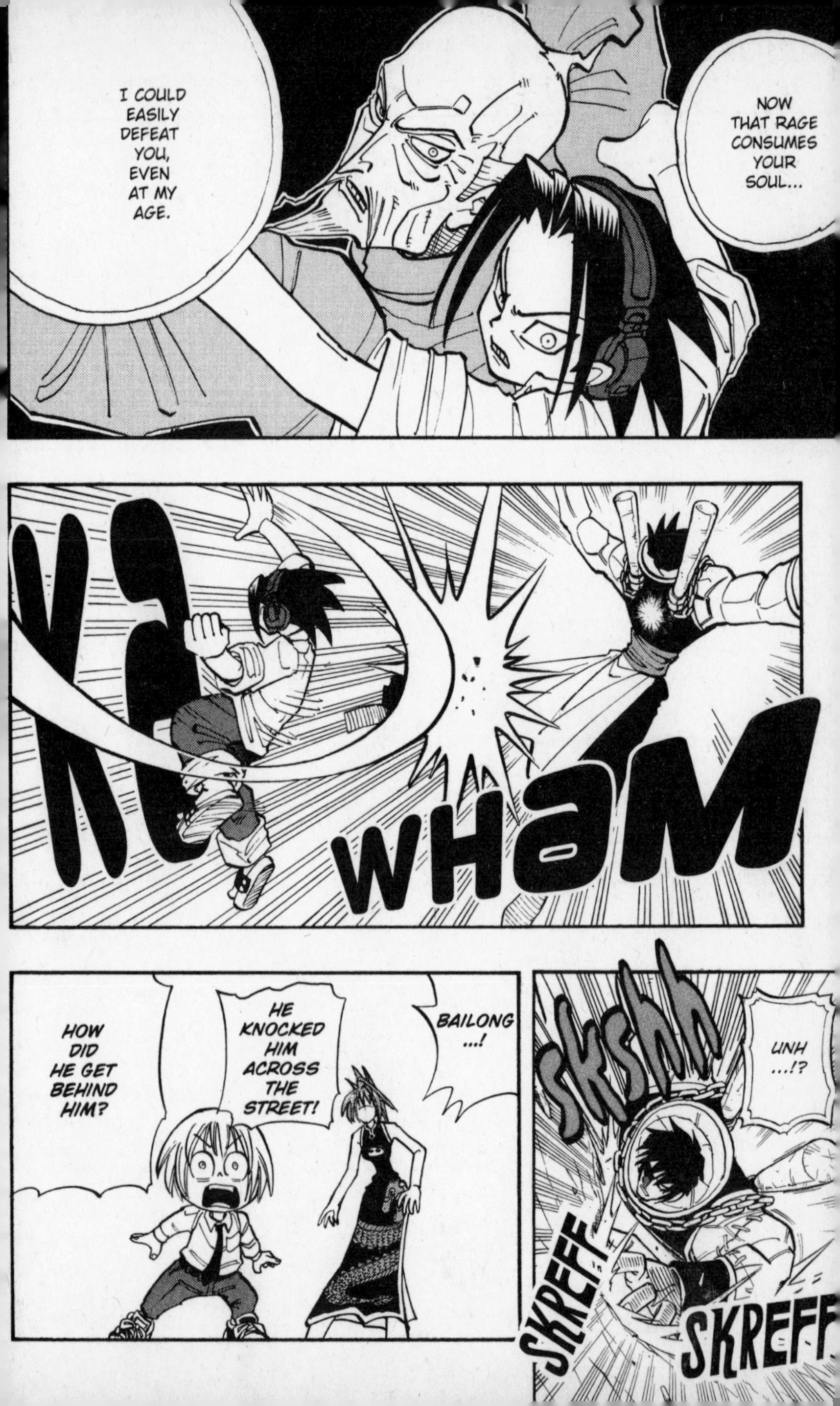
NOW THAT RAGE CONSUMES YOUR SOUL...
I COULD EASILY DEFEAT YOU, EVEN AT MY AGE.
WHAM
UNH ...!?
SKSHH
SKREFF
SKREFF
BAILONG ...!
HE KNOCKED HIM ACROSS THE STREET!
HOW DID HE GET BEHIND HIM?

READ THIS WAY

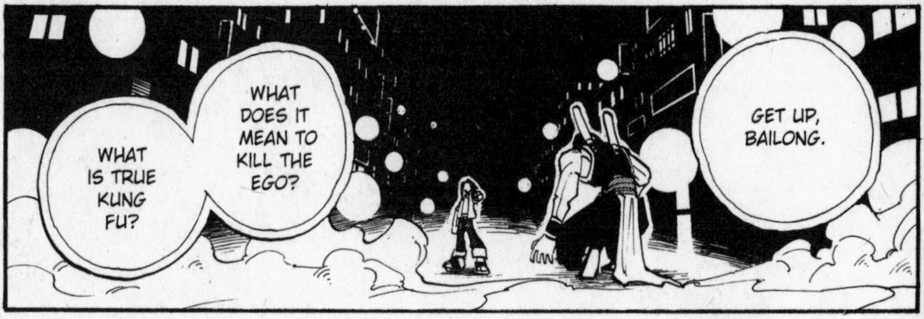
GET UP, BAILONG.
WHAT DOES IT MEAN TO KILL THE EGO?
WHAT IS TRUE KUNG FU?

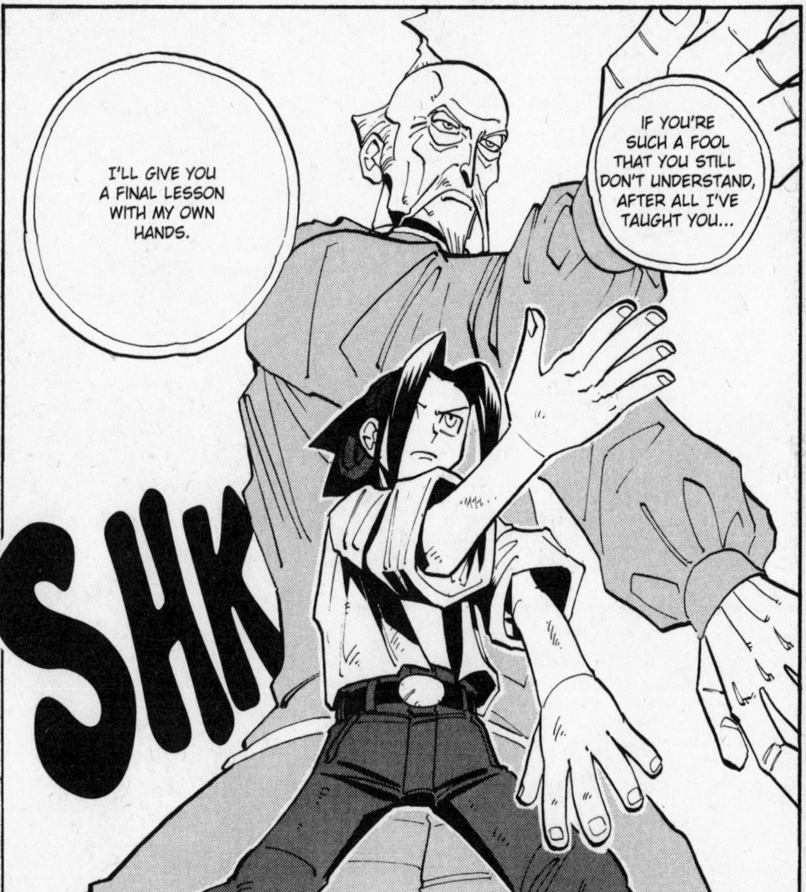
IF YOU'RE SUCH A FOOL THAT YOU STILL DON'T UNDERSTAND, AFTER ALL I'VE TAUGHT YOU...
I'LL GIVE YOU A FINAL LESSON WITH MY OWN HANDS.
SHK

SHAMAN
KING
2

POINTED HAIR
(???????)

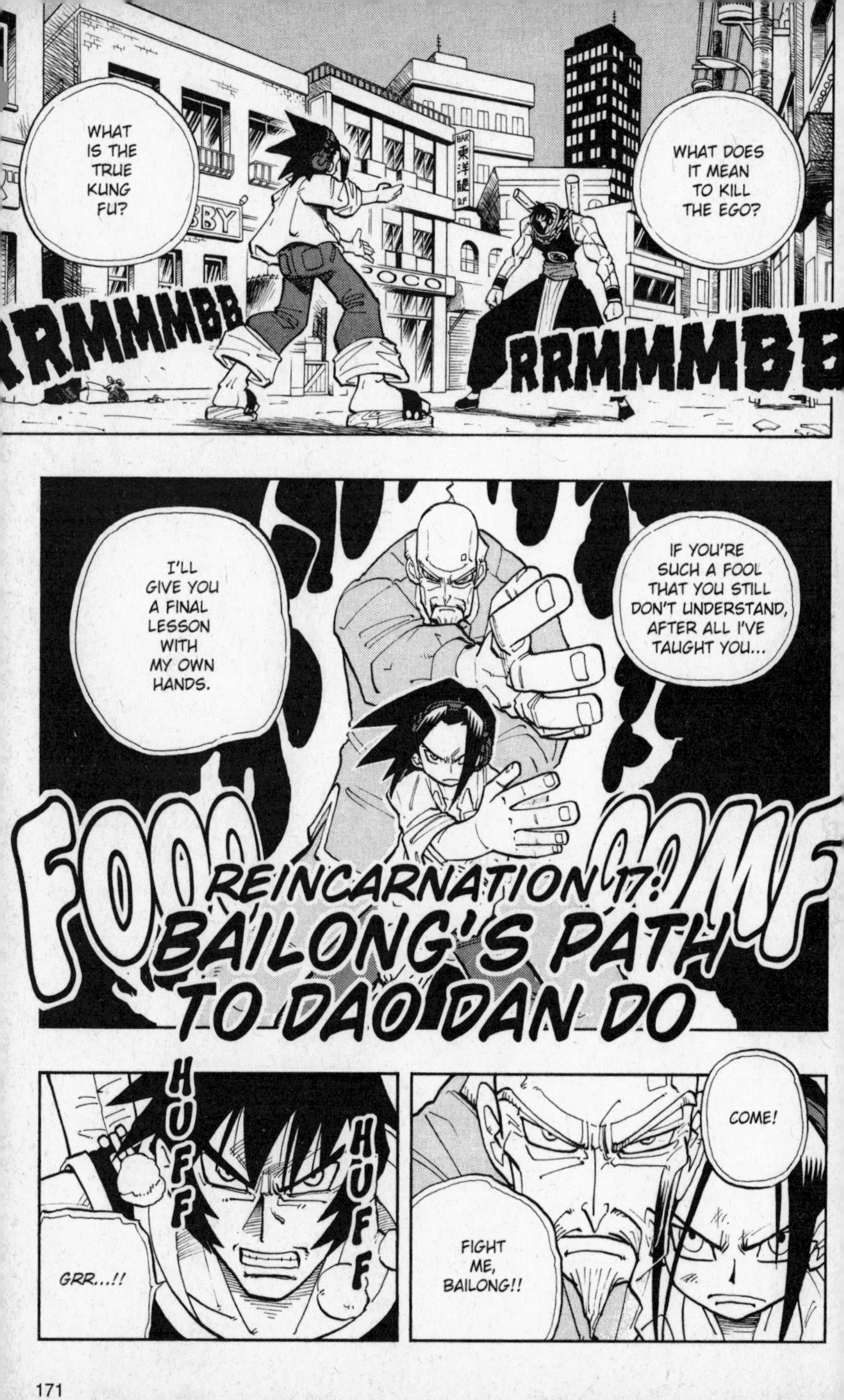
WHAT DOES IT MEAN TO KILL THE EGO?
WHAT IS THE TRUE KUNG FU?
RRMMMBB
RRMMMBB
IF YOU'RE SUCH A FOOL THAT YOU STILL DON'T UNDERSTAND, AFTER ALL I'VE TAUGHT YOU...
I'LL GIVE YOU A FINAL LESSON WITH MY OWN HANDS.
FOO
OOMF
REINCARNATION 17:
BAILONG'S PATH TO DAO DAN DO
COME!
FIGHT ME, BAILONG!!
HUFF
HUFF
GRR...!!

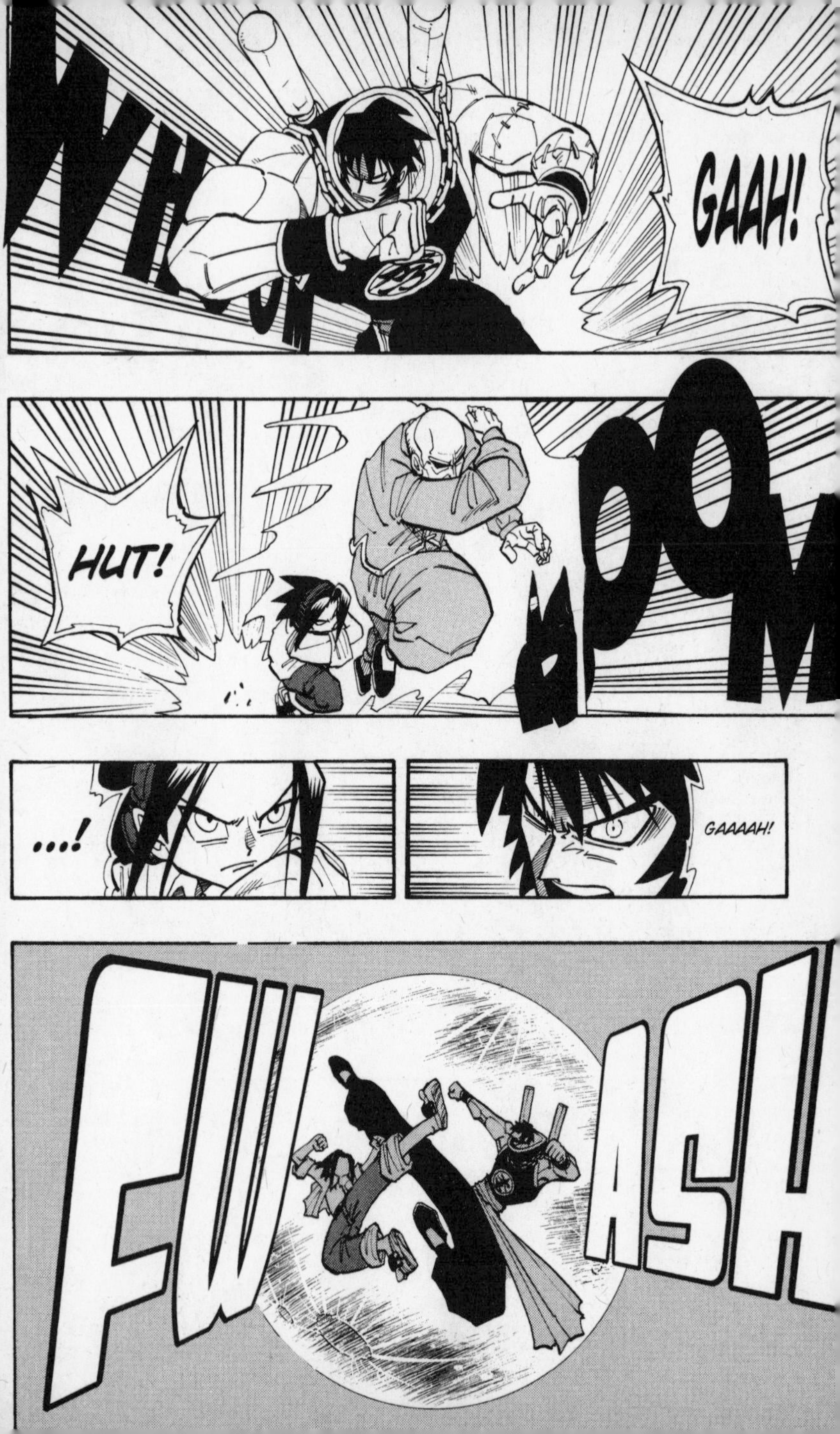
GAAH!
WH
OM
BOOM
HUT!
GAAAAH!
...!
FW
ASH!

Reincarnation 17: Bailong's Path to Dao Dan Do

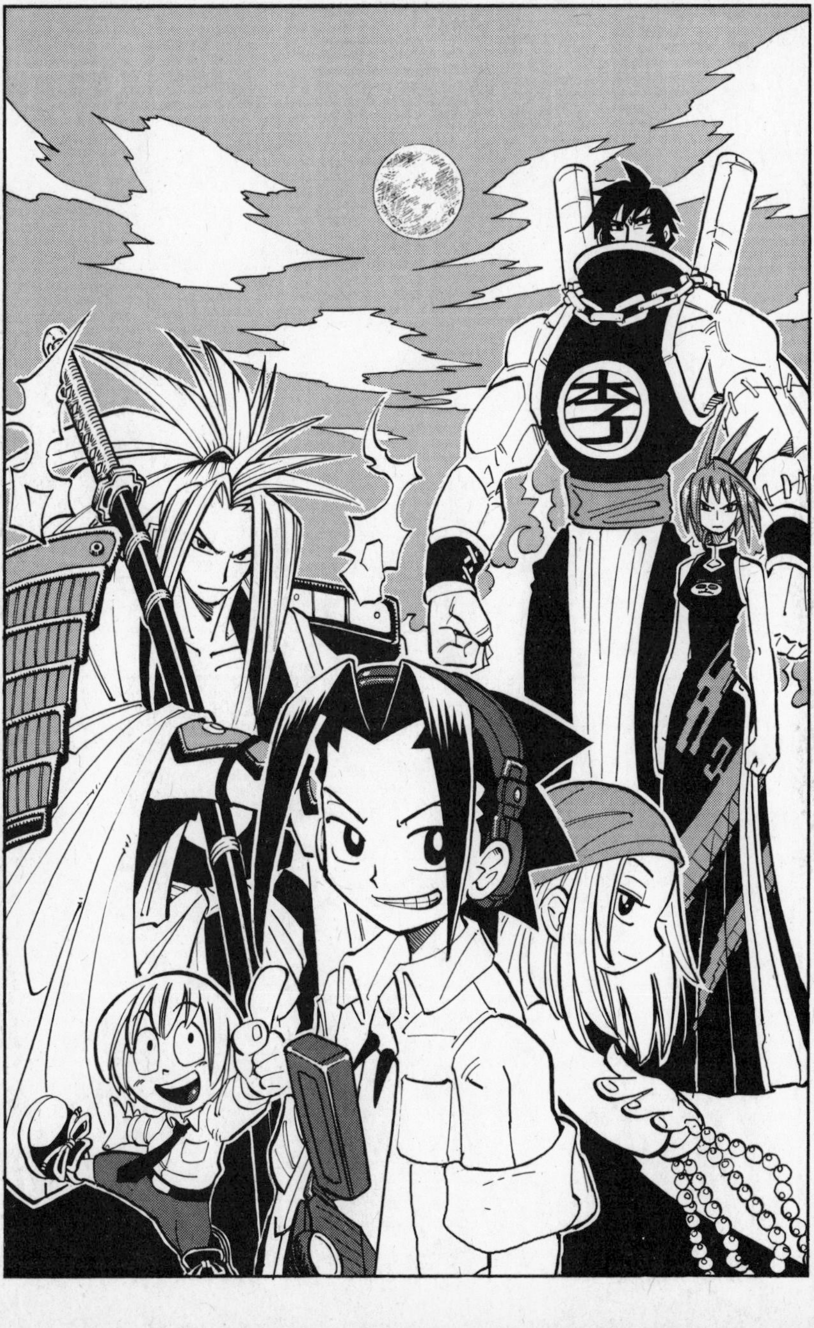

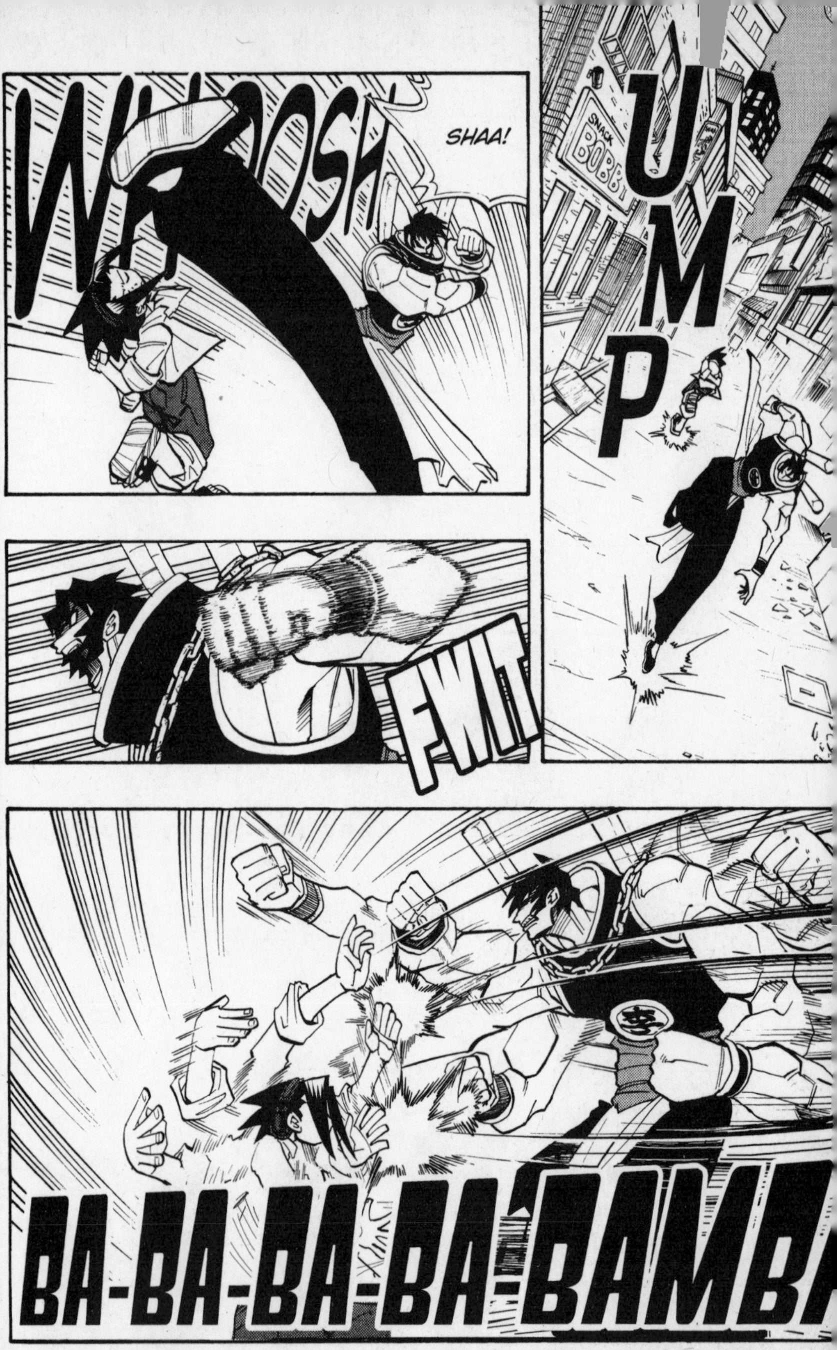
SNACK
BOBB
UMP
SHAA!
FWIT
BA-BA-BA-BA-BAMB

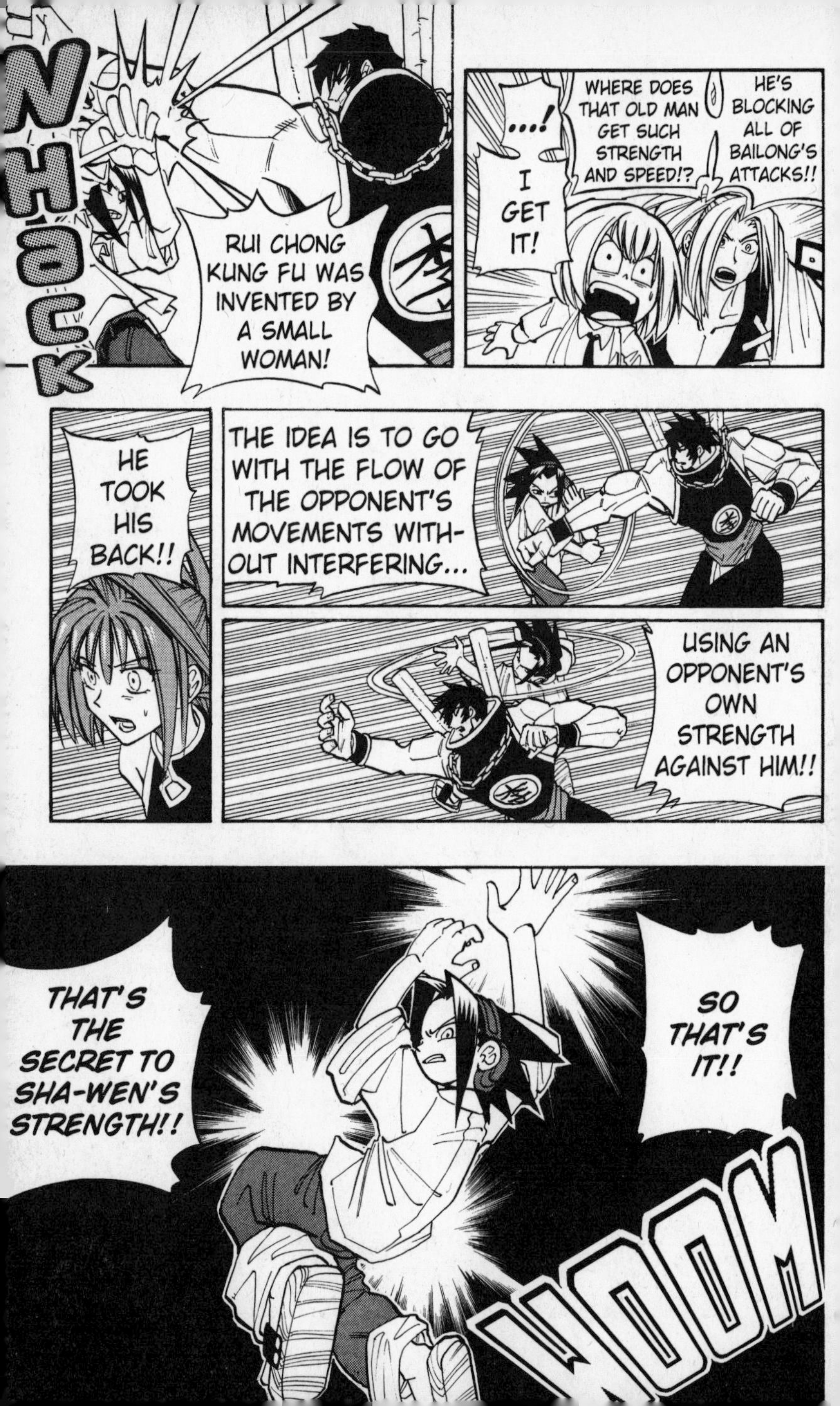
HE'S BLOCKING ALL OF BAILONG'S ATTACKS!!
WHERE DOES THAT OLD MAN GET SUCH STRENGTH AND SPEED!?
...!
I GET IT!
WHACK
RUI CHONG KUNG FU WAS INVENTED BY A SMALL WOMAN!
THE IDEA IS TO GO WITH THE FLOW OF THE OPPONENT'S MOVEMENTS WITH-OUT INTERFERING...
USING AN OPPONENT'S OWN STRENGTH AGAINST HIM!!
HE TOOK HIS BACK!!
SO THAT'S IT!!
THAT'S THE SECRET TO SHA-WEN'S STRENGTH!!
WOOM

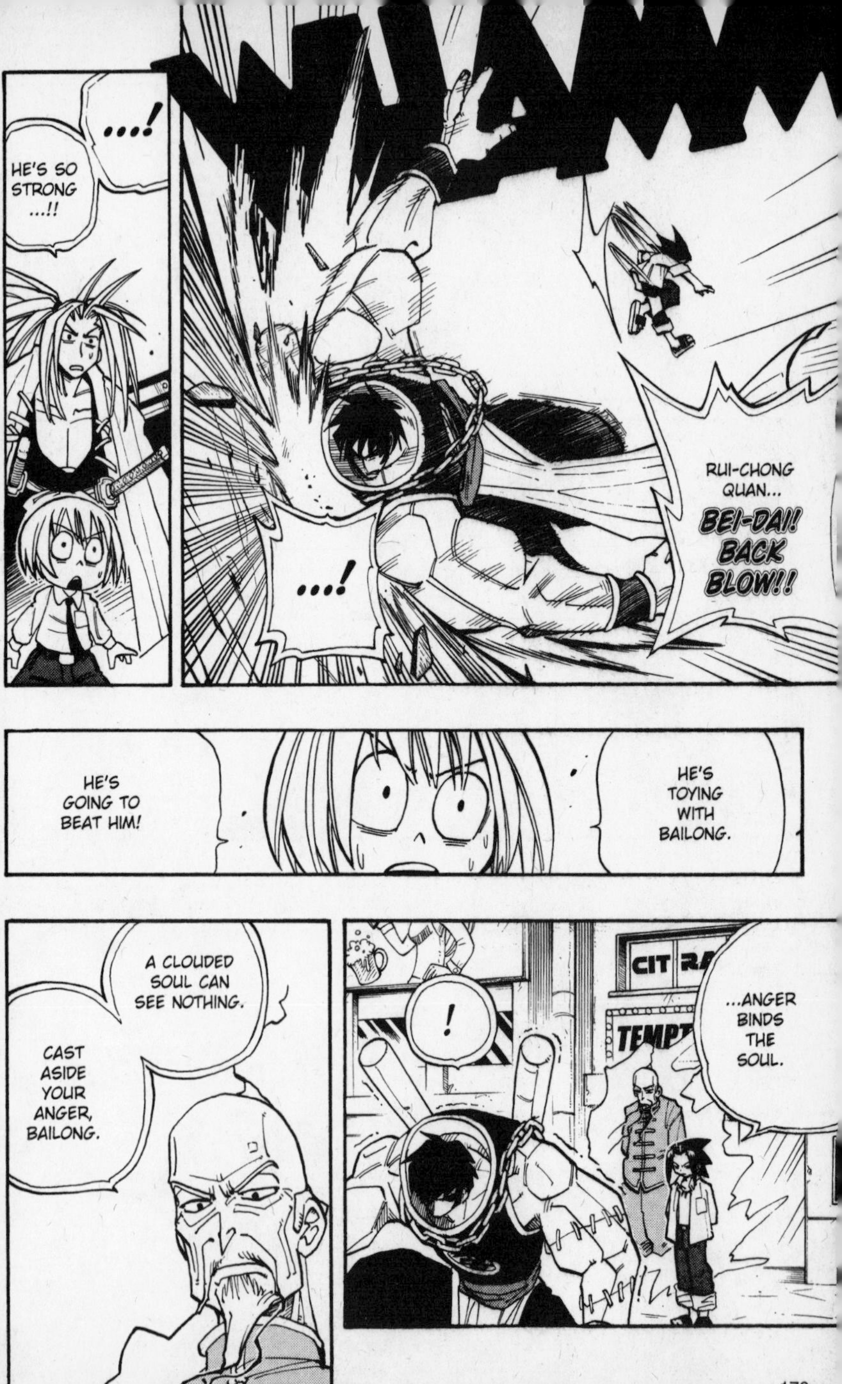
RUI-CHONG QUAN...
BEI-DAI! BACK BLOW!!
...!
...!
HE'S SO STRONG ...!!
HE'S TOYING WITH BAILONG.
HE'S GOING TO BEAT HIM!
...ANGER BINDS THE SOUL.
!
A CLOUDED SOUL CAN SEE NOTHING.
CAST ASIDE YOUR ANGER, BAILONG.

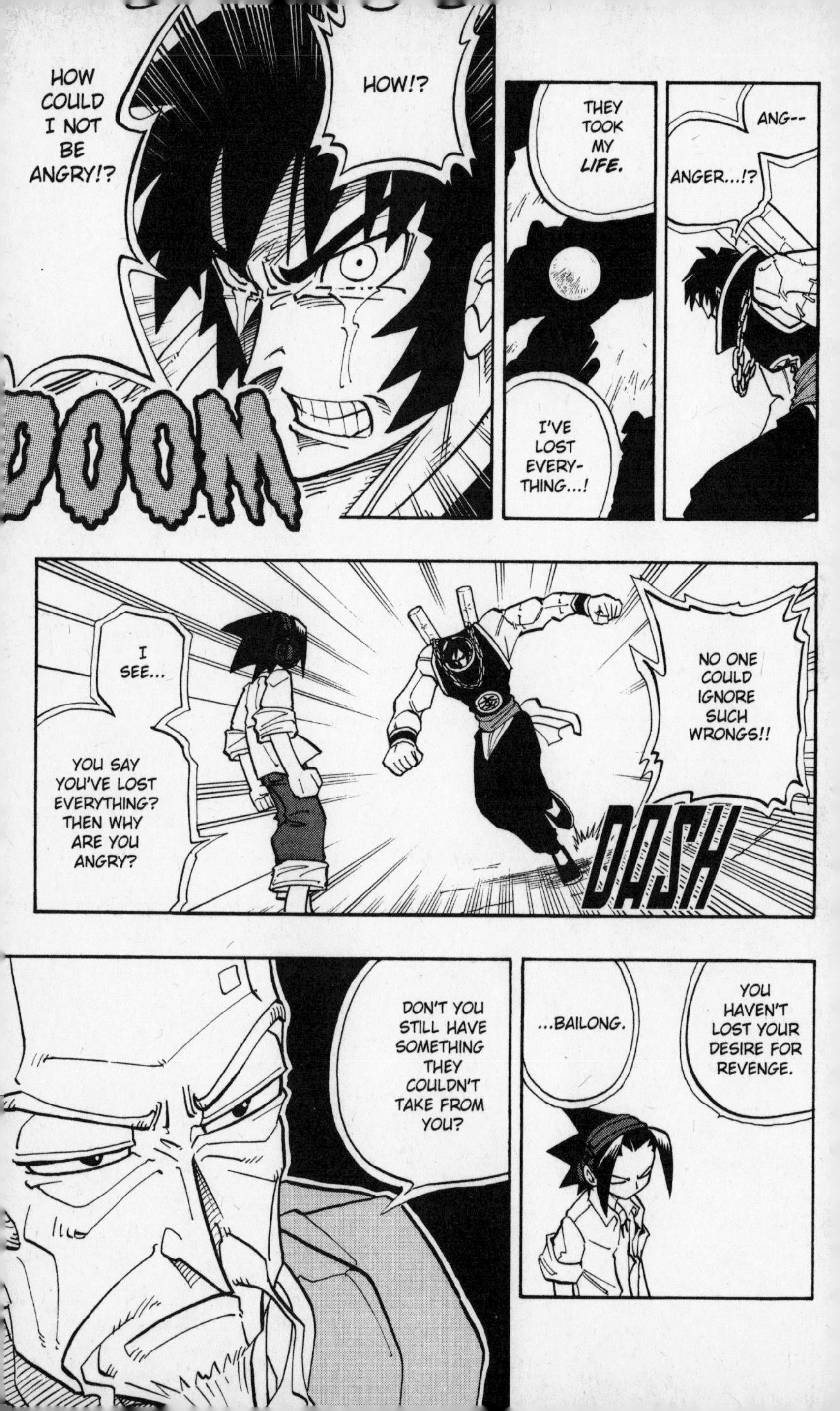
ANG--
ANGER...!?
THEY TOOK MY LIFE.
I'VE LOST EVERY-THING...!
HOW!?
HOW COULD I NOT BE ANGRY!?
DOOM
NO ONE COULD IGNORE SUCH WRONGS!!
DASH
I SEE...
YOU SAY YOU'VE LOST EVERYTHING? THEN WHY ARE YOU ANGRY?
YOU HAVEN'T LOST YOUR DESIRE FOR REVENGE.
...BAILONG.
DON'T YOU STILL HAVE SOMETHING THEY COULDN'T TAKE FROM YOU?

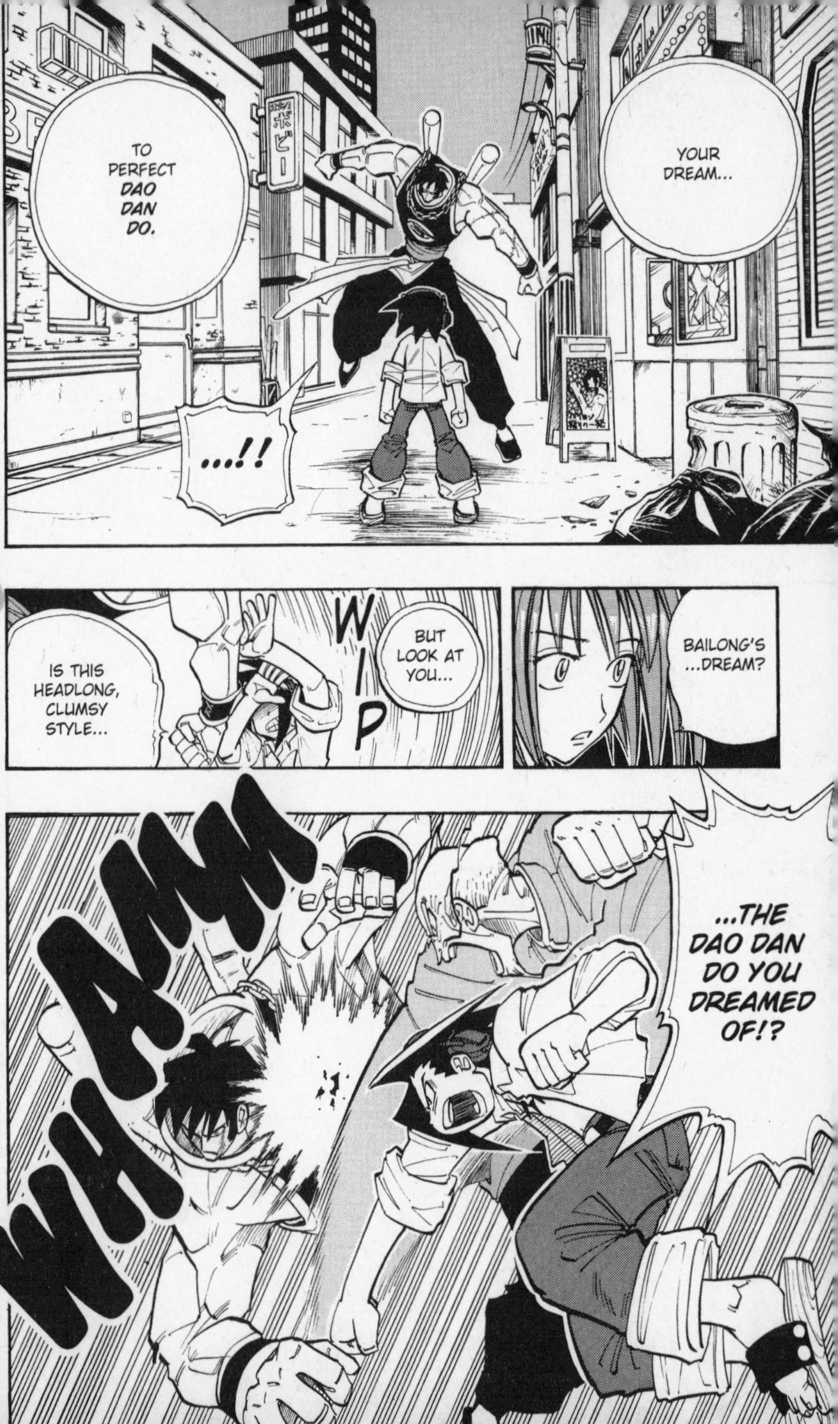
YOUR DREAM...
TO PERFECT DAO DAN DO.
...!!
BAILONG'S ...DREAM?
BUT LOOK AT YOU...
WIP
IS THIS HEADLONG, CLUMSY STYLE...
...THE DAO DAN DO YOU DREAMED OF!?
WHAM

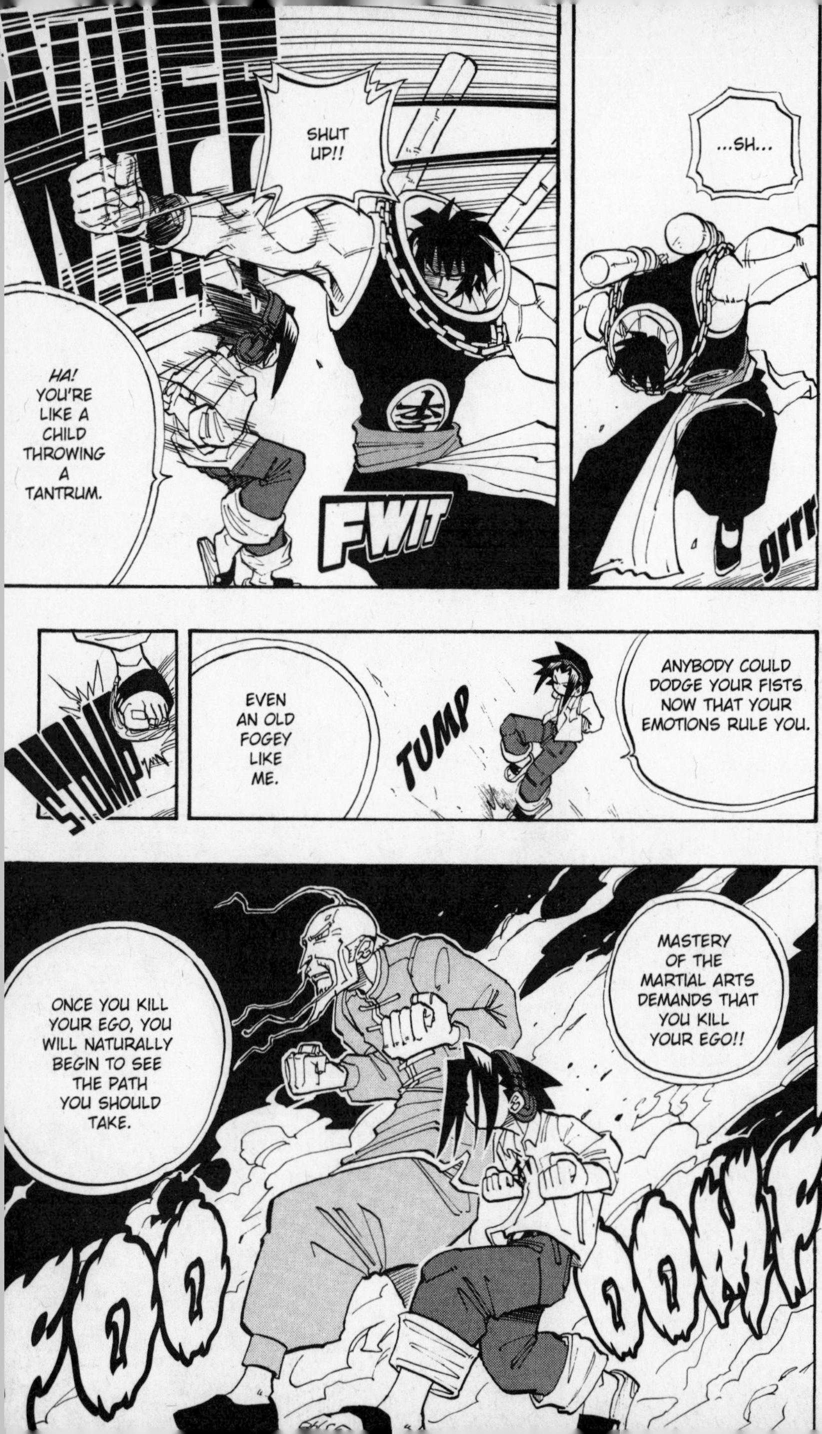
...SH...
grrr
SHUT UP!!
HA! YOU'RE LIKE A CHILD THROWING A TANTRUM.
FWIT
ANYBODY COULD DODGE YOUR FISTS NOW THAT YOUR EMOTIONS RULE YOU.
TUMP
EVEN AN OLD FOGEY LIKE ME.
STOMP
MASTERY OF THE MARTIAL ARTS DEMANDS THAT YOU KILL YOUR EGO!!
ONCE YOU KILL YOUR EGO, YOU WILL NATURALLY BEGIN TO SEE THE PATH YOU SHOULD TAKE.

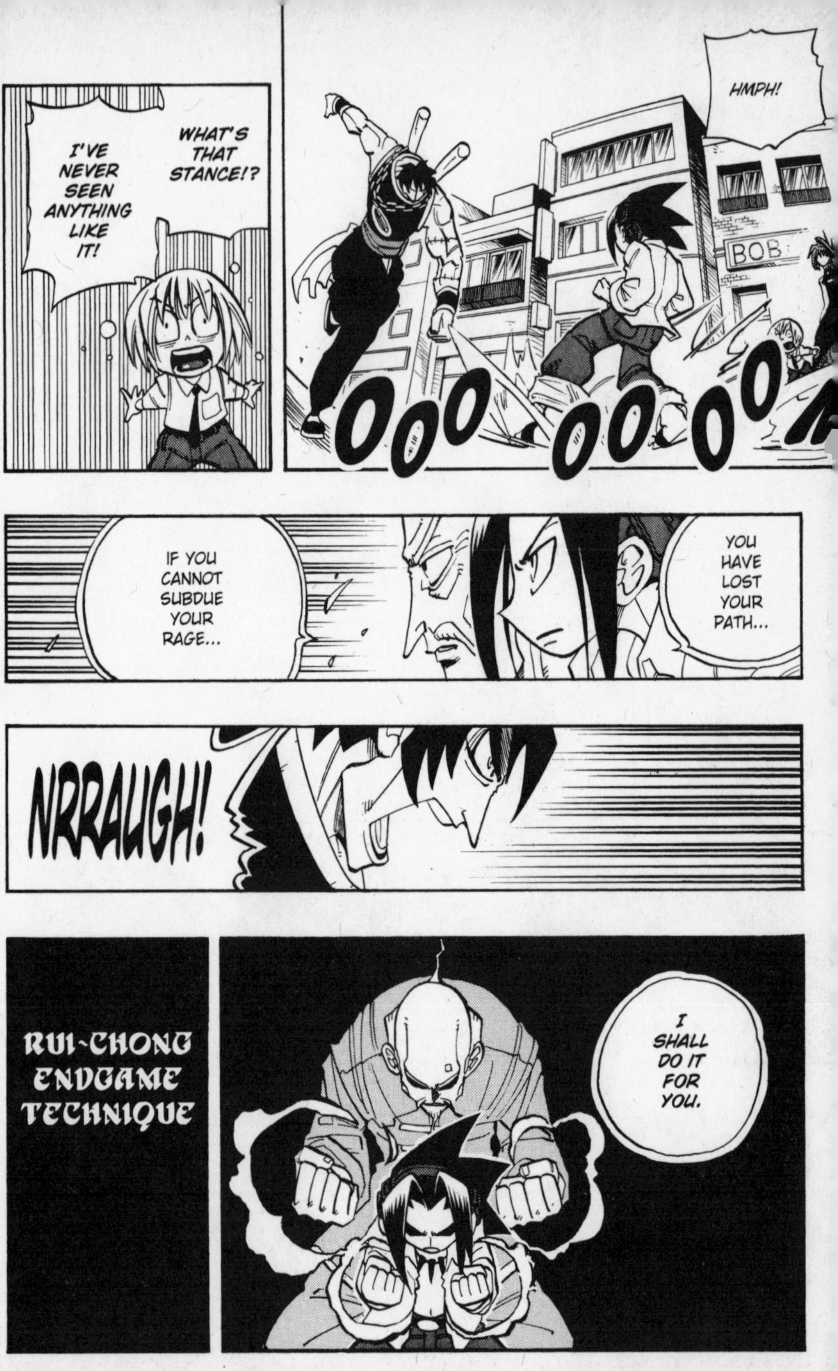
HMPH!
OOOOOOOOO
WHAT'S THAT STANCE!?
I'VE NEVER SEEN ANYTHING LIKE IT!
BOB
YOU HAVE LOST YOUR PATH...
IF YOU CANNOT SUBDUE YOUR RAGE...
NRRAUGH!
I SHALL DO IT FOR YOU.
RUI-CHONG ENDGAME TECHNIQUE

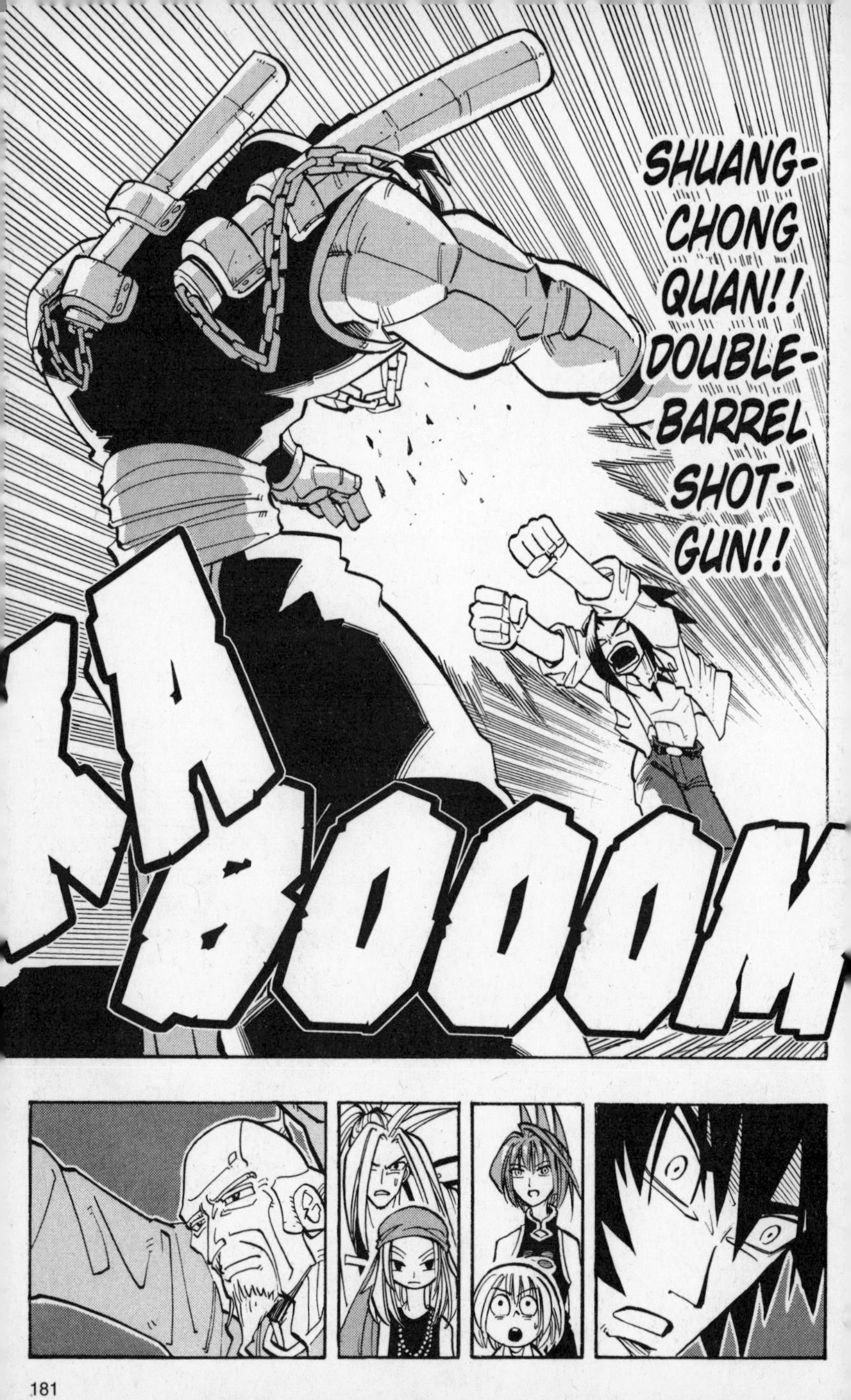
SHUANG-CHONG QUAN!! DOUBLE-BARREL SHOT-GUN!!
KA-BOOOM

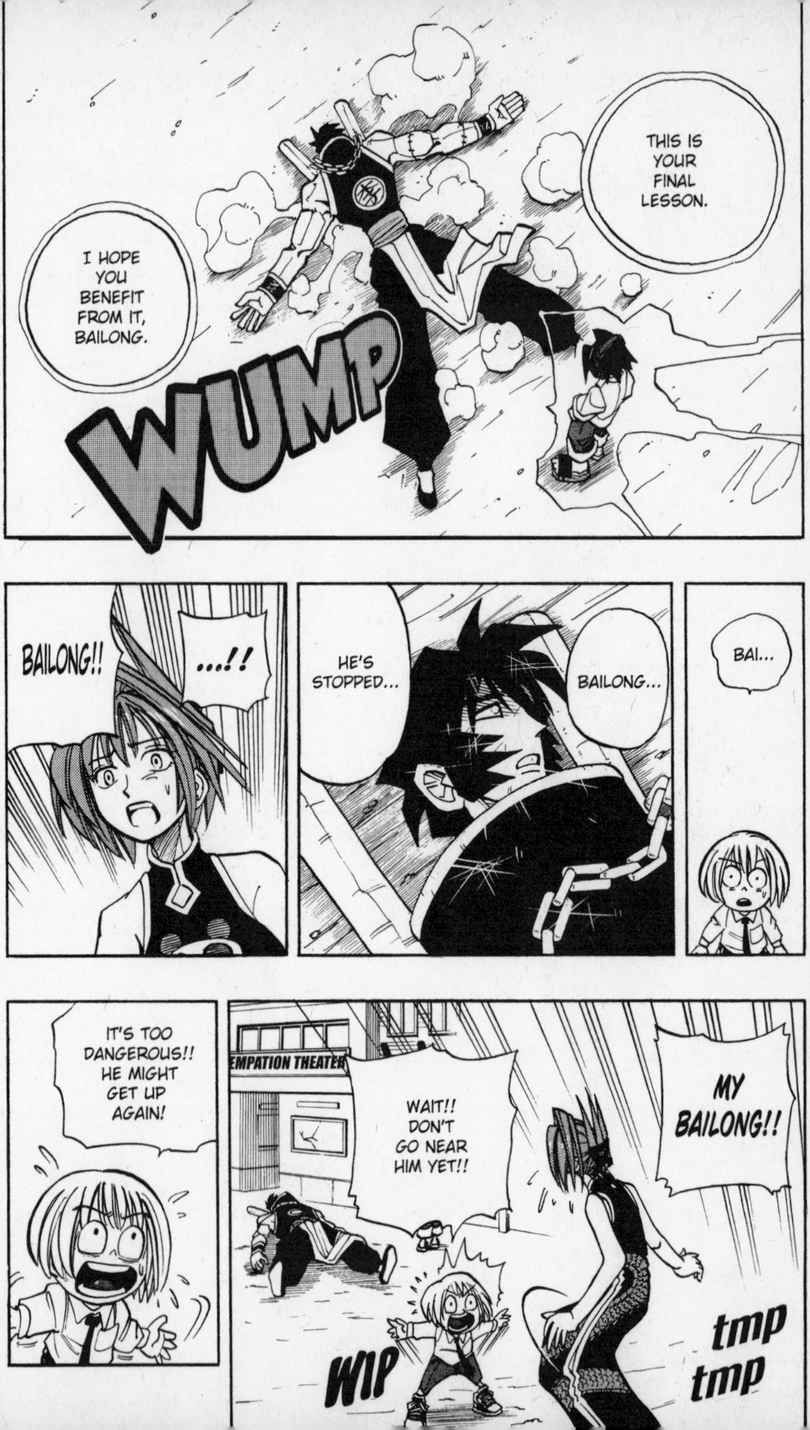
THIS IS YOUR FINAL LESSON.
I HOPE YOU BENEFIT FROM IT, BAILONG.
WUMP
BAI...
BAILONG...
HE'S STOPPED...
...!!
BAILONG!!
MY BAILONG!!
WAIT!! DON'T GO NEAR HIM YET!!
EMPATION THEATER
tmp tmp
WIP
IT'S TOO DANGEROUS!! HE MIGHT GET UP AGAIN!

READ THIS WAY

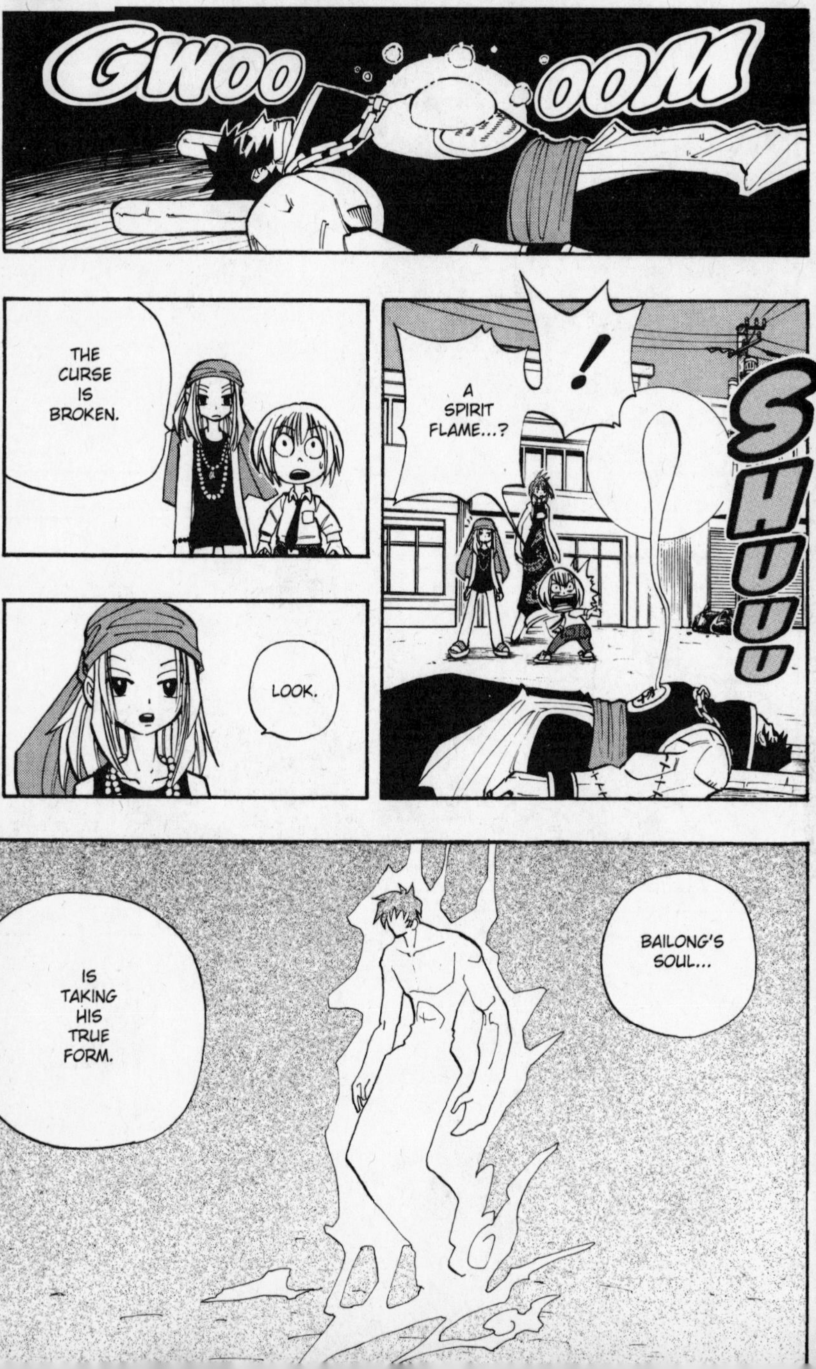
GWOO OOM
!
A SPIRIT FLAME...?
SHUUU
THE CURSE IS BROKEN.
LOOK.
BAILONG'S SOUL...
IS TAKING HIS TRUE FORM.

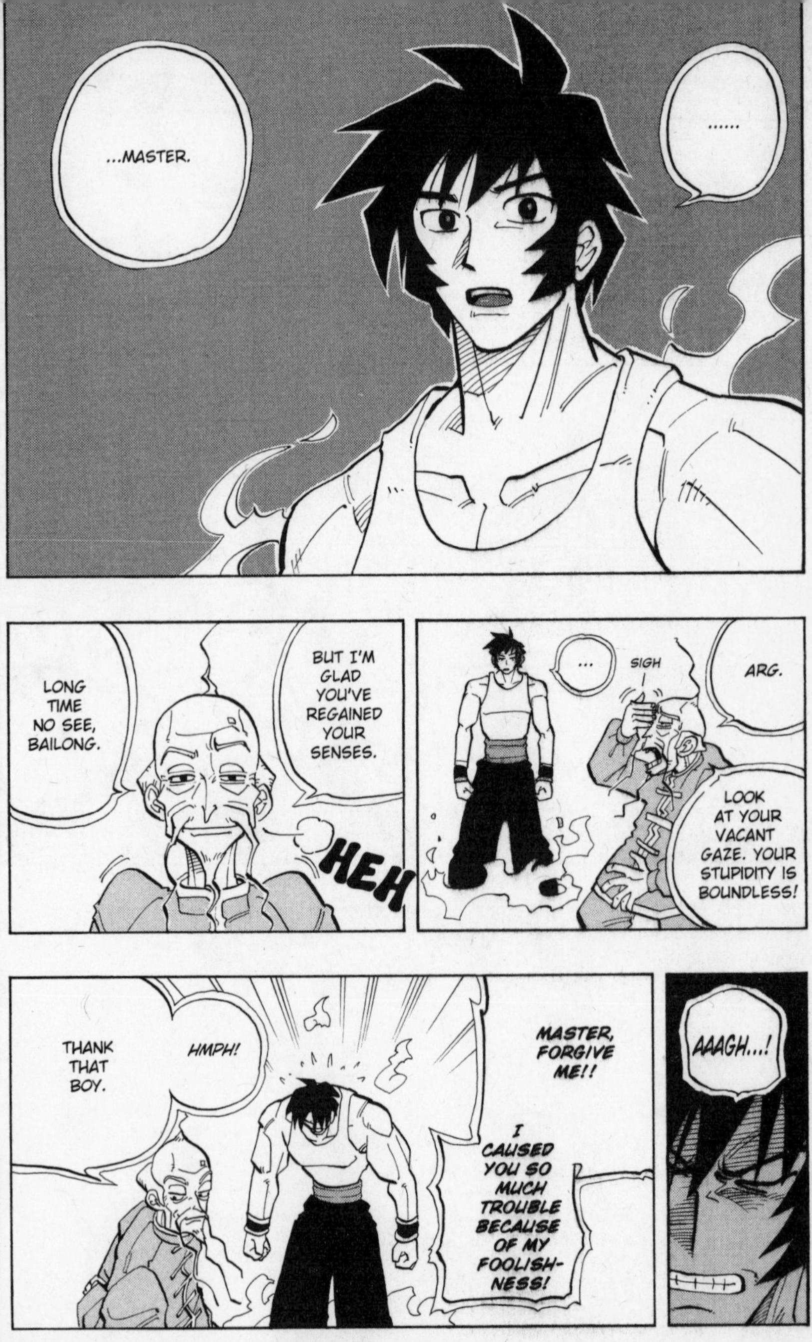
......
...MASTER.
ARG.
SIGH
...
LOOK AT YOUR VACANT GAZE. YOUR STUPIDITY IS BOUNDLESS!
BUT I'M GLAD YOU'VE REGAINED YOUR SENSES.
LONG TIME NO SEE, BAILONG.
HEH
AAAGH...!
MASTER, FORGIVE ME!!
I CAUSED YOU SO MUCH TROUBLE BECAUSE OF MY FOOLISH-NESS!
HMPH!
THANK THAT BOY.

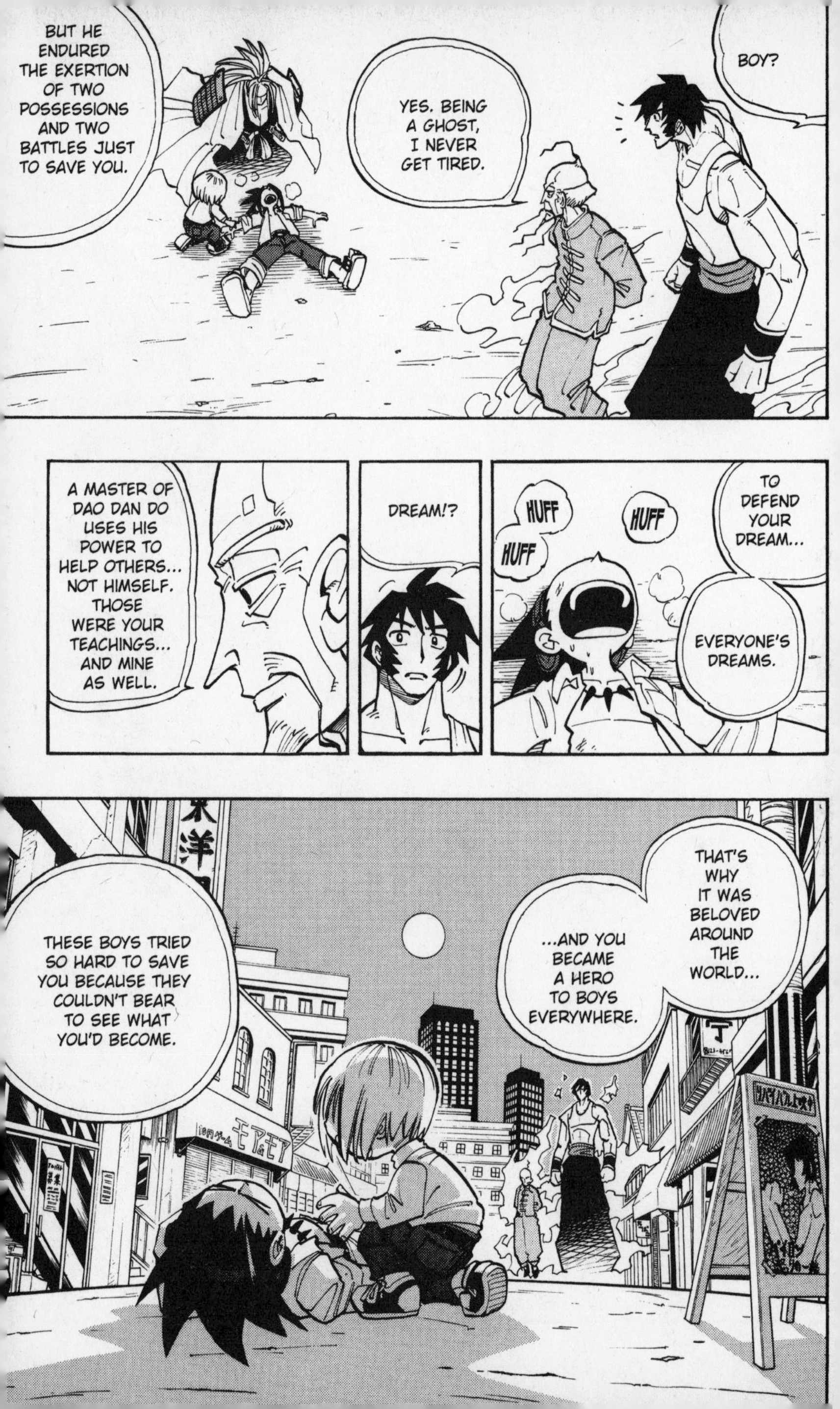
BOY?
YES. BEING A GHOST, I NEVER GET TIRED.
BUT HE ENDURED THE EXERTION OF TWO POSSESSIONS AND TWO BATTLES JUST TO SAVE YOU.
TO DEFEND YOUR DREAM...
HUFF
HUFF
HUFF
EVERYONE'S DREAMS.
DREAM!?
A MASTER OF DAO DAN DO USES HIS POWER TO HELP OTHERS... NOT HIMSELF. THOSE WERE YOUR TEACHINGS... AND MINE AS WELL.
THAT'S WHY IT WAS BELOVED AROUND THE WORLD...
...AND YOU BECAME A HERO TO BOYS EVERYWHERE.
THESE BOYS TRIED SO HARD TO SAVE YOU BECAUSE THEY COULDN'T BEAR TO SEE WHAT YOU'D BECOME.
モア&モア

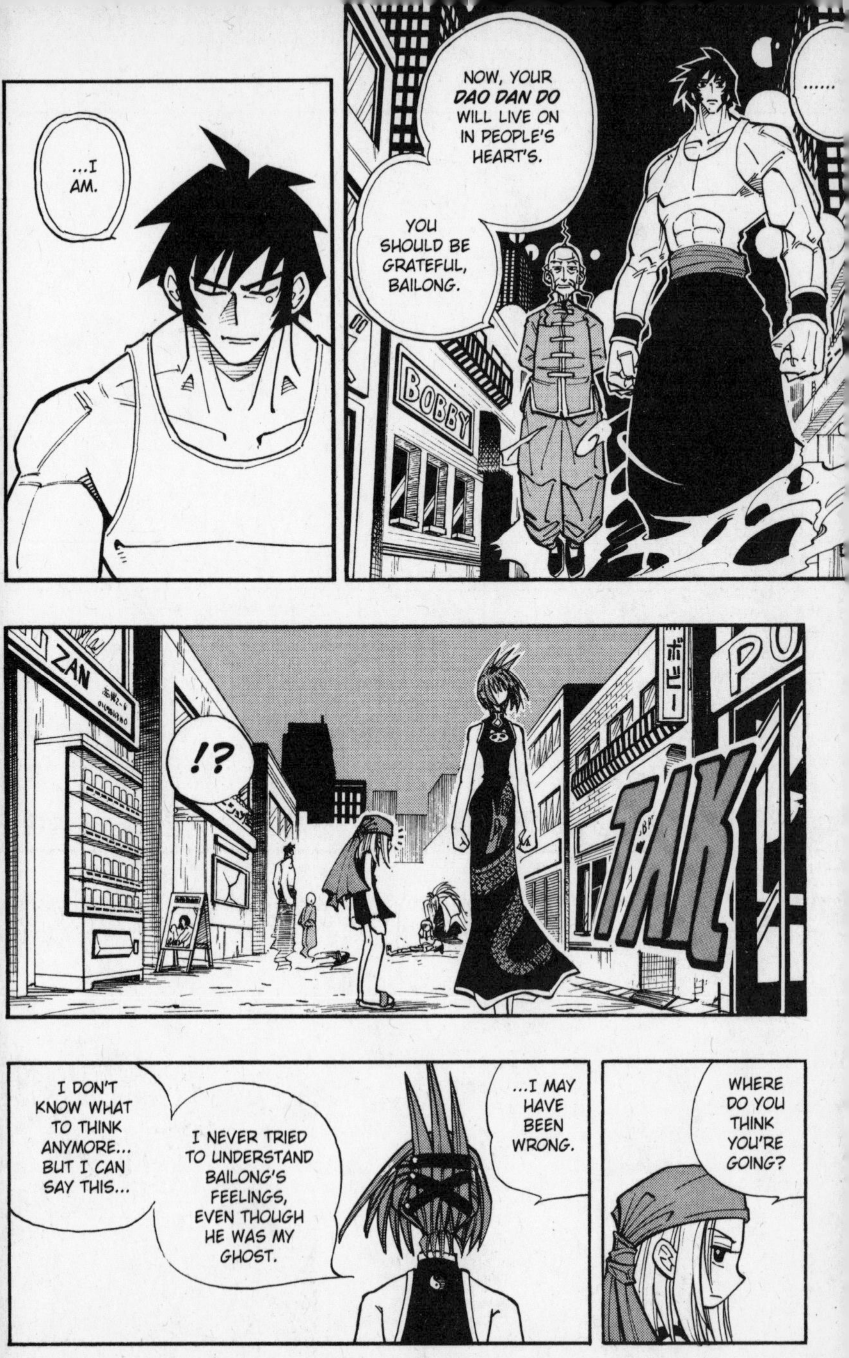
......
NOW, YOUR DAO DAN DO WILL LIVE ON IN PEOPLE'S HEART'S.
YOU SHOULD BE GRATEFUL, BAILONG.
BOBBY
...I AM.
ボビー
PO
TAK
!?
ZAN
WHERE DO YOU THINK YOU'RE GOING?
...I MAY HAVE BEEN WRONG.
I NEVER TRIED TO UNDERSTAND BAILONG'S FEELINGS, EVEN THOUGH HE WAS MY GHOST.
I DON'T KNOW WHAT TO THINK ANYMORE... BUT I CAN SAY THIS...

READ THIS WAY

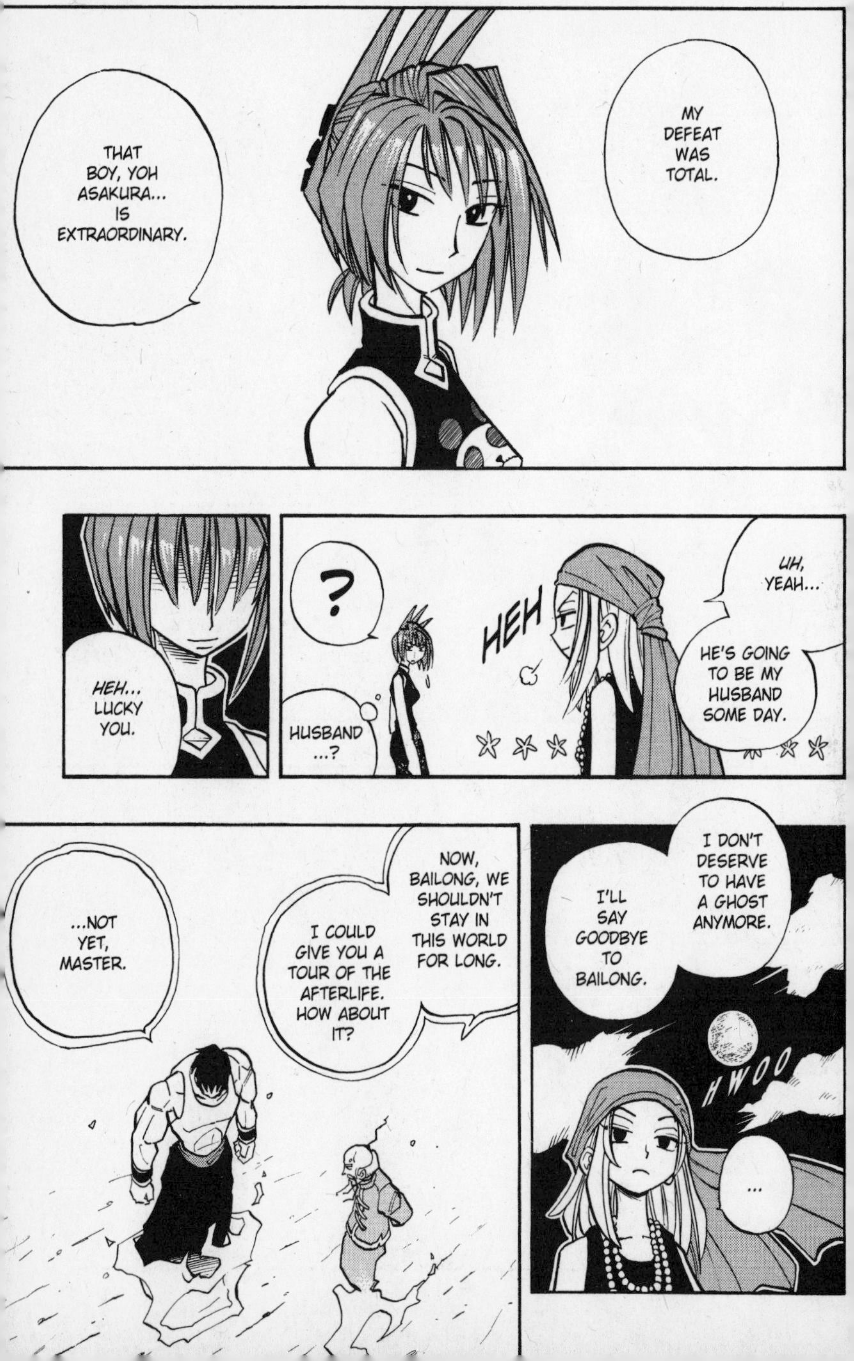
MY DEFEAT WAS TOTAL.
THAT BOY, YOH ASAKURA... IS EXTRAORDINARY.
UH, YEAH...
HEH
HE'S GOING TO BE MY HUSBAND SOME DAY.
?
HUSBAND ...?
HEH... LUCKY YOU.
I DON'T DESERVE TO HAVE A GHOST ANYMORE.
I'LL SAY GOODBYE TO BAILONG.
HWOO
...
NOW, BAILONG, WE SHOULDN'T STAY IN THIS WORLD FOR LONG.
I COULD GIVE YOU A TOUR OF THE AFTERLIFE. HOW ABOUT IT?
...NOT YET, MASTER.

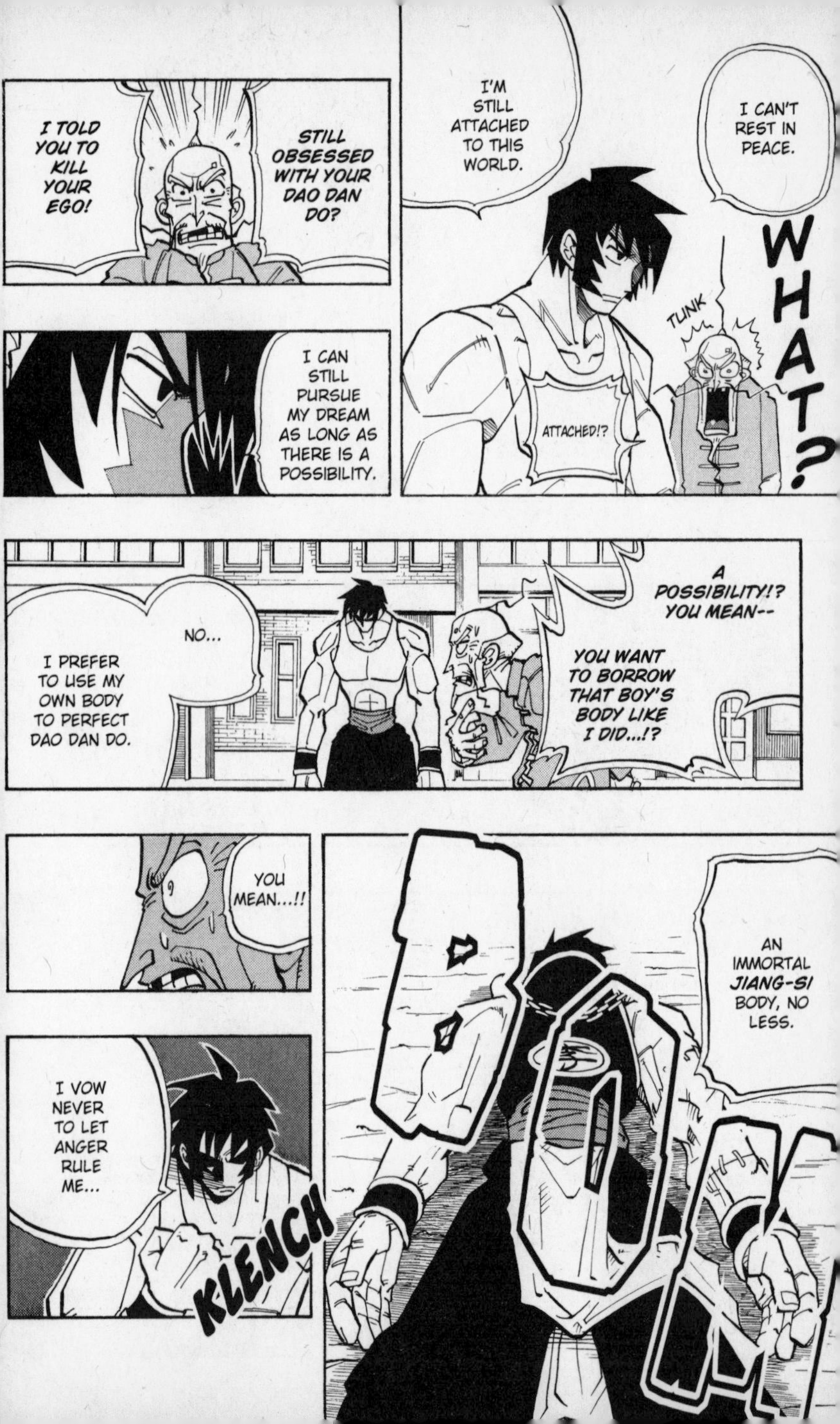
I'M STILL ATTACHED TO THIS WORLD.
I CAN'T REST IN PEACE.
WHAT?
TUNK
ATTACHED!?
STILL OBSESSED WITH YOUR DAO DAN DO?
I TOLD YOU TO KILL YOUR EGO!
I CAN STILL PURSUE MY DREAM AS LONG AS THERE IS A POSSIBILITY.
A POSSIBILITY!? YOU MEAN--
YOU WANT TO BORROW THAT BOY'S BODY LIKE I DID...!?
NO...
I PREFER TO USE MY OWN BODY TO PERFECT DAO DAN DO.
AN IMMORTAL JIANG-SI BODY, NO LESS.
YOU MEAN...!!
I VOW NEVER TO LET ANGER RULE ME...
KLENCH

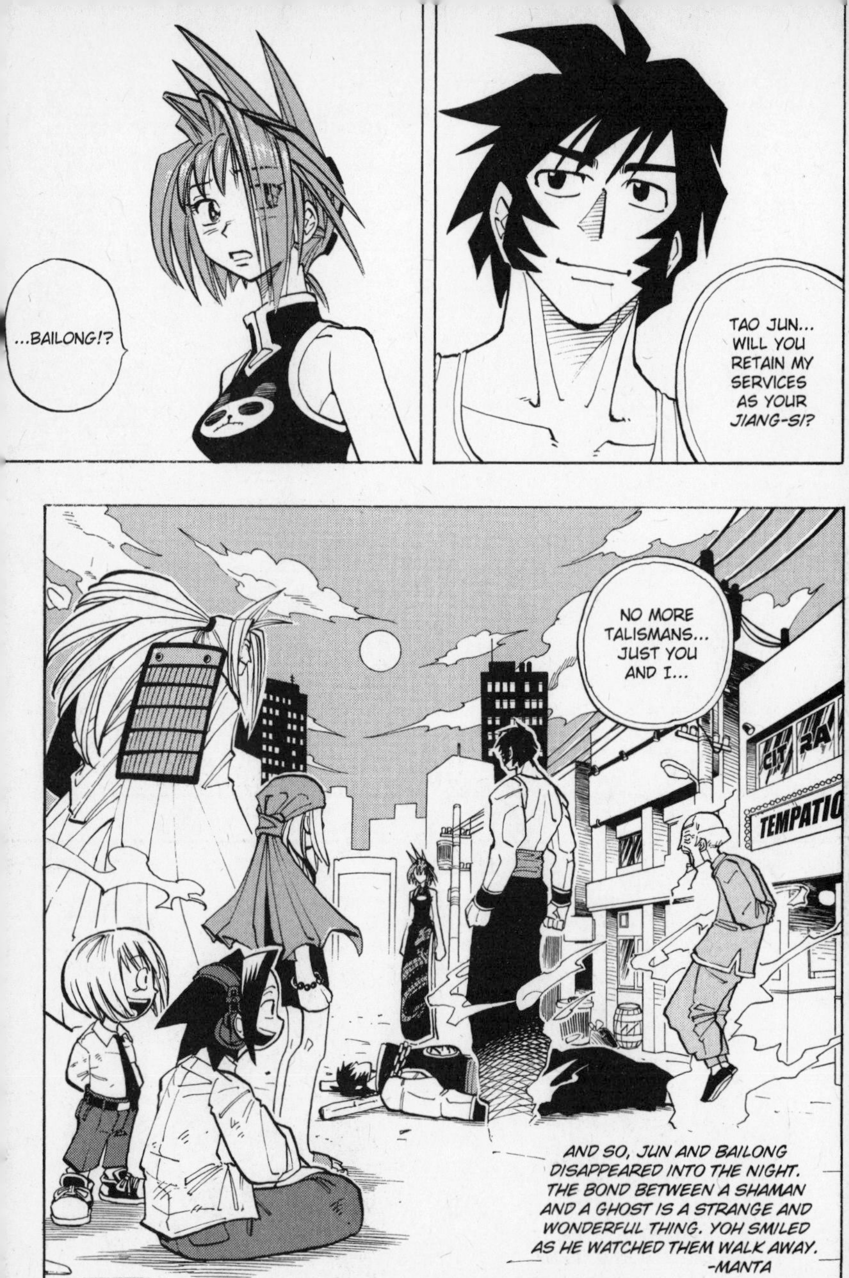
TAO JUN... WILL YOU RETAIN MY SERVICES AS YOUR JIANG-SI?
...BAILONG!?
NO MORE TALISMANS... JUST YOU AND I...
CIT RA
TEMPATIO
AND SO, JUN AND BAILONG DISAPPEARED INTO THE NIGHT. THE BOND BETWEEN A SHAMAN AND A GHOST IS A STRANGE AND WONDERFUL THING. YOH SMILED AS HE WATCHED THEM WALK AWAY. -MANTA

TO BE CONTINUED IN ***SHAMAN KING*** *VOL. 3!*

SHAMAN KING CHARACTER FILE No.9

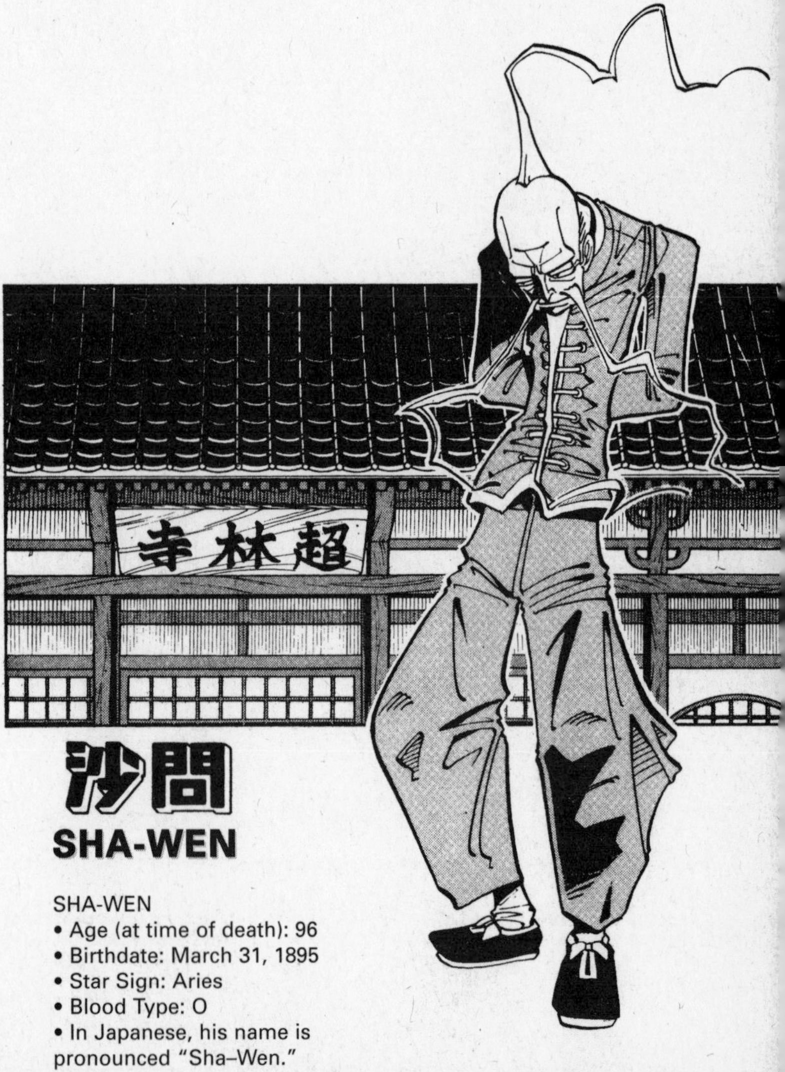

寺林超

沙門

SHA-WEN

SHA-WEN

- Age (at time of death): 96
- Birthdate: March 31, 1895
- Star Sign: Aries
- Blood Type: O
- In Japanese, his name is pronounced "Sha–Wen."

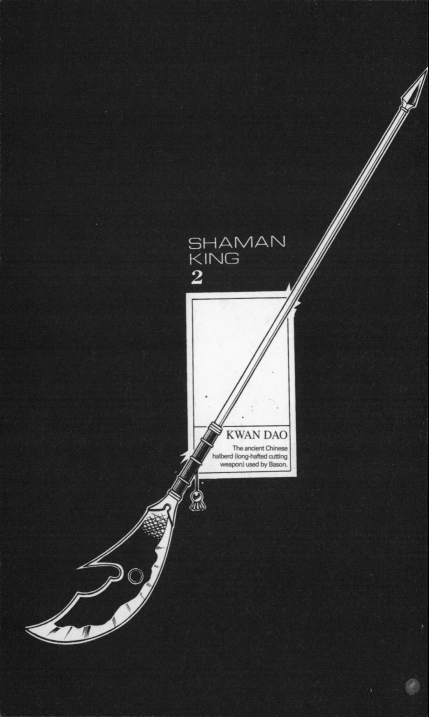

SHAMAN
KING
2

KWAN DAO

The ancient Chinese
halberd (long-hafted cutting
weapon) used by Bason.

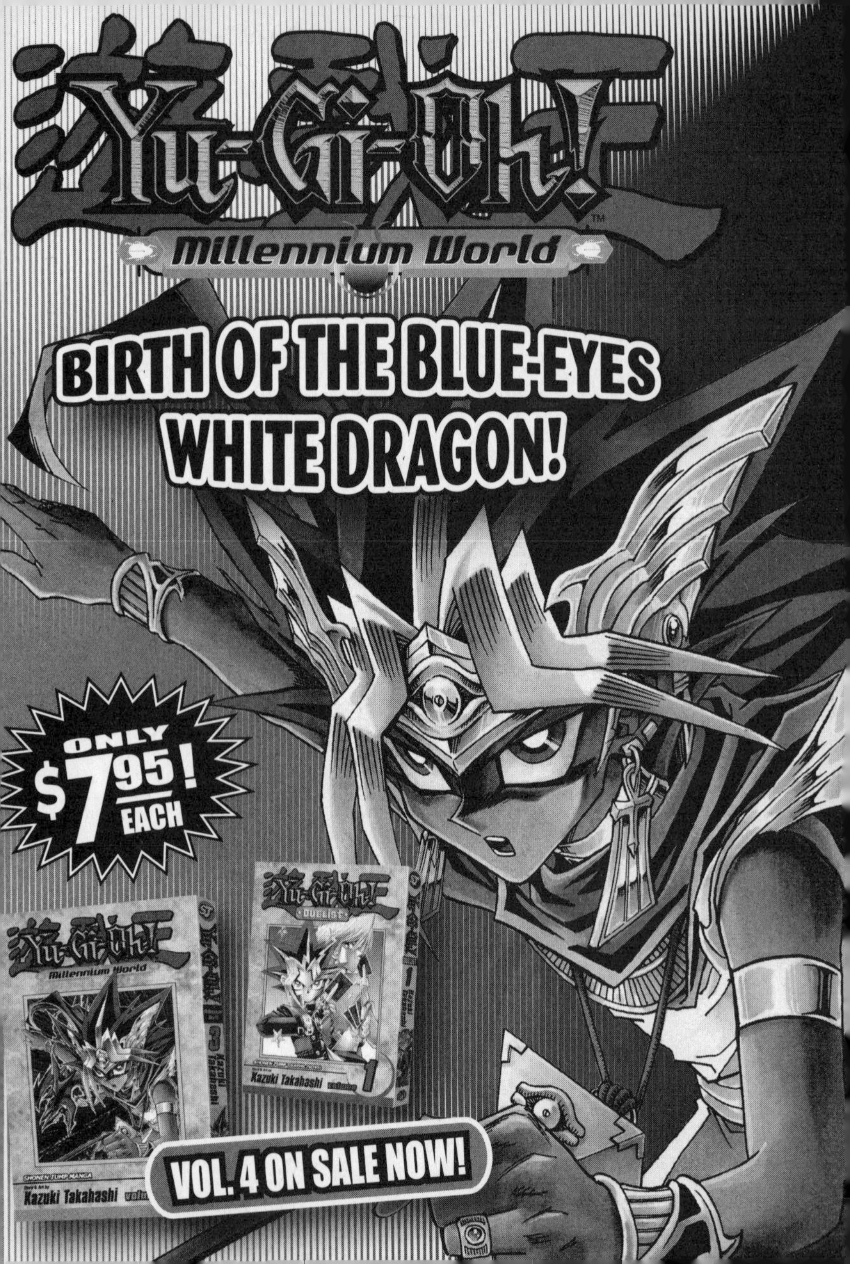

YU-GI-OH!
Millennium World
BIRTH OF THE BLUE-EYES
WHITE DRAGON!
ONLY
$7.95!
EACH
Millennium World
Kazuki Takahashi
DUELIST
Kazuki Takahashi
VOL. 4 ON SALE NOW!

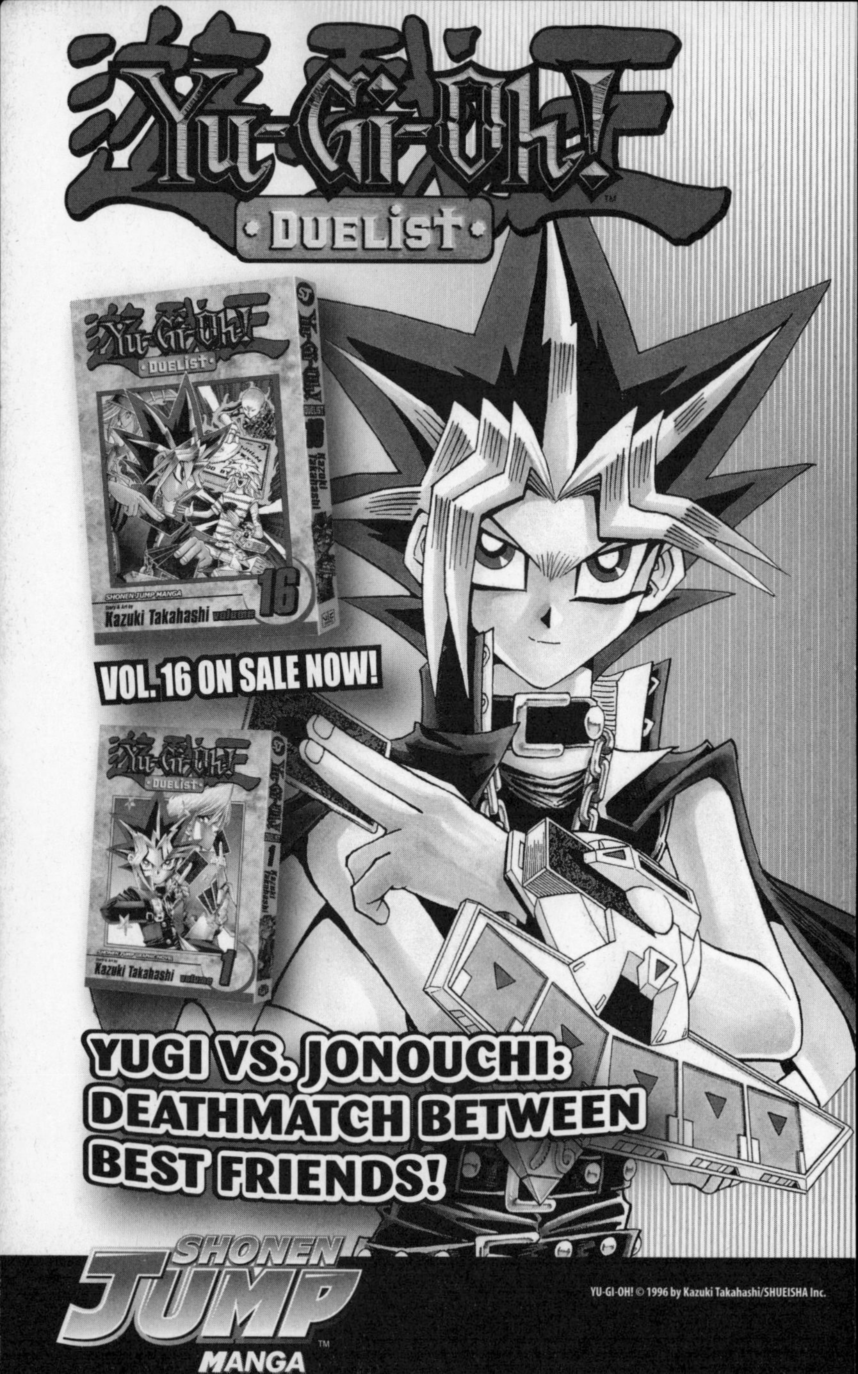
YU-GI-OH! DUELIST
VOL. 16 ON SALE NOW!
YUGI VS. JONOUCHI: DEATHMATCH BETWEEN BEST FRIENDS!
SHONEN JUMP MANGA
YU-GI-OH! © 1996 by Kazuki Takahashi/SHUEISHA Inc.

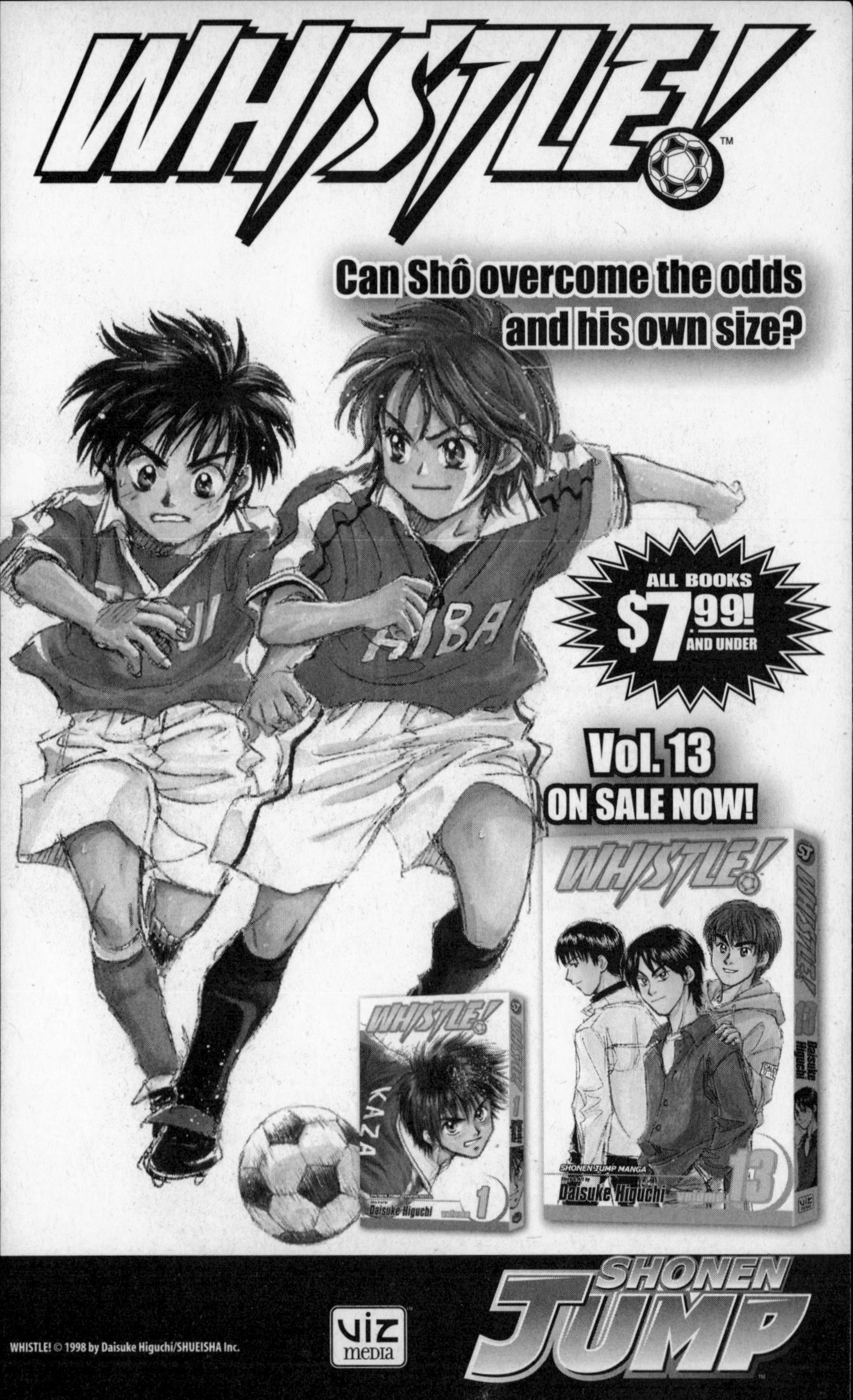
WHISTLE!™
Can Shô overcome the odds and his own size?
ALL BOOKS $7.99! AND UNDER
Vol. 13 ON SALE NOW!
WHISTLE!
Daisuke Higuchi
SHONEN JUMP MANGA
SHONEN JUMP
viz media
WHISTLE! © 1998 by Daisuke Higuchi/SHUEISHA Inc.

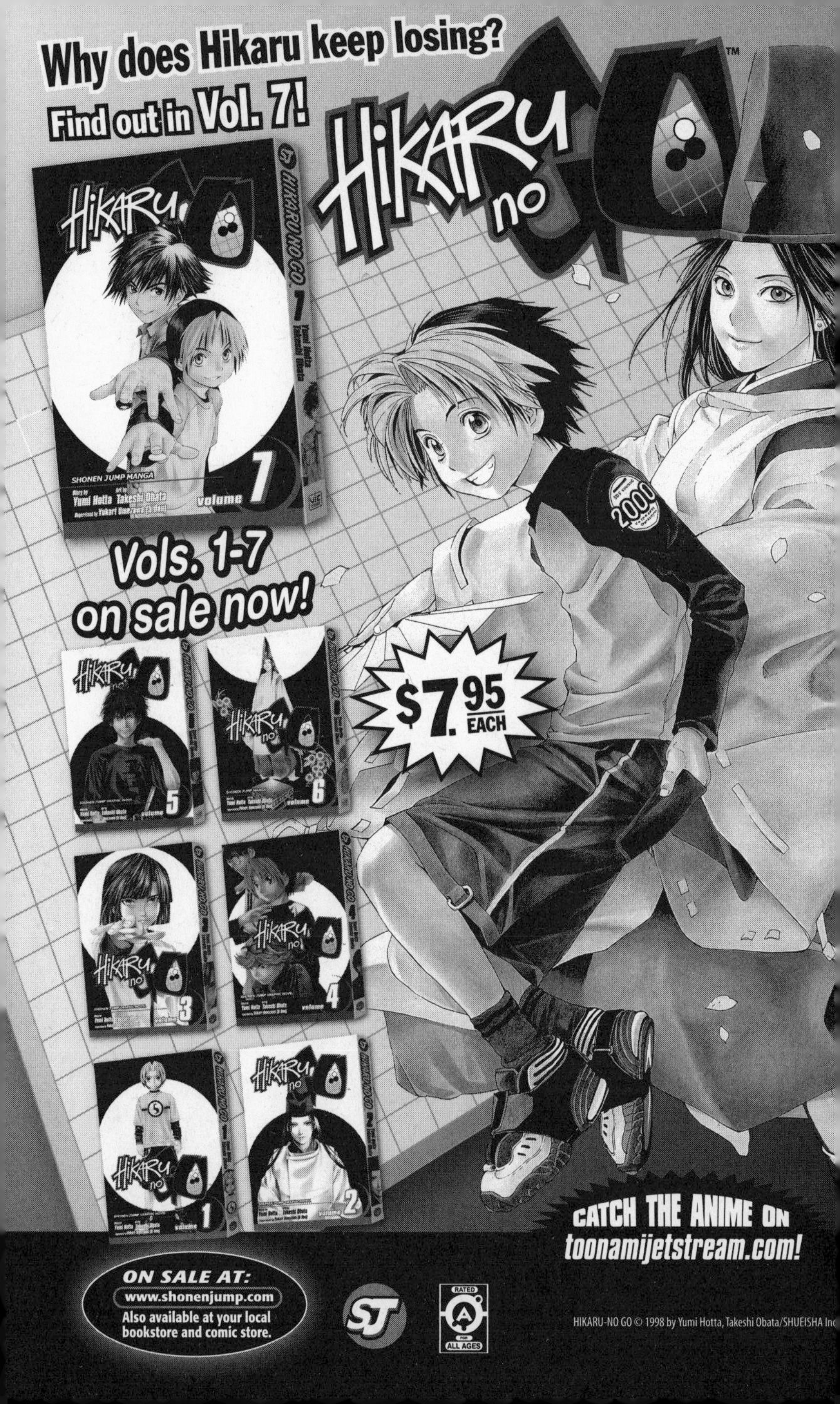
Why does Hikaru keep losing?
Find out in Vol. 7!
HIKARU no
SHONEN JUMP MANGA
Story by Yumi Hotta Art by Takeshi Obata
volume 7
Vols. 1-7
on sale now!
$7.95 EACH
CATCH THE ANIME ON
toonamijetstream.com!
ON SALE AT:
www.shonenjump.com
Also available at your local
bookstore and comic store.
RATED A FOR ALL AGES
HIKARU-NO GO © 1998 by Yumi Hotta, Takeshi Obata/SHUEISHA Inc

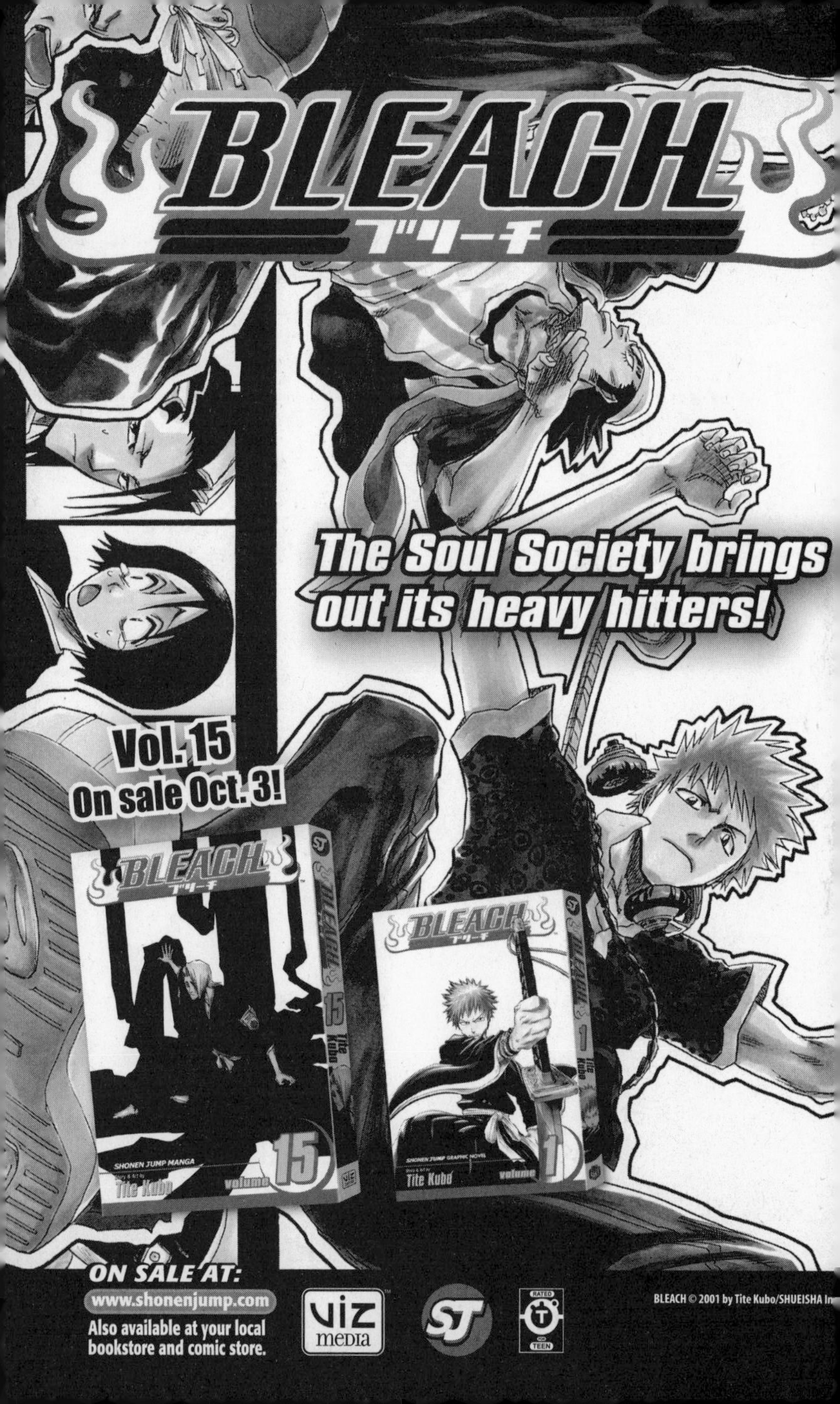

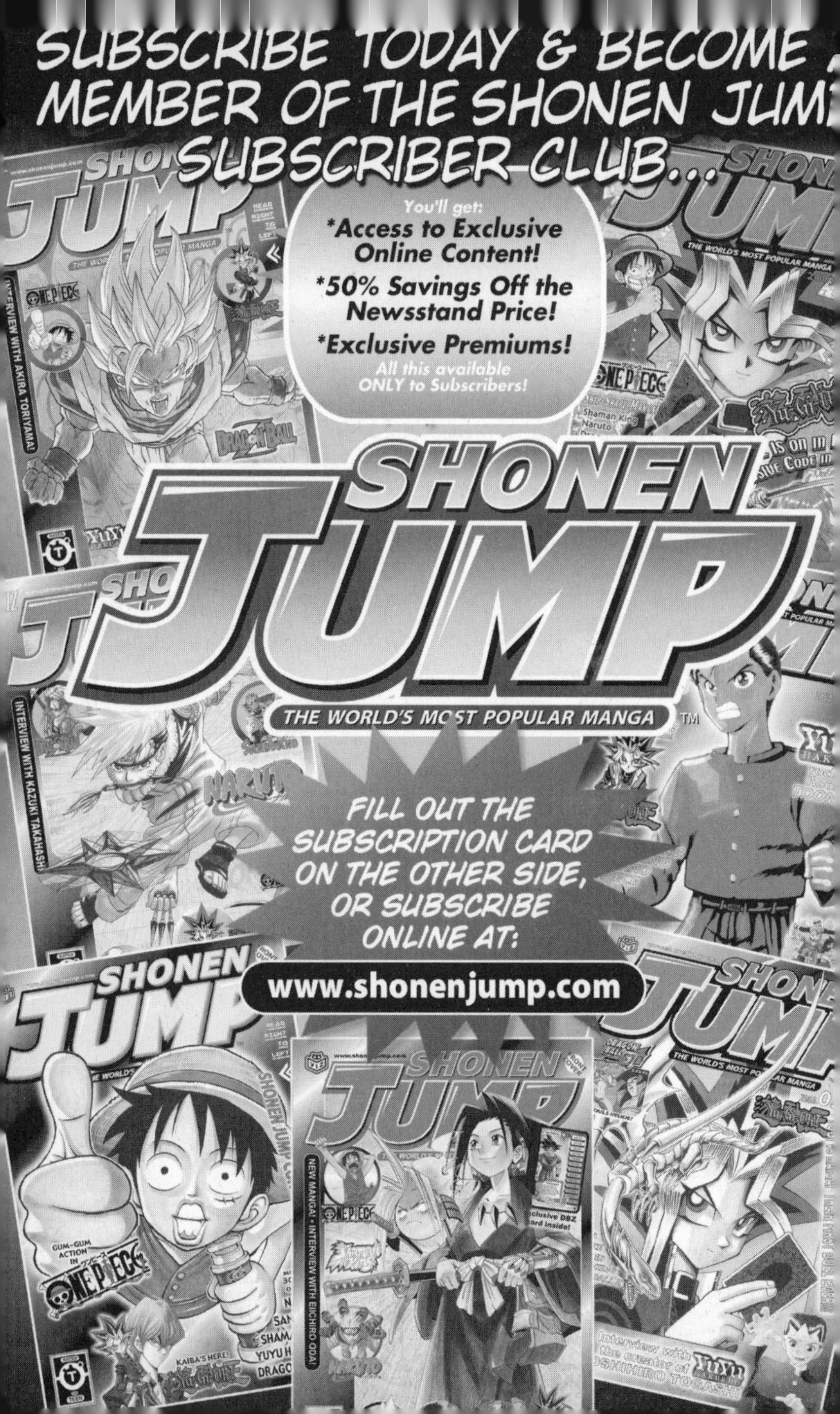
SUBSCRIBE TODAY & BECOME
MEMBER OF THE SHONEN JUM
SUBSCRIBER CLUB...
You'll get:
*Access to Exclusive Online Content!
*50% Savings Off the Newsstand Price!
*Exclusive Premiums!
All this available ONLY to Subscribers!
SHONEN JUMP
THE WORLD'S MOST POPULAR MANGA ™
FILL OUT THE SUBSCRIPTION CARD ON THE OTHER SIDE, OR SUBSCRIBE ONLINE AT:
www.shonenjump.com